CHALLENGING

MODERNITY

CHALLENGING MODERNITY

Robert N. Bellah

Ana Marta González
Philip Gorski
Kyle Harper
Hans Joas
Joel Robbins
Hartmut Rosa
Alan Strathern

Edited and with introduction and conclusion by
Richard Madsen, William M. Sullivan,
Ann Swidler, and Steven M. Tipton

Columbia University Press

New York

Columbia University Press
Publishers Since 1893
New York   Chichester, West Sussex
cup.columbia.edu

Library of Congress Cataloging-in-Publication Data
Names: Bellah, Robert N. (Robert Neelly), 1927–2013, author. |
    Madsen, Richard, 1941– author. | Sullivan, William M, author. |
    Swidler, Ann, 1944– author. | Tipton, Steven M, author.
Title: Challenging modernity / Robert N Bellah ; edited by Richard Madsen,
    William M Sullivan, Ann Swidler, Steven M Tipton.
Description: New York : Columbia University Press, [2024] | Includes index.
Identifiers: LCCN 2023040264 | ISBN 9780231214889 (hardback) |
    ISBN 9780231214896 (trade paperback) | ISBN 9780231560511 (ebook)
Subjects: LCSH: Bellah, Robert N. (Robert Neelly), 1927–2013. |
    Social history—21st century. | Religion and sociology. | Responsibility.
Classification: LCC HN18.3 .B456 23024 | DDC 302.3—dc23/eng/20230922
LC record available at https://lccn.loc.gov/2023040264

Printed and bound by CPI Group (UK) Ltd, Croydon, CR0 4YY

Cover design: Noah Arlow

CONTENTS

Acknowledgments   vii

Preface   ix

Introduction   1
**RICHARD MADSEN, WILLIAM M. SULLIVAN, ANN SWIDLER,
AND STEVEN M. TIPTON**

PART I: DIAGNOSING MODERNITY

1   The Modern Project in the Light of Human Evolution   21
ROBERT N. BELLAH

2   Turning Off Nature's Thermostats: Technology, Ecology,
and Deep History   37
KYLE HARPER

3   *Thermostatlessness*: The Project of Modernity and the Process of
Modernization: Reflections on Robert Bellah's Account of the Late
Modern Predicament   57
HARTMUT ROSA

PART II: THE MODERN PROJECT

4   Prologue in Heaven (or Hell) to the Modern Project   91
ROBERT N. BELLAH

5   Culture and Hope: Reflections on Bellah's Unfinished Project   159
ANA MARTA GONZÁLEZ

6 Axiality and the Critique of Power 182
ALAN STRATHERN

7 Organic Social Ethics: Universalism Without Egalitarianism 225
HANS JOAS

PART III: THE CHALLENGE OF MODERNITY

8 The Tillich Lecture: Paul Tillich and the Challenge of Modernity 265
ROBERT N. BELLAH

9 On the Search for "A Serious Ethical Form of Individualism": Bellah, Tillich, and the Anthropology of Christian Individualism 282
JOEL ROBBINS

10 "Disenchantment of the World" or Fragmentation of the Sacred? 303
PHILIP GORSKI

Conclusion 325
RICHARD MADSEN, WILLIAM M. SULLIVAN, ANN SWIDLER, AND STEVEN M. TIPTON

Contributors 341

Index 345

ACKNOWLEDGMENTS

Thanks to Robert Bellah's daughters, Jennifer Bellah Maguire and Hally Bellah-Guther, who have been friends and supporters of this project throughout and who gave us permission to publish Robert Bellah's final papers, which are the heart of this book.

The Social Trends Institute (STI) at the IESE Business School in Barcelona gave us the opportunity to gather our authors together for extremely creative conversations in an extremely pleasant venue. We are very grateful for their support and to the gracious hospitality provided by Tracey O'Donnell, the STI administrator.

Finally, heartfelt thanks are due to Eric Schwartz and his colleagues at Columbia University Press, who encouraged this project and helped us move it toward completion, and to Kalie Hyatt and her remarkable copyediting team at KnowledgeWorks Global, Ltd.

PREFACE

E dited books often prove disappointing, for readers, sadly enough, and for their editors as well. Not another book about crisis, injustice, and polarization! Instead our experience with this volume has bred something like a slow-moving revelation.

Our work as editors began from our close attachment, at once intellectual and deeply personal, to Robert Bellah. When Bellah died unexpectedly, he left three manuscripts that explored themes of a book he never completed, tentatively entitled, *The Modern Project*. At first we simply wanted to see these seminal papers in print. To accompany them, we thought then, we would invite a group of distinguished scholars—Bellah's peers, not acolytes—to write papers of their own advancing cultural and social inquiry to confront modernity. But this collaborative effort and the resulting volume have transcended whatever we hoped for then to give birth to something deeper and more alive than we could have conceived at the outset.

What do we mean by that? These papers, especially when read in sequence, have had a transformative effect on our own understanding and experience, a transformation we believe readers will share. They have given us new courage to imagine real prospects for facing up to the conflicts and contradictions in the way we live today. By their range of historical reference, their intricacy of exploration into the deep history of modernity, and their rich sense of how everyday practices and transcendent meanings are interwoven, the papers read together renew hope that we can change our way of life and reform our institutions.

What sets this volume apart from other treatments of modern crisis? The papers, in their varied ways, pay close attention to the wellsprings of meaning grounded in rites and sacred symbols we share to galvanize action and drive history. They draw from broad comparative knowledge of cultural resources across civilizations and historical eras, as these ideals frame institutions and inspire the moral drama of immanent practices we live out every day. They seek not only to diagnose the underlying sources of modern crises but to strike sparks of the hope, wisdom, and willingness we need to overcome them.

We find ourselves more interdependent than ever in a smaller world. We sense ourselves in need of an awakening, a change of mind and heart to see our common fate with open eyes and the courage to come together with open hands to remake our future as one species among others on one planet. The papers in this volume help us understand how we came to the present moment not simply by accident or shortfall, but by seeking the seemingly limitless goods of modernity—individual autonomy and a universal right to happiness—that now threaten our shared future. Can we commit ourselves to changing our way of life in practice and reforming our institutions in order to realize our deepest convictions and highest ideals? Yes we can, if we wake up.

CHALLENGING MODERNITY

INTRODUCTION

RICHARD MADSEN, WILLIAM M. SULLIVAN, ANN SWIDLER,
AND STEVEN M. TIPTON

ROBERT BELLAH'S HUMAN PROJECT

In 2013, the day before the heart-valve surgery that ended his life, Robert Bellah wrote to us about his latest intellectual enthusiasm. With his usual combination of self-dramatization and playfulness, he declared that it had been tormenting yet inspiring to read Peter Sloterdijk's *You Must Change Your Life*.[1] When Bellah came to the book's final pages, "they descended on me like tongues of fire. The last two pages swept me completely away and it took me nearly an hour to recover. I just sat there overcome. I see now that the whole book was leading up to those last pages, yet I didn't expect them." He realized that "those pages express exactly what I want to do in my next book, though giving me lots more ammunition. Sloterdijk talks about the PRACTICES we will need to meet the ecological Armageddon, about how they are impossible, but the whole of human history is about attaining the impossible. . . . It was like a giant explosion for me, but not a destructive one, rather a global fireworks display that suddenly shed light on everything."[2]

Bellah's revelation wasn't about some particular issue in his lifelong study of the religious dimension of human experience, nor was it about his understanding that our political dilemmas are at bottom cultural, but about hope and passion in a seemingly hopeless situation. He suddenly saw that it might be possible to

---

1. Peter Sloterdijk, *You Must Change Your Life: On Anthropotechnics*, trans. Wieland Hoban (Cambridge: Polity, 2013), 442–52.
2. Personal communication, July 29, 2013.

transcend the debilitating helplessness of our current political moment. Despite the combined forces of growing economic inequality and injustice, rising nationalism and intolerance, and paralyzing institutional dysfunction, inspired action might still be possible to meet the overwhelming threats to our collective life on earth. This volume aims to extend Bellah's lifelong quest—one that grew more intense as climate catastrophe loomed—to excavate from human history the practical wisdom that our cultural heritages offer to combat concentrated power and transcend the usual limits of our moral vision.

The chapters in this volume, along with the publication of Bellah's unpublished preliminary sketches of his book on modernity, are not hagiography or simple tribute to one of the most important public intellectuals of the twentieth and early twenty-first centuries. Rather, in recuperating Bellah's last project, we aim to extend it: to pose the key questions with which he was grappling and to press forward from there.

Why, in his magisterial final volume, *Religion in Human Evolution*, did Bellah begin with the evolution of life on earth and of humankind to frame the story of religion?[3] He was seeking to foreground the interdependent fate that we share with all life on the planet. He was reminding us (if we need reminding) that the fate of all humanity, and indeed of all life on earth, is now shared. And he was seeking a way to awaken an awareness of that humanity, not so much by preaching it as by immersing readers in the experience of it so it could penetrate us. What was he reaching for in his treatment of religion's fundamental connections to what it means to be human and in his treatment of the universal moral breakthroughs in Israel, Greece, China, and India? In analyzing the symbolic resources that enable transcendence and release the deep wellsprings of human collective action, was he hoping for a new cultural narrative that could break through the confines of late modernity, awaken our common humanity, and allow us to act together to avert our looming fate?

These are the challenging questions that the authors of this volume address. We have gathered a group of brilliant scholars who are Bellah's peers, not his acolytes. This is not a festschrift but rather a collegial engagement of scholars who share Bellah's sense of urgency, his broad range of historical and philosophical

---

3. Robert N. Bellah, *Religion in Human Evolution: From the Paleolithic to the Axial Age* (Cambridge, MA: Belknap Press of Harvard University Press, 2011).

reference, and his sense of dedication to the human project. Drawing on deep scholarly knowledge, individually and collectively, the authors seek to advance the conversation—for Bellah, it was always a conversation, with Tillich, with Weber, with fellow students and fellow citizens—about the fate of modernity and of ourselves as citizens of the modern world. We are, he insisted, responsible for our fate.

CHALLENGING MODERNITY

In the decade since Bellah died, the symptoms of a modern crisis have grown ever more acute and ever more frightening. Populist movements around the world, not least in the United States, have led to authoritarian governments that flout the basic rules of civic decency at home and defy the international institutional arrangements that have maintained, however imperfectly, a modicum of global order since the end of World War II. New centers of wealth and power have arisen in Asia, especially in China, to challenge the balances of national power that have maintained stability even in the absence of globally accepted moral norms. The Coronavirus Pandemic triggered cultural, economic, and political polarization that still handicaps global public health responses to the relentlessly mutating virus. Besides causing immense suffering in Ukraine, Russia's invasion of that country has raised the specter of even wider global conflagration. And looming over all is the apex crisis of global climate change, made ever more visible in deadly heat waves, destructive wildfires, and devasting storms.

These signs of the times are the latest indicators of deep contradictions in the modern project. Bellah, along with such predecessors as Émile Durkheim and Max Weber, wrestled with these chronic contradictions that led to the catastrophic breakdowns of two world wars and the Holocaust. But they were partially obscured by the seeming success of American political and economic hegemony in the first few decades after World War II, celebrated in the modernization theory that dominated American social science in the 1950s and early 1960s.

Most fundamentally, our current crisis reveals limits and contradictions within modernity's signature ambition: the mastery of nature. It has become ever clearer that while humanity has the collective capacity to dominate the planet's natural environment, and thus powerfully reshape the conditions of human life, it lacks the full capacity needed to control the natural processes that it transforms. This problem defines the new period of earth's history, increasingly called the Anthropocene. In this emerging epoch, human activity, especially the extraction of energy by burning fossil fuels, has become the most powerful force shaping the global ecology essential to human survival.

As the dimensions of our predicament have revealed themselves more forcefully, mounting calls for reform have emerged from many quarters. Voices urging a Green New Deal and a new social contract for global climate justice demand a sustainable rebalancing of humankind's relationship with nature and more equal opportunities for collective flourishing and personal dignity. At the same time, the very urgency of these biological, social, and environmental pressures narrows perspectives and shortens the time available to formulate adequate responses.

Bellah's great contribution was not to specify policies for addressing our immediate crises but rather to illuminate their deepest sources. The forces shaping our current maladies are immediately technological and biophysical, but they function as they do only because they are deeply embedded in the structure of our societies, institutions, and cultural traditions. Modern societies, as Durkheim and Weber noted, have grown increasingly complex and interconnected, yet more unequal in their ability to benefit from the global economy and more deeply conflicted. Meeting this crisis, therefore, depends not only on scientific advance and technological innovation but also on our collective capacities for large-scale social cooperation sustained over a long time horizon. Can we develop these capacities sufficiently to provide an ethical matrix for our interdependence? Time grows short.

BELLAH'S VISION

Bellah's work offers two important sources of insight. First is an integrated, multidisciplinary understanding of cultural change that grounds the possibilities for reimagining the present in a theory of cultural evolution that places religion and the experience of the sacred at its center. The other insight directs us toward a constructive if critical reappropriation of inherited traditions to support a more global and pluralistic moral stance of responsibility toward humanity and its role within the larger ecology of our planet.

These two themes—evolution and responsibility—characterize Bellah's work as a whole. But they are especially prominent in his magnum opus, *Religion in Human Evolution: From the Paleolithic to the Axial Age*, which appeared in 2011. In that book, Bellah placed his account of human social and cultural development within the perspective of contemporary biological theories of evolution. His account is one of variation and selection, of humanity's emergence as a species and its consequent adaptation to and role in altering the natural environment. This aspect of his work, therefore, emphasizes the contingent, unpurposeful processes of natural change. It is consciously cast within the epistemological framework of the external and disinterested insights of modern science because they offer the most adequate account of the material world currently available.

Yet Bellah's account is not another version of the deterministic evolutionary brutalism so common today. Instead, he emphasizes that his account, while drawing upon current scientific understanding, unavoidably tells a story. It must do so to make the facts of change over time meaningful. But the meaning and plot of the story cannot be derived simply from the facts of evolution, however necessary those facts are to guiding and checking the narrative. In *Religion in Human Evolution*, the overall perspective is culturally embedded and ultimately involved in the process that it strives to understand. It takes a deliberately internal and consciously concerned stance toward the evolutionary story. This stance is rooted in the recognition that to think about the human situation is finally to think as a living participant in the story, not simply as an observer of facts. This awareness then brings with it a recognition of responsibility toward the other participants and the context in which we participate together, that is, a shared moral commitment.

The deep history told in *Religion in Human Evolution* ends with the breakthroughs to cosmic and moral universalism of the first millennium BCE. The book's conclusion points toward our current crises not with a disinterested pessimism, which could easily be justified, but with engaged criticism of the contemporary state of affairs and advocacy to take responsibility for our shared fate. It urges its readers to take an active part in the debates about our predicament and take responsibility for their conduct and conclusions. The book's account of the emergence of humanity's self-awareness within this larger ecology emphasizes religion—not in the narrow sense of organized religion or patriotic piety evoked in common parlance today, but as the dynamic process of seeking to symbolize humanity's inchoate sense of participation in an encompassing reality and align daily survival with that larger life. In Bellah's account, understanding these processes, analyzed through social scientific and humanistic scholarship, opens up profound questions of moral meaning and responsibility in the present.

Immediately after completing this book, Bellah embarked on a new project to carry forward its account of Axial Age breakthroughs to "pick up the story and see how modernity fits into it." At his untimely death in 2013, he had written a prologue to this book, tentatively titled *The Modern Project*, and given two important lectures that suggest how he planned to develop its arguments.

These writings build upon and begin to move beyond his grand narrative of the development of human culture that, in the first millennium BCE, produced the radical religious innovations of Judaism, Greek philosophy, Confucianism, and Buddhism. In Bellah's telling, these axial breakthroughs develop theoretic cultures that combine disengaged learning and critical ethical reflection to move toward cosmological transcendence, universal morality, and more differentiated individual personhood. All this has inspired some of the greatest achievements and some of the worst disasters of humankind.

Bellah's new book would have taken the narrative into the present and shown how the axial legacies have been transformed but remain relevant today, for better and worse. At the center of our volume, these final papers point toward the envisioned contours of *The Modern Project*. The prologue presents a metanarrative of metanarratives. It outlines grand narratives carried on by pairs of representative philosophers and poets from different eras: Aquinas and Dante, Calvin and Milton, Goethe and Kant, Tolstoy and Max Weber. It concludes with a portrait of human aspirations toward autonomy in a morally fragmented world gripped by overwhelming social forces. But it also begins to explore how the intellectual and ethical breakthroughs of the Axial Age can still provide orientation and grounds for hope in facing the future.

A paper that Bellah presented at Notre Dame University five months before his death, titled "The Modern Project in the Light of Human Evolution," builds on Ian Morris's use of a "social development index" that estimates energy consumption and organizational complexity of societies over time.[4] From 3 units per capita in tribal societies based on hunting and gathering, in premodern agrarian

---

4. Ian Morris, *The Measure of Civilization: How Social Development Decides the Fate of Nations* (Princeton, NJ: Princeton University Press, 2013), 25–143, 238–63.

empires like Rome and Song dynasty China, the index rises to about 43. This marks a kind of limit, as this level of large-scale political and economic consolidation leads to ecological depletion and uncontrollable military conflicts. This hard ceiling gave way only in the Industrial Revolution, with the exploitation of fossil fuels. The index has surged to 1,000 today, and at current rates of growth, it would reach 5,000 by the end of the century. Bellah asks if we are soon going to hit the hardest of all hard ceilings. Our current cultures give us no thermostat to turn off the growth before it is too late.

As Bellah sees it, the crucial problem arises from the modern era's aspiration to attain complete individual autonomy. Its positive potential is institutionalized, however imperfectly, in human rights regimes dedicated to protecting the dignity of every person. But it also inspires a whole complex of institutions that constitute global industrial society and endanger the future of the planet. So Bellah asks:

> The basic question of my project is how do we as a species adapt to a rate of change that no biological species has ever faced before? Can we learn from our own deep past, as I have tried to do in *Religion in Human Evolution*? Are the great role models of our cultural heritage—the Buddha, Confucius, Socrates, Jesus—still relevant to our condition? Are the ethical traditions developed over centuries in the great religions and civilizations capable of meeting the ethical challenges of our rapidly escalating cultural condition? And, perhaps most ominous of all, if we have blown through every hard ceiling that for 16,000 years kept social development at a moderate level, can we go on increasing the social development index forever, or is the mother of all hard ceilings looming not far above us? And if we are facing such a hard ceiling in the not so distant future, can we manage a soft landing or do we face catastrophe?

Bellah's Paul Tillich lecture, "Paul Tillich and the Challenge of Modernity," given at Harvard just three months before he died, turns a discussion of Tillich's life and work toward sharpening a pivotal question of his project: Are the ethical legacies of the Axial Age capable of meeting the challenges of our current condition? Tillich had talked about a dialectic between prophetic and sacramental traditions. Through ritual enactment, the sacramental tradition celebrates the sacredness of what is, and through critical moral judgment, the prophetic tradition pushes beyond that and toward what should be in the future. After inspiring the moral rigor of the Protestant Reformation, in modern societies the prophetic tradition can degenerate. It can lead to an abstract ethical rationalism or to criticism without ethical substance. On the other hand, while the sacramental tradition can sustain a sense of the sacred, it is also liable to become tethered to a static past. Following Tillich, Bellah argues for a living dialectic that encompasses both. We need the kind of deep rationality that can confront our current crises by combining scientific detachment and ethical commitment. Going beyond Weber's "Science as a Vocation," Bellah saw that the task was not simply to hold two incompatible kinds of truth simultaneously.[5] For him, questions about the nature of reality embrace both an external objective reality and the moral reality of our intertwined human fates. He sought a richer kind of rationality that draws on the emotional and moral depth grounded in ritual and myth, as well as the analytic cognition that arises from theory.

Can the universal insights of Axial Age religions and ethics be critically reimagined and restoried, ritually renewed and enacted in modern institutions? Can we thereby realize universal human rights and responsibilities? Through deliberating and deciding in common, can we pursue social goods that are diverse and encompassing enough for all of us to share in order to survive and flourish in practice? At the outset of The Modern Project, the answers to these questions remain far from clear.

The chapters in this book have been inspired by these final papers from Bellah. We have not asked these distinguished scholars, who have from their own disciplinary perspectives addressed some of Bellah's main themes and questions, to try to figure out what he would have said if he had lived to finish his project. Instead, stimulated by his papers and inspired by his vision, they address on their own terms some of the central cultural dimensions of the crises of our time.

RELIGION IN HUMAN EVOLUTION

The theme of religious evolution connects the distinct motifs animating Bellah's papers presented in this volume. This theme recapitulates the larger trajectory of

---

5. Max Weber, "Science as a Vocation," in From Max Weber: Essays in Sociology, trans. and ed. H. H. Gerth and C. Wright Mills (New York: Oxford University Press, 1958), 129–56.

Bellah's work as a sociological theorist of religion and society, and it underlies his career as a public intellectual. Here, we outline the key features of Bellah's understanding of social evolution and the place of culture, particularly religion, within it. While the scheme evolved throughout Bellah's career, the structure perdured even as the issues addressed multiplied and the emphases shifted.

The outline of this framework appeared in his seminal 1964 essay, "Religious Evolution,"[6] but it returned, enriched and greatly expanded, in 2011 as *Religion in Human Evolution*.

In "Religious Evolution," Bellah defines religion as "a set of forms and acts that relate man to the ultimate conditions of his existence."[7] What evolves are the symbols and symbolic acts through which societies have sought to give form to a sense of what is ultimately real. These symbols and acts constitute a moral community by creating bonds and mutual expectations, giving birth to a society with a particular identity and sense of itself. This normative sense of connection among members of society is created and animated through symbolic forms enacted in rites and expressed in myths. As these symbolic forms become more differentiated from embedded social arrangements, human communities gain greater distance to judge and transform their societies, to stand outside received meanings and imagine other possibilities. This is the broad arc of religious evolution. Religion helps form human psyches, civilizations, and social orders alike, giving them energy and moral direction. Thus religion, as Bellah sees it, proves central to the whole process of human evolution.

This set of ideas derives, as Bellah acknowledges, from key figures of the sociological tradition, especially Émile Durkheim, Max Weber, and Talcott Parsons, as well as historians and philosophers of religion, particularly Wilfred Cantwell Smith and Karl Jaspers. "Religious Evolution," however, emphasizes that religion provides a fulcrum for social change as well as a foundation for social stability. Especially important in Bellah's scheme is the increasing differentiation of symbolic systems from social organization so that symbols, especially religion, come to have leverage over social structures rather than simply reaffirming the inevitability of the world as it is. The notion of evolution at work here is borrowed from what Terrence Deacon and others in biology refer to as "emergence" by contrast

---

6. Robert N. Bellah, "Religious Evolution" (1964), in *The Robert Bellah Reader*, ed. Robert N. Bellah and Steven M. Tipton (Durham, NC: Duke University Press, 2006), 23–50.
7. Bellah, "Religious Evolution," 24.

to sheer chance. Later forms are not determined by earlier ones, nor do they represent the logical culmination of a fixed program of development. Rather, under certain environmental conditions, new forms can emerge that show a greater degree of differentiation among their parts, which is made possible by a corresponding increase in the degree to which the parts integrate with one another. The classic biological illustration is the emergence of more complex organisms—with differentiated systems for digestion, reproduction, and so forth—from less complex antecedent organisms composed of undifferentiated conglomerations of identical single cells.

Although they may have new vulnerabilities, these more complex life forms sometimes achieve greater adaptability in the face of environmental changes, and as Bellah notes, they may attain some degree of autonomy in relation to surrounding life forms and conditions. In this analogy, societies have sometimes followed a similar pattern of growing complexity and adaptability in relation to external forces. Importantly, though, Bellah reminds us that earlier forms have continued and flourished. No obsolescence is built into religious forms. "A complex and differentiated form of religious symbolization is not therefore a better or a truer or a more beautiful one than a compact religious symbolization."[8] Bellah uses the model of emergent evolution to give a unified account of how religious expression changes over time in the direction of greater complexity. He shows how these changes are implicated in major historical transformations, sometimes following political or broader cultural changes, and shaping and even instigating them at critical historical points. Bellah delineated five stages of religious evolution:

1. Primitive
2. Archaic
3. Historic
4. Early modern
5. Modern religion

By this account, the great arc of change moves away from less complex, less differentiated forms of religious symbolization and action embedded in

8. Bellah, "Religious Evolution," 25.

hunting-gathering social life and envisioning society as one with the world. It moves toward increased symbolic differentiation from the social and natural worlds in archaic religions in step with increasing social differentiation. Great chieftaincies and agrarian empires emerge in which ruling strata claim descent from and special access to realms of higher powers governing this world from within it but elevated above its commoners and accessible only through sacred symbols and rites tied to separate social ranks. In the historic religions, which Bellah would later call "Axial," religious symbolism shifts from articulating a single hierarchical cosmos into rejecting "this world" as false and evil and exalting another realm of reality as solely true and infinitely good within a framework of cosmological dualism. With the emergence of Hinduism and Confucianism in East Asia, as well as Greek philosophy and ancient Judaism in the West, a sharp symbolic dualism divides the transcendent realm from mundane reality. The historic religions counterpose universal truths and transcendent moral authority to the evils, illusions, and finitude of the earthly order. This higher moral authority has the potential to hold everyone to account, from great rulers to ordinary adherents, in this world and the next.

Early modern religion, in the Protestant Reformation, both intensifies and begins to break down the dualism between transcendent and mundane reality. Especially in its Calvinist form, Protestantism poses an utterly transcendent and unknowable God against an utterly fallen world. This heightened dualism is nonetheless breached by insistence that by submitting to God's will, human beings must make the everyday world manifest God's glory. Thus the claims of the higher are made the demands of the everyday, at least in aspiration. In later Protestantism, salvation is potentially available to every person as an individual of infinite value in direct relationship to God and God's Word. The individual self becomes a bearer of transcendent value, intensifying the differentiation of individual from group.

Modern religion collapses the world-rejecting dualism crucial to all historic religions in favor of accepting this world as a realm of "infinitely multiplex" possibility. What form this collapse of the gulf that separated the transcendent from the mundane is taking and will take—the deification of politicians and rock stars, spiritualization of individual experience, or demystification of a world dominated by science and technology—is a central question raised by the authors in this volume. "Religious Evolution" argues that in the modern period, the forms and acts that relate humans to the ultimate conditions of their existence diffuse across a range of spheres, including science, arts, and politics, leaving human beings in charge of a self-revising personal, social, and cultural order. Bellah concludes his 1964 essay by acknowledging widespread concern for modern developments, characterized as "a collapse of meaning and a failure of moral standards." But he also envisions the modern situation more positively, as "offering unprecedented opportunities for creative innovation in every sphere of human action."[9]

In his 2011 masterwork, *Religion in Human Evolution*, Bellah changes the terminology and the level of detail and complexity grows much greater. But the fundamental idea that evolution provides the most conceptually powerful way of understanding the human condition gains new force.

Drawing on the best contemporary scholarship, the book develops a rich theoretical understanding of how symbols constitute evolving human cultures. Perhaps most significantly, Bellah uses the evolutionary psychology formulated by Merlin Donald to argue for long-term development in human cognition, communication, and group formation.[10] It begins with mimetic gesture, giving rise to full linguistic capacity and then joining gesture and language in myth and story. In the Axial Age, this theory holds, groups were enabled to take a further step beyond earlier forms of ritual and myth by "thinking about thinking" through literacy and related critical capacities for distancing from and thus mastering immediate social realty. In the Greek case most explicitly, this creates a newly detached, self-reflexive stance toward the world that Bellah, following Donald, calls "the theoretic." This stance has come to dominate modern societies.

Bellah then uses contemporary social and psychological theory to understand dynamic forces of cultural evolution. For example, he relates the imaginative construction of the religious cosmos through ritual enactment, which seems so striking to modern students of tribal societies, to recent work among evolutionary biologists. They trace it to "play," the tendency to step temporarily outside the demands of survival that is notable among mammals, especially the young. Alternatives to "everyday reality" prominent in studies of religion,

---

9. Bellah, "Religious Evolution," 45, 49.
10. Merlin Donald, *Origins of the Modern Mind: Three Stages in the Evolution of Culture and Cognition* (Cambridge, MA: Harvard University Press, 1991). On mimetic, mythic, and theoretic stages of culture, see Bellah, *Religion in Human Evolution*, xviii–xix.

though also in science and the arts, can then be speculatively connected to deeper tendencies in animal evolution that humans have developed in new directions.[11] The case is similar for mammalian tendencies toward nurture, on the one hand, and dominance, on the other, as ways of forming and sustaining social groups.

For Bellah, the search for a cultural approach to confronting modernity lies in finding the historical narrative of which we are part. The concept of evolution becomes a central historical narrative that stresses universal aspects of what it means to be human while acknowledging the richness of human difference. Bellah finds that today's idea of cosmic evolution, from the Big Bang forward, is the metanarrative best supported by scientific evidence and experimentation. But then he notes that this account gives rise to debate about its implications even among physical scientists, dividing adherents into what he calls "evolutionary pessimists," for whom there is no human significance to be found in the story aside from a frustration of human hopes, as opposed to "evolutionary optimists," who see a longer-term meaning, especially in the emergence of self-conscious life forms, artificial intelligence, and other recent developments.[12] Others simply accept the account as factual, lacking moral significance.

Bellah makes the key point, however, that all these positions derive from narrative or storytelling, based upon evidence to be sure but necessarily going beyond it. It is this need to construct our understanding as a narrative, with point and direction, that seems to define human rationality. Since science is always revisable, the process of scientific advance takes the form of narrative thinking. So, too, do the phenomena that Bellah's book seeks to study. A definition of religion, rather than a starting point as it was in the essay of 1964, now becomes a revisable part of a narrative that we are constructing—a narrative that gives us a way to experience the connection of human life to all life on earth.

The structure of Bellah's story of religion in human evolution shares the outline of his earlier essay on religious evolution, although it is based on a great deal more information and now sits within the vastly longer metanarrative of cosmic evolution. Taking the story only through the emergence of what he formerly called "Historic Religion," he delineates three stages of religious evolution:

---

11. Bellah, *Religion in Human Evolution*, 2–4.
12. Bellah, *Religion in Human Evolution*, 44–55.

1. Tribal religion
2. Archaic religion
3. Axial religion

The book's historical movement also runs parallel to the earlier essay: from the fully embedded and egalitarian "one world" of tribal religious forms, to the highly stratified archaic societies with their hierarchical articulation of a single cosmos, to the main focus of *Religion in Human Evolution*: the axial religious and philosophical movements of the mid-first millennium BCE. The book culminates in the emergence of the four cases of axial religions—ancient Israel, ancient Greece, ancient China, and ancient India. The early modern and modern religion phases outlined in the 1964 essay are not given direct attention, but modern religion would have been addressed alongside other aspects of modernity in Bellah's projected book on the modern project.

Religion in Human Evolution leads the reader through this long march to recognize the liberatory power but also the problematic character of the very standpoint that it embodies. One trajectory of the axial religions was toward a kind of universal criticism—of dominance hierarchies, of claims to special privilege for groups as well as individuals—and a recognition of universal moral community through new symbols and rites. But the narrative also impresses on the reader that these developments made possible a vast expansion of knowledge and techniques to manipulate both the natural world and other humans. How, then, are we to keep these instrumental capacities from undercutting and overwhelming the potential for wider moral community and a happier human situation?

These disturbing questions, as we have noted, were to have formed the substance of Bellah's uncompleted work on modernity. The prologue and two papers from Bellah that make up the centerpiece of this book were intended as first steps toward that project. These papers present a provocative range of possible approaches and divergent answers, as might be expected if his larger analysis is accurate in its picture of our present situation. Early in *Religion in Human Evolution*, Bellah cites the claim of the philosopher Mary Midgley that the primary thing is "connection," from which "meaning" is derived.[13] These papers do connect, but they do not simply agree. Taken together, they have inspired the dialogue among the contributors to this volume.

---

13. Mary Midgley, *Evolution as a Religion*, 2nd ed. (New York: Routledge, 2002).

ORGANIZATION OF THIS BOOK

We begin with Bellah's Notre Dame lecture, "The Modern Project in the Light of Human Evolution," which powerfully describes our present predicament. It ends by asking how to fit the story of cultural progress as a kind of diffusion of the sacred—conceived in terms of human rights, democracy, and global pluralism— together with the rapid expansion of energy capture that has both accelerated a "thermostatless" economic growth and set off potentially catastrophic planetary destabilization. The problems of modernity come to a head in this crisis, which Bellah linked to the dominance of modern capitalism and its associated cultures.

We continue with two chapters that pick up the theme of "thermostatlessness." Kyle Harper offers an illuminating account of how human societies breached the Malthusian limits that had governed most of human history. Practical knowledge of nature reduced the devastating effects of infectious and parasitic diseases and unlocked the energy of fossil fuels. Now an enormously expanded human population can expect to live longer and more comfortable lives than their forbears, even if famine, pestilence, and war have hardly disappeared. Next, Hartmut Rosa deeply explores how the very mastery of the human condition that we have come to expect generates its own peculiarly modern crises. Modern visions of achieving ever-greater personal autonomy inspire and then come into conflict with the thermostatless drive to achieve ever-greater economic and political progress advanced by modern capitalism and the nation-state. Caught in this conflict, we can weigh Rosa's notion of "resonance" as a possible way out.

We then present the full body of Bellah's prologue to the *Modern Project*. It culminates in a brilliant portrait of Max Weber as the archetypical modern man, who urges us to conjoin an ethic of conviction and ethic of responsibility to meet the competing demands of a morally fragmented world. The prologue ends with the final scene of Lars von Trier's film *Melancholia*. There, as the earth moves toward a fatal collision with a rogue planet, a small group takes care of their child by telling the comforting tale of having a magic tent in which to shelter from the destruction to come. This sacred canopy is presumably annihilated, along with everyone and everything else. "I thought of saying after von Trier's quiet ending, 'not with a bang but a whimper.' (Eliot) But the end of life, even on this planet, is not a whimper," Bellah writes. "However quiet, it is a very Big Bang, one worthy to stand beside that other Big Bang 13.7 billion years ago. Let us hope we won't let it happen."

How did we get to a precarious world where ultimate meaning is violently contested, moral life is fragmented, and we may be hurtling toward final destruction? Both the tragedy and hope of our situation draw on the legacy of the Axial Age. The next three chapters deepen and widen Bellah's story of that legacy. In chapter 5, Ana Marta González undertakes a deep linguistic and philosophical discussion of the original unity (albeit with tension) between sacred logos and the sacred story. She shows how, over the 2,000 years since the Gospel of John opened with "In the beginning was the Word," the distinction between narrative understanding and logical understanding gradually widened, leading after the Enlightenment to the modern divorce between what Bellah called the theoretic and the mythic stages of culture. Our challenge now is to overcome this divorce and ethically reframe technology-driven economic development to serve human goods rather than hinder them.

Next, the comparative historian Alan Strathern widens the story that Bellah told to show how the legacies of all the Axial traditions, not just the Western ones, have played out in the major civilizations of the world. The Axial traditions all posit a transcendent, universal ethic applicable to everyone in the world, including both the powerful and the weak. Rulers are subject to the demands of justice. But in historical practice, Axial transcendence is always embodied in immanent institutions. The universal moral visions of the Axial Age make possible the development of broadly expansive systems of power. They often justify the exercise of such power even as they provide resources for its critique. Strathern shows us how such tension has played out in widely different cultures in different historical circumstances.

Next, the social theorist Hans Joas carefully reconstructs the theoretical background of Max Weber's discussion of an "organic social ethic." Drawing on Otto von Gierke, Wilhelm Dilthey, and Ernst Troeltsch, he highlights the limitations of Weber's conceptualization and his treatment of organic social ethics in Islam and Hinduism. Joas emphasizes how the universalizing ethic of Christian love remained fundamental to the organic social ethic of medieval Europe, thus pointing to the perduring interdependence between a universal morality focused on the dignity of the individual person and the forms of solidarity necessary for a common social life.

The last section of our volume is introduced by Bellah's lecture "Paul Tillich and the Challenge of Modernity." He presents Tillich's version of religious evolution from self-enclosed societies rooted in a sacramental ritual "myth of origin," through a universalizing ethical breakout in Hebrew prophetism, to modern individual autonomy, with its attendant danger of self-absorption. Bellah concludes by endorsing Tillich's call for a modern "theonomy," in which ethical autonomy finds its ground by participating in a cosmic order inspired by divine self-giving. Quoting Tillich, Bellah calls for proclamation of the present as *kairos*, the moment of salvation.

In dialogue with Bellah and Tillich, the anthropologist Joel Robbins shows in chapter 9 how the Axial Christian vision of a universal dignity for all individuals creates tension with the "relationalism" maintained by an isolated language group of Urapmin in Papua New Guinea when they were converted to Protestant Christianity. He uses this ethnography to frame an account of individualism's place in a system of values challenged, in Bellah's and Tillich's terms, by the perpetual dialectic between sacramental myths of origin and prophetic breakthroughs to a universalizing individualism.

Finally, in a chapter that speaks broadly to the whole of Bellah's vision and indeed to many of the other chapters in this volume, Philip Gorski describes the present stage of modernity as one of deeply fragmented sacred symbols—a broader pantheon than the seven "warring gods" that Weber invoked. In a way, it is a development of the vision that Bellah sketched at the end of his original essay "Religious Evolution." There, Bellah wrote, "It is not that life has become again a 'one-possibility thing' but that it has become an 'infinite-possibility thing.' "[14] Gorski now concludes:

> The problem of late modernity, if it is one, is not a "deficit of meaning" so much as a *surfeit* of meanings. Never before has humanity had so many religious and cultural meaning systems—so many competing visions of the sacred—quite literally at their fingertips. Of course, this surfeit of meanings may well involve a loss of "ultimate significance" of a unitary sort. The reverse is also true: the choice for ultimate significance and unity also implies renunciation of multiple meanings and sacred plurality.

This may open up liberating new possibilities of creative hybridity, all made possible through modern moral individualism. But looming global crises like

---

14. Cf. Weber, "Science as a Vocation," 152; and Bellah, "Religious Evolution," 45.

climate change will require solidarity and sacrifice for their solution, Gorski recognizes, and these "are not readily forthcoming in cultures that prize freedom and individualism."

In our conclusion, we analyze the antinomies and contradictions in the chapters' fundamental approaches to modernity, even as we seek to synthesize the overlapping themes developed in these dialogues with Bellah. We wind up by presenting our own views on how the legacy of the Axial Age creates the challenges of late modernity and provides resources for overcoming them. We have sometimes tried to imagine, if Bellah were alive today, how he would have confronted our current moment of peril. He would certainly have raged against the forces of authoritarianism, greed, and political cowardice that seem to dominate our world. But as the epiphany at the beginning of this chapter suggests, he had a profound faith that we can overcome despair, anger, and hopelessness to find the courage and conviction that we need to come together to confront the common threats and pursue the common goods that shape our interdependent fate.

PART I

DIAGNOSING MODERNITY

CHAPTER 1

THE MODERN PROJECT IN THE LIGHT OF HUMAN EVOLUTION

ROBERT N. BELLAH

University of Notre Dame, South Bend, Indiana   March 19, 2013

◆

Just as I was beginning to think about my next book, whose title is very similar to the title of this lecture, a remarkably helpful new book appeared that would change the way I think about modernity and what led up to it. Such surprises are among the great pleasures of scholarship. The book was by a familiar author but its subject matter was, to me, utterly new. The author in question is Ian Morris, trained as an archeologist and historian of ancient Greece, whose work made a major contribution to my chapter on Axial Age Greece in my last book. Morris, British trained but now teaching at Stanford, had sent me helpful comments on that chapter and we had coffee together when he happened to be in Berkeley. But the new book, *Why the West Rules—for Now*, published in 2010, is not about ancient Greece, or it is about ancient Greece and everything else since the end of the last ice age. I knew archaeology has become increasingly quantitative, but I hardly expected such a quantitative book on the whole of human development since the late Paleolithic from a scholar whose insights on ancient Greece had been so suggestive to me. What followed was an e-mail conversation and a request from the Princeton University Press for a jacket comment for Morris's next book, *The Measure of Civilization: How Social Development Decides the Fate of Nations*, which has just appeared.

In terms of the divide between quantitative and qualitative social science, I have always been pretty clearly on the qualitative side, even considered as a "humanistic" social scientist. But Morris's books provide a quantitative perspective that I think gives me a critical framework for everything I want to do in my next book. Morris, taking a very long view, has developed a social development index. There are four components of his index: the first and most important is energy capture per capita, to put it roughly, how much energy does a single human require to keep body and soul together? His index is based on the number of calories required, the details of which I can't go into, but the index number for 14,000 BCE is 4. At that point and for a long time after, the index number of the other three measures that go into his overall index—degree of organization measured by size of urban settlements, degree of information technology, and degree of war-making capacity—are close to zero because there were no cities, information technology remained at the level of the human voice, and humans fought with sticks and stones. Since the amount of energy capture makes possible the development of the other three measures, it is still the most fundamental measure even in societies that have large cities, developed information technology, and effective war-making capacity.

So Morris estimates that at 14,000 BCE when humans were just emerging from the last ice age, energy capture per capita, at that point the only component of his social development index, was at 4. Twelve thousand years later it had reached about 20 in 2000 BCE, that is, after the development of agriculture in several parts of the world, the growth of cities, the earliest non-alphabetic forms of writing as an information technology, and the development of bronze weapons. Going from 4 to 20 in 10,000 years is certainly an indication of development, though much of it, like metallurgy and writing was quite late in that 10,000 years. So it is a sign of significant social development, but at a speed, compared with the present, that seems hardly better than the proverbial snail's pace. That, however, is probably the wrong comparison. The changes we can measure in those 12,000 years are cultural, not biological, and far faster than the development of biological capacities in any known species.

But then if we look at the 2000 years between 2000 BCE and the turn of the Common Era, we find that the index doubles and then some, reaching 43 in first century Rome, which turns out to be roughly the first century of the Roman Empire. But then for the following 1800 years we find something new. Morris hypothesizes that 43 was a kind of ceiling (I will have more to say about ceilings later) because Rome declined back to the upper 20s and no Western society reached 43 again until well into the eighteenth century. Further, China, which had been behind the West when Rome was at 43, not only pulled ahead of the West after several centuries, but itself reached 43 in the Song Dynasty around 1000 CE, before falling back as the West had done before. Then again, by about 1750, both China and the West reached 43, and yet all the indications were that they were both heading for hard ceilings and would not break through that number.

While there is a long-term tendency for the scale to rise, the rises are followed by declines, and for most of the two millennia after Rome reached 43, the index fell or, if it got back to 43, fell again. To me this was entirely counterintuitive. I had imagined a long slow climb of civilizational development from the time of Christ until the nineteenth century, when, in fact, the social development reached 43 early on and then dropped back to where it had been a thousand or more years before Christ, and kept on bumping up and down but never getting above where it had been at the beginning of the common era.

This is where we need to understand what Morris means by a "hard ceiling," one produced by what he calls "the paradox of development." That is, the very success of pre-modern societies seems inevitably to have led to overpopulation, famine, plague and war. Even so long ago, environmental damage led to decline in various areas. Southern Mesopotamia was the homeland of the first cities and probably the first written script, as well as a number of other "firsts" that led the great scholar Samuel Noah Kramer to call his 1956 book *History Begins at Sumer*, Sumer being the oldest large city in southern Mesopotamia. But the flourishing of southern Mesopotamia was dependent on an elaborate system of canals to bring water to rich agricultural areas with little rain. Over the centuries those canals either silted up or became salinized and Southern Mesopotamia never regained its preeminence. The Mayans in the first millennium CE created a great civilization with a number of important cities and the only system of writing invented in the New World, but then collapsed as an advanced civilization. All the details are unclear, but the spread of agriculture into marginal areas and the cutting down of the forests seem to have denuded the environment to the point where it would no longer support a major civilization.

Another endemic problem, one that plagued both Rome and China during the first and much of the second millennia CE, was barbarian invasion. Large empires, as Rome and China were, had enormous boundary problems. Tribal movements from inner Asia could send whole peoples crashing into those borders. Since the cost of military defense of such extensive borders was enormous, it seemed politic to use barbarians to fight barbarians. So both empires armed what were intended to be client groups to patrol the borders and keep out more distant invaders. Civilized weapons were better than what the barbarians had, but not much better, and once the client groups acquired that military technology they could turn on their sponsors and conquer the empires themselves. This happened to China for centuries after the fall of the Han Dynasty about 200 CE, and to the Western Roman Empire from about 400 CE.

Of course the conquerors created new empires and drove the social index up, but they, in turn, were subject to the same forces that brought down the empires they conquered. So it begins to become apparent why there was no long, slow, continuous rise in the social index for most of the first 2000 years of the Common Era. Within the technological and organizational constraints operating at that time, each effort to rise in the social index created the very conditions of the hard ceiling that brought it down again.

It is as if there were a built-in thermostat that put a break on continuous development at each stage of development, a rather harsh thermostat operating through war, famine and plague, but one that didn't stop growth, only kept it from exceeding certain limits.

It seems that there was only one way to reach modernity and that involved going through a certain set of stages each with its own conditions and its own limits. In what follows I will be quoting occasionally from Morris's *The Measure of Civilization*:

> The index reveals not only a very clear progression from foragers to farmers to factory workers and beyond but also a series of hard ceilings limiting how far development could go under each broad form of organization. No foraging society has developed much beyond six or seven points on the index; no agricultural village society much beyond ten to twelve points; and no agrarian empire beyond the low forties. No society has leapt from foraging or agricultural villages directly to industrialism without going through the stage of agrarian empires—unless it comes under the influence of another society that has already gone through these stages . . . (Morris, *Measure*, 258)

As I have said, by the late 18th century both the West and China had reached 43 again, but seemed headed for another hard ceiling. This time, however, something new under the sun happened. Up until 1773 the only sources of energy were human and animal muscles with some help from wind and water. What happened in 1773 was the invention of the steam engine, used first to pump out the water that accumulated in coal mines, but then setting off the industrial revolution, itself probably only possible due to the scientific revolution which began in the West in the 17th century. This development did not occur everywhere in the West at once. It occurred initially in Britain, and was not followed immediately even in the continental countries closest to England, partly due to the Napoleonic wars and their lasting consequences. Development has been uneven ever since and though it began in Britain, which is surely in what we call the West, it spread first of all to the Netherlands, Western Germany and Northern France, from about 1850, but other parts of Europe, in the east and south lagged behind, while in Asia, the Japanese by the end of the nineteenth century were rapidly industrializing and by 1905 had decisively beaten a major European power, Russia, showing that modern development was no longer Western or Eastern but global, though uneven development continues to this day.

In any case where it did take hold, this new development not only blew through the hard ceiling of 43 by the end of the 18th century, but by 2000 it was reaching 1,000, an advance totally unheard of in pre-modern times. And in the last 50 years the information revolution increased at a rate that makes the industrial revolution look slow, with consequences we can hardly imagine. In fact Morris estimates that if social development continues at the rate of the last few decades it will reach 5000 by the end of the twenty-first century:

> The most significant implication of projecting twentieth-century trends forward is that social development will reach five thousand points in the next hundred years. Between 14,000 BCE and 2000 CE, development rose by nine hundred points. This took humanity from Paleolithic cave paintings to the Internet. [But] between 2000 and 2100 CE development will rise by a further four thousand points; and if anything, this may be an underestimate. All the signs in the dozen years since the new century began suggest that development is increasing exponentially, not just as a linear extension of what the last century saw . . .
>
> The five-thousand-point scenario assumes that humanity has permanently escaped Malthusian constraints, but there is an obvious alternative interpretation of post-Ice Age history: that industrialization merely pushed these

constraints outward. It did so dramatically . . . but all the same, this reading of the index would suggest, industrial societies will face built-in hard ceilings, just like the hard ceilings that constrained the growth of agrarian societies.

The Roman and Song agrarian empires faltered and failed when their social development rose above forty points, and perhaps modern societies will encounter a new hard ceiling somewhere between one thousand and five thousand points. And if development stagnates in a world of ten billion people, unpredictable climate change, nuclear proliferation, and rapid, unevenly distributed advances in robotic, cyber-, and nano-warfare, the consequences could be even more catastrophic than when development stagnated in the agrarian age. (Morris, *Measure*, 262–263)

What this quantitative picture of modernity compared to all previous societies has done for me is to dramatize the uniqueness of the modern condition. Humans have the same bodies as we did two hundred years ago, though that is beginning to change due to a variety of implants and insertions, but the notion that intelligent computers will take over the planet appears nothing more than science fiction. We have the same basic needs and dispositions that humans have had for hundreds of thousands of years. Language, the greatest technological advance in history and the one on which all the later ones depend, is plus or minus 100,000 years old, writing a few millennia old, printing 550 years old, and electronic media are so recent that we have to think in terms of decades, though the rate of change is so rapid that even decades seem slow.

The basic question of my project is how do we as a species adapt to a rate of change that no biological species has ever faced before? Can we learn from our own deep past, as I have tried to do in *Religion in Human Evolution*? Are the great role models of our cultural heritage—the Buddha, Confucius, Socrates, Jesus—still relevant to our condition? Are the ethical traditions developed over centuries in the great religions and civilizations capable of meeting the ethical challenges of our rapidly escalating cultural condition? And, perhaps most ominous of all, if we have blown through every hard ceiling that for 16,000 years kept social development at a moderate level, can we go on increasing the social development index forever, or is the mother of all hard ceilings looming not far above us? And if we are facing such a hard ceiling in the not so distant future, can we manage a soft landing or do we face catastrophe?

I don't have time to give you a short course in environmental degradation but I can presume that this audience is already aware of all that, which makes it all the more remarkable that so many of our world leaders are still in denial, or are just afraid to talk about it. During our long presidential campaign last year [2012] both parties were absolutely afraid to talk about global warming, except for a few who thought it politically expedient to ridicule the idea. None of our national leaders was able to take the political risk of talking seriously about this issue.

But just to give you a quick reminder, let me cite some alarming statistics. After 1800 something remarkable begins to happen which is clearly related to modernization and industrialization: human population, which previously had taken hundreds, sometimes thousands of years to double, doubles from one billion in 1800 to two billion in 1927, faster than ever before—the industrial revolution was underway—but still slow in terms of what was coming. I was born in 1927 when the world's population reached two billion. In October 2011, when I was 84, the world's population reached seven billion. That is, it grew three and a half times in my lifetime, and if I live even a few more years I could see it reach eight billion and so quadruple in my lifetime. How marvelous! How adaptive! What an achievement we have made in out-producing any possible rivals for our primacy! Or is it? Most scientists in the world today believe that this enormously rapid increase in population and the geometric increase in the use of energy that made it possible are signs of profound vulnerability, that we have already crossed the line of sustainability where the costs are outrunning the benefits. Rather than shouting Hurray, they see giant red lights flashing and sirens going off. What worries them is not that geometrically rapid population growth is "against evolution." It is explained perfectly by evolution; it's just that evolution itself is very complicated and simple contrasts between what is adaptive and what is maladaptive are not always helpful. Evolution goes on at many levels; unless we keep the levels in mind we will not understand either the achievements or the dangers.

What is clearly the case, and I can only touch on it in one short lecture, is that the enormous increase in energy available to humans and the enormous increase in population that that increase has made possible, could not have happened without an equally enormous increase in human knowledge, science, obviously, but organizational knowledge in order just to manage such massive change. What I want to question is whether the kind of knowledge that has made it possible for our social development index to go from 43 to close to 1000 in 200 years is really able to cope with its own achievements.

Gregory Bateson, a significant, though neglected, twentieth century thinker, who happens to have been my sophomore tutor at Harvard, argues for the fatality of the fact that the scientific breakthrough came in physics and to some degree in chemistry, where linear thinking (A causes B by hitting it), leads to the apotheosis of one-way causation and loses the sense of circular causation that is essential in biology and sociology. Modern civilization actually misinterpreted the scientific advance which made it possible by seeing it in purely instrumentalist terms, which means, to put it simply, that success means the more, the more. And though the rise of cybernetics, system theory, chaos theory, etc., since WWII has tried to right the balance it has had limited success.

Think of it this way: the world of science and capitalism has removed the thermostat on global warming so that we keep on getting hotter and hotter and nothing turns off the heat because there is no functioning thermostat. It's as if you had a furnace in your home that you couldn't turn off, or that you would need the cooperation of the whole world to turn off, but no thermostat. So your house would just keep getting hotter, and hotter, and hotter . . . I don't need to tell you what would happen if this went on very long. The whole idea of unlimited growth is thermostatless and ultimately self-destructive, though there are arguments for sustainable growth that would create an effective thermostat, but at the moment pretty speculative and with enormous power mobilized against them. In fact, if it weren't such an ugly word, I could call my next book "Thermostatlessness."

So far I have described modernity in almost completely materialist, statistical terms. This leaves out two important questions: How can we explain this sudden abrupt rise in the social development index, not just describe it as I have done, but explain it? What about the cultural side of modernity, the new understandings about human meaning that began to crystallize even before the great takeoff really got started? And are the answers to these two questions related, so that one helps explain the other? Obviously in a few minutes I can only point to these questions, not answer them.

Let me look quickly at the various causes that have been suggested. Karl Marx explained this historical shift as having been caused by a new kind of economy, called capitalism. Even Max Weber, who was much more multi-causal than Marx, tended to speak of recent society as "capitalist," suggesting that he, too, found capitalism to be the primary causal factor. Marx, but particularly Weber, were well aware that economies involving large-scale markets and mediated by money can be found all the way back to ancient times. Ancient Rome, for example, couldn't possibly have functioned without massive commodity production and exchange throughout the Mediterranean and beyond. Commercial agriculture was essential if the great cites were to be fed, and a few landowners grew enormously wealthy. Still Weber was inclined to distinguish what he called "modern capitalism" from an economic system based on slavery as in the ancient world. The notion that slavery made for an inefficient economy that could not compare with an economy based on wage labor was long taken for granted until economic historians pointed out that the slave economy that existed in the Caribbean and the ante-bellum South was highly efficient, and that its efficiency and high profit level made it very difficult to eliminate. So maybe "modern" capitalism wasn't so different from ancient capitalism.

But then we have learned more about the history of Asian economies, which were supposed to be quite different from the modern Western economy. Even Adam Smith knew that China was a huge market economy, larger than that of Europe, and as we have learned more about the Chinese and Japanese economies as late as the eighteenth century, we see that they were quite comparable to the European economy in those days. They involved very efficient commercial agriculture and large amounts of manufacture, in textiles, ceramics, even alcoholic beverages, and their products were quite competitive with those of Europeans before the industrial revolution. Indeed the British had to prohibit the importation of Indian textiles as, for a long time, they were of superior quality to what they could produce even with machines. If you want to know why East Asian economies, and to an only slightly lesser degree, South Asian economies, are so powerfully competitive today you can't forget that they were as advanced as Europe at the dawn of industrialization and as soon as they had the new technology would be competitive again.

Weber offered a cultural alternative to Marx's materialist explanation. He found the Reformation and the Protestant work ethic to which it gave rise as crucial to modern capitalism. I wrote my doctoral dissertation to show that Japanese religion in the immediately pre-modern period had a work ethic comparable to that of Protestantism, and my book is still in print 55 years later. At the time I wrote it I thought only the Japanese had such a work ethic, but I didn't realize that what the Japanese had was shared throughout East Asia and that under the right conditions could support a modern economy everywhere that it existed.

I have said that both Europe and China, the two largest markets in the world, were heading for a hard ceiling late in the eighteenth century. The Rev. Thomas Malthus, who published his *Essay on the Principle of Population* in 1798, just before the industrial revolution, explained why. If population growth exceeds the capacity of a society to produce food, the result will be mass starvation and social decline: it had happened many times before and he predicted it would happen again. His essay went into six editions, the last of which was published in 1826 and he died in 1834, old enough to see the beginnings of the industrial revolution. Malthus was not wrong, he just had no idea of what the industrial revolution was going to do by applying new energy to more efficient farming. Nonetheless, the Rev. Malthus has been standing at the door ever since with the bill in his hand. The "green revolution" of the late 1960s to the late 1970s led to a general increase of agricultural productivity of over 3 percent per year for several decades. However it has not been replicated and agricultural productivity is increasing at only 1 percent per year or less, while drought, floods and the decline of the glaciers that feed the major rivers of China and India, among other things, suggest that the hard ceiling was raised but is still there. One cannot say that there is no technological fix, but remember that the world's population is increasing by 85 or 90 million persons a year, the equivalent of the entire population of Vietnam, or two-thirds the population of Japan. Malthus is still waiting.

So if we want to understand why industrial civilization occurred when it did, where it did, as I have said, in England in the first half of the nineteenth century, the explanation cannot be capitalism or religion if we look only at the work ethic, because those things were at a comparable level elsewhere, outside the West altogether, in the decades just before the industrial takeoff. So where else can we look? Clearly science was an important factor. The first steam engine required skilled craftsmen, but those again were numerous in east and west. James Watt, however was an instrument maker employed by the University of Glasgow and trained in the new physics. His invention of an effective steam engine was the result of a marriage of traditional craft skills and modern science, possible anywhere in Europe, but perhaps especially in Scotland. However Watt had a great deal of trouble raising money for his new project until in 1775 he found an English manufacturer, Matthew Boulton, who was willing to go in partnership with him to produce practical steam engines that would actually work, first to pump out the water that accumulated in British coal mines, and then to make steam engines for railways and produce the industrial revolution. So entrepreneurial capital was, in fact, another key ingredient. Government sponsorship could have had the same effect and later on would be essential for many new developments, but at the time no bureaucrat apparently had the imagination to get involved.

So we can now, apparently, solve our first questions: it took an advanced, highly monetized, capitalist economy, plus skilled workmanship arising from pre-industrial manufacture, plus a strong work ethic, together with, critically, modern science to make the breakthrough that would produce the society that would rise with an acceleration that only increases as we approach the present.

Still, what did people make of all this? What kind of society did they think they lived in or wanted to live in? Most remarkably we have a series of great cultural changes, we could even call them without exaggeration, cultural revolutions, arising just before the industrial takeoff, yet in no obvious sense causing it. Still, when we speak of modernity, we don't just point to the industrial revolution and all its subsequent technological developments. We are pointing to a new kind of society, one that can be described in many ways, but that has a very important ethical/political content, so important that it is this that we primarily mean when we speak of "the modern project." And the center of this project is a new understanding of the human person, the human individual, an understanding that is religious as well as ethical and political. We can speak of individualism, a highly ambiguous word, but must remember that the emergence of the person as an ethical focus occurred well before the term individualism was invented, that is before Alexis de Tocqueville's *Democracy in America* of 1830. Hans Joas has a new book that gets at this focus and its title is *The Sacredness of the Person: A New Genealogy of Human Rights*. It is being published by the Georgetown University Press and should be available at any minute. It is a good place to begin.

Joas argues that the search for the origins of the modern human rights movement cannot look only to the history of ideas. The idea of the sacredness of the person is to be found in ancient Israel very early in the book of Genesis where God is said to have created human beings in his own image and likeness. What could be more sacred than that? For the ancient Greeks there is something in the soul of every human being that is identical to the soul of the universe. In early India there were influential thinkers who proclaimed the identity of the atman, the self, with Brahman, the ultimate reality of the universe. And Confucius proclaimed that all under Heaven are brothers. So the axial age certainly proclaimed the sacredness of the person. But while this idea motivated individual piety and acts of charity it nowhere, outside private religious communities, became the standard of social and political practices and institutions. Rather, the very traditions that proclaimed the sacredness of the person lived side by side with and often validated harsh practices of inequality and violence: slavery, ethnic discrimination, the inequality of women, torture and indiscriminate violence against civilians in the maintenance of internal order and external warfare. The ideas were not meaningless and gave rise to prophetic criticism and social protests, but never were institutionalized even in a single society. Joas begins his genealogy of human rights from the moment of their actual translation into practices and institutions, beginning with their codification as potentially enforceable claims.

Here I can merely touch on the rich history which Joas recounts. He begins by dismissing the two most often cited sources of modern human rights: beliefs of the Enlightenment, especially for those who look to France as the birthplace, and beliefs of Christianity, especially for those who look to America. For one thing, idea systems do not produce human rights regimes, important though they may be as sources. Joas pinpoints the Declaration of Independence as the first significant codification of universal human rights, and points out that though it was a document drafted by Jefferson, it was amended by other members of the committee assigned to produce it and so was a collective document representing a wide spectrum of the colonial leadership. Taking the Declaration together with the revolutionary state constitutions drafted soon after the Declaration was proclaimed and that spelled out more specific rights than the great general rights to "life, liberty and the pursuit of happiness," and specifically the right to the free exercise of religion that would later be incorporated in the First Amendment, he sees the early American Republic as the birthplace of the institutionalization of universal human rights. And as to where the impetus for that great innovation came from he holds that both of the usual suspects were involved. Organized Christianity in the American colonies, especially the non-established groups such as the Baptists and the Quakers, had waged an urgent battle for religious freedom through much of the eighteenth century, but it was only in alliance with some of the Deist Founders of the new republic with their strong commitment to Enlightenment values, but who had on specific points the same agenda as the Christian groups mentioned above, that what had been ideas became values with constitutional force. Nor does Joas want to slight the role of the Declaration of the Rights of Man and of the Citizen at the very beginning of the French revolution, though he points out that its drafters were fully aware of the American documents and were themselves motivated by Christian as well as secular ideals. Both the American and the French Declarations would have world-wide influence. The degree to which they were effectively institutionalized even in their home countries as well as in other countries which adopted similar declarations was always far from perfect, but it is the intention that they be normative for whole populations, not simply ideals of specific groups, including the intention that they should ultimately be universal in all countries, that is what made the genealogy of modern human rights different from the history of ideas.

Joas is very interested in institutionalization and practices rather than ideas alone, yet institutionalization was often very limited in its effects. "All men are created equal" was at the beginning of the American experiment, but the Constitution not only did not abolish slavery, it counted slaves as three-fifths of a person in counting populations for representation. Yet the codified values of the equality of persons expressed in the American and French revolutions led to world-wide movements for abolition, movements in which the British were conspicuous early leaders but soon followed by the abolitionist movement in the United States. These movements over time led to the global abolition of slavery, though we know that various forms of slavery still exist today in ways that are marginal or not so marginal.

My point here is that institutionalization though importantly a matter of law is not confined to legalization. Human rights as a value demanding institutionalization gives rise to social movements, because existing institutionalization is never wholly adequate. We can see this clearly in the fact that the Emancipation Proclamation of 1863 that formally freed the slaves did not erase powerful forms of racism that continued for another century, requiring the Civil Rights Movement of the late 1950s and 1960s to create a new set of legal norms, while significant forms of racism continue to this day. One could see the same pattern with the Women's Suffrage movement that gave women the vote, but the lingering practices of sexism required further work from the Women's Movement of the late twentieth century, and victory is still only partial.

I would like to add one more dimension that is often not included in the human rights agenda, though it is closely related to it, and that is the rise of democracy as the only acceptable form of government, something that began with the American Revolution, though at the beginning the new government was not called a democracy, still a pejorative term at time of the American founding. It was only with the French Revolution that the term took on its modern positive meaning, though it wasn't until after World War II that democracy finally achieved the status as the only acceptable form of government, almost, but significantly not entirely, globally. Here again democracy as a form of government and democracy as a value, namely that the people should govern themselves, have been and still are two different things. In the United States today, two very different things, but nowhere completely identical.

Joas placed a great deal of weight on the Declaration of Independence and the Declaration of the Rights of Man and the Citizen, whose consequences continue to reverberate to this day. He closes his book, however, with a discussion of a third document, The Universal Declaration of Human Rights adopted by the United Nations General Assembly on 10 December 1948 at the Palais de Chaillot in Paris. Although both the 18th century documents were addressed to "all men" they came from particular countries and they drew on particular traditions, in both cases a combination of Christianity and Enlightenment philosophy. The fact that the Universal Declaration was written at all is something of a miracle. It was clearly a response to the unprecedented horrors of World War II, including but not only the Holocaust. But the United Nations was a very new and uncertain institution and some of its most powerful members, not only the Soviet Union, for obvious reasons, but the United Kingdom because of the still-existing empire, and the United States because of the still legal segregation in much of the country were very nervous about universal human rights. That the Declaration could happen at all was because it occurred in that brief intermission between the end of World War II and the beginning of the Cold War. In the end the Soviet Union abstained, but it did not veto. Along with the Soviet Union, the United States and the United Kingdom were insistent that the declaration have no provisions for enforcement, and if it had it would certainly not have been ratified by the United States Senate, so jealous in protecting American sovereignty. It also had to speak in a language that could include all the world's cultures, so had to avoid particular religious or secular references. Jacques Maritain was involved in a group of philosophers charged with writing something like a substantive preamble but concluded that such proved unnecessary since the only expedient way of reaching an agreement was "not on the basis of common, speculative ideas, but on common practical ideas, not on the affirmation of one and the same conception of the world, of man, and of knowledge, but upon the affirmation of a single body of beliefs for guidance in action."

It was widely believed that the Universal Declaration was forced on the world by the United States, in part because of the active role of Eleanor Roosevelt. What was not widely known is that the American State Department was a most reluctant partner that repeatedly warned Eleanor Roosevelt that she had to make it clear that she did not speak for the US government. Joas shows that the initiative in the drafting came largely from small or non-Western countries. One of the chief drafters was a member of the Chinese delegation who was a Confucian and another was Charles Malik, a Lebanese philosopher and an Eastern Orthodox Christian. It was a woman delegate from India who urged the use of inclusive language so that the Declaration speaks of "all human beings," not "all men." In spite of the care with which the great powers kept any enforcement provision out of the Declaration, from the moment of its appearance a variety of activist groups demanded implementation. One observer noted, "[The Declaration] has come to achieve a significance it was carefully designed not to have at the time." I cannot here give you a sense of how great the consequences of that Declaration have been, not just because of its words, but because those words called out for realization in practice and so stimulated many groups in many parts of the world that were determined to do just that.

Finally I would like to add a fourth document to the three that Hans Joas has found so important but that he doesn't mention, namely *Gaudium et Spes*, the Vatican II Pastoral Constitution on the Church in the Modern World of 1965. It was *Gaudium et Spes* that for the first time declared the Church unequivocally committed to the idea of modern human rights. Further, like the Universal Declaration, though in its own way, it was speaking not only to fellow Catholics, or to Christians of whatever allegiance, but to believers of all kinds, including secularists, so far as they, too, were committed to the realization of those rights. The global reach was evident from the very beginning: "[T]his Second Vatican Council, having probed more profoundly into the mystery of the Church, now addresses itself without hesitation, not only to the Sons of the Church and to all who invoke the name of Christ, but to the whole of humanity."

For me the special value of *Gaudium et Spes* is its constant awareness of how rights language can be interpreted in an individualistic and self-serving way but how although the dignity of the human person as created in the image and likeness of God is always at the center, that dignity is never realized except in relation to others, in societies that include the Church but many other social forms as well.

Gaudium et Spes was not issued by a nation or by the United Nations, but I think it deserves a place alongside those other documents because it shows the largest religious body in the world finally giving its assent, qualified to be sure, to the modern human rights regime about which it had been from the beginning ambivalent to say the least. I don't want to overlook the history of modern Catholic Social Teachings going back at least to Leo XIII's *Rerum Novarum* of 1891, which in many ways indicates a Catholic presence in the growing consensus. But *Gaudium et Spes* put its seal on that process as the last and longest document of the Second Vatican Council.

So, with my limited time, I must leave you with two enormously important facts that are to some degree related in time but neither of which explains the other: modernization as the greatest and most rapid material change in human history, and an idea of the sacredness of the person that has changed the values of the world though unevenly and incompletely.

Since I am at the beginning of my task in writing this next book, *The Modern Project in the Light of Human Evolution*, I must leave you with this extraordinary fact of which I was unaware before I started but that has only become clearer the more I learned:

The great religious-ethical-political change that moved us from traditional hierarchical, often despotic, societies, to societies that, at least in principle, though so far never completely in fact, respect the dignity of every single member of society and allow them to participate on an equal basis in the government of their own society, had been outlined in principle and even begun to be put in practice in traditional agricultural societies whose social development index had barely changed for 1800 years. But some decades later the discovery of steam power began a series of industrial revolutions, economic historians now count three, that dramatically and totally changed our material world, led to enormous population growth and a series of technical changes that have greatly improved the life of some of us while they threaten all of us with the greatest hard ceiling in history. How to make sense of this story, how to see its two apparently disparate parts fitting together, is the task I have only begun to face. So, more than usual in academic discourse, I leave you with a great question whose answer, to me at least, is still very far from clear.

CHAPTER 2

TURNING OFF NATURE'S THERMOSTATS

Technology, Ecology, and Deep History

KYLE HARPER

INTRODUCTION: HISTORY'S THERMOSTATS

In 2013, Robert Bellah gave a lecture at the University of Notre Dame titled "The Modern Project in the Light of Human Evolution."[1] Looking forward to a future book project, he reflected on modernity as a kind of breakdown, or breakthrough, of certain long-standing limits on human growth and expansion. He repeatedly used the vivid metaphor of a "thermostat" that had kept humanity in check until modern times. In his words:

> It is as if there were a built-in thermostat that put a break on continuous development at each stage of development, a rather harsh thermostat operating through war, famine and plague, but one that didn't stop growth, only kept it from exceeding certain limits. . . . The world of science and capitalism has removed the thermostat on global warming so that we keep on getting hotter and hotter and nothing turns off the heat because there is no functioning thermostat. . . . The whole idea of unlimited growth is thermostatless and ultimately self-destructive. . . . In fact, if it weren't such an ugly word, I could call my next book "Thermostatlessness."[2]

1. Robert N. Bellah, "The Modern Project in the Light of Human Evolution," University of Notre Dame, South Bend, IN, March 19, 2013. Chapter 1 in this volume.
2. Bellah, "The Modern Project," 24, 28.

"Thermostatlessness" is indeed an ugly word for a big and stimulating idea. The metaphor of modernity as the breakdown of natural limits can act as a starting point to reflect on the contours of human history. In other words, it is a chance to reflect on some of the major themes that occupied Bellah's scholarly talents throughout his career and to try to pull together some of the loose ends that he was thinking about in his later years. This chapter is an effort to think about "thermostats" in nature and in human history. It will argue that doing so requires a kind of interdisciplinary approach to big-picture human history. To think about "thermostats" in human history is necessarily to think about our past in concrete, biological terms. It requires us to see the human story as part of, not something apart from, nature.

A thermostat is a regulatory device invented by humans to maintain temperature at a set equilibrium. Nature, too, is full of regulatory mechanisms at all scales, from individual cells to entire ecosystems.[3] Critically, populations of animals are regulated in nature. The number of individuals of any species fluctuates within certain bounds but cannot increase in an uncontrolled fashion. Humans are different—though as we will see, it is important to be careful and specific on this point because our distinctiveness can be overstated and misunderstood to our peril. But there are nearly eight billion of us, which is truly astounding for a large-bodied mammal. In fact, aggregate human biomass is now more than ten times higher than the biomass of all wild mammals combined.[4] We have been called, justly, "the dominant animal."[5] Why are there so many of us? Why is it not instead a world dominated by gorillas, or gibbons, or geckos?

Rather than starting with the human side of these questions, consider why animal numbers are limited—why there is a built-in "thermostat" for other organisms. There are, for instance, a few hundred thousand chimpanzees. Their numbers have been reduced by habitat loss in recent times, but chimp populations probably never exceeded a million or two, despite the fact that these apes are quite intelligent.[6] The reason why is because in nature, all populations are

3. Sean B. Carroll, *The Serengeti Rules: The Quest to Discover How Life Works and Why It Matters* (Princeton, NJ: Princeton University Press, 2016).

4. Yinon M. Bar-On, Rob Phillips, and Ron Milo, "The Biomass Distribution on Earth," *Proceedings of the National Academy of Sciences* 115 (2018): 6506–11.

5. Paul R. Ehrlich and Anne H. Ehrlich, *The Dominant Animal: Human Evolution and the Environment* (Washington, DC: Island, 2009).

6. Samantha Strindberg et al., "Guns, Germs, and Trees Determine Density and Distribution of Gorillas and Chimpanzees in Western Equatorial Africa," *Science Advances* 4 (2018): 2964.

regulated.[7] This means that rates of population change are density-dependent. In simple terms, populations grow or decline based on differences in the birth rate (fertility) and death rate (mortality). When births exceed deaths, populations increase, and vice versa. But birth rates and death rates are influenced by a number of factors, some of which are determined by the size of the population itself. Consider a few of these mechanisms.

As a population grows, the availability of food will decrease, and as food consumption per capita declines, birth rates and death rates eventually will be affected. Chimpanzees, for instance, are adapted to eat insects, fruits, and occasionally small monkeys in their tropical forest environments. There cannot be runaway population growth because if chimp numbers were to escalate, food availability per "chimp capita" would decline. As chimps became hungrier and hungrier, they would have trouble reproducing (fertility decline) or experience higher levels of sickness and death (mortality increase). Population numbers would then fall. They might fall to an extent that food availability was high, which in turn promotes fertility and depresses mortality.

The scarcity of energy and nutrients is perhaps the most important density-dependent mechanism that regulates animal populations—the most important natural thermostat. But scarcity is not the only such regulatory mechanism, and the forces of parasitism and predation are also powerful. Simply, any population that is successful will attract more parasites (giving parasites evolutionary incentives to learn to exploit the successful hosts). Similarly, any population that is successful is likely to attract more predators (giving them evolutionary incentives to learn to take energy from the successful prey population). As the biologist E. O. Wilson has aptly put it, parasites *are* predators that eat their prey in units of less than one.[8] In natural populations, parasites and predators act to keep populations in check. Like energy scarcity, they prevent populations from experiencing runaway growth in the long run; like energy scarcity, predators and parasites are part of nature's thermostat.

In the rest of this chapter, I ask what these ideas can tell us about human history. Doing so is necessary to bring to bear concepts and terms from very different fields and traditions of study. The study of population regulation belongs

---

7. Peter Turchin, *Complex Population Dynamics: A Theoretical/Empirical Synthesis* (Princeton, NJ: Princeton University Press, 2003).
8. E. O. Wilson, *The Meaning of Human Existence* (New York: Liveright, 2014), 180.

to the field of ecology; the study of mortality and fertility belongs to demography; the study of growth belongs to economics; and the study of modernization belongs to sociology. But to understand the human condition requires us to draw from all of these fields and traditions—to find a way to make their concepts and terms interoperable. That, it seems to me, is what Bellah was trying to do in the loose threads of his late work—and what we can try to continue in the same, large spirit.

THE MALTHUSIAN THERMOSTAT

Thomas Robert Malthus was the first great ecological thinker. An English country parson by profession, Malthus's family connections and education exposed him to the broad European currents of Enlightenment thought.[9] He was a contributor to eighteenth-century political economy, and although some of his ideas were presaged by thinkers like Benjamin Franklin, his *An Essay on the Principle of Population* (first published in 1798 and repeatedly revised and reissued thereafter) was a sensation and a watershed. And although its enduring influence has been most evident in the field of economics, it is worth noting that Malthus had a profound impact on the thinking of Charles Darwin, who realized that competition and differential mortality under competitive conditions and scarcity were the ultimate context of natural selection.[10]

To put his argument in ecological terms, Malthus held that human populations were regulated by energy availability. He postulated an endogenous relationship between population movements and the food supply that kept the total population in check. Human populations were capable of growing faster than output could grow in the agricultural sector, so population growth eventually meant decline in per capita wages—impoverishment. As people became poorer,

---

9. Alison Bashford and Joyce Chaplin, *The New Worlds of Thomas Robert Malthus: Rereading the Principle of Population* (Princeton, NJ: Princeton University Press, 2016).

10. As Darwin put it in his autobiography: "I happened to read for amusement Malthus on *Population*, and being well prepared to appreciate the struggle for existence which everywhere goes on from long-continued observation of the habits of animals and plants, it at once struck me that under these circumstances favourable variations would tend to be preserved and unfavourable ones to be destroyed. The result of this would then be the formation of new species. Here, then, I had at last got a theory by which to work." Charles Darwin, *The Autobiography of Charles Darwin* (London: John Murray, 1892), 40.

they could limit reproduction or mortality would increase. Malthus called the first mechanism the "preventative check"—societies could forestall the impoverishment of the population by limiting fertility. He called the second mechanism the "positive check." As a population became progressively impoverished, mortality would rise due to famine or to the indirect effects of poverty like plague and violence. The positive check is, of course, why Malthusianism has something of a reputation for being a bleak and pessimistic social philosophy. In the words of Malthus himself:

> The power of population is so superior to the power of the earth to produce subsistence for man, that premature death must in some shape or other visit the human race. The vices of mankind are active and able ministers of depopulation. They are the precursors in the great army of destruction, and often finish the dreadful work themselves. But should they fail in this war of extermination, sickly seasons, epidemics, pestilence, and plague advance in terrific array, and sweep off their thousands and tens of thousands. Should success be still incomplete, gigantick inevitable famine stalks in the rear, and with one mighty blow levels the population with the food of the world.[11]

And, of course, the Malthusian positive check is precisely what Bellah called "a rather harsh thermostat operating through war, famine and plague."[12]

It is a great irony in the history of social thought that Malthus provided one of the best models for social dynamics—but was wrong in the case of his own society, where runaway modern growth had already begun, where the thermostat was turned off (or was being turned off). But as a picture of premodern social dynamics, the Malthusian model remains powerful. It is probably fair to say that its influence remains highest among economic historians (and to a certain extent among historical demographers). Why is that so, and why is the Malthusian hypothesis so important for understanding the long-term social dynamics of human societies?

Like any good model, the Malthusian one helps to identify the mechanistic relationship among a few critical variables and to illuminate what otherwise

---

11. Thomas Robert Malthus, *An Essay on the Principle of Population: The 1803 Edition* (New Haven, CT: Yale University Press, 2018), 276.
12. Bellah, "The Modern Project," 24.

might lie hidden. The most important prediction of the Malthusian model is that, in the long run, there is no per capita economic growth—the real wage level will be held at the subsistence line because population and wages are in homeostatic equilibrium. The Malthusian model predicts that if a population for any reason enjoys some transient prosperity, fertility will go up or mortality will go down until the population rises and reduces the people to misery. Then there will be poverty, hunger, famine, war, or pestilence, so the population may fall enough to bring back prosperity. But the long-term equilibrium is set by a wage level that is around the line of minimal biological subsistence for the human population.

The best empirical confirmation of the Malthusian model is in fact that per capita incomes remained so devastatingly low across the entire preindustrial period.[13] The world before the Industrial Revolution was Malthusian in the sense that it was defined by populations that subsisted near the bare minimum. The Malthusian world was one of dire poverty that has become difficult to imagine or evoke. For most of the people, everywhere, most of the time, incomes (in today's terms) were about five hundred dollars per person, per year. Life expectancies were also miserably low—probably close to twenty years in tropical regions, a bit higher (mid-to-high twenties) in temperate climes.[14] Precision and quantification can be almost descriptively meaningless here. What matters is that for most of our history, most people lived close to the biological minimum necessary for survival—bouncing around a bit, above and below the subsistence line, but without long-run trends of improvement or increase.

To say the same thing in other words: for most of human history, there was stagnation, not growth. Down to ca. 1750, levels of per capita consumption remained *mutatis mutandis* where they had been since the origin of our species on the African savannah some 300,000 years ago. Even aggregate population growth rates, when measured from the very beginning, were negligible (a point that we will qualify momentarily). That is why the economic historian (and die-hard Malthusian) Gregory Clark could say that down to the Industrial Revolution, growth rates in human economies were, to a first-order approximation,

---

13. Angus Maddison, *Contours of the World Economy, 1–2030 AD: Essays in Macro-Economic History* (New York: Oxford University Press, 2007).
14. James C. Riley, *Rising Life Expectancy: A Global History* (New York: Cambridge University Press, 2001).

zero.[15] This is the "hockey stick" view of history—a long period of flat, near-zero growth, followed by exponential increase.

In my experience, as an ancient historian who spends lots of time with other premodern historians, it ruffles feathers to say that to a first-order approximation, the only thing that happened before 1750 was that population growth swallowed up everything else. The question, though, is not whether the Malthusian model annoys us or flatters the periods that we study. The question is whether it is a valuable heuristic, a meaningful picture of social dynamics that helps us identify mechanistic relationships and otherwise hidden connections. And in those terms, Malthusian social theory is indispensable.

The Malthusian prediction of zero growth can be usefully confronted with two empirical findings that are in apparent tension with the model. First, by 1750, there were nearly a billion humans on earth, which implies some kind of growth.[16] Second, there seem to have been phases of the past (the high Roman Empire, the Abbasid Caliphate, and Song China, to name a few) when broad parts of the population, not just a tiny extractive elite, enjoyed real wages significantly above the subsistence level. Both of these realities prompt important clarifications of the strict Malthusian model.

In response to the first issue, economic historians have helpfully distinguished between extensive growth and intensive growth.[17] "Extensive growth" can be defined as an increase in the aggregate output of an economy, generally caused by an increase in inputs, such as population. In other words, there is more product because there are simply more people, but the output per person has not changed. "Intensive growth," by contrast, can be defined as an increase in the per capita output of an economy. Intensive growth is "real" growth. It is growth on a per person basis that allows the possibility of a population enjoying life above the level of mere biological subsistence (though of course, the distribution of income is structured by institutions and social arrangements). Importantly, the Malthusian model only predicts that there is no long-run intensive growth.

15. Gregory Clark, *A Farewell to Alms: A Brief Economic History of the World* (Princeton, NJ: Princeton University Press, 2007).

16. Massimo Livi Bacci, *A Concise History of World Population*, 5th ed. (Chichester, UK: Wiley Blackwell, 2012).

17. Peter Temin, *The Roman Market Economy* (Princeton, NJ: Princeton University Press, 2012), provides a helpful primer. More generally, see Oded Galor, *Unified Growth Theory* (Princeton, NJ: Princeton University Press, 2011).

Premodern history, then, witnessed successive and cumulative technological innovations that increased output—at times on a per capita basis, but only transiently. In the Malthusian economy, technological progress could change the level of the population, but not the level of the average income. By 1750, then, what humanity had to show for all of its technological innovation was simply more people, not greater average prosperity.

What about the second issue, the fact that history presents so many "golden ages" when the most dire predictions of the Malthusian model seem hardly in evidence? Indeed, there are phases of the past that seem to defy the law of gravity of the Malthusian economy, when a broad, middling group living well above the biological minimum is attested. The sociologist Jack Goldstone has characterized these periods as ages of "efflorescence" and sees the phenomenon not as a fatal contradiction of the Malthusian model but an important qualification.[18] In those periods of civilization when things went right (peace, institutional stability, or even a favorable climate), trade and technological innovation did allow intensive growth. And, significantly, these phases of intensive growth could last for decades, or even a century or two. The Malthusian world thus had significant cushion, and the long run inevitability of renewed misery could be put off for significant stretches of time. But, crucially, not forever. And in fact, the category of historical "efflorescence" underscores the difference between premodern and modern growth. Periods of premodern growth were bounded and slow, whereas modern growth has been sustained and fast. None of the premodern efflorescences led to breakaway growth, to sustained intensive growth such as characterizes the post-Malthusian economy. To put it back in Bellah's terms, the thermostat was always there, in the background, even if it was a bit clunky and imperfectly effective. (The room might warm up, a bit, for a while, but eventually the regulatory mechanisms would kick back in and cool things off.)

I have argued for another important extension or qualification of the Malthusian model—one that helps address issues raised by historical demographers and also goes to the heart of how biology can enrich political economy. Empirically, the causal relationship between population movements and changes in the wage level is robust. In premodern economies, when the population rose, wages

18. Jack A. Goldstone, "Efflorescences and Economic Growth in World History: Rethinking the 'Rise of the West' and the Industrial Revolution," *Journal of World History* 13 (2002): 323–89.

declined; and when the population fell, wages rose; and in the long run, techno-logical advance resulted in population growth but income stagnation. But the reverse relationship has been shown to be weak or unsupported, that is, changes in the wage level only sometimes and only partly seem to drive changes in fertil-ity and mortality. Malthusian theory predicts that when wages decline, fertility will decline (people will marry later or practice natural fertility limitation) and/ or mortality will go up (people will starve or get sick and die). Conversely, when wages go up, people in a Malthusian economy should have more babies or die at a lower rate.

In general, premodern societies do not seem to obey these latter predictions very well. Fertility rates were too conservative, too unresponsive to changes in the wage level. In premodern societies, the greatest (but not the only) control on fertility was nuptiality; delaying marriage was the primary means of reduc-ing fertility; and deeply embedded cultural customs shaped marriage patterns, so the system was not highly responsive to short-term movements.[19] Mortality rates, by contrast, were relatively variable—sometimes wildly variable. And yet movements in the death rate seem strangely disconnected to changes in the level of per capita income. In more formal terms, the mortality rate was exogenous to the wage level. The Malthusian model seems particularly bad at predicting pestilence, yet pestilence was one of the main factors affecting the mortality rate. Premodern population movements seem to be essentially random, driven by unaccountable, exogenous factors. In the words of the economic historian Jan de Vries:

> The periodic *crise de subsistence* were real enough in their short-term effects but seem incapable of explaining the larger patterns of population growth and decline. Periodic crisis-mortality notwithstanding, overall mortality rates in England were lower in the sixteenth and early seventeenth centuries (resulting in average life expectancy at birth of more than thirty-eight years) than they would be again until well into the nineteenth century. Mortality rates rose significantly during the seventeenth century in England, and they appear to have done so in much of Europe, and, indeed, much of Eurasia as well. Epidemiological factors, substantially exogenous to the socioeconomic

---

19. Christer Lundh and Satomi Kurosu, eds., *Similarity in Difference: Marriage in Europe and Asia, 1700–1900* (Cambridge, MA: MIT Press, 2014).

systems of the time, appear to have dominated mortality and, hence, the overall course of population change. Thus, rather than a crisis provoked by endogenous processes, unique to the technologies, institutions, and reproductive practices of particular societies, the seventeenth-century demographic crisis appears to have had a proximate cause that was exogenous—infectious-disease vectors possessing a history of their own, and before which societies stood powerless.[20]

It is a stark limitation of the Malthusian model that population movements are so weakly dependent on changes in the wage level. But this is a limitation that is inherent in the fact that Malthus was a political economist and not, in fact, an ecologist (a field that did not exist, of course, until the twentieth century). In nature, animal populations are regulated both by food availability and by the role of predators and parasites. The conventional Malthusian model predicts that human populations are regulated by the availability of food (expressed in terms of the real wage level since consumption in populations living near the subsistence line is dominated by food). But conventional Malthusianism has nothing to say about the other mechanisms of population regulation—predators and parasites. But these mechanisms too are an important part of nature's thermostat, providing checks that prevent runaway population growth.

For humans, predators have never been a serious demographic factor. That is because even before the evolution of *Homo sapiens* some 300,000 years ago, hominins had become apex predators. Like gray wolves or great white sharks, we are hunters who are not hunted, despite the occasional mishap with a tiger or shark. In itself, this is quite remarkable, given our physiology—our pathetic teeth and unintimidating "claws" (aka fingernails). But early hominins developed technologies—namely, the control of fire and ability to make weapons—that gave us leverage over predators such as the saber-toothed cats that *had* been a regulating factor in the very deep past.[21]

Parasites, by contrast, have been an enormously important demographic factor throughout the human past. Down to the twentieth century, most people,

20. Jan de Vries, "The Economic Crisis of the Seventeenth Century after Fifty Years," *Journal of Interdisciplinary History* 40 (2009): 151–94.
21. For example, Sally Reynolds, Ronald J. Clarke, and Kathleen Kuman, "The View from the Lincoln Cave: Mid- to Late Pleistocene Fossil Deposits from Sterkfontein Hominid Site, South Africa," *Journal of Human Evolution* 53 (2007): 260–71.

most of the time, in every society, died of infectious disease.[22] Infant mortality was grievously high, and life expectancies were low. Bacteria, viruses, protozoa, and helminths accounted for the vast majority of human deaths, directly and indirectly. Plague, smallpox, dysentery, tuberculosis, typhoid fever, typhus, syphilis, malaria, and various worm infections were among the great killers. Diseases like plague, smallpox, and typhus were especially prone to wild oscillations—sudden, sharp increases in mortality that we call "epidemics," when a disease spreads through a susceptible population rapidly. In premodern times, life was both short and unpredictable because death was mostly caused by invisible microbes against which populations were basically helpless.

Thus, rather than seeing the mortality rate as determined by purely exogenous, random forces, we can recognize that human populations were partly regulated by the natural force of parasitism. Population growth was constrained because death rates were high and because occasionally they were *exceptionally* high. The Black Death, most notoriously of all, wiped out approximately half of the population of Europe, the Near East, and North Africa (and its effects beyond are still being debated).[23] Plagues like this could take decades or even centuries to recover from. And these kinds of events were *ecological* rather than *economic*—that is to say, we can best understand them as natural events shaped by the expansion of human populations and our relationship with parasites rather than the endogenous effects of changes in the wage level.

Malthusian theory, in short, is not sufficient to explain how premodern regulatory mechanisms—thermostats—constrained the growth of human populations. But Malthus *plus* microbes brings us closer to a full ecological model of premodern human populations. Including the microbes in the scope of the model can also help us understand the transition to "thermostatlessness," to modern breakaway growth, which is hard to explain without accounting for the control of infectious disease and the modern decline in mortality that accompanied it.

Sociological models can help us understand the dynamics of past societies, and the ecological perspective enriches one of the most powerful models

22. Kyle Harper, *Plagues upon the Earth: Disease and the Course of Human History* (Princeton, NJ: Princeton University Press, 2021).
23. Ole J. Benedictow, *The Black Death, 1346–1353: The Complete History* (Woodbridge, UK: Boydell, 2004).

of premodern societies. I have tried to bring it to bear to help us understand the Roman past—and particularly the big, long-run dynamics of Roman history. Even a process as complex as the "fall of the Roman Empire" can be understood in terms of the interplay of natural and sociopolitical factors.[24] The fall of Rome was in reality a process of state failure and stagnation that unfolded—with fits, starts, and reversals—over the course of several centuries. The Roman Empire at its height fostered a period of efflorescence, when both population and per capita output increased. The power of the state—fiscally, demographically, militarily— benefited from the phase of growth, which fueled the expansion and flourishing of the empire. But starting in the middle of the second century, the congeries of agrarian societies around the Mediterranean that made up the Roman Empire experienced a series of major, interregional shocks. These shocks were ecological as much as social disruptions, which marked the beginning of a new period of Roman statecraft.

The first shock was brought on both by the end of a long period of climate stability (known even to paleoclimatologists as the Roman Climate Optimum) and the beginning of a period of greater instability. Even more potent was the onset of a pandemic, known as the Antonine Plague, in the middle of the 160s.[25] The pandemic arrived at a moment when real wages were still rising (at least in Egypt, where the survival of papyri allows quantitative estimation; the story could have been different elsewhere), so it can hardly be considered a strictly Malthusian shock. The biological agent of the Antonine Plague remains a mystery, perhaps an ancestral form of the smallpox virus.[26] Regardless, it seems to have been the biggest mortality event—both spatially and in terms of magnitude—in centuries. The pathogen that triggered this mortality seems to have arrived in the Roman Empire from beyond Roman borders, very likely transported on the intercontinental trading networks that connected the empire to Africa and Asia.[27] And once the pandemic reached the Roman world, it found

---

24. Kyle Harper, *The Fate of Rome: Climate, Disease, and the End of an Empire* (Princeton, NJ: Princeton University Press, 2017).
25. Elio Lo Cascio, ed., *L'impatto della "peste Antonina"* (Bari, Italy: Edipuglia, 2012).
26. For a discussion of this point, see Rebecca Flemming, "Pandemics in the Ancient Mediterranean World," *IsisCB Special Issue*, ed. Stephen P. Weldon and Neeraja Sankaran (2021), https://pandemics .isiscb.org/essay.html?essayID=13.
27. Brandon T. McDonald, "The Antonine Crisis: Climate Change as a Trigger for Epidemiological and Economic Turmoil," in *Climate Change and Ancient Societies in Europe and the Near East*, ed. Paul Erdkamp, Joseph G. Manning, and Koenraad Verboven (Cham, Switzerland: Palgrave Macmillan, 2021), 373–410.

a densely settled and highly interconnected population that proved highly susceptible to the transmission of the disease.

The sudden loss of a significant part of the population (although estimating
death tolls is nearly impossible), especially of able-bodied adults who did most
of the agrarian labor and military service, was a serious blow to Roman fortunes. The Antonine crisis was thus a multifaceted disaster that marks a point
of caesura between the efflorescence of the high empire and the more troubled
age that followed. The Roman Empire would go on to experience other crises, as well as phases of resurgence. And the most severe crisis of all awaited
in the sixth century, when an episode of severe, volcanically induced cooling
was immediately followed by the beginning of a centuries-long pandemic of
bubonic plague. But the ultimate lesson of these chapters of the past is that
human and natural systems are interdependent. This has been true throughout
our history, both during the long, essentially Malthusian period, when populations lived on the knife's edge of subsistence, and in the uncertain present of
runaway growth.

Bellah's interest in the idea of a thermostat was piqued in part by the work of
another ancient historian, Ian Morris, whose *Why the West Rules—for Now* argues
for a "social development index" as a measure of growth and progress over long
timescales.[28] Morris is a neoevolutionist whose social development index is a useful effort to capture the scale and tempo of material progress. What struck Bellah
about Morris's index was both how slow and limited growth was before modern
times and how strong, technological limits imposed themselves again and again.
And that is, essentially, the lesson of the Malthusian model: human societies were
strongly constrained by their energy-extraction technologies, which in turn were
a function of their limited knowledge of the natural world and limited ways
(technologies) to exploit it. The transition to modernity can be considered from
many angles, but it was certainly a transition from a slow-moving and highly
energy-constrained world to a fast and more unbounded period of growth.
Humans, in short, learned to turn off nature's thermostat.

One of the great questions of historical sociology must be—how did we do
that?

---

28. Ian Morris, *Why the West Rules—for Now: The Patterns of History, and What They Reveal about the Future*
(New York: Picador, 2010).

MODERNITY SEEN FROM ANTIQUITY: TURNING THE THERMOSTAT OFF

The transition to modern growth brought the Malthusian world of stagnation to an end. In crude terms, this transition is defined by rapid increases in population (there are now almost eight billion humans on the planet) and massive increases in energy and resource usage (the average individual American, for instance, consumes about the same amount of energy per day as a herd of gazelles). The economist Angus Deaton characterized the transition to modern growth as "the great escape" because it was an escape from the Malthusian trap of stagnation, a world of general poverty and early death.[29] The economic side of the transition—the shift to an age of industrialization, of constant Schumpeterian innovation—is relatively familiar. But it was accompanied by an equally important and instrumental transition in human demography—the demographic transition, a shift from high-mortality, high-fertility societies to low-mortality, low-fertility societies.[30] The relationship between modern economic growth and the demographic transition is intricate and inseparable. Ecologically, it is imperative to reckon with both transitions and the complex causal links between them to have an adequate description of how the thermostat was turned off.

When Malthus first published his essay in 1798, there were around one billion humans on the planet. Life expectancies were low and stagnant. In fact, in the first edition, Malthus claimed that "with regard to the duration of human life, there does not appear to have existed from the earliest ages of the world to the present moment the smallest permanent symptom or indication of increasing prolongation."[31] As with so much else about his model, Malthus was right about the world that was starting to pass away—and wrong about the world that was coming into being.

---

29. Angus Deaton, *The Great Escape: Health, Wealth, and the Origins of Inequality* (Princeton, NJ: Princeton University Press, 2013).
30. Richard A. Easterlin, *Growth Triumphant: The Twenty-First Century in Historical Perspective* (Ann Arbor: University of Michigan Press, 1996); Robert William Fogel, *The Escape from Hunger and Premature Death, 1700–2100: Europe, America, and the Third World* (Cambridge: Cambridge University Press, 2004); Galor, *Unified Growth Theory*.
31. Thomas Robert Malthus, *An Essay on the Principle of Population* (Oxford: Oxford University Press, 1798), chapter 9.

The mortality transition refers to the more than doubling of average life expectancy that has been achieved since Malthus wrote. In broad terms, the mortality transition was achieved by human-influenced changes in the main causes of morbidity and mortality.[32] Death by infectious disease has declined dramatically, and instead most people now die of organ diseases (neurodegenerative disease, cardiovascular disease, liver disease, diabetes, and others) and neoplastic diseases (various cancers). This transition happened first (and most slowly) in Western Europe and the United States, and in the twentieth century, it has progressed globally (and more rapidly). It remains incomplete, of course, and in many underdeveloped countries, infectious diseases still account for a significant burden of morbidity and mortality.[33] Yet even the lowest country-level average life expectancies are in the sixties, more than double (and almost triple) their pretransition levels.

The mortality transition is undoubtedly one of the great accomplishments of our species. It has relieved countless humans from suffering and early death and allowed them to reach their full potential; it has spared countless parents from the anguish of burying their children. So how was it achieved? To some extent, the control of infectious disease was a direct effect of modern economic growth, which freed populations from bare-bones, subsistence-level existence.[34] But close study of the question has emphasized that economic growth did not play a leading role.[35] Instead, a series of overlapping innovations in public health and biomedicine have prolonged human life and pushed the threat of infectious disease toward the margins. Quarantine, vaccines, sewers, water treatment, hygiene, antibiotics, insecticides, oral rehydration therapy, and other improvements in primary care and therapeutics have liberated us from the doom of early death.

32. Classically, see Abdel R. Omran, "The Epidemiologic Transition: A Theory of the Epidemiology of Population Change," *Milbank Quarterly* 49 (1971): 509–38. Alexander Mercer, *Infections, Chronic Disease, and the Epidemiological Transition: A New Perspective* (Suffolk, UK, and Rochester, NY: University of Rochester Press and Boydell & Brewer, 2014); Harper, *Plagues upon the Earth.*

33. James C. Riley, "The Timing and Pace of Health Transitions Around the World," *Population and Development Review* 31 (2005): 741–64.

34. This position was defended by Thomas McKeown, *The Modern Rise of Population* (New York: Academic Press, 1976). Fogel, *The Escape from Hunger and Premature Death*; Roderick Floud, Robert W. Fogel, Bernard Harris, and Sok Chul Hong, *The Changing Body: Health, Nutrition, and Human Development in the Western World since 1700* (Cambridge: Cambridge University Press, 2011).

35. David N. Weil, "Health and Economic Growth," in *Handbook of Economic Growth*, vol. 2B, ed. Phillippe Aghion and Steven N. Durlauf (New York: Elsevier, 2014): 623–82. See also Harper, *Plagues upon the Earth*, chapters 10 and 12.

From an ecological perspective, the control of infectious disease removed one of nature's thermostats.[36] Just as fire and weaponry had once freed us from the dangers of predators (for the most part), so modern innovations in public health and biomedicine gave us the upper hand over parasites that had held our numbers in check. The result was a breakdown of a natural mechanism of population regulation—and we have multiplied accordingly. There are now almost eight billion of us and counting. Fertility has *declined* in modern times, of course. The proximate cause of modern population growth is the decline of mortality. Human beings have multiplied deliriously not because they "suddenly started breeding like rabbits: it is just that they stopped dying like flies."[37]

The modern rise in population would have been checked if there had not been an equally consequential breakthrough to modern economic growth. As Bellah notes, it was the transition to fossil energy, which has fueled modern growth, that allowed humans to break through the Malthusian ceiling that had made progress slow and halting throughout our history. From the perspective of deep history, what made the Industrial Revolution so transformational was the development of technologies that harnessed the potential of fossil fuels—first coal, later hydrocarbons—to augment or replace humanity's dependence on living phytomass as a source of energy. In the words of John McNeill, "the adoption of fossil fuels made us modern." Since the onset of industrialization, human energy use has increased 100-fold.[38] The transition from a Malthusian economy to a Schumpeterian economy was enabled by fossil energy. It is impossible to imagine modern growth without its ecological basis in the power unlocked in the form of congealed sunlight stored underground.[39]

36. Kyle Harper, "Deep History and Disease: Germs and Humanity's Rise to Planetary Dominance," in *Altered Earth: Getting the Anthropocene Right*, ed. Julia Adeney Thomas (Cambridge: Cambridge University Press, 2022), 106–29.

37. Geoffrey Lean, Don Hinrichsen, and Adam Markham, *Atlas of the Environment* (London: Helicon, 1990). Generally, see Tim Dyson, *Population and Development: The Demographic Transition* (London: Zed Books, 2010). The vivid quote about "dying like flies" comes originally from Nicholas Eberstadt, "Too Many People?," International Policy Network, 2007, https://www.aei.org/wp-content/uploads/2011/10/20070712_Too_Many_People.pdf, 6.

38. See Robert C. Allen, *The British Industrial Revolution in Global Perspective* (Cambridge: Cambridge University Press, 2009), for an overview of the transition to industrial growth. Also see John R. McNeill, "Energy, Population, and Environmental Change since 1750: Entering the Anthropocene," in *The Cambridge World History: Volume 7: Production, Destruction and Connection, 1750–Present*, ed. John R. McNeill and Kenneth Pomeranz (Cambridge: Cambridge University Press, 2015), 53.

39. Vaclav Smil, *Energy and Civilization: A History* (Cambridge: Cambridge University Press, 2017).

Descriptively, then, the transition to modern growth was characterized by a shift from a long period without sustained trends in life expectancy or per capita economic output (a "period" that lasted from the origins of our species until the eighteenth century!) to a period with dramatic improvement in human longevity and sustained intensive or per capita economic output. But description is not explanation, and in his Notre Dame lecture, Bellah then turns briefly to ask, what might explain such a momentous transformation? We should separate hypothesized causes into proximate and distal explanations; sometimes there has not been adequate or sufficiently careful inquiry into the proximate causes of the transition, and yet, to be convincing, any big distal or ultimate explanations (e.g., capitalism, imperialism, individualism, or whatever) should have to account for the proximate mechanisms that in fact drove the transition to healthier and more prosperous societies.

Bellah rightly calls attention to the importance of modern science in effecting this transition. Had he been able to pursue his project, he would surely have drawn on the extensive literature in economic history seeking the origins of modern growth and the prolongation of human life. And indeed, some of the most convincing accounts of both industrialization and the decline in mortality highlight the rapid, accelerating growth in human knowledge of the natural world. After all, coal does not cause modern growth; rather, the scientific knowledge of how to build machines that exploit fossil energy catalyzed dramatic and sustained increases in per capita output. Ever-growing scientific knowledge then underwrote the Second Industrial Revolution, the wave of innovations led by electricity, hydrocarbons, the internal combustion engine, big steel, and industrial chemistry.[40] Along the same lines, science (modern, empirical, Enlightenment science) allowed the development of effective technological interventions like vaccines, water filtration, and pharmaceuticals to control infectious disease and extend average human lifespans.[41]

In a word, science is a highly credible, *proximate* explanation for how humans turned off the thermostats of nature. It was knowledge of nature that simultaneously allowed us to figure out how to transcend the powerful ecological limits

---

40. Joel Mokyr, "The Second Industrial Revolution, 1870–1914," in *Storia Dell'economia Mondiale*, ed. Valerio Castronovo (Rome: Laterza, 1999), 219–45; Vaclav Smil, *Creating the Twentieth Century: Technical Innovations of 1867–1914 and Their Lasting Impact* (Oxford: Oxford University Press, 2005).

41. Harper, *Plagues upon the Earth*, 375–416, 466–90.

of human and animal power, as well as how to overcome the threat of deadly microbes. In the words of the economist David Weil, "The contemporaneous advance of income and health in the leading countries over the last several centuries (after millennia of stagnation) is explained largely by changes in knowledge. More specifically, productive knowledge and health knowledge advanced together, driven by the underlying advance of science and the spirit of experimentation born of the Enlightenment."[42] None of this should seem surprising from the perspective of basic physics. All life on earth is a system far from thermodynamic equilibrium that stores and processes information (mostly in DNA) to extract free energy from the environment to create order and organization. Information about the environment is fundamental to growth in the biosphere. Similarly, human cultures have progressively acquired and stored information about the external environment to create greater and greater local reductions in entropy—to grow.

From my perspective as a historian who has mostly studied the other—Malthusian—side of the great transition, this proximate explanation is compelling. What limited the Romans—what precluded the possibility of breakaway economic or population growth—was the lack of rapid, sustained technological innovation, rooted in their limited knowledge of the natural world.[43] Roman medicine never came remotely close to the breakthroughs of modern medical science. Roman technology advanced, but only by inches—aqueducts, improvements in animal breeding, wind- and water-powered machines. These innovations never triggered a sustained, accelerating breakthrough in how to extract and exchange energy from the environment. In a way, the great value of the Malthusian-ecological model is to help us see what was not there, and thus why the thermostats worked in antiquity, as they did for the vast majority of our history as a species.

If science-led technological innovations are the best *proximate* explanation for the revolutionary changes in life and death experienced by human societies over the last two and a half centuries, what *distal* or *ultimate* explanations can account for their appearance, so sudden in relative terms, after millennia of stagnation? Why did practical knowledge of nature gain pace? Why then (slowly from the

---

42. David N. Weil, "A Review of Angus Deaton's *The Great Escape: Health, Wealth, and the Origins of Inequality*," *Journal of Economic Literature* 53, no. 1 (2015): 102–14. Richard A. Easterlin, "Industrial Revolution and Mortality Revolution: Two of a Kind?," *Journal of Evolutionary Economics* 5 (1995): 393–408; Easterlin, *Growth Triumphant*; Deaton, *Great Escape*.
43. Richard P. Saller, *Pliny's Roman Economy: Natural History, Innovation, and Growth* (Princeton, NJ: Princeton University Press, 2022).

seventeenth century, more evidently from the eighteenth, and stunningly fast from the nineteenth), and why there (Western Europe and its offshoots first, particularly Britain, and then most of the rest of the world, particularly in the twentieth century)? What conditions triggered the transformation?

Any number of materialist, institutional, and ideological explanations have been mooted, most of them permutations of answers adumbrated by Adam Smith, Karl Marx, and Max Weber. The question will likely keep historically inclined economists and sociologists employed until the dying sun swallows the earth. Satisfying answers are unlikely to be simple, which is why "isms" like capitalism or individualism are so frequently adduced, and why the direction of causal links between materialist and ideological realms is such a venerable question. Bellah, for his part, points to the "two enormously important facts that are to some degree related in time but neither of which explains the other: modernization as the greatest and most rapid material change in human history, and an idea of the sacredness of the person that has changed the values of the world though unevenly and incompletely."[44]

Without going further, we can conclude by remarking that any satisfying answer will benefit from trying to make terms and arguments developed in various disciplines interoperable. Ideas from the history of science—for instance, the arguments of Michael Strevens about the rise of the modern "knowledge machine," or empiricist discursive rules about what counts as truth—have much to offer.[45] In parallel, the work of economic historians like Joel Mokyr, who has emphasized the culture of "useful knowledge" that took shape in the early phases of the transition, is also illuminating.[46] And a truly physicalist materialism that traces the flow of energy and materials through modernizing human societies has much to offer.[47] In short, the question of how humanity attained enough knowledge of nature to turn off the regulatory mechanisms that hold in check every other species is, in the words of Bellah, "a great question whose answer . . . is still very far from clear," and one that will continue to require different kinds of expertise to approach.[48]

---

44. Bellah, "The Modern Project," 36.
45. Michael Strevens, *The Knowledge Machine: How Irrationality Created Modern Science* (New York: Liveright, 2020).
46. Joel Mokyr, *The Lever of Riches: Technological Creativity and Economic Progress* (New York: Oxford University Press, 1990).
47. Vaclav Smil, *How the World Really Works: The Science Behind How We Got Here and Where We're Going* (New York: Viking, 2022).

CONCLUSION: AXIAL AGE MORALITY IN THE ANTHROPOCENE

The fact that humanity has turned off nature's thermostats is a fundamentally ambiguous achievement. The "great escape" has liberated humanity from the doom of poverty and early death. Leave aside here the important distributional questions that must also force us to ask about the equity of modern growth both within and between societies. The breakdown of nature's regulatory systems that held humanity in check is also responsible for modern environmental degradation—resource depletion, pollution, global warming, and the ongoing massive loss of biodiversity known as the Sixth Extinction. It is clear from his final essays that Bellah was going to explore the moral dimensions of this challenge with characteristic breadth and insight. In his words:

> Are the ethical traditions developed over centuries in the great religions and civilizations capable of meeting the ethical challenges of our rapidly escalating cultural condition? And, perhaps most ominous of all, if we have blown through every hard ceiling that for 16,000 years kept social development at a moderate level, can we go on increasing the social development index forever, or is the mother of all hard ceilings looming not far above us? And if we are facing such a hard ceiling in the not so distant future, can we manage a soft landing or do we face catastrophe?[49]

We can regret that we will face these questions without the mind that posed them here so perspicaciously. As we reckon with them, the deep history of our species can help us come to terms with our past to understand who we are and what we have done to the planet. Deep history can give us a sense of the vertiginous acceleration of human ecological impact in modern times—and hopefully a sense of urgency and solidarity as we chart our way into the future.

---

48. Bellah, "The Modern Project," 36.
49. Bellah, "The Modern Project," 26.

CHAPTER 3

THERMOSTATLESSNESS: THE PROJECT OF MODERNITY AND THE PROCESS OF MODERNIZATION

Reflections on Robert Bellah's Account of the
Late Modern Predicament

HARTMUT ROSA

INTRODUCTION

In one of the last lectures that Robert N. Bellah gave to the academic world, his Notre Dame lecture, he made it exceptionally clear that a full account of modernity as a historical social formation, and with it an acute diagnosis of our late modern predicament, require a dual analysis, or a combination of two distinct perspectives.[1] This duality is indicated already in the title of his lecture: "The Modern Project in the Light of Human Evolution." With the latter term— "Human Evolution"—the focus is, so to speak, on a *third-person perspective*. With the help of the social development index formulated by the archaeologist Ian Morris,[2] Bellah recounts the history of civilizational advance from an "outside," structural perspective that observes the historical changes in the patterns of *energy production and consumption, social organization, war-making capacity,* and *information technology*. But with the first half of the title—"The Modern Project"—the

---

1. Robert N. Bellah, "The Modern Project in the Light of Human Evolution," University of Notre Dame, South Bend, IN, March 19, 2013. Chapter 1 in this volume.
2. Ian Morris, *Why the West Rules—for Now: The Patterns of History, and What They Reveal about the Future* (New York: Picador, 2010); Ian Morris, *The Measure of Civilization: How Social Development Decides the Fate of Nations* (London: Profile Books, 2013).

spotlight is on the *first-person perspective*: it denotes the modern aspiration toward a good life couched in moral and ethical terms, drawing on the hopes and fears motivating this project from cultural and hermeneutical perspectives. Here, Bellah recounts the evolution of the idea of autonomy and the accompanying principle of human rights, which were finally institutionalized in the twentieth century. This latter perspective clearly is dominant in the prologue to Bellah's planned book (chapter 4 in this volume), centering on the philosophical and ethical conceptions of philosophers and poets alike, and it is also dominant in his Tillich Lecture (chapter 8 in this volume).

Now, with a considerable degree of amazement, Bellah observes that there are two very different revolutionary turns that have come to define the social formation of modernity, with each of these revolutions visible from only one of the two perspectives. Thus, the closing paragraph of his lecture reads like this:

> I must leave you with two enormously important facts that are to some degree related in time but neither of which explains the other: modernization as the greatest and most rapid material change in human history, and an idea of the sacredness of the person that has changed the values of the world though unevenly and incompletely. . . . I must leave you with this extraordinary fact of which I was unaware before I started but that has only become clearer the more I learned: The great religious-ethical-political change that moved us from traditional hierarchical, often despotic, societies, to societies that, at least in principle . . . respect the dignity of every single member of society . . ., had been outlined in principle and even begun to be put in practice in traditional agricultural societies whose social development index had barely changed for 1800 years. But some decades later the discovery of steam power began a series of industrial revolutions . . . that dramatically and totally changed our material world, led to enormous population growth and a series of technical changes that have greatly improved the life of some of us while they threaten all of us with the greatest hard ceiling in history. How to make sense of this story, how to see its two apparently disparate parts fitting together, is the task I have only begun to face. So, more than usual in academic discourse, I leave you with a great question whose answer, to me at least, is still very far from clear.[3]

---

3. Bellah, "The Modern Project," 36.

Since Bellah sadly left us before he could take up the challenge formulated here, I would very much like to jump in for him and try to give an answer to the question that he ends with: How do the two parts fit together? I actually believe that no account of modernity can claim to be convincing, let alone comprehensive, if it does not manage to combine these two sides (i.e., the cultural-hermeneutical and the structural-institutional perspectives). Conceptually, I propose that we should start by distinguishing the two parts as the ethico-political *project of modernity*, centered on the notion of autonomy, on the one hand (the cultural perspective); and the *process of modernization*, which yields the escalatory increases in energy capture as well as the organizational, war-making, and information-technological capacities that Morris and Bellah wonder about, on the other hand (the structural perspective). The pressing question, then, is this: How do the project of modernity and the process of modernization fit together?

THE PROJECT OF MODERNITY AND
THE PROCESS OF MODERNIZATION

The question of whether modernity is first and foremost a *cultural project*, driven by moral and intellectual ideas and validity claims formulated most succinctly by the Enlightenment thinkers, or a structural process, driven by the logic of either capital accumulation or functional differentiation, has been one of the core defining questions of sociology ever since its beginning. This question, as Bellah notes, is not equivalent to the dichotomy between materialist and idealist accounts of modernity, but of course it is connected to it. And as in the latter debate, most social theorists tend to agree that both tendencies, the cultural and the structural, go together in producing the modern social formation. Nevertheless, the question *how* the two sides exactly are interwoven, and hence, which element takes the lead, remains utterly unresolved. In the humanities, it is often taken as self-evident that the Enlightenment principles and validity claims gradually reshape not just our conceptions, but step by step also our practices and institutions in science, politics, law, the economy, and everyday life. By contrast, in sociology we find the opposite tendency: taking it for granted that certain structural processes—be they variations of differentiation as in the conceptions of Émile Durkheim, Talcott Parsons, or Niklas Luhmann, or of capitalist appropriation in (neo-)Marxian theories—led to necessary adaptations in the realms of politics or culture and in the form of individual subjectivation. To complicate matters, it is not even clear whether the relationship between the project and the process is historically and geographically variable or not: it is certainly conceivable, for example, that in the eighteenth century (as Bellah suggests), the project took shape and started to exert a transformative influence on social structures in Europe, while in the twentieth century, in some East or Southeast Asian regions, the structural impacts of the globalizing process of modernization have (re-)activated elements of the cultural project. It is also possible that in the twenty-first century, the two sides have turned against each other, such that insisting on the validity claims of individual and political autonomy in the Enlightenment sense now has become an obstacle to unbridled modernization—and vice versa, that the dizzying demands of ever-increasing acceleration undercut the cultural and institutional safeguards of moral autonomy.[4] To even begin to contemplate such questions, of course, it is of paramount importance to clearly define the contours of the project, as well as the features of the process. I want to start with the former.

A SPIRITUAL DECLARATION OF INDEPENDENCE: THE PROJECT OF MODERNITY

Following thinkers such as Charles Taylor,[5] Jürgen Habermas,[6] and Bellah, one could claim, perhaps, that at the heart of the modern project is a *spiritual declaration of independence.*[7] This declaration is an emanation of the claim to autonomy not in a narrow, Kantian sense, but, as Bellah points out, in a broader sense of self-determination against the powers that be. These powers include all forms of religious or political paternalism or unjustified authority, but also the limiting forces of nature and history. To be autonomous in this sociological sense means to be capable of making decisions and implementing them independent

---

4. This is something that has been suggested by Richard Sennett, for example; see Richard Sennett, *The Corrosion of Character: The Personal Consequences of Work in the New Capitalism* (New York: Norton, 1998).
5. Charles Taylor, *Sources of the Self: The Making of the Modern Identity* (Cambridge, MA: Harvard University Press, 1989).
6. Jürgen Habermas, *The Philosophical Discourse of Modernity* (Cambridge, MA: MIT Press, 1987).
7. I borrow this term from Taylor, who uses it much in the sense that I develop here, but with the stress on *independence from nature*; see Charles Taylor, "Legitimation Crisis?," in *Philosophical Papers, Vol. 2: Philosophy and the Human Sciences* (Cambridge: Cambridge University Press, 1985), 277.

of, or against, the will of others. Hence, it is not just "a new understanding of the human person, the human individual, an understanding that is religious as well as ethical and political,"[8] as Bellah has it, but it also implies a new conception of the relationship between self and world, a new spiritual and habitual stance of being in the world—with the world encompassing everything "out there," outside the subject.[9]

Thus, as a political project, modernity is propelled by the idea that human beings as citizens should by themselves determine their fate by shaping society and the spatial and material environment independent of the demands of tradition, custom, or even nature. *Self-determination* thus appears to be the key promise of modernity, and social acceleration figures as a crucial means to break free from the inertia of tradition, custom, and convention and to overcome natural scarcities and social barriers to true autonomy.

The principle of autonomy, which in the collective realm is equivalent to the principle of *sovereignty*,[10] thus lies at the heart of the modern form of *being-in-and-to-the-world*, and it is equivalent to a fivefold spiritual declaration of independence: it implies making decisions which are, at least to some extent, independent of, or against, (1) the precepts of history, (2) the limitations of nature, (3) religious or political authorities, (4) family or community traditions or conventions, and (5) transcendent powers.

Now what I want to claim in the following is that scientific progress, technological acceleration, economic growth, political dynamization, and cultural innovation—in short, the processes that can be identified as "modernization"—in this cultural (or first-person) perspective were the cardinal tools by and through which this form of comprehensive sovereignty over nature, space, social life, and history has been pursued in the course of modernity. But to understand our current predicament, it is of vital importance to realize that the *cultural* (or "spiritual") disposition, which can be called the *paradigm of autonomy or sovereignty*, gradually has been turned from a moral claim and value into *an institutional requirement*. Let us look at this process a little more closely.

---

8. Bellah, "The Modern Project," 31.
9. Hartmut Rosa, *Resonance: A Sociology of Our Relationship to the World* (Cambridge and New York: Polity, 2019), 31–37; on this point, also cf. chapter 9 of this volume.
10. Hartmut Rosa, "Resonant Sovereignty? The Challenge of Social Acceleration—and the Prospect of an Alternative Conception," in *Sovereignty: A Global Perspective*, ed. Christopher Smith (Oxford: Oxford University Press, 2023), 323–42.

Quite obviously, the social and cultural expectation that it should be individuals themselves who decide on the basic goals, norms, and patterns of action that direct their lives is not self-evident. Quite on the contrary, in fact—while autonomy does not *require* that individuals break with the traditions and conventions of their communities, it does tie the latter's normative validity to the consent and ethical will of the former. To repeat it once again: in this sociological reading, autonomy should not be read as moral self-legislation in the deontological sense of Kant, but rather as a socially effective *principle of structuring social practice according to individual decisions*. This, however, eventually requires that there are practices and institutions within which individuals can develop and shape, as well as apply, their ethical will. It requires, in other words, subjects who claim to decide on the basic parameters of their lives—such as *where to live, whom to live with, what to believe in, what to strive for and to consume*, and *what to pursue*—and social institutions that allow and operate on such decisions. For autonomy in this sense to become a culturally as well as institutionally operative principle, a whole, complex array of intellectual, moral, religious, economic, legal, and political developments needed to converge in the revolutionary change of social fabric that marks the transition from an estate-based to a genuinely modern society. This convergence in Europe took effect mainly from the eighteenth century onward. Before that, the basic premise of life, the sociocultural, religious, and economic position of an individual, was predetermined at birth. There simply were no social institutions that made sense of things like a political choice or position, a religious stance, consumer choices, or professional careers. Who and what you are, what you believe in, and what you strive for were, in terms of social practice, basically decided beforehand. What gained ground with Enlightenment thinking, with "individualizing" religious ideas,[11] and in bourgeois claims to political power then evolved into a forceful cultural principle and ethicopolitical claim that perhaps found its paradigmatic expression in the famous formulation of the Declaration of Independence by the American colonies in 1776 that postulated the pursuit of happiness as an inalienable *individual right*. However, this claim to autonomy in the eighteenth century was still more a fighting creed than a social and institutional reality: it was met with considerable political, religious, and social opposition, and more important, it lacked the

---

11. Charles Taylor, *A Secular Age* (Cambridge, MA, and London: Harvard University Press, 2007), 146–58.

institutional underpinning to really *give* individuals the freedom of choice. You need markets (and an independent educational system) to allow producer and consumer choices, a democratic party system to allow political choice, freedom of movement to allow the choice of a place to live, and social practices that allow the free choice of spouses and family-founding, etc. Hence, as Peter Wagner[12] would have it, in the first phase of modernity as a social formation, autonomy was a powerful normative principle, an agent of change, but not yet a form of life or an institutional reality.

By the mid-twentieth century, however, in what Wagner calls "organized modernity," this situation in many parts of the world had changed significantly on both ends. Culturally, individuals habitually incorporated the claim to autonomy in their normative expectations and social practices. By that time, in so-called Western societies, it was not just the male bourgeois entrepreneur, but increasingly also women and workers who assumed and required that it *was* their individual right to decide where to live and whom to live with, what job to seek, what clothes to wear, whom to love, what to believe in, and whom to vote for in elections. The whole concept of *what it meant to lead a life and to have an identity* had changed. This, in turn, was possible only because social institutions had changed significantly too. Individuals now were *expected* and *required* to make all the relevant choices by schools and firms, by shops and supermarkets, parties and authorities, and other institutions. Without individuals capable of making choices and habitually willing to take responsibility for their choices, neither a supermarket nor a party system, let alone an advanced capitalist educational and career system, could work, and not even the institutions of the welfare state could function. The basic demand that society makes on the individual is that they *find* and *define* their position (or, better, their *positions*) within the social framework. *Find a job*, for example, has become a cardinal task for young men at first, but soon for young women, too. This does not make sense in an estate-based structure where sons inherit the professional positions from their fathers (and daughters were often tied to the positions of mother and/or wife). The same holds true for the second core task: *found a family*, or *found your own nuclear family—and find a place to live*! This, again, was pretty much confined at first to bourgeois groups but then spread out to most or all segments of the population.

---

12. Peter Wagner, *A Sociology of Modernity: Liberty and Discipline* (London: Routledge, 1994).

But, most interestingly, the same principle of autonomous positioning also oper-
ated for things like *find your political position*, which meant something like find
out whether you are a liberal, a conservative, or a socialist citizen; and *find your
stance toward the religious world*. Most significant for such individual development
were the social institution of adolescence as a phase of individual "positioning"
and the corresponding conception of a "normal biography" or, respectively, a
regular (i.e., standardized) life course.[13]

In adolescence, the young would question, challenge, and leave the positions of
the previous generation and reposition themselves. Thus, social change and social
innovation became a generational project. But the classical modern institutions
were geared toward a conception of autonomy that made the basic life choices a
more or less singular process. After one takes a profession, founds a family, and
becomes a political and religious citizen, one's position was supposed to be stable
and settled, so one's life could develop along the expectable paths of professional
and family "careers."[14] Hence, autonomy was culturally defined and institutionalized more or less in the sense of a life project. It meant directing one's life toward
the goals that were defined by one's professional, familial, political, and religious
choices. This did not deny the possibility of revision or conversion. Of course,
the ethical basis of modernity allowed a repositioning (e.g., through divorce or
religious conversion), but this was perceived as an institutional exception, as the
correction of an error; and after the repositioning, stability was sought to be
regained. Autonomy in the sense developed by and in the institutions of classical
modernity was supposed to consist in the definition and pursuit of individually
set, but quite robust and time-resistant, norms and goals.

However, due to processes of progressive acceleration and dynamization—to
the institutionalization of the process of modernization, to which I will turn
later in this chapter—the social and institutional fabric of the social formation
of modernity has since changed quite significantly once again. The neoliberal,
the political, and the digital revolutions around 1990 induced new levels of performative social competition and hence new pressures to consistently optimize
and readjust behavior. Hence, in the twenty-first century, the speed of social,

---

13. Martin Kohli, "Social Organization and Subjective Construction of the Life Course," in *Biographical
Research Methods, Vol. II*, ed. R. L. Miller (London: SAGE, 2005), 39–63; Martin Kohli, "The Institutionalization of the Life Course: Looking Back to Look Ahead," *Research in Human Development* 4
(2007): 253–71.
14. Zygmunt Bauman, *Liquid Modernity* (Cambridge: Polity, 2000), 113–18.

technological, and institutional change has reached a pace beyond the speed of generational change.[15] As a result, individuals are now forced to reposition themselves along all the axes of self-determination—work life, family life, political life, consumer choices, place to live, and political position, among others—in an ongoing, performative mode. Markers of identity are made potentially reversible and are thus temporalized. One no longer "is" a baker, a Protestant and a conservative, living in, say London, but one *has been working* as a baker for the last five years (but might lose or leave the job soon), is living in London right now (but is about to leave for Manchester), has been voting Conservative last time (but might vote UKIP in protest next time), and experiments with Buddhist mindfulness in a course next spring.

Of course, all this does not necessarily imply that those parameters of life or identity actually *do* change all the time; it only means that individuals now are aware and expect that they *can* change any time, through either their own decisions or the decisions of others. This is what the diagnoses of increasing flexibilization in individual life courses boil down to: the "normal biography" now reckons with shifts and ruptures—and *leading a life* means permanently monitoring one's standing, options, and resources. Individuals are (culturally as well as institutionally) expected to performatively make judgments about whether it is time for a reorientation or repositioning with respect to their place, job, family, political or religious position, and consumer choices, but also with respect to much more mundane things, such as their banking arrangements, retirement, health, communication contracts, Internet provider, and newspaper preference. As authors like Alain Ehrenberg[16] and Axel Honneth[17] have suggested, this implies the danger that instead of bestowing a strong sense of agency, self-efficacy, and coauthorship of their lives to individuals, modern subjects tend to feel worn out and tired, close to suffering fatigue or burnout.

By consequence, and this is of crucial importance for the project of modernity, the high speed of social change and the ensuing instability of patterns of association, forms of practice, and packages of knowledge force subjects to renounce

---

15. Hartmut Rosa, *Social Acceleration: A New Theory of Modernity* (New York: Columbia University Press, 2013), chapter 4.
16. Alain Ehrenberg, *The Weariness of the Self: Diagnosing the History of Depression in the Contemporary Age* (Montreal: McGill-Queens University Press, 2009).
17. Axel Honneth, "Organisierte Selbstverwirklichung: Paradoxien der Individualisierung," in *Befreiung aus der Mündigkeit: Paradoxien des gegenwärtigen Kapitalismus*, ed. (Frankfurt, Germany, and New York: Campus, 2002), 141–58.

the classical conception of autonomy as a life project. The social psychologist Kenneth Gergen makes this point quite forcefully. In a section aptly titled "Out of Control," he writes: "Slowly I am learning the pleasures of relinquishing the desire to gain control of all that surrounds me. *It is the difference between swimming with deliberation to a point in the ocean—mastering the waves to reach a goal—and floating harmoniously with the unpredictable movements of the waves.*"[18] In fact, this image suggests that there are two possible forms of experiencing the life course in late modernity: one is the conception of the surfer who rides the waves. She does not try to sail to a specific point or island in the ocean; she simply watches the waves and observes the wind, and when there is a challenging and promising opportunity, she jumps the waves, staying on top and in some form of control, not in control of the overall direction, but nevertheless in control of choices and movements. Translated into social practices, this means that surfers decide when to quit a job, terminate an intimate relationship, move out, or other decisions. Mastering the waves of modern life in this sense certainly still bestows a sense of self-efficacy and autonomy, albeit not the autonomy that served as a yardstick in classical modernity, or in the Enlightenment sense of the term. However, this requires a high level of cultural, economic, social, and physical (i.e., body-related) capital. Individuals who lack these resources are in danger of becoming "drifters," in the sense suggested by Richard Sennett in his book *The Corrosion of Character.*[19] A drifter either lacks the resources to make profitable and informed choices or lacks actual options altogether. He or she is simply subject to the unpredictable and sometimes wild currents of the waves—and hence, in no significant sense an "autonomous" subject, regardless of whether he or she is held responsible for his or her positionings. Responsibility without any control certainly is not autonomy.

Interestingly, it seems that this loss of control and sovereignty is mirrored in the political or collective sphere too. The modern aspiration to dominate, use, and control nature appears to have led to a situation where the runaway effects of climate change, resource depletion, and environmental pollution have created a situation where the modern social formation helplessly awaits the "hammer of doom" in form of an ecological disaster; the aspiration to achieve economic

18. Kenneth Gergen, *The Saturated Self: Dilemmas of Identity in Contemporary Life* (New York: Basic Books, 2000), xviii (emphasis added).
19. Sennett, *The Corrosion of Character.*

growth has turned into a structural and institutional necessity that has become harder and harder to fulfill—even negative interest rates, by themselves an economic perversity, no longer seem to power the engines—which leaves politicians and markets in an anxious expectation of an escalating economic crisis; and finally, the aspiration to break free from history and politically shape the future has turned into a desperate attempt to prevent the worst. Politics no longer appears to be about shaping the future society, but rather about handling the fire extinguisher.

So what we have here, it seems, is the project of modernity—the spiritual aspiration toward sovereignty and autonomy over nature, history, religious and political authority, traditions and conventions, and transcendent powers—turning against itself. The very same processes and tools that at first appeared to further and operationalize that aspiration now seem to undermine it. How are we to explain this?

DYNAMIC STABILIZATION: THE PROCESS OF MODERNIZATION

In my view, the image of modern society that I sketched out in the previous section is significantly incomplete if one leaves out its "third-person counterpart": the structural institutionalization of what I call the "process of modernization." Robert Bellah in his paper observes an almost unbelievable escalation and acceleration of "social development" in the sense of Ian Morris, that is, an escalation of energy production and consumption in the improvement of war-making capacities, of organizational skills and technologies, and of information technology, such that the social development index has risen from 43 in the late eighteenth century to more than 1,000 by the year 2000. This growth of the human "ability to get things done in the world"[20] is all the more spectacular when we consider that 43 points on the development index had been reached by the Romans almost 2,000 years ago, and by the Chinese around the year 1000 too, but it never was surpassed before 1773 (the invention of the steam engine)—and that 1,000 does not even appear to be the limit on the score. If we do not "hit the ultimate hard ceiling," as Bellah has it, it might go up to 5,000 within the next eighty years. So, Bellah asks, what is driving this escalation?

---

20. Morris, *The Measure of Civilization*, 5.

From the account of modernity that I am suggesting here, the reason for the almost blind persistence of patterns of growth, innovation, and acceleration from the eighteenth century onward is that acceleration and dynamization have become a *structural necessity* for modern society. Looked at in purely structural terms, *a society should be called modern*, I suggest, *when its mode of stabilization is dynamic*—that is to say, *when it systematically requires economic growth, technological and social acceleration, and (increasingly) cultural innovation to reproduce its structures and to maintain its institutional status quo.*[21] As the reader will notice, this definition does *not* require or include any cultural or normative ideals or principles such as autonomy or sovereignty. It is a definition formulated exclusively from the third-person perspective.

When we look at it historically, it turns out that the shift from an adaptive to a dynamic mode of stabilization can be observed as a systematic transformation in all cardinal spheres of social life occurring, despite some historic predecessors, mainly from the eighteenth century onward, that is, parallel with the evolution of the modern conception of autonomy. Most obviously, of course, it can be found in the realm of economy. The accounts of both Max Weber and Karl Marx vividly focus on this transformation. In a capitalist economy, virtually all economic activity depends on the expectation and promise of an increase in the form of profit of one sort or another. Money–Commodity–Money' (m-c-m'), is the short formula for this, where the prime (') signifies the increased return. It is realized, of course, either through exploitation or through *innovation* (of product or process) and *acceleration*, mostly in the form of increased productivity. The latter can be defined as an increase in output (or value production) per unit of time (i.e., as acceleration). I do not want to go into the details of economic theory here, which can show that the need for innovation, acceleration, and growth really is *intrinsic* to the logic of capitalist production, to the logic of competition, and even to the logic of the modern monetary and credit systems.[22] The net result of this is that without steady growth, acceleration, and innovation, at least under late-modern conditions of globalized economic and financial markets, capitalist economies cannot maintain their institutional structures: jobs are lost, companies close

---

21. Hartmut Rosa, Klaus Dörre, and Stephan Lessenich, "Appropriation, Activation and Acceleration: The Escalatory Logics of Capitalist Modernity and the Crisis of Dynamic Stabilization," *Theory, Culture and Society* 34 (2017): 53–74; Rosa, *Resonance*, 404–13.
22. Rosa, *Social Acceleration*, 161–73.

down, tax revenues decrease, while state expenditures (for welfare and infra-structural programs) increase, which in turn tend to cause a severe budget deficit at first, and then a progressive delegitimation of the political system.

All of this can be seen in the present crisis in southern Europe, particularly in Greece and Spain, where the institutional structure of the health system, the educational system, pension schemes, the arts and sciences, and other aspects of the society are all in disarray or even decay due to the lack of economic growth. Thus, not just the economic system in a narrow sense depends on the *logic of escalation* as the consequence of the mode of dynamic stabilization, but also the welfare state and the system of democratic politics. As Luhmann[23] showed more than thirty years ago, the latter is based on the logic of dynamic stabilization too. Not only has the rather static monarchic order—where kings or queens rule for their lifetime and then are simply replaced in a dynastic succession that preserves order in an identical fashion—given way to a democratic system that requires dynamic stabilization through reiterated voting every four or five years, but, much more dramatically, elections (and hence legitimation) can be won only on the basis of political programs that promise an increase—in income, or in jobs, or in universities, houses, or hospital beds, for instance.

Interestingly, the same is true for the way that modern society perceives and produces *knowledge*. Quite independent of the escalatory logic of capi-talist reproduction, the modern conception of *science* displays a similar shift to a dynamic mode of stabilization that transforms its institutional order. In previous social formations, even past the axial shift, knowledge quite regularly was considered and treated as a social possession, or a treasure, that needs to be carefully handed down from one generation to the next. This knowledge in most communities is traced to some ancient or sacred source, such as to "holy scriptures," or "the wisdom of the ancients," and there almost invariably is an attempt to preserve this knowledge in pure form. It is knowledge about *how things are done*—for example, how one builds a home, or produces clothing and food, when to sow or to reap or how and when to hunt game, and, not least, how to perform the sacred rituals. Knowledge is transmitted from one generation to the next either simply by imitation and participation or in some form of schola. By contrast, modern societies shift from *Wissen* (knowledge) in this sense to

23. Niklas Luhmann, *Politische Theorie im Wohlfahrtsstaat* (Munich: Olzoc, 1981).

Wissenschaft (science). As the "schaft" in the German word indicates quite nicely, the central form and art of knowledge in modernity are not about preservation and schooling, or treasuring, but it is about systematically *pushing the borders*, increasing the volume of the known, and transgressing into the yet-unknown. Science is about looking further into the universe than ever before, deeper into the microstructures and particles of matter, closer into the workings of life. The sacred spaces of knowledge have moved from the schola to the laboratory. Science is reproduced dynamically through growth, increase, and transgression. Just as the propelling dynamics of m-c-m′ lie at the heart of the modern economy, a similar process of *knowledge-research-increased knowledge* (kn-r-kn′) provides the basis for modern science.

In "Science as a Vocation," as Bellah reminds us in his prologue, Max Weber[24] formulated this point quite forcefully:

> In science, each of us knows that what he has accomplished will be antiquated in ten, twenty, fifty years. That is the fate to which science is subjected; it is the very meaning of scientific work, to which it is devoted. . . . Every scientific "fulfilment" raises new "questions"; it asks to be "surpassed" and outdated. Whoever wishes to serve science has to resign himself to this fact. Scientific works . . . will be surpassed scientifically—let that be repeated—for it is our common fate and, more, our common goal. We cannot work without hoping that others will advance further than we have. In principle, this progress goes on ad infinitum.[25]

Finally, even in the arts, the picture is quite similar. After millennia of a predominantly mimetic art, for which the goal of artistic creation is the emulation either of nature or of some traditional style or ancient mastery, there is a marked shift in literature and poetry, as well as in painting, dance, and music, that puts the onus on innovation and originality. As in science—and quite contrary to what Weber thought—going beyond what others have done before becomes the central challenge in the arts as well.[26]

---

24. Max Weber, "Science as a Vocation," in *From Max Weber: Essays in Sociology*, trans. and ed. H. H. Gerth and C. Wright Mills (New York: Oxford University Press, 1958), 129–56.
25. Weber, "Science as a Vocation," 138.
26. Cf. Boris Groys, *On the New* (London: Verso, 2014).

In sum, the point that I want to make here should be clear: the structural logic of dynamic stabilization has become the hallmark of modern society in toto. It is translated into individual subjects' lives via the logic of competition. In the end, it is we humans who have to achieve growth, acceleration, and innovation through incessant optimization and rationalization, and we play this escalatory game through the endless accumulation of economic, cultural, social, and body-related capital. As with Weber's capitalist entrepreneur, modern subjects find themselves unavoidably "on their way down," as if on a downward escalator or on a slippery slope, if they do not run uphill to improve their standing and keep up with the changes around them.[27]

As a consequence, the acceleration cycle between technological acceleration, the acceleration of social change, and the corresponding acceleration of the pace of life that results from dynamic stabilization has become a self-propelling mechanism in modernity.[28] It maintains the socioeconomic order, as well as the institutional structure of the market system, of the welfare state, of science, art, and education via a substantive escalation of its productive power and substantive output. This is what explains the escalatory tendency that Bellah is so puzzled about. Needless to say, the stability achieved in and through this dynamic is remarkable; it has kept the machines going for more than 250 years—just as Weber predicted when he observed the "overwhelming force" of this "pulsating mechanism," which, he suspected, could keep on going "until the last ton of fossil fuel has burnt to ashes."[29]

However, the operational logic of dynamic stabilization also explains what Robert Bellah calls the "thermostatlessness" of modern society.[30] The fact that there is absolutely no inbuilt, endogenous limit to the processes of growth and acceleration (and with it of energy consumption), and furthermore, the fact that the ensuing increases—in extraction and pollution, production and consumption, traffic and waste—display escalatory tendencies, made him state that "the whole idea of unlimited growth is thermostatless and ultimately self-destructive. . . . If it weren't such an ugly word, I could call my next book 'Thermostatlessness.' "[31]

---

27. Cf. Rosa, *Resonance*, 414–20.
28. Rosa, *Social Acceleration*, 151–59.
29. Max Weber, *The Protestant Ethics and the Spirit of Capitalism*, trans. Stephen Kalberg (Chicago and London: FD Publishers, 2001), 123.
30. On this aspect, see the much more detailed account by Kyle Harper in chapter 2 of this volume.
31. Bellah, "The Modern Project," 28.

STRUCTURAL IMPERATIVES AND CULTURAL YEARNINGS

Quite obviously, the fact that there is no social "thermostat," that is, absolutely no endogenous limitation to the structurally necessitated, escalatory processes of growth, acceleration, and dynamization, entails the risk that this social formation, despite its amazing institutional robustness, paradoxically will turn out to become increasingly fragile, too. It can be undermined any time, either because of its externalities (such as ecological costs), because of a failure of social integration despite growth and acceleration (such as in phenomena of "jobless growth" and increasing social *precarization*), or because of problems created by desynchronization between the social and institutional spheres, to which I will return in a moment. In short, dynamic stabilization resembles a ride on a bicycle: the faster the wheels go, the more robust the bike is in its course (a slow bike can be made to tumble at the slightest push from the side, but not so for a fast one)—but the higher the risk of severe accidents too.

In my view, the logic of dynamic stabilization creates two escalating pathological tendencies that affect the structural process as much as the cultural project. The former is threatened by tendencies of growing socioeconomic desynchronization. Not all spheres and aspects of the world are equally speedable. Some processes can easily be accelerated, while others remain slow or even decelerate. The problem of desynchronization arises whenever and wherever fast and slow systems, groups, or processes interact (i.e., at the intersections). For example, what is discussed as the ecological crisis of the Anthropocene can be reinterpreted as a growing desynchronization between the tempo and rhythms of nature and the speed of socioeconomic processes. We cut down trees, catch fish in the oceans or rivers, and deplete valuable raw materials at a pace that simply is too high for them to reproduce; and we fill in the wetlands and pollute the air at a pace that is too fast for the self-cleansing of the environment. Thus, global warming, in fact, is literally an acceleration of the molecular movement up in the atmosphere due to the incessant socioeconomic acceleration down on earth. But more than this, it appears that even within the social world, there are serious forms of desynchronization, particularly between the speed of the markets and the media on one hand and the pace of democratic politics on the other. Democracy in itself is a time-consuming process of collective articulation, deliberation, and decision-making that cannot be sped up at will. As a result, the current crisis of Western democracies might well be explainable by such problems of desyn-chronization.[32] Finally, rising rates of depression, stress disorders and burnout, and the widespread cultural fear of such forms of overheating might indicate a growing desynchronization between late modern, high-speed social structures and the "souls" or psyches of the human subjects lagging behind. This is the sense, of course, in which Alain Ehrenberg has diagnosed "The Weariness of the Self."[33]

As for the cultural project of modernity, we have already seen how there appears to be a paradoxical backlash, in which the search for autonomy in the sense of self-determination and control over our life circumstances seems to result in a progressive *loss* of control. Furthermore, it even seems to lead to a loss of "vibrant connection" and responsivity in our contact with nature, with the future, with others, and in the end with ourselves—in short, to growing forms of *alienation*.[34] This is not the place for an extensive discussion of these forms of alienation as a loss of resonance with the world—suffice it at this point to observe that instead of reaching true spiritual independence from nature, his-tory, and social pressures, the modern social formation seems in danger of being encapsulated by self-created pressures beyond control.

To fully understand this contemporary predicament, and to contemplate how a "thermostat" could be brought to bear, we need to look a bit more closely at how the project and the process actually interact.

Historically, as Bellah notices, the project clearly precedes the escalatory tech-nological achievements of the process of modernization. But the shift toward a mode of dynamic stabilization obviously precedes the Industrial Revolution, too. Thus, the invention of the steam engine, and soon after of the railway, for exam-ple, are the *result* rather than the *cause* of a changed institutional relationship with the world—and this change has cultural and structural elements. As we can learn from Georg Simmel as well as from Max Weber, even though the project and the process clearly are analytically separate, it might well turn out to be impossible to disentangle the two when it comes to the identification of first causes.

However, there can be no doubt that in the early phases of Western moder-nity, the cultural project and the structural logic pointed in the same direction.

---

32. Hartmut Rosa, "The Speed of Global Flows and the Pace of Democratic Politics," *New Political Science* 27 (2005): 445–59.
33. Ehrenberg, *The Weariness of the Self*.
34. Taylor, "Legitimation Crisis?" Also see Taylor, *Sources of the Self*; and Rosa, *Resonance*, 307–56.

The progress of science, the advancement of technology, the explosion of economic productivity, and the institutionalization of human rights and democracy could be perceived as the wheels of progress by which the realization of spiritual independence—of autonomy and sovereignty—became a plausible goal. Modernization's promise was the overcoming of hunger, cold, and scarcity, of ignorance and poverty, of dependence and disease. Thus, it would be utterly wrong to think of the machines of modernization as driven only by the logic of competition, by the fear of losing out. No social formation can subsist in the long run if its only motivational source is fear—there always needs to be a propelling aspiration too. This is all the more true for modern society: as I have tried to point out, the mode of dynamic stabilization requires incessant growth, acceleration, and innovation—but institutions cannot grow, accelerate, or innovate by themselves. They depend on the motivational energy of subjects to do so. So what is driving modern subjects? In part, the answer is clear: it is the project of modernity. But how exactly does it translate into a desire for ceaseless increase?

For this, we have to turn to the dominant modern conception of the good life. As we know from social theorists ranging from Alasdair MacIntyre[35] to John Rawls, there is no shared "comprehensive doctrine of the good" anymore.[36] Instead, in the face of ethical pluralism, the good has been *privatized*. What are worthwhile goals and pursuits in life, which of the "value spheres" (art, religion, politics, family life, work life, but also sports and other pursuits) should be given which weight in one's life, are questions that teachers as well as parents tell kids to find out for themselves. What there is, however, is a range of "primary goods" of which it is always better to have more rather than less. This is John Rawls's definition of primary goods such as money, health, rights, relationships, and knowledge.[37] Thus, parents can tell their offspring (and in fact, themselves): *No matter what you will be or aspire to in the future, be it a pianist, a physicist, or even a*

35. Alasdair MacIntyre, Donald P. Kommers, and W. David Solomon, "The Privatization of Good: An Inaugural Lecture," *Review of Politics* 52 (1990): 344–77.

36. John Rawls discusses this idea in John Rawls, *Political Liberalism: Expanded Edition* (New York: Columbia University Press, 2005); and John Rawls, *The Law of Peoples: With "the Idea of Public Reason Revisited"* (Cambridge, MA: Harvard University Press, 1999).

37. "Regardless of what an individual's rational plans are in detail, it is assumed that there are various things which he would prefer more of rather than less. With more of these goods men can generally be assured of greater success in carrying out their intentions and in advancing their ends, whatever these ends may be." John Rawls, *A Theory of Justice, Revised Edition* (Cambridge, MA: Belknap Press, 1999), 79.

terrorist, whether you will have a family with kids or live alone or as a couple, it is better to have more rather than less money and social relationships, physical health, attractiveness and strength, and cultural knowledge and capabilities in addition. One could also couch this in Bourdieusian terms: subjects are constantly seeking to accumulate economic, social, cultural, and body-related capital. In a social world that is dynamizing incessantly, there in fact is no other way to keep up the aspiration for long-term autonomy and independence. Only through incessant investment in these realms can one entertain hopes to be able to remain a sovereign subject even in a future full of economic, technological, social, and cultural changes and uncertainties. And in fact, of course, in a society that escalates dynamically there can *never be enough* of these forms of capital if one wants to *really* be safe and independent.

In this way, the structural imperatives of increase and expansion are translated into individual hopes and fears. As a consequence, the modern conception of the proper way *to lead a life*, of the ethically and morally correct stance in the world, has come to converge with the imperatives of dynamic stabilization. The good is perceived as everything that expands the horizon of what is *available, accessible, and attainable*—we could call this the "Triple A Approach to the good life." It explains, for example, why *money* is attractive to modern subjects. In fact, the Triple A horizon for the individual to a large extent is defined by the balance in his or her bank account. If it has a lot of money in it, the whole earth (or, if you are Elon Musk, even Mars) is within reach—but if it is overdrawn, even the puniest apartment or a bus ticket to the nearest town might be out of reach.

Similarly, the Triple A conception of the good life helps to explain the attractiveness of the metropolis to modern subjects. It is in the big city that the whole world of art and science, of entertainment and adventure, of sports and shopping, and other realms comes within reach. Finally, the attractiveness of new technologies is almost always grounded in their promise to increase the horizon of accessibility. For example, when you got your first bike as a kid, your physical world literally expanded: you could now visit your friends, or the communal swimming pool, or the far side of town; and when you got a car, it literally exploded, just to be dwarfed again by what came into the horizon of options by plane or other transport. And smartphones today have become so irresistible because they actually grant easy and immediate access to all the music, literature, and movies that have ever been digitized, to all the world's knowledge, and to most of the people we know, all with just a click. What a spectacular increase of the Triple A horizon!

Thus, when Bellah asks how the two "apparently distinct parts" fit together, this is my answer: the cultural longing for an increase in the horizon of availability, accessibility, and attainability—resulting from the modern project of spiritual independence—converges with the structural requirement for incessant growth, acceleration, and innovation. The project of modernity in this sense is still propelling the process of modernization. But, as we have seen, the logic of escalation paradoxically has also started to *undermine* the stability of the process (by economic or ecological disaster), as well as the promise, of the project. The expansion of the Triple A horizon was supposed to be the vehicle for the ultimate end of autonomy, or spiritual independence. This latter aspiration, I believe, was the yardstick that, albeit in a barely articulated way, defined the meaning of *progress*. It is evident in the conviction of many generations of parents that their hard work and sustained efforts secured a better and brighter future for their kids. This idea, this sense of *moving forward* toward a better (i.e., more autonomous) form of life, in a way actually meant that modern society felt that it was moving toward an earthly "New Jerusalem." This hope, obviously, is now betrayed by the fact that for the first time in modern history, in all highly industrialized societies from Europe to North America to Japan, the majority of parents no longer are driven by the ambition, hope, and desire for their kids to have a better life than themselves, but by the desperate attempt to enable them to *keep the standards they have achieved already*.[38] This means that subjects now feel they have to run faster and faster just to stay in place, not to make headway, while they worry that the future might be bleaker despite their efforts. This feeling resembles running up a down escalator. As soon as we relax, we start losing ground. The same holds true for collective political experience. Political parties and programs have turned defensive in the sense that they justify reforms and projects as *necessary adjustments* to preserve and protect what we have.

---

38. Bruce Stokes, "Public Divided on Prospects for the Next Generation: Americans, Canadians and Europeans Generally Pessimistic," *Pew Research Center Report: Global Attitudes and Trends*, June 5, 2017, https://www.pewresearch.org/global/2017/06/05/2-public-divided-on-prospects-for-the-next-generation.

I have called this the perception of a "frenetic standstill" on the individual as well as the collective level.[39] But in fact, it is worse than a standstill. It is not just that we no longer run toward a bright horizon; rather, we are running from an abyss that closes in frighteningly from behind. Year after year, we have to muster more physical, psychological, and political energy to keep the engines going, while the price we pay and the dangers we face on all three levels—environmental, political, and individual—loom ever larger. This, so to speak, is the downside of Ian Morris's spectacular story of modernity's success, and one starts to wonder in what sense future increases in his social development index really can be understood as *social development* or *progress*.

CONCLUSION: HOW TO INSTALL A THERMOSTAT

If this analysis of the modern social formation and its current predicament is correct, we should ask a different question than Bellah. "The basic question of my project is how do we as a species adapt to a rate of change that no biological species has ever faced before?" Bellah asks, and then he adds: "Can we go on increasing the social development index forever, or is the mother of all hard ceilings looming not far above us?"[40] In my view, we should not ask whether we are able to adapt to ever-higher rates of speed, change, and innovation, and we should not seek to achieve these ever-higher rates until we hit the ceiling. It is impossible to simply insert a "thermostat" into the fabric of modern society. What modernity really needs is a move that puts it beyond the logic of escalation—that is, it needs to shift to a different mode of stabilization. I would like to call this alternative an "adaptive mode of stabilization," for it seems to be self-evident that a society should be *able* to grow, accelerate, or innovate whenever there is a good reason to do so—that is, when there is a need or desire to change the status quo (e.g., when there is a shortage or lack of something important, or when there is a change in its environment or a new vision of an important improvement). But it should not be *forced* to grow, accelerate, and innovate incessantly just to keep its institutional status quo. This shift in its basic institutional fabric, of course, and quite far-reaching reforms in the realms of the economy and politics appear to

---

39. Rosa, *Social Acceleration*, 299–322.
40. Bellah, "The Modern Project," 26.

be inevitable. Bellah goes on to ask whether "the great role models of our cultural heritage—the Buddha, Confucius, Socrates, Jesus—[are] still relevant to our condition? Are the ethical traditions developed over centuries in the great religions and civilizations capable of meeting the ethical challenges of our rapidly escalating cultural condition?"[41]

My suggestion would be that perhaps these ancient traditions in fact might help not to satisfy the requirements of our *rapidly escalating cultural condition*, but to *transform* this cultural and ethical condition altogether, to correct its pathological tendencies. For this, I think, we also need a revision of, or at least an addendum to, the spiritual declaration of independence that founds the modern project. What I have in mind here is a change of our basic "spiritual stance" toward the world.

The mode of dynamic stabilization with its institutionally inbuilt "pleonexia," as Plato undoubtedly would have called it, habitually enforces as a default mode a stance of domination, or more than that, even of *aggression* toward the world. The need to incessantly increase, improve, innovate, and optimize to fulfil the imperatives of growth and acceleration and to preserve society's institutional fabric leads to aggression against nature in the guise of ever-expanding extractive industries and increasing pollution, but also toward ourselves. Studies show that contemporary subjects don't feel at home in their bodies;[42] they increasingly are ready to enhance themselves through surgery, drugs, or implantations, and by working on themselves in ways that often lead to burnout and depression. Aggression even seems to define the basic stance that people take toward the political world, as the bitter oppositions between Democrats and Republicans in the United States or between Brexiteers and Remainers in the United Kingdom testify.[43] Part of the reason for this is that in the daily struggle imposed by the imperatives of dynamization, everything that gets in our way is seen and treated as an obstacle that needs to be conquered and controlled—or overcome

---

41. Bellah, "The Modern Project," 26. Compare this to Alan Strathern's reflections on the relationship between axiality and power in chapter 6 of this volume.
42. Elvira Ebert, "Zur Entwicklung des Konsums in den neuen Bundesländern von 1990–1994/95," in *Wohlstand für Alle?*, ed. Wolfgang Glatzer and Gerhard Kleinherz (Opladen, Germany: Leske & Budrich, 1997), 166–69; Thomas Gunzelmann, Christa Brähler, Aike Hessel, and Efmar Brähler, "Körperleben im Alter," *Zeitschrift für Gerontopsychologie & -psychiatrie* 12 (1999): 40–54.
43. Michael Bruter and Sarah Harrison, "Inside the Mind of a Voter: Do People Still Respect Democracy?," *LSE Brexit*, June 15, 2020, https://blogs.lse.ac.uk/brexit/2020/06/15/inside-the-mind-of-a-voter-do-people-still-respect-democracy/.

and destroyed. And as we can learn from Horkheimer and Adorno's[44] account of modernity, this stance of aggression dovetails with the project of modernity insofar as the desire for autonomy is tied to an attitude of domination and control toward the world we live in.[45]

So how could it be otherwise? It is important to notice here that the problem that causes the environmental destruction that Bellah is so strongly concerned with[46] is not so much rooted in the *values and ideals* that people consciously hold. Individuals rarely or never advocate an aggressive stance toward nature, and in value surveys all over the world, they reveal an ever-growing concern about the environment. Sustainability has become one of the most important values for voters all across the early industrialized societies at least.[47] The millions of young people turning out for the "Fridays for Future" demonstrations or events concerning agreements such as the Paris Climate Accord testify to this. However, from what is known as the gap between environmental awareness and corresponding action, we can learn that it is precisely those social classes for whom sustainability ranks highest on their value scale who have the worst (i.e., largest) carbon and environmental footprints.[48]

We find a similar value/action gap in other segments of social life, too; it opens up between concern for social justice and economic behavior, for example, or between valuing slowness and leading accelerated lives. It seems as if the institutional imperatives of the "iron cage"[49] are almost completely immunized against people's ethical ideals and convictions.[50] While they value an environmentally

---

44. Theodor W. Adorno and Max Horkheimer, *Dialectic of Enlightenment* (London: Verso, 1997).

45. Of course, similar arguments have been brilliantly formulated and extensively elaborated in recent strands of feminist literature and debate; see, for example, Jessica Benjamin, *Beyond Doer and Done To: Recognition Theory, Intersubjectivity, and the Third* (Milton Park, UK, and New York: Routledge, 2017); Donna Haraway, *Simians, Cyborgs and Women: The Reinvention of Nature* (Milton Park, UK, and New York: Routledge, 1991); Catriona Mackenzie and Natalie Stoljar, eds., *Relational Autonomy: Feminist Perspectives on Autonomy, Agency and the Social Self* (New York and Oxford: Oxford University Press, 2000).

46. Compare Bellah's sense of urgency in these matters to the introduction to this volume.

47. Katrina Running, "Examining Environmental Concern in Developed, Transitioning and Developing Countries—A Cross-Country Test of the Objective Problems and the Subjective Values Explanations," *World Values Research* 5, no. 1 (2012): 1–26, http://www.worldvaluessurvey.org.

48. Ludger Heidbrink, Imke Schmidt, and Björn Ahaus, eds., *Die Verantwortung des Konsumenten: Über das Verhältnis von Markt, Moral und Konsum* (Frankfurt, Germany, and New York: Campus, 2011).

49. Max Weber, *The Protestant Ethic and the Spirit of Capitalism*, trans. Talcott Parsons (New York: Scribner's, 1958), 181.

50. In my view, this dilemma is what motivated the book *The Good Society*. Robert Bellah, Richard Madsen, William M. Sullivan, Ann Swidler, and Steven M. Tipton, *The Good Society* (New York: Vintage, 1992); cf. their introduction, titled "We Live through Institutions," 3–18.

sustainable, socially just, and moderately paced life, they also create environmental destruction, growing inequality, and a madly rushed life.

So when I call for a revision of the project of modernity, I do not mean a revision of core values such as human rights, but rather a fundamental change in the incorporated, habitualized as well institutionalized default mode of being in the world. The change that I envision would be a shift not in the goals we seek or in the goods we accumulate, but in the core mode of relating to the world, and it would be a shift from a relationship of domination and control—or comprehensive spiritual independence—to resonance.[51] *Resonance* is the form of relationship that ultimately characterizes living organisms. Whether or not something is alive can be tested by touching it; being alive means being receptive to touch and responding to it in ways that cannot be predicted mechanically. Aliveness is a special form of relationship to one's environment, and, as I will argue in a minute, my claim is that we can gain a new, globally viable conception of the common good when we focus on this form of relationship.

Resonance contains four distinctive elements:

1. Af←fection:[52] Being open and receptive to things that are touching or voices that are calling us.
2. E→motion: Being capable of answering and reaching out to the call or touch in a way that is characterized by self-efficacy. Thus, (1) and (2) conceptualize a dynamic relationship of mutual listening and responding.
3. Transformation: Being transformed in this interplay of call/touch and answer, as well as being capable of exerting a transformative influence on the environment, too.
4. Uncontrollability: The fourth element is the open-endedness, the uncontrollability and unpredictability of this process. Resonance is not a stimulus-response or cause-effect form of relationship, but a dynamic and creative interplay. It is uncontrollable and unpredictable in two dimensions. First, it is impossible to "engineer" it (i.e., to bring it about instrumentally). For example, we buy the most expensive tickets to our

---

51. This shift is what my book *Resonance: A Sociology of Our Relationship to the World* is about.
52. The arrows in af←fection and e→motion indicate a two-way dynamical movement between a subject and the world. Some alien reality touches and moves the subject form the outside, while it reacts with an opposite motion of reaching out.

favourite concerts, or for a cruise, in hope of a truly touching and deeply transformative experience, but it might very well be that nothing of this sort happens. The relationship stays "mute"—we remain untouched and untransformed. Second, if there really is a resonant encounter, it is unpredictable what kind of transformation we will experience.

Resonance in terms of its temporality, as well as with regard to its outcomes, is an open-ended process, and as such, it is in its essence contrary to the imperatives of dynamic stabilization, which always call for goal-directed optimization and acceleration. Hence, the modern predicament, of course, will not dissolve by a change in attitude alone. On the contrary, as I have tried to argue all along in this chapter, individual attitudes remain quite powerless with regard to the *institutionalized* (i.e., institutionally required and habitualized dispositions).[53] But the concept of resonance, which is not at all a new cultural idea but just an articulation of the most basic form of human existence, of being in and relating to the world,[54] could break the intrinsic link between that institutionalized logic and the culturally dominant conception of the good or the good life—and thus provide a yardstick for the inevitable institutional reforms.

Unlimited growth and acceleration, Bellah says, is "thermostatless and ultimately self-destructive." So when he asks, "Can we manage a soft landing or do we face catastrophe?"[55] he basically suggests that modern society eventually will have to overcome the mode of dynamic stabilization—either by design (*soft landing*) or by disaster (*catastrophe*). So the question is: How can we *design* a resonant instead of an ultimately destructive social future? It will not do to simply install a thermostat into an otherwise unchanged social formation. This, as I have tried to show, is structurally as well as culturally impossible. What we need, then, is a structural-cum-cultural, or institutional-cum-individual, turn from instrumental

---

53. Bellah et al., *The Good Society*.
54. This view actually finds confirmation not just in philosophical, phenomenological, or religious conceptions, but also from child development research. Long before human beings are reasonable beings or language animals, and certainly before they are possessive individualists, they are beings that are searching and longing for resonance. They need to be touched and held (affection), and they need to experience self-efficacy in the form of yielding a reaction from the world in response to their voice, looks, or gestures (emotion, or self-efficacy); see, for instance, David Skuse, Helen Bruce, and Emma Dowdney, eds., *Child Psychology and Psychiatry: Frameworks for Clinical Training and Practice* (Hoboken, NJ, and Chichester, UK: Wiley-Blackwell, 2017).
55. Bellah, "The Modern Project," 28, 26.

control and domination (i.e., spiritual independence) to attentive listening and responding. *Listening and responding* is the default mode of a resonant relationship to the world. Perhaps we could call this a mode of *respons-a-bility* because it necessarily involves an element of care for the natural, material, social, and historical environment. Let me explain.

There is almost universal agreement in the social sciences by now that we cannot define a societal common good in substantive terms because it would involve a more or less essentialist definition of the good life. On the other hand, however, democratic politics necessarily needs to keep a sense of struggling for the common good, because otherwise politics cannot be distinguished from the pursuit of private interests. Hence, I want to suggest that we can use the notion of resonance to arrive at a nonessentialist concept of the common good defined not in substantive terms, but as a specific type of relationship.

The *listening society* that I have in mind as an alternative to the current regime of dynamic stabilization, then, would be a society establishing "axes of resonance" in at least four dimensions: social (as a relationship of resonance between citizens), temporal (as a relationship of resonance toward the past and the future, that is, toward history), spatial/material (as a relationship of resonance toward the natural and built environments), and vertical (as form of relationship, or a spiritual stance, toward life or the world as such). The common good, then, would be realized *not* by being in control of the world, but rather by being in resonance with it.

In social terms, a listening society would be a society in which citizens are in resonance with each other. This does not mean that they share a predefined set of values, interests, or experiences, let alone that they live in harmony or unity—it just means that they encounter each other as beings that are able and willing to reach out to each other; to listen, and to respond, equipped with voices and ears. This, of course, has always been the essence of the republican conception of democratic politics. And this process of listening and responding is not just about seeking compromise—it is about being touched and transformed. It is about joint political action transforming the positions, voices, and even identities of those involved, such that it becomes possible to create a shared community that goes beyond compromises or the will of the majority.

From a temporal perspective, the common good is thus achieved when a resonant relationship to both the past and the future materializes. With regard to the past, this means that the common good implies that, as citizens, the history of the community "concerns us" and has "something to tell us"; that we are in a responsive relationship with that history; and, in fact, the success of the democratic process where this common good is attained is conditional on this. This involves all four principles of a relationship of resonance defined previously: the past event affects or moves us. By no means do we have to be moved in a positive or pleasant way, however. For instance, someone visiting a concentration camp museum or Holocaust memorial, or the site of a battle against Indigenous peoples, may experience an existential obligation arising from a memory of the past brought to life by the location. The individual may react with a response that is transformative, one that affects who they are at present and how they will act in the future, despite the fact that they would not be able to specify exactly what the obligation is that arises from this situation (elusiveness/uncontrollability). Such resonance creates a link, however—an axis of resonance between the past and the future.

When someone feels a vibrant and responsive connection not only with past but also future generations, they have a direct sense, as it were, both emotional and physical, of the relevance of their actions for those who come after them. Once again, the consideration of future needs and interests stops being an irksome obligation or a cost that outweighs the benefits, and instead creates an experience of accessible and transformative self-efficacy. I am therefore of the opinion that the quality of a democratic system can most certainly be measured by the quality of the transhistorical connection. The common good tends to be achieved where there is a vibrant axis of resonance spanning the past and the future. This axis of resonance does not determine each action in the present; rather, it inspires and motivates those actions.

However, what emerges in the mode of transformation and uncontrollability is a shared world arising from joint political actions, in line with Hannah Arendt's concept.[56] The sociopolitical system—its rules and institutions—thus becomes a structure that is in resonance with the citizens, a structure that is appropriated. Again, when I say a structure that is appropriated, this does not mean that that system is fully consistent or in total harmony with all their desires, needs, and

---

56. Hannah Arendt, *Zwischen Vergangenheit und Zukunft: Übungen im politischen Denken* (Munich: Piper, 1958); also Hannah Arendt, *Vita activa oder Vom tätigen Leben* (Munich: Piper, 1994 [orig. 1960]); for a detailed account, see also Paul Sörensen, *Entfremdung als Schlüsselbegriff einer kritischen Theorie der Politik: Eine Systematisierung im Ausgang von Karl Marx, Hannah Arendt und Cornelius Castoriadis* (PhD diss., Friedrich-Schiller-Universität Jena, 2015).

interests, but rather that there is a constitutive, responsive relationship between the citizens and all the institutions and practices, spaces and buildings, and rules and traditions. Here, opposition or conflict is an important and inevitable form of this response, without contradiction, and this applies to our context too; there can be no transformation or encounter without the opposition of an other, and there can be no experience of resonance.

If we redefine the conceptual pairing of the common good and democracy as a multidimensional relationship of resonance, one fundamental problem of the notion of the common good initially remains unchanged: Where are the boundaries of the community whose good we are referring to; how does this community relate to the social or material outside world? My thesis (and hope) here is that a society cannot be unjust, violent, repressive, or destructive to the outside world if it wishes to maintain the capacity to be resonant within itself. If we define the common good using the concept of resonance, resonance describes a way of relating to the world as a whole, as a way of being in the world. Repression, violence, and suppression, however, force not only the victims, but also (and particularly) the perpetrators into an objectifying, repulsive mode of relating to the world. This relationship is characterized by the dispositional suppression of resonant relations in oneself and in others and the ruthless obliteration of the corresponding impulses. This repression and violence impose a relationship with the world in which the transformative listening to the voice of the genuine other is systematically impeded or rendered impossible, while the echolike amplification of our own unvarying voice is systematically promoted or enforced.[57]

Interestingly, the exact same point also applies to our relationship with the natural world and our environmental/spatial surroundings. Those who treat the material (and especially the living) environment simply as a resource to be exploited and processed, to be used instrumentally and to be shaped, cannot experience that environment as a sphere of resonance or a vibrant other that is in a lasting and responsive reciprocal relationship with us as human beings. The reverse also holds true: those with a stable resonant relationship with the natural world (whatever your definition of that might be) need not force themselves to protect or sustainably manage the environment. This is something that they will

---

57. For a detailed account of this, see Hartmut Rosa, "Politik ohne Resonanz: Wie Wir die Demokratie wieder zum Klingen Bringen," *Blätter für deutsche und international Politik* 61 (June 2016): 97–108.

do automatically to avoid rendering inaudible the voice of that "other," losing their own voice in the process.[58]

I am thus proposing that we try to grasp the democratic common good as the creation of axes of resonance in an encompassing sense, and furthermore, I claim that being in resonance with a sphere of life inevitably entails a relationship of care. Actors will always seek to preserve the "voice" that they hear and resonate with. Resonance involves an ethics of care. If we take this approach, then the common good and an ethics of care indeed prove to be complementary reciprocal conditions and the key components of a successful democracy.[59] The phrase "ethics of care" then describes people's capacity for and openness to resonance. The common good, however, is achieved where the social and temporal, material and spatial conditions allow the four axes of resonance to be established and maintained.

How could this provide a yardstick for institutional reforms? In fact, when we look at institutions and practices across the full gamut of social activities, we find that there is always a tension, an uneasiness, between two conflicting orientations; between the need for parametric measurement, reliability, and optimization, or the logic of increase, on the one hand, and the sense of or desire for resonance with objects and participants of social action on the other hand. Just think of our conceptions of education, and of the cultural and political struggles about it. On the one hand, there is the attempt in educational policy to define, measure, and improve objective levels of skills, such as in the Programme for International Student Assessment (PISA) scales of the Organisation of Economic Co-operation and Development (OECD). On the other hand, teachers have and defend a strong sense of what it means, and what is required, to not just create an atmosphere of resonance in schools and classrooms, but also to enable students to enter into resonance with the subject matters taught in school. In this sense, education is about opening the axes of resonance between students and history, the arts, the natural sciences, politics, and other subjects. Similarly, everybody involved in care institutions like hospitals or nursing homes feels the tension between imperatives of efficiency and transparency and the appeal for

58. Hartmut Rosa, "Die Natur als Resonanzraum und als Quelle starker Wertungen," in *Welche Natur brauchen Wir? Analyse einer anthropologischen Grundproblematik des 21. Jahrhunderts*, ed. Gerald Hartung and Thomas Kirchhoff (Freiburg and Munich: Karl Alber Verlag, 2014), 123–41.

59. On this point, see the four volumes published by Herfried Münkler, Harald Bluhm, and Karsten Fischer, eds., *Gemeinwohl und Gemeinsinn* (Berlin: Akademie Verlag, 2002).

resonance, which is perceptible as soon as we look into someone's eyes. It is small wonder that we find the highest rates of burnout in teachers and caregivers, who are constantly exposed to these conflicting demands in their everyday actions.

But beyond this, we can see the institutional gap between practices and relationships aiming for resonance and those following the imperatives of parametric optimization, perhaps most clearly in the way that we institutionalize our interactions with animals. On the one hand, in industrial farming, there is a pure, instrumental orientation toward increase and efficiency, while on the other hand, pets serve no other purpose than as being sources of resonance for us. Now, we can obviously start to rethink the ways in which we organize schools, hospitals, and agriculture to improve their resonance qualities. A lot of attempts are already underway that seek to alter our institutionalized relationships in these domains (e.g., organic farming or novel conceptions of schooling and caring) and to create resonant and still efficient institutions.

Most interestingly, research in labor studies shows that even beyond the sphere of interaction with living things, workers (even in industrialized environments) constantly try to create axes of resonance not just with coworkers and clients, but also with the materialities they interact with when they give names to their machines, for example, or when they talk about "listening and responding to the motor," or to the structure of the wood or stone that they work on. They tend to measure the quality of their work not least by the opportunities that they find to experience self-efficacy and responsiveness in their social and material interactions, and they complain bitterly when the imperatives of acceleration, innovation, or optimization destroy those established and experienced axes of resonance.[60]

And finally, if it is true that the current dynamics of incessant growth, acceleration, and optimization is driven by fear rather than greed, that is, by the fear of losing one's job and income, and thus one's legitimate place in the social order, which serves as a cardinal axis of vertical resonance connecting us in a self-efficacious way to the social whole—then the introduction of an unconditional basic income might serve as an institutional starting point for creating a more resonant social reality.[61] In any case, paying attention to the conditions of resonance

---

60. Graham S. Lowe, *The Quality of Work: A People-Centred Agenda* (Oxford: Oxford University Press, 2000); Richard Sennett, *The Craftsman* (New Haven, CT: Yale University Press, 2009); Mark Williams, Ying Zhou, and Min Zhou, *Mapping Good Work: The Quality of Working Life Across the Occupational Structure* (Bristol, UK: Bristol University Press, 2020).

61. Rosa, *Resonance*, 434–43.

in the institutional fabric of society can open up an alternative way of defining the quality of social life beyond the imperatives of parametric optimization. And this, it seems to me, comes very close to what Bellah and his team suggested quite a while ago when they diagnosed a defining crisis of modern attention[62] from the fact that our relationships to the natural, as well as the institutional, worlds have become almost exclusively instrumental. By contrast, they claim that "democracy means paying attention."[63]

The Good Society that they were seeking thus could be one that is in resonance with (instead of having a spiritual independence from) nature, history, political institutions, and social "others" of all kinds. Resonance here decisively does not mean harmony, fusion, or union. Visions of harmony and unity actually critically misconstrue what resonance is about. They confuse resonance with "echo," that is, with an amplification of the ever-same and the affirmation of a given identity, while resonance means the transformation of identity through an encounter with others who are essentially different and uncontrollable. This, as we might well learn from the "great role models of our cultural heritage—the Buddha, Confucius, Socrates, Jesus"—eventually is the essence of life: being touched and transformed by a reality that always transcends our horizon of control and domination.

62. Andy Kaplan, "Editor's Introduction: The Essential Institution," *Schools: Studies in Education* 15, no. 2 (2018): 201.
63. Bellah et al., *The Good Society*, 254.

PART II

THE MODERN PROJECT

CHAPTER 4

PROLOGUE IN HEAVEN (OR HELL) TO THE MODERN PROJECT

ROBERT N. BELLAH

Bellah: Modern Project   April–July, 2012

The most incomprehensible thing about the universe is that it is comprehensible.

—Albert Einstein

The more the universe seems comprehensible, the more it seems pointless.

—Steven Weinberg

E instein and Weinberg are famous for being theoretical physicists, that is, their work is in, for most people, the most theoretical field there is. But the two epigraphs with which I begin this Prologue would seem to imply narrative. Maybe not so clearly with Einstein; "comprehensible" could mean only theoretically comprehensible. But for Weinberg, who is clearly responding to Einstein, the narrative aspect of what he says is evident. A point is something one reaches in time. To say the universe is "pointless," even though comprehensible, would seem to mean it has no narrative direction. We know from the larger passage from which this sentence comes that it specifically means the universe is not organized to end up with us. Rather, "human life is just a more-or-less farcical outcome of a chain of accidents."

Merlin Donald has indicated that narrative and theory are the two highest cultural capacities that humans have attained, making use of language to culminate a history of new cultural capacities that began with episodic culture, the capacity to know what kind of episode one is in, followed by mimetic culture, by which one enacts or embodies meaning non-linguistically.

Theoretic culture leads to the possibility of a theory of everything, what is sometimes called today, grand theory. Narrative culture leads to the idea of a story of everything, what is sometimes today called metanarrative. This book and its predecessor draw on grand theory, or at least depend on a lot of it, and are obviously metanarratives. Metanarratives don't try to understand literally everything, just the big picture: beginnings, possible endings, and everything in between, and, like myths, which in good part they are, they are inescapable. They have come into bad odor of late because, it is claimed, they are forms of power, openly or tacitly trying to convince people that some particular story is true when it actually is an apology for the status quo. There is such a multiplicity of metanarratives today, including sharply contradictory ones (think creationism vs. evolution), that no one of them poses a great danger, although since some are more dangerous than others we should not forget that possibility. In this prelude I will give a brief overview of metanarratives, some old and some relatively new, that are almost all in one way or another still alive, still influencing the way we think and act, whether we know it or not. But I want to make it clear that the metanarrative that I will offer in this book claims to be no more than an extended hypothesis, at every point more or less true and always open to contestation and correction.

Whatever their dangers, metanarratives are needed since human beings will always ask the questions Where are we? Where have we come from? Where are we going, and is it going to be great or disastrous? Given the state of the world, such questions can hardly be avoided and are being constantly asked and answered in both popular and academic culture today. So before I pick up the story that I left in my last book at a point some 2000 years ago, and try to move it to the present and especially to consider how our most recent history, our modernity, fits into it, I thought it might be helpful to offer a meditation on this kind of story and the vicissitudes of some of these stories over time.

In the beginning . . . Many such stories begin with such words. We are very familiar with the story that begins, "In the beginning, God . . ." but we are hardly less familiar with the story that begins with the Big Bang, and there are more than one version that combine the two, Teilhard de Chardin's for example. Some have contrasted stories of creation from above, as from God in Genesis, or from below, as from lower forms of life in Darwin or from the explosion of an intensely hot, extremely small entity, as in the Big Bang theory.

Very common are stories that see the beginning as a kind of chaos into which God or other primal beings bring order. It is probable that Genesis 1 really begins with this kind of story:

> In the beginning when God created the heavens and the earth, the earth was a formless void and darkness covered the face of the deep, while a wind from God swept over the face of the waters. NRSV Gen. 1:1–2.

Or in Everett Fox's translation:

> At the beginning of God's creating of the heavens and the earth,
> when the earth was wild and waste,
> darkness over the face of Ocean,
> rushing-spirit of God hovering over the face of the waters— Gen. 1:1–2[1]

The idea that God created the cosmos out of nothing became orthodox for both Jews and Christians, but the earliest appearance of that idea is found in 2 Maccabees, a book that dates from the late second century or early first century BCE, and was heavily influenced by Greek thought:

> I beg you, my child, to look at the heaven and the earth and see everything that is in them, and recognize that God did not make them out of things that existed. NSRV 2 Macc 7:28.

Daniel Boyarin has discovered what he calls a "Palestinian Targumic [Aramaic] poetic homily on the 'Four Nights,' " referring to the four days/nights of Genesis 1,

---

1. *The Five Books of Moses*, The Schocken Bible, Vol. 1, trans. Everett Fox (New York: Schocken, 1995), 13.

dating from the first or second centuries CE, that seems to retain the older version of what was already there when God began to create:

> Four nights are written in the Book of Memories: The first night: when the Lord was revealed above the world to create it. The world was unformed and void and darkness was spread over the face of the deep; and through his *Memra* [Word] there was light and illumination, and he called it the first night.[2]

We will have more to say about the Prologue to the Gospel According to John, which begins with "In the beginning was the Word . . ." after we discuss some other beginnings.

If Genesis 1 does really begin with formlessness and chaos to which God gives form, but which was already there when God began to create, it would be similar to creation myths found in many parts of the world. In the ancient Near East in the beginning there was often water, and we might remember that Thales, called the first Greek philosopher, believed that water was the fundamental element from which all things came. Karl W. Luckert posits the idea of a "pre-human flux" as a kind of baseline for hunter beliefs, not only in North America, but perhaps everywhere. By this term he points to a "time" when all things were interchangeable: not only powerful beings, humans and animals, but insects, plants, and features of the natural environment such as mountains, were all "alive," and could take the form of one another. Eventually some of the powerful beings shaped the earth and separated the "peoples" (including animals, plants, mountains, etc.) into their present forms.[3] Hesiod's version of Greek cosmogony starts with chaos, which gives rise to Gaia, the earth, which in turn gives rise to Uranus, the heavens, with which Gaia lies in close embrace so that she must be separated from Uranus for other entities to emerge. I could go on to discuss origin narratives generally, or concentrate on those found in the four axial civilizations discussed in my previous book. That, however would lengthen this Prologue unduly in light of the fact that this book is supposed to be relatively short. Modernity, which is something I will be spending a lot of time delineating, is a global phenomenon,

---

2. Daniel Boyarin, "*Logos*, A Jewish Word: John's Prologue as Midrash," in *The Jewish Annotated New Testament*, ed. Amy-Jill Levine and Marc Zvi Brettler (New York: Oxford University Press, 2011), 547.

3. Karl W. Luckert, *The Navajo Hunter Tradition* (Tucson: University of Arizona Press, 1975), 233–42.

but the breakthrough to unprecedented modern development occurred first in Western Europe in about 1800. Why that should be true will concern us greatly later on in this book, but for now it is my excuse to focus on the metanarratives that dominated the West for over 2000 years and not consider the very interesting metanarratives that were current in other societies, many of them in economic or political terms at least as advanced as the West as late as the eighteenth century.

Creation myths are by definition narratives, yet they raise questions that give rise to reflection, to thought, to theory. In the case of Thales, water is both something that was there from the beginning and from which everything came, but, perhaps even more important, water was a principle, a constituent of everything, or everything is a form of water. So from a narrative context it is possible to move toward abstraction. The Greeks would call it physics, by which they meant something richer and more amorphous than our modern meaning of physics would imply, and so it is often translated with the more polysemous word "nature." Something similar has happened to Word (Gr. *Logos*) in the Prologue to John:

1. In the beginning was the Word,
     And the Word was with god.
2. And the Word was God.
     He was in the beginning with God.
3. All things were made through him,
     and without him was not anything made that was made.
4. In him was life, and the life was the light of men.
5. The light shines in the darkness, and the darkness did not receive it.[4]

Boyarin argues that although it is the first verses of Genesis 1, culminating in v. 3, "And God said: Let there be light, and there was light," that is the text on which this to him perfectly normal Jewish midrash is based, there is another subtext in the Scriptures upon which it is also commenting, Proverbs 8:22–31, where Wisdom is equated with the Logos [*Memra*] of the opening of Genesis 1. In Proverbs

---

4. John 1:1–5, as given in Boyarin, "*Logos*," 548. Boyarin has used the Revised Standard Version (RSV) translation, not the New Revised Standard Version (NRSV) text, which is used in *The Jewish Annotated New Testament*. However, though the words are identical to those in the RSV, Boyarin has given them a poetic form and has slightly changed the RSV punctuation. A glance at the NRSV translation shows why Boyarin chose the RSV: the NRSV may have the latest scholarship, but its literary qualities are often inferior to the RSV, as is the case here. To those who own a copy of the RSV: don't throw it away.

8:22 Wisdom says "The Lord created me at the beginning of his work, the first of his acts of old," and in 8:30 Wisdom says "and I was beside him," just as John 1:1 says "the Word was with God." Boyarin also tells us that Philo (20 BCE–50 CE), the Hellenistic Jewish philosopher who lived in Alexandria at the time of Christ, like others, identified *Sophia* [Wisdom] with *Logos* as a single entity. Seeing *Sophia/Logos* as an entity, with or beside God, but also so closely identified with God as to be in some sense also divine is, in Boyarin's view, the likely Jewish source for the Christian idea of Christ as the "second person" in the trinity,[5] and if Christ could be the second person, then *Sophia* could be identified with the third person, though without the female identity it had in Hebrew and Greek. The Trinity is one of the most difficult doctrines in Christianity and has over time successfully resisted full rational explanation. Furthermore, though God the father and God the Son as well as the Holy Spirit are all found in the New Testament it is hard to say that there is any exposition of something that could be called "the Doctrine of the Trinity," but when there was, the possible Jewish origins of the idea were as forgotten by Christians as they were rejected by the rabbis. The fact that Stoicism, one of the most influential Greek philosophical traditions, identified the *Logos* with God, and even with Zeus, only adds to the complex background of the term.

Both Genesis and the Gospel According to John (in the Jewish Septuagint Greek translation of the Hebrew text dating from the third century BCE, and in the original Greek text of the New Testament) begin with the Greek words "*En arche* . . ." which clearly means "In the beginning." However, *arche* has more than one meaning. Surely it has a temporal meaning that "beginning" correctly translates. But *arche* refers not only to what is primary chronologically but also to what is primary logically. *Arche* in Greek philosophy, which was part of the cultural atmosphere for both Jews and Christians in New Testament times, can be translated as "beginning, starting point, principle, ultimate underlying substance (*Urstoff*), ultimate undemonstrable principle."[6]

While *arche* never loses its meaning as "beginning" because of its close connection with *logos*, "word," which can also mean "principle," already in commentary on both Genesis 1–2 and John 1, leads to understanding of the world in terms of first

---

5. Boyarin, "Logos," 548–49.
6. F. E. Peters, *Greek Philosophical Terms: A Historical Lexicon* (New York: New York University Press, 1967), 23.

principles rather than temporal beginnings, an idea that develops over the whole course of Christian thought, but also Jewish and Islamic to some extent as well.

What is striking is that even the most fundamental abstractions, such as *logos* as word or meaning, can also be expressed in narrative terms, for example as command. A trope that will have great resonance in later history is the fusion by Denys the Areopagite[7] of two narratives that also have theoretical implications, Plato's Allegory of the Cave in *Republic* 7 (it is interesting that the most famous passage in the first great theoretical philosopher should be a narrative, a parable) and Moses's ascent of Mount Zion in Exodus 19–20. Denys compresses the Exodus account in which God called to Moses "out of the mountain" and was told to bring the people to the foot of the mountain on the third day.

> On the morning of the third day there were thunders and lightening and a thick cloud upon the mountain, and a very loud trumpet blast, so that all the people who were in the camp trembled. Then Moses brought the people out of the camp to meet God; and they took their stand at the foot of the mountain. And Mount Sinai was wrapped in smoke, because the Lord descended upon it in fire; and the smoke of it went up like the smoke of a kiln, and the whole mountain quaked greatly. And as the sound of the trumpet grew louder and louder, Moses spoke, and God answered him in thunder. And the lord came down upon Mount Sinai, to the top of the mountain; and the lord called Moses to the top of the mountain, and Moses went up. Ex. 19:16–20

God gave Moses the Ten Commandments which he was to transmit to the people. But the people were frightened by what they had seen and heard:

> Now when all the people perceived the thunderings and the lightnings and the sound of the trumpet and the mountain smoking, the people were afraid

---

7. Usually referred to as Pseudo-Dionysius the Areopagite because the Greek text, probably written by a late fifth-century monk in Syria, claimed the authorship of the figure of Dionysius the Areopagite, named in the book of Acts to have been converted by Paul while he was in Athens, Acts 17:34. It was not until the sixteenth century that humanists on philological grounds proved conclusively that the book could not have been written by a contemporary of Paul, and Dionysius's name was subsequently preceded by "Pseudo-." Since through the High Middle Ages the writer was referred to as Dionysius the Areopagite, or, more frequently as Denys, some contemporary writers prefer to use that name rather than the more scientifically accurate one. See Denys Turner, *The Darkness of God: Negativity in Christian Mysticism* (Cambridge: Cambridge University Press, 1995), 12.

and trembled; and they stood afar off, and said to Moses, "You speak to us, and we will hear; but let not God speak to us, lest we die." and Moses said to the people, "Do not fear; for God has come to prove you, and that the fear of him may be before your eyes, that you may not sin."

And the people stood afar off, while Moses drew near to the thick darkness where God was. Ex. 20:18–21

Denys, using imagery from Plato (427 BCE–347 BCE) in Book 7 of *Republic*, says that at the top of the mountain Moses "plunges into the truly mysterious darkness of unknowing. Here, renouncing all that the mind may conceive, wrapped entirely in the intangible and the invisible, he belongs completely to him who is beyond everything. Here, being neither oneself nor someone else, one is supremely united by a completely unknowing inactivity of all knowledge, and knows beyond the mind by knowing nothing." The would-be philosopher, released from his chains in the cave where he could see only illusion, not reality, goes up to the real world, but is blinded by the light so that at first he can't see anything. Denys relates Moses to Plato's would-be philosopher in that both ascend from the world of illusion to the world of reality, but it is only through darkness that they can find the light. Denys was by far not the first to think of Moses as the proto-philosopher. Philo, the Alexandrian Jewish/Hellenistic philosopher, already found the profundity of Moses to have been the true source of the Greek philosophy, Plato in particular, whom Philo thought had plagiarized Moses.

But there was another parallel between Moses's ascent of Mount Zion and Plato's Allegory of the Cave: what was revealed to Moses and to Plato's proto-philosopher was above all ethical. Not only the ten commandments were revealed to Moses, but the whole Torah, which we can translate as "instruction" rather than as the more usual "law," since it was the whole pattern of life under the Covenant that God gave to Moses, and also because Christians have often compared a (harsh) law to a (gentle) gospel, thus giving a pejorative meaning to a word otherwise rather central in moral philosophy. But what did the one who ascended from Plato's cave see at the highest point in the real world? The form of the Good. Good can be translated here as truth or reality, or even as God, but the etymology makes clear that the basic meaning is ethical, is the Good in the deepest sense. Plato did not spell out in specific rules what the good was in his philosophy, but all the dialogues taken together give a sense of what the good life is for human beings, what virtue is in the deepest and broadest sense.

Yet in both in Moses and in Plato we can find very short and succinct summaries of the central teachings of the two traditions. It is implied in the discussion with Thrasymachus in Book I of *Republic* and elsewhere in Plato but is very explicit in *Gorgias* (469b–c) that "It is better to suffer injustice than commit it," even though Socrates is assured by Thrasymachus and Callicles that someone who says that is likely to be killed. And in the very midst of Leviticus which is often seen as a collection of highly specific cultic and other obligations, we find the central Chapter 19, in which are the two great ethical commandments: "You shall love your neighbor as yourself" (Leviticus 19:18), and "You shall love the alien as yourself, for you were aliens in the land of Egypt" (Leviticus 19:34). Whether in extended or compact form, the teaching of Plato and the Hebrew Scriptures, however concerned with the nature of the cosmos, are, above everything, about the good life for human beings.

In the great texts of the axial traditions we find cosmology, the description of the universe, inextricably mixed with ethics, what is, compared with what should be. And if Socrates is told that the one who suffers injustice rather than commit it will not thrive in this world, Socrates is sure that such a person will be rewarded in Heaven, as described in the last book of *Republic*.

Westerners were stuck with a double tradition, Hebrew and Greek, as we have been seeing, that was a constant source of perplexity and creativity. God in the Pentateuch, from the very beginning of Genesis, is a sovereign God who wills and decides. After each of his acts of creation God finds that what he created was good, so that after the word, "Let there be light," there was light and God saw that the light was good. But was there an independent standard of good such that God measured the light and saw that it was good, or was it good because and only because God had created it? Of course there were ways of answering that question that caused no problem at all, yet it lingered for Jews, Christians and Muslims right up to the present day.

The Greeks did not take their highest mythical god, Zeus, and turn him into the creator of the universe, though the Stoics would still call the Logos, one of their commonest terms for God, Zeus on occasion. What served as the Greek basis for later creation stories was *Republic* in just the place already discussed, but also even more centrally in *Timeaus*, a late, and to moderns, minor dialogue. *Timeaus* from ancient to early modern times was more frequently translated and commented on than any other Platonic dialogue mainly because it was the only place Plato discussed cosmology. In it the narrator describes the action of a

Demiurge who created the universe and all its parts, but for some commentators, the Demiurge was simply a mythical story that contained the real teaching, that the Universe itself is an expression of the World Soul, the *Nous* that underlies everything that is.

Later Christians would see in the Demiurge a Platonic counterpart of Yahweh, that is, a creator God, but Gregory Vlastos points out how surprising it is that Plato would choose the term *demiourgos* for the creator of the universe, since *demiourgos* was simply the Greek word for craftsman. Craftsmen, for both Plato and Aristotle, were not very dignified figures, often slaves and even when free were denied full citizenship in the polis.[8] Perhaps Plato made this surprising move just because the Demiurge was not the highest figure in his understanding of the universe. Even if one translates *demiourgos* as artist, it is still the case that he does not create anything on his own. Beyond the cosmos altogether are the Forms (*eide*) to which the Demiurge constantly looks for the patterns of what he is creating since, as Vlastos says, "he was not the inventor of new form, but the imposer of existing form (Forms) on as yet formless material." It is furthermore surprising that the Demiurge was not a "jealous god" in the sense that Zeus and the other Greek gods were jealous of humans when they punished Prometheus for helping them. Rather, as Plato said, "he was good and in the god there can be no envy at any time about anything." (Timaeus 29e).[9] The Form, that is the model, the Demiurge chooses for the universe is the Ideal Form of a Living Creature, so far as possible (Plato insists that whatever he intends, the Demiurge is not entirely free as he must deal with necessity) because such a model is both good and beautiful, the terms in Greek being hard to separate.[10] Note that this is not an early Platonic version of the Gaia hypothesis since it is not the earth but the whole cosmos which is alive and has a world-soul (*psyche tou pantos*, literally, "the soul of all").

What is even more amazing about this dialogue (it is actually largely a monologue), often overlooked because it is so outdated as cosmology, is the degree to which Plato took the best astronomy available at his time, added touches from his own metaphysics, above all that the circle is the most perfect and beautiful form, and created the cosmology that all the best astronomers for 2000 years,

---

8. Gregory Vlastos, *Plato's Universe* (Seattle: Washington University Press, 1975), 26.

9. Vlastos, *Plato's Universe*, 27.

10. Vlastos, *Plato's Universe*, 29.

Greek, Jewish, Christian and Muslim, would rely on. In spite of recurring problems with it, it was so much closer to reality than the void and random atoms of Democritus and Epicurus, that the latter never were in competition until the great discoveries of the sixteenth and seventeenth centuries. The key idea was that the universe was composed of successive spheres around the earth at the center, spheres for the moon, sun, planets and finally the celestial sphere of the fixed stars, that is, the stars studded like gems in a single sphere, with souls and thus alive, but moving in perfect harmony with reality. Both Plato and Aristotle recommended contemplation of the fixed stars as good for the soul because representative of the highest truth.

Still, we must remember that whatever later monotheists might wish, Plato himself did not think of the Demiurge as a Highest Being, perhaps the mere act of making is beneath the dignity of the Highest Being, but gave us for that a number of terms in different dialogues that scholars have still not entirely reconciled. We have already mentioned the Forms, but there were also the concepts of the One (*hen*), Being (*On*) and sometimes Intellect or Mind (*Nous*). Neo-Platonism would develop a triad of hypostases, that is, forms of highest being, with Plotinus holding the One as the highest reality, completely, indescribably, without qualities, and therefore without even the attribute of goodness. As the source of all reality, which is good, the One may be presumed to be good even though beyond qualities, but all realities below the One lack the fullness of the reality of the One, and in fact form a perfect hierarchy of decreasing fullness down to the most inert piece of matter, an idea that gave rise to the Great Chain of Being into which all existing things could be arranged without a break.[11]

Although Neo-Platonism had a powerful influence on the philosophy that developed within the monotheistic religions, theologians could never accept the central idea of Plotinus, which they saw as describing an emanation of everything from the One. The idea that the very nature of the One, indescribable though it is, must necessarily lead to the emanation of the whole of the existing world seemed to them to deprive God of the absolute freedom that they took to be the truth of Creation. As we noted, this problem emerges from reflection on the very first verses of the first chapter of Genesis: was the light that

---

11. Arthur O. Lovejoy's *The Great Chain of Being: A Study of the History of an Idea* (Cambridge, MA: Harvard University Press, 1936) is still worth reading for an idea that was still very much in play at least until the eighteenth century.

God created good in itself or only good because God had created it? Augustine (354–430 CE), the greatest theologian of the Latin West before the Middle Ages, had early been influenced by Manichaeans to believe that Christian scriptures were full of primitive fables. He was finally convinced by Neo-Platonism that it was the Manichaeans who were followers of fables and that a philosophical, as he heard Ambrose say, a figural, interpretation of scripture revealed its profundity. Augustine got around the problem of emanation by arguing that the sheer absence of any qualities in Plotinus's One meant that it had to be the God of Israel, who could not be circumscribed by any human understanding and was thus utterly free, whatever the Neo-Platonists thought.

Augustine is a fascinating figure, at times, as is often the case with persons of extraordinary creativity, a maddening one. With his *Confessions* he made a great contribution of the understanding of the self in Western thought, though we must remember that that book is an extended prayer to God which we are privileged to overhear, but it is what it says about God not about Augustine that he wants us to hear. Similarly, his *City of God* is a great contribution to the understanding of society (can we call Augustine an early sociologist?) but again we must remember that it is the City of God, not the City of Man to which he calls our deepest attention. Both books and many of his others remain alive in our intellectual life today.

But the Middle Ages saw a great expansion of thought when Thomas Aquinas (1225–1274) and others finally recovered most of Aristotle, in some cases from Byzantium, most often at first from Arabic translations. By incorporating Aristotle in their thought they legitimated the study of the secular world as part of the responsibility of religiously serious scholars. Denys Turner has clarified Thomas's somewhat hasty treatment of the five arguments for the existence of God by showing that what Thomas meant by reason was richer than the modern, post-Kantian, version of "pure reason," and so proving that God existed didn't seem such a big deal to him.[12] What was most important to Thomas was that we could know *that* God existed but not *what* God is. We know God has many important attributes—truth, goodness, beauty, justice, reason—yet we understand these attributes only in human terms and cannot understand what they mean in God, where they are not separate attributes but united in one. God for

---

12. Denys Turner, *Faith, Reason, and the Existence of God* (Cambridge: Cambridge University Press, 2004).

Thomas is Being, or Being Itself, and from that many things follow. Yet what at the most basic level Being means is as distant from our capacity to understand as were the highest terms of Plato or Philo or Plotinus or Augustine or the many others who have thought about these things over the centuries.

Partly out of this situation where our highest knowing is a kind of unknowing came, especially in the early Middle Ages, what has come to be called negative theology, the *via negativa*, drawing heavily on Denys the Areopagite. Here again, Denys Turner is a reliable guide, not letting us turn negative theology into some Death of God, New Age speculation, but not letting us avoid the fact that the highest affirmation and the highest negation both must be overcome if we are to get even a glimpse of what the tradition was trying to describe.[13]

It would seem that in certain cases a great theologian finds a complementary figure in a great poet, a poet who can often teach us as much as the theologian, though in a different way, and Dante (1265–1321) is the obvious poet to pair with Thomas. They shared the same cosmology, one that is central to Dante's poem, divided as it is into three parts, each a major segment of the cosmos: Inferno, Purgatorio, Paradiso. And that cosmos, at least its astronomy, is still basically the same as that of Plato's Timaeus, which would continue to reign for several centuries after Dante, though finding a place for purgatory would present a problem and lead to a strange geology not foreseen by Plato or Ptolemy.

Dante's Inferno, Hell, is within the earth and consists of ever deeper circles as Dante and Virgil visit criminals of worsening degree, with the bottom of hell, as most of us know, being bitterly cold rather than hot. At the very center of the bottom level, the circle of treachery, is Lucifer, the traitor to God, half embedded in ice with three faces each of whose mouths is chewing on the worst human traitors: the central face on Judas Iscariot, with Brutus and Cassius, murderers of Julius Caesar, being chewed on the left and right face.

The idea of purgatory, a place where sinners could make up for their sins through various forms of punishment and their own continuing repentance, was foreshadowed by a few passages in the Bible that speak of sinners being cleansed by punishments, and was developed as an idea later on, but as an actual place

---

13. Turner, *The Darkness of God*, 44, where Turner quotes Denys as saying that the Cause of all is "beyond assertion and denial."

with an importance that puts it alongside Heaven and Hell as Dante does, its origin is late in the Twelfth Century, so only a century or so before Dante.[14] The origin of Purgatory is intimately related to the origin of Hell in Dante's cosmography. When Satan was thrown out of Heaven for rebelling against God, for which we have an actual Gospel source in Luke 10:18: "And he said to them, 'I saw Satan fall like lightning from heaven,'" he hit the earth at Jerusalem but entered with such force that he created a great cone-like space narrowing at the bottom to the very center of the earth. The sides of this vast cone, now invisible below the earth's surface, are the nine circles of Hell and their subdivisions. But although somehow the surface of the earth survived this impact intact, it pushed out in the southern hemisphere, which according to Dante was entirely covered by water, exactly opposite to Jerusalem, a cone-shaped mountain existing as an island in this otherwise watery half of the earth. That mountain was the mountain of Purgatory, which likewise was divided into circles as was Hell. How Dante and Virgil got from the middle of the earth to the island of Mount Purgatorio is complicated, but suffice it to say it involved climbing over the body of Satan and holding on to his hair so as not to slip down and then reversing themselves as, having passed the center of the earth, what had been down had now become up, and proceeding through a long passage, emerging at the southern island.

Having traversed the circles of Purgatory, and on the way cleansing himself, though others notice that he casts a shadow which the spirits don't and so is still alive, Dante reaches the top which consists of the earthly paradise, where Virgil, as a pagan, can go no further but turns Dante over to Beatrice, his ideal love, whose early death he had lamented in his poetry, as his guide to Heavenly Paradise which resides in the skies. Heaven consists in successive spheres, much as described in Plato's Timaeus, with the sphere of the fixed stars, alive for Dante as for Plato, as the sphere of saved souls. Beyond that there is a sphere of angels, whose ontological status is not entirely clear to me, but beyond that there exists, if that is the right word, a realm beyond time and space where God is "seen" by all the angels and souls in terms that can only be metaphorical in a realm beyond our imagination. At this level Beatrice has turned Dante over to Bernard, who was said to have seen God on this earth, as his guide as he is the greatest

14. See Jacques LeGoff, *The Birth of Purgatory* (Chicago: University of Chicago Press, 1984 [1981]).

master of contemplation.[15] Bernard manages to get Dante permission to have a glimpse of God himself, the *Visio Dei*, which turns out to symbolize the Trinity, but whose details escape Dante's memory after his breathtaking vision. Yet he is still granted the possibility to return home and write up all his travels for the edification of mankind.

We tend to imagine a Middle Ages that goes on for several centuries under the supreme guidance of Thomas and Dante. It is impossible to defeat narrative with argument, but new narratives may qualify the authority of older ones, and we shall consider some that later rivaled Dante in scope and influence. Argument, however, and never more than in the High Middle Ages, always leads to more argument. The authority of Thomas would last for centuries, and in a sense, and this is true of Aristotle as well, until the present. But not unchallenged. And the challenges were from early on unsettling. Long before the Reformation or the scientific revolution or all the other things that have unsettled moderns, doubt was cast on Thomas's whole approach. This is not the place to even glance at those doubts, which focus initially on the problem of the truth of universal concepts and were raised by those called "nominalists" who argued that truth is found only in individuals, as against the "realists" who attribute some reality to concepts. The nominalists who questioned the capacity of metaphysical systems to supply firm truths, often turned to the Bible as their only reliable source, thus pointing the way to the Protestant Reformation but without questioning the authority of the church. Nor will we stop to consider those who did begin to question that authority and can be seen as proto-Protestants, such as John Wycliffe (1320–1384) and Jan Hus (1369–1415). Rather than at Martin Luther (1483–1546), whose importance for the beginning of the Reformation is indisputable, we will look briefly at John Calvin (1509–1564), a thinker if anything even more rigorous than Luther and a greater influence on English-speaking Protestantism.

The Protestant Reformation of the Sixteenth Century marked a major transformation of European society, one often seen as a background factor to modernity. Later in this book we will have to consider why more closely. The

---

15. Beatrice, after giving Dante a last smile, takes her place in the giant rose that the vast throng of angels and souls have created around the Godhead, to which she, with everyone else, looks with rapture. Since this is outside of time and place, from our limited view it will go on "forever," though that is because eternity is hard for humans to grasp. It is worth noting, however, that Dante's conception of Paradise can give little comfort to those who expect to be "reunited with their loved ones" in heaven. Heaven, it seems, is about the love of God, and nothing else.

Reformation does not obviously seem to be caused by any of the other major background factors for modernity: the scientific revolution was barely getting started in the Sixteenth Century and the industrial revolution was centuries in the future. The New World had been "discovered" at the end of the Fifteenth Century, but its consequences had been minor when early in the Sixteenth the Reformation broke out. While the European economy had been growing slowly for some time, nothing in this century indicated any marked increase. William Bouwsma, in his remarkable book about Calvin, indicates nonetheless that Calvin's century saw "a momentous cultural crisis" that "was at the heart of the Renaissance as well as the Reformation and as crucial for Catholic Europe as for the peoples that separated from the Roman Church." Bouwsma writes, "For me the century was tense, driven, fundamentally incoherent, and riven by insoluble conflicts that were all the more serious because they were as much within as between individuals and parties."[16] He suggests the turmoil of the century on his first page with his list of Calvin's near contemporaries: Machiavelli, Thomas More, Erasmus, Rabelais, Michelangelo, Copernicus, Cervantes, Montaigne and Shakespeare. While Bouwsma is surely right that the crisis was greater than the Reformation itself, it would be hard to overestimate the importance of the dramatic end to the cultural hegemony of the Roman Catholic Church which had for centuries provided unity, fragile and uncertain to be sure, but was now denounced by much of Europe as the Whore of Babylon.

Calvin himself was an unlikely leader of so drastic a revolution. Raised in a well-to-do French provincial family, but with a mother who died when he was four or five and a father who sent him to relatives to be raised and was neglectful except that he did give him an excellent education. He was training for the priesthood at his father's behest when, at his father's whim, he was sent to study law instead. Of fragile health, nervous and anxious all his life, pious and studious, he seemed to prefer the life of a quiet scholar to anything as demanding as a role in the Reformation that not only involved leadership but the very formation of the terms of the new dispensation itself.

---

16. William J. Bouwsma, *John Calvin: A Sixteenth Century Portrait* (New York: Oxford University Press, 1988), 4. The subtitle is suggestive of the fact that the book is as much about the century as about the man. I am sorry to say that Bill gave me a copy at the time of publication but it is only now that I have read it so I cannot thank him for his important work.

Like several of his young friends, and young men all across Europe, Calvin was attracted to Erasmus (1466–1536), whose call for reform was moderate, based on the new Humanism in which classical antiquity was understood in its own terms, yet devoutly Biblical, Erasmus having done important work on the Greek text of the New Testament and made a far more accurate translation than that of Jerome. Erasmus's criticism of the existing order was more in sorrow than in anger and he never lost his sense of humor. As the Reformation progressed Luther pressed Erasmus to take sides, which he evaded doing as long as he could, until it was clear that he was not going to leave the old church. He always affirmed his intention not to take sides, in spite of immense pressure from both parties to do so. Near the end of his life he moved from Catholic Freiburg to the more cosmopolitan Protestant Swiss city of Basel where in 1536 he died surrounded by Protestant friends and, as far as we know, without benefit of Catholic clergy.

The young Calvin, well educated and well read, nonetheless lacked Erasmus's worldliness and, succumbing to pressure, made the decisive leap to Protestantism, still hoping to survive in his beloved France. When it became clear that that was no longer safe he accepted the call from the Protestant French-speaking Swiss city of Geneva to become pastor of its congregation. For the rest of his life he was embroiled in controversies he never sought but felt he could not avoid, and in spite of his anxious nature, found he was more gifted for political leadership than he imagined, even helped by a temper that was, to his dismay and regret, at times ungovernable. In the midst of all his many duties to church and state, not only in Geneva but in Protestant Europe as a whole, he nonetheless continued to study and write and it is to Calvin as an enormously influential thinker that we must turn however significant his leadership in the new movement may have been.

Calvin was educated as a Renaissance humanist in the Greek and Latin classics; quotations from Cicero or Virgil could fall from his tongue at any time. He was also schooled in the history of Christian thought from the early Church Fathers (for him Augustine always remained central), whom he admired but held not to be above criticism, to the scholastic theologians of the High Middle Ages, whom he, like other humanists, criticized for engaging too much in quibbles. Yet Bouwsma could quote approvingly John Dillenberger's comment, "Calvin can be said to be the least systematic of the systematic theologians." Instead, Calvin was, according to Dillenberger, "a biblical theologian *par excellence*." That is, much of his theology is to be found in his sermons and commentaries on most of the books of the Bible, and even his most systematic work, *Institutes of the Christian Religion*, was more a commentary on the Creed than a systematic work. In terms of the argument in my previous book, *Religion in Human Evolution*, we could see Calvin as trying to return to and capture the essential breakthrough of the axial age, not denying all that had come since, but using the Axial standard to judge the validity of everything else, pagan or apparently Christian.

There is one claim that he found central to biblical teaching and that became the critical standard, and that was the absolute sovereignty of God. Bouwsma points out that, like Machiavelli with whom he differed in so many other ways, "he saw power as supreme throughout the universe," and it was earthly political power that provided him with many of his analogies, as when he wrote that "all sovereign power and empire remain his [God's]," and the entire world "is in his hand and he governs it as he will."[17] Though the analogy is earthly, no king, however much he may claim to be powerful and even all-knowing, is, as God is, absolutely omnipotent and omniscient. From this the doctrine of predestination, even double predestination (the idea that God has decided before the beginning of time which humans will be saved and which will be consigned to eternal punishment in hell) necessarily follows. Calvin didn't particularly like this doctrine. Indeed he was appalled by the idea that only a few would be saved and the rest consigned to hell, and he preferred that people not spend time discussing it. But if God knows everything and controls everything from the beginning to the end, how can such a doctrine be avoided? Calvin did see some empirical evidence for this painful doctrine when he looked around him and saw how many were the wicked and how few the just, though he knew neither he nor any human could know the fate of anyone, for that was in the hands of God alone. He repented of his tendency to think he could discern those condemned to the lower realm, which in moments of wrath he was tempted to do.[18]

From this one central doctrine almost everything else followed. All intermediary powers between God and humans were denied. Christ could be a kind of

---

17. Bouwsma, *Calvin*, 162–63. Calvin quotes are from sermons and commentaries.
18. Bouwsma reminds us that "total depravity" does not mean quite what we assume it means: "Total Depravity means, not that there is no capacity for good in human beings, but that no human activity is altogether blameless" (*Calvin*, 139). We still carry the image and likeness of God with which we were created, but there is no part of us that is free from sin. Sin is in our intellect as well as in our sensual desires. It is in that sense that it is total, not in the sense that everything we do is bad.

intermediary, but Christ was one of three persons in the One God. The Virgin Mary and all the saints, however admirable, could not intercede for humans. And the absolute sovereignty of God required a drastic rethinking of the church, which could no longer be seen as having any powers of its own other than bringing the Sacraments and the Word of God to humans. The fury with which the Protestants rejected the Pope is perhaps explicable in that the Pope was the only figure in Christendom who seemed to resemble the divine king of archaic empires. For Calvin not only the Bishop of Rome, but all bishops were, according to scripture, mere caretakers, whose office was not essential, but could continue or be abolished at the will of the believers.

One might imagine that so extraordinarily exalted a notion of the power of God would be used by analogy to justify absolute monarchy on earth. To the contrary, although the moderate Calvin enjoined respect for all superiors, from wives to their husbands, from children to their parents, especially their fathers, from believers for their pastors, and from subjects for their rulers. Yet such respect could never be absolute. A superior who denied God's commands had no claim on obedience. Ultimately all are equal in the sight of God and all temporal distinctions are merely for convenience. Calvin denied the right of the populace to rebel against their ruler, but he taught that the magistrates were justified in replacing a monarch who had become tyrannical, a modified version of the right of rebellion. Further, though Calvin was aware that most polities were monarchies and that is what believers would have to deal with, he preferred republics to monarchy and was glad that, with all its problems, he lived in the Republic of Geneva. Here again, Calvin was no democrat. One of his model republics was Venice, where a variety of elite councils governed, not the people. Nonetheless, for his day, and excepting the sectarians of the Radical Reformation, he was a man of the left in current terminology. He could rival the Hebrew prophets in denouncing the sins of the rich and powerful toward the poor and lowly, though he justified the validity of wealth and power rightly used. He even said that the rich would wrench the sun out of the sky for their own use, leaving the poor in the dark, if they could.

Any notion that the doctrine of predestination would necessarily give rise to fatalism and indolence can only show an inadequate understanding of what the sovereignty of God requires. Whether saved or damned, and we can never know, we must obey God's commandments or face the consequences in this life. Calvin was all too aware of how hard those commands are, among others that we love our enemies, and how often we fail to conform to them. Though perfection is required of us we lack the power to achieve it and so must live in awareness of our failures, and undertake a life of repentance as a result, none more in his own eyes than Calvin himself. And, yes, Weber was right: among the many commands was the command to work in a calling, work diligently and without shirking. For Calvin the calling of a farmer or a craftsman or a mechanic was an honorable calling, as honorable as the calling of a merchant, a preacher or a ruler. And for all of them diligence was required. Calvin, who in spite of his rigorism believed in the "middle way" thought one could even work too hard and endanger one's health. On top of his enormous schedule he lectured on weekday mornings at 6 AM on the old Testament and the New Testament in alternate weeks, allowing in the winter for class to begin at 7 AM, and in Latin as there were many exiles in Geneva, some of whom didn't speak French. On this point he didn't seem to take his own advice and he died at the age of 57, in part surely because of overwork. Yet indolence appalled him. He even suspected our need to sleep, to which we return all too easily if allowed. To Calvin sleep is close to death, necessary and inevitable, but not desirable.

Of course I have given a totally abbreviated version of Calvin's teaching, inadequate for any but the narrowest purpose. But I think I have not missed the main point, the recognition of the absolute sovereignty of God and all that it implied. And even why such a recognition would lead to a radical and sweeping revolution in church and state. Calvinism is not Calvin. His own teachings were stern enough; they could be turned by his followers into formulas, formulas that would sooner or later be abandoned, but the spirit of Calvin is the spirit of the Protestant Reformation and all Europeans whether Catholic, Protestant, or non-believers live in a world radically changed by it.

We can ask one question that won't go away even long after the Reformation. Did Calvin and his fellow Protestant leaders throw out too much? Did they not heed the maxim that "nothing is ever lost"? Given that all post-Axial civilizations were compromises between profound axial commitments and pre-Axial tribal and archaic elements, including aspects of ritual and myth? Interestingly, Calvin himself wanted weekly communion in his church in Geneva, though the council of ministers and his own congregation blocked him. Calvin had a profound understanding that communion is a deep expression of union in the body of Christ, but he also had a strong disciplinary understanding of it: he would not serve the unrepentant. Perhaps the weekly humiliation of not being served was too much for some of his congregants. In any case only two sacraments were left as the other five previously recognized were deemed not biblical, and even the two remaining sacraments, communion even more than baptism, became almost vestigial in a religion that emphasized the word above all. Eamon Duffy in his *Stripping of the Altars* pointed out all that was lost in the English Reformation of the Sixteenth Century, in particular the relation between the living and the dead as masses for the dead were declared magical and forbidden.[19]

For a poetic parallel to Calvin I find I must jump ahead to the Seventeenth Century. I am tempted to consider Blaise Pascal (1623–1662), who was not a systematic theologian or philosopher, and whose *Pensées* were aphoristic and even poetic. He was one of the first to express eloquently the painful effect on him of the new understanding of the universe as a result of the work of Copernicus (1473–1543) and Galileo (1564–1642), not the idea of a heliocentric solar system but a sense of the vast emptiness of space brought on by the collapse of the idea of a sphere of fixed stars and the realization instead that the stars are randomly scattered, incredibly distant, and our place in the universe insignificant. But because Milton's *Paradise Lost* is a kind of Protestant *Divina Commedia*, a narrative sharing many themes with Dante's poem, it is an appealing choice.

John Milton (1608–1674), like Calvin, came from a well-to-do commoner family and was sent to Cambridge, to study for the Anglican priesthood. From early on he was very studious, learned Latin and Greek as well as Italian, and even as a teenager began to write poetry. At Cambridge he learned Hebrew, French and Spanish as well, and was known for his erudition and also for his poetry. His education included classical humanism and biblical and theological studies. His father's wealth allowed him to study and to write, and at the age of thirty to undertake an extended trip to France and Italy. But as Milton was growing in learning and poetic accomplishment, England was gripped with increasing religious and political controversy, especially after the accession of Charles I in 1625, leading ultimately to the English Civil War of 1642–51. Milton was deeply engaged in these controversies and took the side of the Long Parliament against the king, and of the Puritans against the Anglican bishops. He became a vigorous pamphleteer in defense of the Long Parliament, then of the Commonwealth of England (1649–53) and finally the Protectorate under Oliver Cromwell, in whose

---

19. Eamon Duffy, *Stripping the Altars: Traditional Religion in England c.1400–c. 1580* (New Haven, CT: Yale University Press, 1882).

government he served as a cabinet secretary. As Milton grew successively more radical, he wrote in defense of the execution of Charles I by Parliament and supported a republican form of government for England. His early support of Cromwell weakened as the latter became in Milton's eyes, too authoritarian.

His falling out with Cromwell, however, would not save him from harsh treatment after the restoration of Charles II in 1660. His writings defending the execution of Charles I and supporting republicanism were publicly burned. He emerged from hiding after a general amnesty had been proclaimed, but he was still briefly imprisoned and might have been executed except for the intervention of powerful friends. He lived the remaining fourteen years of his life in obscurity and became completely blind. He had had thoughts of a poem on the theme of *Paradise Lost* from an early age but it was only now that he could bring it to completion, speaking to secretaries who took down his verses and correcting them when they read them back, ironically returning to the oral composition that characterized early epic poetry.[20]

Paradise Lost is the poem that we will pair with Calvin as we did the *Divina Commedia* with Thomas. If Dante's poem contained just about everything known in the Middle Ages, Samuel Barrow in an introductory note printed in the second edition of the poem in 1674, the year of Milton's death, eight years after the first edition, tells all future readers: "You who read *Paradise Lost*, the sublime poem of the great Milton, what do you read but everything? This book contains all things and the origin of all things, and their destinies and final ends."[21] Both poems are truly metanarratives. Milton was surely less loyal to Calvin than Dante was to Thomas, but however far his independent mind strayed, Calvin was his starting point as he was for English Puritans generally. Nonetheless, the mid-Seventeenth Century was a very different time from Calvin's day. Copernicus, Calvin's contemporary, was a relatively marginal figure compared to Galileo who was born after Calvin's death, but Calvin had heard enough to harshly assert that those who hold "that the sun does not move and that it is the earth that moves and turns," are possessed by the devil and aim "to pervert the order of nature." Most tellingly, Calvin insisted that "However widely the circuit of the Heavens

---

20. Of course, we should remember that before modern times many prolific writers dictated to secretaries. Augustine could never have completed the immense number of works he produced without a corps of secretaries to take down what he said, even when he was in his bath. And Henry James dictated his novels in more recent times.

21. John Milton, *Paradise Lost*, ed. Barbara K. Lewalski (Malden, MA: Blackwell, 2007), 6.

extends, it still has some limit."[22] Milton, on the other hand, visited Galileo in Florence and in *Paradise Lost*, though he uses the Copernican universe as part of his stage scenery, clearly accepts the new astronomy.

Milton's universe is far less coherent than Dante's in large part because he tells a very different story. Dante's universe is already there from the beginning, and in the *Paradiso* Dante tells us that God created everything, including the angels, at the same time, so there was nothing "before" creation. One might ask, with Satan securely frozen at the bottom of hell, what tempted so many mortals to sin and continue to people the circles of hell? But that is not the problem with which Dante is concerned. Milton's world begins in "heaven" before the creation of the cosmos as we know it, so it's not a "place" with any clear location. When Satan has decided to rebel, he withdraws "to the north" where his numerous followers reside. But with no Ptolemaic cosmos, where is "north"? The poem itself actually begins with Satan and his followers having already lost their war of rebellion, and having been cast "down" through a terrible chaos into an abyss, in complete darkness, chained in a burning sea. So Hell is not within the earth as the earth and the cosmos of which it is part have not yet been created: there is only Heaven, chaos, and Hell. Our cosmos, once it has been created, is "suspended by a golden chain" from Heaven. This is the stuff of fiction, not astronomy. Just one more example of the purely fantastic cosmography that Milton gives us: In Book 10, after the fall of Adam and Eve, God releases Sin and Death from their confinement at the gates of Hell so that they can now inhabit the new world that God had created. Satan's minions then construct a highway or bridge over chaos to conveniently connect the extra-cosmic Hell to earth, unintelligible under the laws of physics and perhaps invisible as hard to locate its connecting point on this earth.

When in one of his long conversations with Raphael, Adam asks about the cosmos, Raphael tells him not to worry about whether the sun goes around the earth or vice versa but to attend to more practical matters, suggesting to some that Milton hadn't yet made up his mind, but to others that his cosmological picture was complicated enough and he just didn't want to get into it.[23]

Dante's Satan is completely immobilized in ice and can't even speak as his three mouths are chomping on the three greatest traitors. Milton's Satan,

---

22. Bouwsma, *Calvin*, 72.
23. Barbara Lewalski, in her edition of *Paradise Lost*, cites the several places where Milton uses, inconsistently, Ptolemaic or Copernican understandings of the universe.

however, wakes in fury, casts off his chains, and calls his many legions of followers (we learn later that one-third of the myriad angels of heaven had followed him) to awake as well and hear what he has to say. Recognizing the
terrible situation they find themselves in compared to the delights of heaven,
Satan nevertheless accepts his reality and plans his revenge. He proclaims to
his followers:

> The mind is its own place, and in it self
> Can make a Heav'n of Hell, a Hell of Heav'n.

And finally:

> To reign is worth ambition though in Hell:
> Better to reign in Hell, then serve in Heav'n.[24]
>   (PL I)

Here already early in Book I, Satan sounds disturbingly attractive. Just before
the second quotation above Satan says "Here at least we shall be free."[25] Since
Milton's God is, or almost is, Calvin's God, whose sovereignty is absolute, and
who even foresaw and foreordained Satan's rebellion and punishment, we can
see that he is an earthly monarch absolutized beyond human imagination. Yet
Milton, unlike Calvin, believed angels and humans have free will, which somehow still leaves God as absolute sovereign. But if Calvin did not believe human
kings were absolute as God is absolute and authorized judicious rebellion against
tyrants, Milton declared human kings no better than any other humans, subject
to the same laws and justly executed if they have committed crimes worthy of
that punishment. Calvin had no patience with what he believed to be error and
even approved the execution of Servetus as a heretic, though disapproving the
Genevan Council's decision to burn him at the stake as inhuman and calling, in
vain, for a less cruel form of execution. Milton, however, wrote in *Areopagitica*
one of the earliest defenses of freedom of speech, in this case freedom to publish
without censorship, though it may surprise us to learn how narrowly his freedom extended: Catholics, Jews and Muslims were not included; only Protestant

---

24. *Paradise Lost* (hereafter PL), 1.254–5, 261–2. All quotations are from the Barbara K. Lewalski edition.
25. PL 1.258–9.

thought was to be allowed. Still, it is no wonder that many have thought Satan was Milton's true hero, whether he knew it or not.

Dante's world is mainly spatial: the leading characters, Dante, Virgil, and Beatrice, move in the poem through three levels of the universe, referring back to this earth as they go. Neither God nor Satan can be seen as major actors. *Paradise Lost*, however is much more focused on time: its major actors—God, Satan, Adam and Eve—unfold in time in a series of dramatic interactions. God and the angels, who seem to be countless, already exist when the poem starts, and the opening of Book I depicts Satan cast into Hell by the action of a God who is absolute sovereignty personified. According to the traditional view, angels are entirely intellectual, that is, they have no material bodies even though they can appear to humans as embodied. Since sensuality, including desire and hatred, were thought to reside in the body and not in the intellect, it is hard to see how angels could have the deep hatred that Satan has for God. Nonetheless, angels have free will and intelligence and that seems to have been enough to arouse dark feelings in one of the highest-ranking and beloved angels, Lucifer, the "light-bearer," as he was called before his rebellion led to his new name of Satan.

All of this we learn later in the poem, but the last straw for Lucifer was God's announcement to the assembled angels of his only begotten Son, Jesus Christ, to whom all worship was due and every knee should bow.[26] Lucifer apparently had enough trouble dealing with the unrivalled sovereignty of God, but having now not even the possibility of being God's favorite was too much. Kenneth Burke in his great essay on the first three chapters of Genesis points out the power of language in human thought, especially the power of the negative, of "no," "not," and "nothing," none of which have counterparts in the natural world but without which human language, and particularly interpersonal language, would be impossible.[27] We know that among animals, who know what dominance is but have no idea of sovereignty, those dominated are resentful and the alpha male will eventually be met with a challenge and overthrown. But for humans the idea of a just and righteous sovereign order raises the inevitable possibility of a negative order, a disorder or a counter-order. Satan is consumed with jealousy of God

---

26. It would seem that God "begot" the Son some time after Heaven and the angels were created, for Milton has God say in his announcement to the assembled angels, "This day I have begot whom I declare / My onely Son" (PL 5603–4).

27. Kenneth Burke, "The First Three Chapters of Genesis," in his *The Rhetoric of Religion* (Boston: Beacon Press, 1961).

and of Christ and would himself replace them if he could. This is an emotional, but also a terminological, as Burke puts it a "logological," inevitability. Thus the whole narrative shape of the poem is established before Adam and Eve are even created. They are central in the poem because we are descended from them—humans are neither divine nor angelic. Yet Adam and Eve are in a sense pawns in the titanic battle between God and Satan.

The central issue in *Paradise Lost*, as we would suspect in a Calvinist poem, is original sin, in particular the violation in Genesis 3 of God's prohibition of eating from the fruit of the tree of good and evil, first by Eve and then by Adam. For Milton (though not for Calvin) Adam and Eve and therefore all humans, have free will. God knows that Satan will tempt Eve and then Adam successfully, and allows it to happen, yet Adam and Eve were free to resist temptation, but failed to do so. This might seem to make Satan still a part of the heavenly court, sent to tempt Adam as he was at a later time to tempt Job. Satan in Job does not have the quality of absolute evil that he has in *Paradise Lost*, and we should remember that in Genesis 3 the tempter is not Satan but a snake and the snake's punishment is not to be frozen forever in Hell, but rather to have to crawl on his belly forever (we are not told his previous mode of locomotion), to bruise the heel of man, but to have his head crushed by man in return. While Genesis 3 knows nothing of Satan, Milton sees Satan as taking the form of a snake when tempting Eve.

However, in Genesis 3 as well as in *Paradise Lost* there is a terminological (logological) problem. God after creating all the plants and animals and fish on the earth creates Adam, and then from his rib, Eve, places everything else he has created under their command, and then settles them in an earthly paradise, Eden, a garden with every possible kind of fruit, telling them that they can eat whatever they please, but just not (thou shalt not) eat of the tree of the knowledge of good and evil. In this wonderful ideal world, there is only one commandment (*mitzvah*). Since in their natural innocence, Adam and Eve had no proclivity to do anything that might need to be forbidden, it almost seems as though God had to make up something to forbid. The assumption is that unless they ate of that tree they would never know what good and evil are. This would be very bad for the story which would come, at this point, to an abrupt end: there is nothing to tell about a life of eternal "dreaming innocence."

However, things do seem a bit more sinister than that. I think we all know what would happen if you put a couple of children (and Adam and Eve in their innocence are rather like children) in a room filled with wonderful toys and said to them you can play with any toy in the room except *this* one. Even if you told them they would be severely punished if they played with *this* one, we can be quite sure that as soon as the door is closed the children will head straight for *this* one. Who needs the snake when God has already set up such an enormous temptation? And can we really believe that before they eat the fruit of the forbidden tree they don't know the meaning of good and evil? The very words of the prohibition, "Don't eat of the tree of the knowledge of good and evil or you will die," is *already giving them* the idea of good and evil.

So then we have to reconsider the idea that God set them up to sin. Without their sin the story could not begin, they would not be punished, and there would be no need for a redeemer who would sacrifice himself for their sins. Traditionally this was called the *felix culpa*, the "happy fall."[28] Terrible though the consequences—they were given only one little commandment and they couldn't even keep that—without their original sin there would be no metanarrative, only the beginning of a story but no middle and no end.[29] And after all, Satan is not superfluous, for the story is not about whether to eat a certain apple or not but is about the gigantic struggle between Good and Evil, remembering, of course that it is not Manichaean, not a struggle between two equal principles, because Satan never ceases to be in God's control and is an actor in a drama designed by God from Beginning to End. This, however, does not mean that Satan is not attractive or that the word "no," so essential in bringing up children, does not always have a certain alluring quality, as though it not only means "Don't do it" (thou shalt not) but "Do it if you can get away with it!"

There is much in this great poem worthy of our attention, but there is only one more point that there is space for here. The whole story of the temptation in the garden is a blame story: Adam blames Eve for tempting him and Eve blames the snake, though it was the snake's promise that she would not die, but be like

---

28. PL 12.469–478. Lewalski, unaccountably, holds that these lines do not affirm the *felix culpa* because earlier we had been told that if Adam and Eve had not sinned, their bodies would gradually have turned into pure spirit and there would have been no difference between the earthly and the Heavenly Paradises. PL 496–503. But, in that case the poem would have ended before it began: no conflict, no plot, no interest. And, equally important, humans would never have experienced a life of both suffering and joy denied even to the angels.

29. One poignantly Calvinist element of the *felix culpa* is Adam's recognition that the part of his punishment that requires that he earn his living from the soil by the sweat of his brow (instead of just eating the fruits of Eden) is maybe not so bad after all: "with labor I must earne / My bread; what harm? Idleness had bin worse" (PL 10.1054–5).

God in the knowledge of good and evil, and so his appeal to her selfishness that succeeded in tempting her.

But Milton gives Genesis 3 a slightly different twist: the snake tempts Eve and she gives in to him, but Adam does not eat because Eve tempts him. When he sees that Eve has eaten of the forbidden fruit, some of which is still in her hands, he is horrified. Raphael has given him a long talk, to which Eve was not privy, about how absolutely important it was to obey God's one commandment and how truly awful the consequences would be of disobeying it. Remember that Adam was created first by God shaping the dust of the earth and blowing spirit into him, and that Adam was pleased with everything except that he felt alone. All the animals had mates but he had none. God graciously accedes to Adam's wish, takes a rib out of Adam's side to create Eve, and sets up a lovely impromptu marriage service in which he says that they will be of one flesh and that in all future generations the male and female will "forsake all others" to be with each other. Adam, when he sees what Eve had done and that the punishment for her sin is death, says he will not leave her behind, but will also eat of the fruit so that he will be with her in death as in life, for they are of one flesh. Adam's sin, therefore, is based on love, not selfishness. One could see Milton's version as just one more twist in an already misogynistic story, letting Adam off the hook and blaming Eve all the more, or one could remember that Eve did manage to tell Adam the snake's essential message before he ate, so whatever he said, he was probably tempted too. Nonetheless, it seems to me that the expression of Adam's deep and self-sacrificial love for Eve at this critical moment is not without importance. So far in this story everything has been about dominance. Suddenly we have the appearance of love. But maybe love has also been there all along, at least since the creation of our universe, for when God created each thing on successive days, "he saw that it was good," and so Creation itself can be seen as the expression of God's love. And we are also told that God, when faced with the sin that would lead to further sin and death for humans, asked his divine council if anyone would take on the sin of humans so that in the end they could be saved, and Christ volunteered, so that the ultimate love was also there almost from the beginning. As I said, Dante unfolds in space, Milton in time. For both of them divine power and love are one.

It is true that after they have eaten the forbidden fruit Adam and Eve fall to bickering. Even though Adam had chosen to be with Eve until death, he can't refrain from blaming her for the fatal sin. She, in turn, blames him for not forbidding her more clearly not to eat the fruit. They are both quite miserable when they learn that they will have to leave Eden and make their way in a much harder world than they have ever known before. But as they are preparing to leave the angel Michael comes to tell them what lies ahead in history. He recounts the results of their sin over many generations, but then the coming of Christ who will have taken all the sin upon himself and so will be the savior of the world. Michael points out that Jesus will be born of a human woman, the Virgin Mary a descendent of Eve. Very near the end of the poem, PL 12.620–624, Eve reminds Adam and herself that "though all by mee is lost/ . . . By mee the Promis'd Seed shall all restore." A few lines later at the very end of the poem, they walk out of Eden hand in hand, but it is the image of Eve that stays most strongly in our minds.

So far, at least in the tradition that begins with Moses and Plato, continues with Denys the Areopagite and Plotinus, then with Augustine (whose *Confessions* are his own narrative poem, paired with his doctrinal works), then with Thomas and Dante, ending so far with Calvin and Milton, God is the primary actor in this succession of metanarratives. Something happens in the eighteenth and nineteenth centuries that changes that scenario: God is not missing, but is now off-center, so to speak, has to contend with other actors for primacy. We now see a whole slew of philosophers for whom God is as much a problem as an answer: Descartes, Spinoza, Locke, Leibniz, leading up to the great culmination of early modern philosophy in Immanuel Kant. But amazingly, in the early nineteenth century we have a major poem that still deals with the whole world and its contents, and in which God is an important but not a central actor: Goethe's *Faust*.

Immanuel Kant (1724–1804) is perhaps the most important European thinker since Calvin, or perhaps, since Thomas, and his influence is so pervasive that it is hard to sum it up succinctly. If one looks over everything that Kant published in his life one will quickly note that he was one of those who wanted to know everything. It is hard to think of any subject of importance in his day that he didn't touch on. He said of himself, "I am an inquirer by inclination. I feel a consuming thirst for knowledge, the unrest in the desire to progress in it, and satisfaction at every advance in it."[30] Still it is not wrong to see in Kant a new

---

30. Immanuel Kant, *Practical Philosophy*, trans. and ed. by Mary J. Gregor (Cambridge: Cambridge University Press, 1996), xvii.

emphasis compared to the thinkers we have considered before. Although he was deeply interested in religion and published a lot about it, I think it is fair to say that, compared to Thomas or Calvin for example, God is no longer the center of his concern; reason is. That is why one can say that Kant is the central figure of the Enlightenment, with which we will have to deal further later in this book. He published his most important book, his *Critique of Pure Reason*, in 1781 at the age of 57, and, receiving almost instant fame with this book, spent the rest of his life developing his thought even more extensively (he had published a great deal earlier, in what is called his "pre-critical" period), and it is on the late works, especially the three *Critiques*, that interest has centered.

It is certainly not the case that Kant ignored God or religion; his publications in that area are extensive.[31] But "pure reason," in Kant's view cannot say anything about God or religion, so has no theological basis. One must qualify this by noting that his practical, that is ethical, philosophy, does require the existence of God as a postulate of pure practical reason, along with the postulates of freedom and the immortality of the soul. Further, Kant also says in his *Critique of Practical Reason*:

> Thus, in the union of pure speculative reason with pure practical reason in one cognition, the latter has primacy, assuming that this union is not *contingent* and discretionary but based a priori on reason itself and therefore *necessary* . . . [O]ne cannot require pure practical reason to be subordinate to speculative reason and so reverse the order, since all interest is ultimately practical and even that of speculative reason is only conditional and is complete in practical use alone.[32]

So in one sense, if practical reason is primary and the postulate of the existence of God is necessary for it, God remains (though alongside the postulates of freedom and the immortality of the soul), at the basis of the primary form of reason. We must remember, however, that for Kant, the existence of this God

---

31. See, for example, in the Cambridge Edition, Immanuel Kant, *Religion and Rational Theology*, trans. and ed. by Allen W. Wood and George di Giovanni (Cambridge: Cambridge University Press, 1996), which contains several works, of which the most important is *Religion within the Boundaries of Mere Reason*, though by no means everything he wrote about religion.

32. Immanuel Kant, *Critique of Practical Reason*, in Immanuel Kant, *Practical Philosophy*, trans. and ed. by Mary J. Gregor (Cambridge: Cambridge University Press, 1996), 237–38.

cannot be proven by speculative reason, that is, by traditional metaphysics, and further cannot be proved by revelation, for which, Kant claims, there is no rational basis. Kant's God, it turns out, is a rather special form of the philosophers' God, and appears only as a necessary postulate of practical reason. This is not Thomas's God, or certainly, Calvin's. It has been said that Kant denies the possibility of philosophical theology, and certainly biblical theology, as rational systems. What is left is the philosophy of religion, though, as usual (nothing is ever lost), philosophical and biblical theologies continued to be written even though Kant said they were impossible.

Kant argues that it is "morally necessary to assume the existence of God," because only God can be identified with the highest good, and it is our duty to strive "to produce and promote the highest good in the world," even though, as human beings, we have a "continuing propensity to transgression or at least impurity," and so "nothing remains for a creature but endless progress." The postulate of the immortality of the soul is necessary because, such a creature must be justified in "hoping for his endless duration." While the assertion of the depth of human imperfection suggests some similarity to Calvin, a posthumous existence of endless progress rather than a final separation of souls into eternal bliss or eternal perdition surely doesn't. And while God is termed "all powerful" and even the "Creator," God is not the absolute monarch of Calvin's view, but, since all humans are autonomous, even God cannot transgress that autonomy:

> It now follows of itself that in the order of ends the human being (and with him every rational being) is an *end in itself*, that is, can never be used merely as a means by anyone (not even God) without being at the same time himself an end, and that humanity in our person must, accordingly, be *holy* [*heilig*] to ourselves . . . For, this moral law is based on the autonomy of his will, as a free will which, in accordance with its universal laws, must necessarily be able at the same time *to agree* to that to which it is to *subject* itself. 245–246

If Kant did not quite see God as the absolute sovereign that Calvin and Milton did, he joined them in believing that on this earth republics are preferable to monarchies. Living in nearly despotic Prussia and always with the censor in mind, Kant called for no revolutionary uprising, but urged gradual reform. If anything, in his late years his interest in politics grew, even international politics, and he proposed as the basis for "perpetual peace" a global confederation of republics. Republics as he defines them, are based on three principles: the free-dom of all members of society; the dependence of everyone on a single common legislation; and the principle of legal equality of everyone. In such societies, Kant believes, since it is the people themselves who would decide whether to go to war or not, and since they would be most aware of the burdens of war on ordinary people, they would be most likely to hesitate to resort to force in solving inter-national problems.[33]

What is most striking about Kant's view is its "unqualified egalitarianism" as Allen Wood puts it.[34] Kant, remembering when he thought his "thirst for knowl-edge constituted the honor of humanity," wrote:

> I despised the people, who know nothing. Rousseau set me right about this. This binding prejudice disappeared, I learned to honor humanity, and I would find myself more useless than the common laborer if I did not believe that this attitude of mine can give worth to all others in establishing the rights of humanity.[35]

For Kant any opinion of superiority creates inequality, depriving those who are felt to be inferior of their inherent dignity. He would not even allow a sense of superiority on the basis of virtue. Virtue can give one a sense of inner worth, but it is no excuse for looking down on others: "One always talks so much of virtue. One must, however, abolish injustice before he can be virtuous. One must set aside comforts, luxuries and everything that oppresses others while elevating myself, so that I am not one of those who oppress their species. Without this conclusion all virtue is impossible."[36] If Calvin could be harsh to the wealthy, Kant could be equally so:

> In our present condition, when general injustice is so entrenched, the nat-ural rights of the lowly cease. They are therefore only debtors, the superiors

---

33. Immanuel Kant, "Perpetual Peace: A Philosophical Sketch" (1795), in Immanuel Kant, *Political Writ-ings*, ed. H. S. Reiss (Cambridge: Cambridge University Press, Second Edition, 1991), 99–102 (93–130). Would that that were the case in the American Republic, though it is far from clear even here how much control "the people" have over decisions of war and peace.

34. Allen Wood, "General Introduction," in Immanuel Kant, *Practical Philosophy*, trans. and ed. by Mary J. Gregor (Cambridge: Cambridge University Press, 1996), xvii.

35. Kant, *Practical Philosophy*, xvii.

36. Kant, *Practical Philosophy*, xviii.

owe them nothing. Therefore these superiors are called "gracious lords." But he who needs nothing from them but justice can hold them to their debts and does not need to be submissive.[37]

And speaking of debts, we can remember how much we owe Kant and his teacher in this respect, Rousseau, when we use today the language of human rights as almost our only way of talking about global justice.[38]

Johann Wolfgang von Goethe (1749–1832), Kant's only somewhat younger contemporary, was a product of many of the same influences as his elder, including the influence of Kant himself, as well as the responses to him. Like Kant, Goethe is a true child of the Enlightenment. For Goethe as for Kant, Rousseau's "Profession of Faith of a Savoyard Vicar" from *Emile*, was a defining statement of what is rational in religion.[39] Goethe was influenced by Voltaire and the more radical critics of traditional religion as a youth when he went through a phase of strong negativity toward Christianity. Although never professing religious faith himself, showing particular hostility to the Catholic Church, late in his life he showed greater sympathy with Christianity and was impressed with some open-minded but devout Catholic believers. Yet *Faust*, which occupied him off and on through most of this life, is still a religious poem.[40]

Though *Faust* played a central role in his life and it is not inappropriate to focus on it, Goethe was a prodigious writer of fiction, lyric poetry, and biological speculation, as well as being through his sheer personality, an overwhelming (and to some at times an oppressive) figure in German cultural life. Tolstoy, though in an entirely different way, was also a commanding personality, and I will use the persona he created, "Tolstoy" as against Tolstoy, later in this chapter. Although Goethe created in the same sense "Goethe," there is a simplicity in "Tolstoy" that

---

37. Kant, *Practical Philosophy*, xix.
38. See Ernst Cassirer's valuable essay, "Kant and Rousseau," in his *Rousseau, Kant, Goethe: Two Essays* (Princeton, NJ: Princeton University Press, 1945).
39. Jean-Jacques Rousseau, "Profession of Faith of a Savoyard Vicar," in *Emile or On Education*, trans. Allan Bloom (New York: Basic Books, 1979), 266–313. The "Profession" caused Rousseau to be persecuted in Catholic France and Protestant Geneva, but within years its enlightened view of religion was shared by most of educated Europe.
40. My treatment of Goethe, and of *Faust* in particular, would be even more amateurish without the help of Nicholas Boyle's two extraordinary volumes of his *Goethe: The Poet and the Age* (Oxford: Oxford University Press): Vol. 1, *The Poetry of Desire (1749–1790)*, 1991, and Vol. 2, *Revolution and Renunciation (1790–1803)*, 2000. Since Goethe died in 1832, my only regret is that we don't yet have volume 3 (or maybe 4 as well?).

allows my compressed explication, whereas "Goethe" is far too complex for easy summary. We will therefore stick to *Faust*.

For our purposes Goethe as narrative poet makes a perfect pair to Kant, not only because their beliefs were substantively parallel, but because his *Faust* overlaps in theme and characters with Dante's and Milton's poems. Here again we have God, Satan, and humans somewhere in between. The differences, already great between Dante and Milton are all the greater between Goethe and the earlier poets. Interestingly enough, the most theologically orthodox, or at least Catholic, of the three poems, the *Divina Commedia*, takes place in a space defined by God and Satan as the poles between which all the action occurs, but neither actually has much of a part. The actors are primarily Dante, Virgil, and Beatrice, though the scores of characters they meet along the way and their memories of their lives on earth, create much of the interest of the poem. In *Paradise Lost*, however, God and Satan are major actors, along with Adam and Eve: there are many minor characters but it is these four who dominate the action. *Faust* differs from both the others in giving God a minor part—he doesn't appear again after the Prologue in Heaven, but Satan (whom Goethe calls Mephistopheles), a primary part, along with Faust, himself the principal actor. Margaret or Gretchen is critically important in the action of the play which in many ways centers around her, yet her part in terms of number of lines is small.

Mephistopheles, a name associated with the Faust legend from the sixteenth century, may have started out as a devil subordinate to Satan, but in *Faust* it is fair to say he is Satan. Goethe seems to model the " Prologue in Heaven" on the Prologue to Job, in that Mephistopheles is on good terms with the Lord, if not, as in Job, an actual member of his court. The Lord acknowledges Mephistopheles's wager that Faust will choose evil and end in hell, without accepting it, assuring Satan that Faust will escape him because he is "A good man in his darkling aspiration," and that he "Remembers the right road throughout his quest." (Part I 328–329) In allowing Mephistopheles to tempt Faust as long as he lives, the Lord adds, "Man errs as long as he will strive." (I 317) The German verb for "strive" is *streben*. It is a key to understanding Faust and returns in his final judgment at the end of Part II.

After the Prologue, Part I of *Faust* begins with a long monologue by Faust lamenting his wasted life in mastering all existing knowledge. Since traditionally Dr. Faustus lived in the sixteenth century, Goethe's play often seems set in that time, though on occasion it also often seems much more modern. The fields of knowledge that Faust claims to have mastered, however, are the traditional fields established in the Middle Ages and still describing university education in the sixteenth century: philosophy, law, medicine, and "worst of all" theology. (I, 354–356) But while Kant claimed to find satisfaction in every advance in knowledge, Faust finds his knowledge meaningless, ashes in his mouth. He has been teaching students for ten years but he finds "that for all our science and art/ We can know nothing." (I 364–365) Since his life is empty he decides to turn to magic

> That I might see what secret force
> Hides in the world and rules its course
> Envisage the creative blazes
> Instead of rummaging in phrases.

It is not to books that Faust turns, but to nature and the spirits, invoking the Spirit of the Earth so that he may "plunge into the world, to bear/ All earthly grief, all earthly joy." (I, 464–465) But the Earth Spirit is not impressed with Faust, calls him mockingly a would-be *Übermensch* (an interesting use of the term before Nietzsche) who is in fact "A miserably writhing worm" and refuses to help him. (I 490, 498, 513)

In despair Faust contemplates suicide, for the meaninglessness of his life as it is is unbearable. We must remember that suicide is a recurring theme in Goethe's life and work, and that in his first and by far most famous novel, *The Sorrows of Young Werther*, his hero at the end dies of suicide. Faust, thinking that his willingness to die, even if it means to consign himself to hell, will prove his human dignity in the face of meaninglessness, lifts the poison bowl to his mouth but in that instant hears the bells and chorus of Easter morn and puts the bowl down. Hearing the choir sing "Christ is arisen," Faust says "Although I hear the message, I lack all faith or trust/ And yet these chords, which I have known since infancy:/ Call me now, too, back into life." (I, 765, 768–770) But the spell doesn't last long and Faust is distracted by others. While taking a walk with his assistant, Wagner, Faust finds that a black dog, a poodle, has attached himself to them.

Faust, at home alone with the dog circling around him, considers whether a supernatural revelation will help him. Famously, he opens the Bible to the words "In the beginning was the *Word*." But he is unsatisfied. It is just words that have failed him. He thinks of other translations: "In the beginning was the *Mind*," and "In the beginning there was *Force*," but he is still unsatisfied. Finally he thinks the spirit helps him and he translates: "In the beginning was the *Act*" (*Im Anfang wardie Tat!*) (I, 1224–1237) It is not knowledge, not the Word, that will save him, he thinks, but deeds. Above all he wants not to be but to do.

Finally Faust thinks the unquiet dog may be some kind of devilish spirit and utters the spell that might call him forth (I, 1273–1276). Mephistopheles (or Mephisto) appears but Faust is wary of him. Earlier, Faust, looking at the sun, had said "Oh, that no wings lift me above the ground/ To strive and strive (*streben* again) in his pursuit!" (I, 1074–1075) Mephisto reveals his nature plainly:

> I am the spirit that negates . . .
> Thus everything that your terms, sin,
> Destruction, evil represent—
> That is my proper element. (I, 1338, 1342–1344)

So that Faust can say,

> What would you, wretched Devil, offer?
> Was ever a man's spirit in noble striving (*Streben*)
> Grasped by your like, devilish scoffer? (I, 1675–1677)

Mephisto, however, is beguiling. He promises to be Faust's servant and allow him what other humans have never been allowed to do, to satisfy every desire for women, wealth and power, to "strive" to his heart's content. Faust knows that the Devil is no philanthropist, and wants to know what his conditions are. Mephisto's answer is simple: "*Here* you shall be the master," but in the "*beyond*,/ Then you shall do the same for me." (I, 1656, 1658–1659) Faust replies quickly that he cares only about this world and doesn't care at all about any other. Mephisto promises to give him "more/ Than any man has seen before." (I, 1673–1674) But he adds, "the time comes when we would/ Recline in peace and feast on something good." (I, 1690–1691) But Faust replies that if Mephisto ever finds him in sloth or sheer pleasure "Then break on me, eternal night!/ This bet I offer." And Mephisto: "I accept it." Faust then affirms the deal even more clearly:

> If to the moment I should say:
> Abide, you are so fair—(*Verweile doch! Du bist so schön!*)
> Put me in fetters on that day . . .
> As time comes to an end for me. (1, 1699–1701, 1706)

Much of the rest of Part I is concerned with Faust's seduction of the attractive young Margaret (or Gretchen) which ends in total disaster, giving rise to Gounod's famous opera and many spin-offs. I can give only the most abbreviated account of this first fruit of what Mephisto can do for Faust. After Mephisto by magic manages to make Faust thirty years younger, Faust accosts a very young, innocent, and not at all educated girl, Gretchen. She instinctively turns away from him, but is flattered by his attention and more responsive when Faust tries again. She agrees to meet him in her bedroom but fears her vigilant mother. Mephisto suggests Faust give Gretchen a sleeping potion for her mother, so she will be unaware of the tryst. However, unknown to Faust, he supplies poison instead, so Gretchen's mother dies. Just the first example of Mephisto's inadvertence (radical evil) that Faust chooses to overlook. Then Faust and Mephisto encounter Gretchen's brother in front of her house after the brother had discovered that his sister is pregnant. In the ensuing fight Faust and Mephisto kill the brother. Faust must flee to avoid a murder charge. Gretchen, abandoned, with her mother and brother dead, decides the pregnancy would bring ill repute on her and might harm Faust as well. She drowns the baby, which she loves, soon after its birth, but she is discovered, sentenced to death for murder, and imprisoned.

Faust is shaken with guilt and begs Mephisto to help him rescue Gretchen before it is too late. Mephisto manages to get the prison keys so that Faust can find Gretchen and get her out before daylight when there would be too many people around for them to escape. Faust tries to persuade Gretchen to come with him but she is convinced of her guilt and the justice of her sentence. Moved by Faust's concern, she seeks comfort from him and a kiss, but he is frozen and can't respond. Mephisto insists Faust leave or he too will be caught. In spite of Faust's efforts she still resists, but calls him "Heinrich" in her despair. Mephisto says "She is judged," but a voice from above says, "is saved." Faust leaves with Mephisto, while a voice from within, fading away, says "Heinrich, Heinrich." (I, 4610–4614) These are the only three times in the poem we hear Faust's first name.

Part II opens in a "pleasing landscape," where Faust seems to be recuperating in the arms of nature, without thought of the sad scene he has left behind. Soon both Faust and Mephisto are taken up in a massive imperial court scene with many actors and intrigues but both find imperial favor. Part II is both longer and far more complex than Part I (it was written much later) and the central event, occurring in Act 3, is the conjuring up of Helen of Troy, Faust's ideal of the most beautiful woman who ever lived, far too multi-leveled for me to try to untangle here. I will only summarize briefly the events in Act 5 that bring the story to its conclusion.

With Mephisto's help, Faust has been doing a lot of striving, becoming powerful at the emperor's court, leading the incompetent imperial army against a disciplined invading army, which he nonetheless defeats with Mephisto's magic aid. In Act 5 we find Faust engaged in a massive land reclamation project, draining swamps the emperor gave him, even building dikes to reclaim land from the sea, and becoming enormously wealthy as he sells his reclaimed land to new settlers.

But at the beginning of the Act we find a "wanderer," who must be the spirit of Zeus, discovering the dwelling of Baucis and Philemon who took him in so many years before, and are offering him hospitality once again. Contemporary readers of *Faust* would know the classical myth of Baucis and Philemon, who, when Zeus and Hermes, wandering through a village as it was getting cold and dark and had been turned away by the other villagers, took them in and gave them food and shelter. After enjoying the visit Zeus revealed himself and asked them what favor they might request. Baucis and Philemon consulted quietly and returned with the request that they be allowed to die at the same time, something any loving elderly couple might ask, and Zeus not only grants their wish but sets them up in a lovely marble temple to spend their final years.

Readers would also know of the gentle way that Baucis and Philemon end their days in the old myth, but Faust provides another ending. He has long admired the lovely hill where Baucis and Philemon dwell with their temple that has become a chapel, and wishes to have it as a lookout from which he can survey all the land he has reclaimed, offering another place to Baucis and Philemon. The latter, however, insist on the sacredness of their dwelling and refuse to move. Finally Faust orders Mephisto and three of his thug companions to remove Baucis and Philemon by force, which they do by burning them alive in their dwelling, thus ironically and wickedly fulfilling the promise that they would die together. Faust is horrified—he seems to have learned nothing of his servant's true nature—and Mephisto excuses himself on the grounds that Baucis and Philemon resisted efforts to remove them. Faust curses Mephisto and his thugs, but soon turns his attention away. He never seems to cling to guilt.

In the face of worrisome suggestions about mortality from the Spirit of Care, Faust once again affirms his commitment to constant action, and determines to extend his reclamation efforts even further. In the face of all distraction he declares his creed:

> Freedom and life are earned by those alone
> Who conquer them each day anew,
> Surrounded by such danger, each one thrives,
> Childhood, manhood, and age lead active lives,
> At such a throng I would fain stare,
> With free men on free ground their freedom share. (II, 11575–11580)

But just at the height of his self-assertion, he is tempted to go one dangerous step further:

> Then, to the moment I might say:
> Abide, you are so fair . . . (*Verweile doch, du bist so schön*)
> As I presage a happiness so high,
> I now enjoy the highest moment. (II, 11581–11582, 11584–11585)

Faust has lost his bet and falls down dead. Mephisto's minions are already digging his grave. Mephistopheles has what he thinks is his last word:

> Now it is over. What meaning can one see?
> It is as if it had not come to be,
> And yet it circulates as if it were,
> I should prefer—Eternal Emptiness. (II, 11600–11603)

However, it is not over. According to the beliefs of the day, the spirit does not necessarily leave the body immediately. Mephisto calls his minions to help him watch carefully so that when the spirit leaves Faust's body they can grab it and put it in hell. But then a chorus of young male angels descends from above, strewing roses. The minions are distracted and Mephisto tells them to watch more closely, but then he finds himself attracted to the beautiful youths, "such charming boys," and singling out one—"You, tall one, are the fairest boy I've ever seen"—asks him to throw him a kiss. (II, 11763, 11794) But just as he is thinking only of the boys, the young angels steal Faust's spirit and take it up to heaven. Mephisto is disgusted with himself:

> Absurd feelings of love, a vulgar lust
> Has turned the tough old Devil's head. (II 11838–11839)

But, recovering himself, he affirms:

> Saved are the Devil's noble parts—for sin;
> The love spook went no deeper than my skin. (2 11813–11814)

But then we hear the angel's choir, carrying Faust's immortal spirit on high, sing:

> "Whoever strives [streben] with all his power,
> We are allowed to save." (II, 11936–11937)

This is more than a little disconcerting. The Lord in the Prologue had warned that to strive is to err ("Man errs as long as he will strive." (I, 317). Faust has committed countless sins and has never repented. In any orthodox theology he should be damned forever and has no right to be saved. Whatever we make of the changed valence of "striving" near the end of Part II, Act 5, there is something else going on in heaven.

In fact, the Heaven at the end of Part II is quite different from the Heaven depicted in the Prologue in Heaven that begins Part I. For one thing, there is no Lord present. The ruler here seems to be Heaven's Queen [Die Himmelskönigin], (II, 119995) It is the "Virgin, beautifully pure,/ Venerable mother," who is "Our chosen queen." (II, 12009–120011). Among the many women there are the famous Penitent Women, from the Bible, the woman who washed Jesus's feet with her tears, and the Samaritan woman by the well, along with the later Mary of Egypt, above whom the Mater Gloriosa floats in the air. (II 12037–12065) But then there is one more Penitent woman, whose name was formerly Gretchen, and who, nestling Faust, says:

> He whom I loved in pain
> Now returns free from stain,
> Comes back to me. (II, 12073–12075)

It would seem that her intercession, her abiding and undivided love, was what saved Faust.

It is not for me to solve the meaning of *Faust*. Mephistopheles is relatively easy to understand, urbane, with a sense of humor, he might seem likable, but in the end is even less attractive than Satan in *Paradise Lost*, for he has no grudge against God; he is simply pure evil and negation. Faust himself is surely no hero. His need to do is not accompanied by any need to do good. He can construct, but his willingness to call on Mephisto's help infects every one of his constructive projects. Is all the land he has reclaimed worth the murder of Baucis and Philemon? Not only does Faust lack a will toward the good, he seems unable to love. Lust on a grand scale he has, but when his victim, Gretchen, in her misery in the prison, needs his simple affection, he can't give it.

Since the heaven of Part II, Act 5, is almost purely feminine, one must suspect Goethe is making some kind of gender distinction. Faust and Mephistopheles are both into power; both want above all to dominate. We have seen Faust's inability to care for Gretchen in the great prison scene at the end of Part I, and we have seen the superficial lust of Mephisto in his attraction to the beautiful boy angels, but neither of them have any capacity to love, to nurture. For Mephisto the very idea is repulsive, but Faust just seems tone deaf in that sphere.

As opposed to the severe limitation of the leading males in the poem, and the complete absence of the Lord at the end of it, there is an increasing importance of the feminine in Part II. Earlier than Act 5 there is the mysterious appearance of the Mothers, whose meaning Goethe himself refused to explain, but seems to imply an undercurrent of the feminine even when the masculine seems to be running riot. And then there is the great final Chorus Mysticus at the very end of the Poem, that defies explanation yet which one cannot forget. I give here only the opening and closing lines:

> Alles Vergängliche
> Ist nur ein Gleichnis;

> What is destructable
> Is but a parable;

And then at the end:

Das Ewig-weibliche
Zieht uns hinan.

The Eternal-Feminine
Draws us up.[41]

It has been my practice so far, especially since the discussion of Aquinas and Dante, to begin with the great theorist and then go to the great poet. In my final pair I am reversing my habit by beginning with Tolstoy and then going to Max Weber, mainly because Tolstoy was a significant figure for Weber, and we need to understand Tolstoy first to see why.

Leo Tolstoy (1828–1910) whose world stature is comparable to that of Goethe, was born just four years before Goethe's death.[42] It is remarkable how much they share; both were profoundly indebted to Rousseau and deeply influenced by Kant. Although Tolstoy read Goethe at several times in his life, there is no indication that he particularly liked him or was influenced by him. But since Tolstoy didn't much care for Shakespeare, we shouldn't make too much of his lack of enthusiasm for Goethe. Although Goethe came from a wealthy merchant family in Frankfurt, and Tolstoy from an upper aristocratic family with large country estates, there were clear similarities between them in spite of the obvious differences: neither ever really had to worry about money, and both profited from the best available education of their times.

Tolstoy says at the beginning of *What I Believe* that from the age of 14 or 15, before which he had had the faith of childhood, up until the age of 50, when he " 'began to believe in the doctrine of Christ," he had been a "nihilist."[43] But such a dramatic claim is an illustration of what I meant when I wrote earlier that Tolstoy was deeply interested in creating "Tolstoy": the claim to have been completely changed by a conversion adds much drama to a story. However, when

---

41. Walter Kaufmann, whose translation I have used throughout, here translates "Lures to perfection," but I chose to be more literal. *Goethe's Faust*, translated and with an introduction by Walter Kaufmann (bilingual edition) (Garden City, NY: Doubleday Anchor, 1961). Kaufmann is usually so close to the German that I am not tempted to interfere.

42. On the comparison between the two, see Thomas Mann, "Goethe and Tolstoy," in *Essays by Thomas Mann* (New York: Vintage, 1957), 176–79. Mann, addressing a German audience in 1922, has to argue against the idea that Tolstoy does not deserve comparison to Goethe, insisting that he is Goethe's equal.

43. Leo Tolstoy, *What I Believe*, trans. C. Poppov (New York: Cosimo, 2007 [1885]), 1.

I say Tolstoy created "Tolstoy," I don't just mean as an image for others, as in this case. No. Tolstoy was involved from an early age in creating an image of himself for himself, and comparing himself, usually as deeply unsatisfactory, with the image he was trying to be. There is some of this in the Augustine of the *Confessions*, but it is hard to think of anyone else who from such an early age, was so continuously concerned with such a project.

Tolstoy's constant critical concern with his own behavior is evident in his early trilogy, *Childhood*, *Boyhood*, and *Youth*.[44] The trilogy was a "novel," though written in the first person, and many significant details, as well as names, including his own, were fictional: for example Tolstoy's mother died when he was two years old, so he had no personal memories of her, while in *Childhood* she dies when he was nine and is clearly depicted. Nonetheless we know that Tolstoy wept when rereading parts of the trilogy in later life so we can see it as psychologically autobiographical, though not literally so. Nor can we be sure that what he attributed to the young boy was what he really felt at the time or what Tolstoy, when he was writing, thought he ought to have felt. It is worth remembering how young he was at that time: *Childhood* was published when he was 24, *Boyhood* when he was 26, and *Youth* when he was 29: these are not the reconstructions of an old man, but of a young man in his twenties, still close to what he is describing.

It is typical of Tolstoy's arrogance, but also his fear of rejection, that he sent the manuscript of *Childhood* to the best literary magazine in Russia with a note saying that if they didn't like it they could tell him why, but he didn't care if they published it or not, and giving only false initials but not his real name as the author. He need not have feared—the book was an immediate success and left Turgenev and other writers in the dark as to who this remarkable new talent was. It really was remarkable that someone who had previously published almost nothing was making significant innovations in Russian fiction, using colloquialisms that were previously avoided to give a powerful sense of immediacy to his story. I will comment shortly on moral sensitivities in the trilogy that point to his much later fully developed persona, but there is even earlier evidence of Tolstoy's conscious effort at self-creation.

Through much of his life Tolstoy was an inveterate diarist. The earliest diary is dated somewhat uncertainly as 1846 or 1847, but seems likely to be of the later

---

44. Leo Tolstoy, *Childhood, Boyhood, and Youth*, trans. Judson Rosengrant (London: Penguin, 2012).

date, when Tolstoy was 18 and studying at the university in Kazan. It begins while he is in the hospital with what turned out to be a minor illness, but which gave him time "outside of society," as he put it, to think about his own life. Writing that some change must come in his way of life, he says:

> Yet that change must not come of an external circumstance—rather, of a movement of spirit: wherefore I keep finding myself confronted with the question, "What is the aim of man's life?" and, no matter what I take to be life's source, I invariably arrive at the conclusion that the purpose of our human existence is to afford a maximum of help towards the universal development of everything that exists.

He goes on to say that nature does this unconsciously but that man, also a part of nature, "is gifted with consciousness, and therefore bound . . . to make conscious use of his spiritual faculties in striving for the development of everything existent."[45] That word "striving" again, but not, as in Faust, for himself, but for "the universal development of everything that exists." The most striking thing about this passage is that it contains a form of the question that will haunt Tolstoy during his whole life, and will call him to Weber's attention: "What is the aim of man's life?" He gives a tentative answer here, and "the universal development of everything that exists" might make one think of evolution, but this is over twenty years before the publication of *Origin of Species*. It is an answer that he never rejected but he finally found too vague, so he had to keep on searching.

In *Childhood* we find an awareness of status differences, between family and hired tutors, between family and serfs, and between a boy his age whose father is lower middle class and himself, and a sense of their injustice, which only deepened during his later years. He also recounts in *Boyhood*, how, at the age of 14 he was captivated by skepticism:

> I imagined that except for me, no one and nothing else existed in the whole world . . . There were moments under the influence of that "fixed idea" when I reached such a degree of extravagance that I would suddenly turn around, hoping to catch nothingness (*néant*) by surprise where I no longer was.[46]

45. Leo Tolstoy, *The Diaries of Leo Tolstoy*, trans. C. J. Hogarth and A. Sirnis (London: Dent, 1917), 30–31.
46. Tolstoy, *Childhood*, 185.

While this was a passing moment of playful solipsism, it suggests that Tolstoy's quest for faith would never leave doubt behind and that he thought about nothingness as well as truth. On the first page of *Youth* we find a concern for virtue that is a constant for the rest of his life:

> The idea of virtue I examined with my cherished friend Dmitry . . . had appealed only to my intellect, not to my feelings. But the time came when those ideas entered my mind with such a fresh power of revelation that it scared me to think of how much time I had wasted, and I wanted at once, wanted that very second, to apply them to life with the firm intention of never betraying them.
>
> And it's that time I consider the beginning of *youth*.[47]

However wavering Tolstoy's pursuit of virtue turned out to be, these are not the words of a nihilist, whatever he said later.

I dealt with their great poems in the case of Dante, Milton and Goethe. Of course, Tolstoy wrote no *Faust*, only the two greatest novels ever written, but are not *War and Peace* (1867–9) and *Anna Karenina* (1877) also great poems? Granted that they are far too huge to be parsed in a few paragraphs here, aren't they, too, a part of Tolstoy's creation of "Tolstoy"? Yes, of course, but even dealing with them in that sense, except for one central character in *Anna Karenina* as we will see in a moment, would take us too far afield.

Tolstoy had thought to complete his trilogy with a fourth short novel that would have dealt with his early adulthood, but he never got around to it and eventually produced his two masterpieces instead. But he did, in 1878 at the age of 50, just after the publication of *Anna Karenina* in 1877, start to write a long autobiographical essay, *A Confession*, that would eventually be published abroad as it could not pass the censor in Russia. It is there that we will find the beginning of an outline of the late Tolstoy, the teachings that will make him world famous, and that will continue to flow from his pen almost up to his death in 1910.

Just a brief comment on the title: Tolstoy must have known what he was doing when he chose a title that so closely resembled the books of St. Augustine and Rousseau, both of which were called simply, *Confessions*. Rousseau is

---

47. Tolstoy, *Childhood*, 213 (Tolstoy's emphasis).

credited with having written the first modern autobiography, one distancing itself from the pious concerns of Augustine and dealing with secular life instead. At the very beginning of the book he famously wrote: "I have resolved on an enterprise which has no precedent, and which, once complete, will have no imitator. My purpose is to display to my kind a portrait in every way true to nature, and the man I shall portray will be myself."[48] And yet, can we take him so simply at his word? Rousseau was, and knew he was, a teacher, one with enormous influence. His *Confessions* is not so simply just a book about "myself." It is a model, a teaching, complex and needing to be untangled to be sure, yet in its own way as didactic as the book of Augustine whose title he chose for his own book. Here, clearly, Rousseau shows that in this book he will create "Rousseau," something a little more than just "myself." And so in Tolstoy's *A Confession*, we will find something other than just an autobiographical sketch. What we get instead is an introduction to his mature world of thought, a world he wanted to share with others.

Much of *A Confession* consists of a harrowing description of how he was feeling as he approached the age of fifty. First he gives us, as does Augustine, an account of the depraved life he lived as a young man. "When I was sixteen," he writes, "I ceased saying my prayers, going to church or fasting of my own accord. I no longer believed in what I had been taught as a child." He adds that he did not deny God and Christ but had no idea what they meant. As he grew into manhood he found that "Ambition, lust for power, self-interest, lechery, pride, anger, revenge were all respected qualities. As I yielded to these passions I became like my elders and I felt that they were pleased with me."[49] He then describes his life as he began to publish and gain recognition as a writer. As his mission he took up the common belief of writers in his day that in his work he was promoting "progress," but he had no idea what progress meant as it seemed to mean only "We are being carried somewhere."[50]

---

48. Jean-Jacques Rousseau, *The Confessions*, trans. J. M. Cohen (Harmondsworth, UK: Penguin, 1953), 17. I considered Rousseau as a major subject for this chapter—in terms of influence he certainly would deserve it, and it was only the arbitrary pressure of space that led to his omission. For a treatment of Rousseau's ethics, politics, and religion see Robert N. Bellah, "Rousseau on Society and the Individual," in *The Robert Bellah Reader*, ed. Robert N. Bellah and Steven M. Tipton (Durham, NC: Duke University Press, 2006), 181–202.

49. Leo Tolstoy, "A Confession," in *A Confession and Other Religious Writings*, trans. Jane Kentish (London: Penguin, 1987), 21–22.

50. Tolstoy, "A Confession," 26.

Approaching fifty, with fame as a writer and a rich family life, he nonetheless entered a period of dread. He kept on living but it seemed there was nothing he wanted: "It was as if I had carried on living and walking until I reached a precipice from which I could see that there was nothing ahead of me other than destruction." The only truth he could find is "the truth that life is meaningless."

> And it was at this time that I, a fortunate man, removed a rope from my room where I undressed every night alone, lest I hang myself from the beam . . .and I gave up taking a rifle with me on hunting trips so as not to be tempted to end my life in such an all too easy fashion.
>
> All this was happening to me at a time when I was surrounded on all sides by what is considered complete happiness: I was not yet fifty, I had a kind, loving and beloved wife, lovely children, and a large estate that was grow-ing and expanding with no effort on my part . . . I was praised by strangers and could consider myself a celebrity without deceiving myself . . . Physically I could keep up with the peasants tilling the fields; mentally I could work for eight or ten hours at a stretch . . . And in these circumstances I found myself at the point where I could no longer go on living and, since I feared death, I had to deceive myself in order to avoid suicide.[51]

It is in this passage that I see a parallel with Levin, the Tolstoy character in *Anna Karenina*, who had recently married the woman he loved and was engaged in the improvement of his estate, but who experienced a profound sense of mean-inglessness and contemplated suicide, like Tolstoy, hiding things that might have helped him do so. Levin recovers from this experience after a conversation with one of his serfs, whose naïve faith inspires Levin to reexamine his life. He works out his salvation through identifying with his peasants and deciding to devote himself to their welfare, a very Tolstoyan solution.

Tolstoy tells us in *A Confession* that he undertook a desperate search for knowledge in order to answer his persistent questions: "what am I? or: why do I live? or: what must I do?"[52] He came to an answer not too different from the one we found facing Faust at the beginning of Goethe's play and that led him too to contemplate suicide:

---

51. Tolstoy, "A Confession," 30–31.
52. Tolstoy, "A Confession," 37.

I searched all branches of knowledge and not only found nothing, but was convinced that all those who had searched the realms of knowledge like myself had likewise found nothing. Not only had they found nothing, but they had plainly acknowledged the same thing that had led me to despair: the meaninglessness of life as the only indisputable piece of knowledge available to man.[53]

One of the hardest things for me to understand about Tolstoy is that, from this point on he tends to dismiss his earlier work, including the two great novels, as mere entertainments, not to be taken seriously. There is nothing that Tolstoy ever wrote that did not engage with the immediacies of life intensely such that the reader finds a deep sense of truth. It is not surprising that he didn't find answers to his questions in the findings of empirical science or the reflections of metaphysical philosophers, though he surely tried. Those were simply not his ways of knowing as he eventually saw. Yet he never connected the immediacy of experience that finally led to his answers with the work that he had done before. Genius can indeed be maddening.

It was the realization that most of the world didn't share his existential anxieties and his concern to find out why, that is, his turn not to the intellectuals, but to the common people, that provided his breakthrough: "It seems so strange to me now, so utterly incomprehensible, that in my reasoning of life I should have overlooked the life of humanity that surrounded me on all sides."[54] He realized that ordinary people who lived lives that those in his elite circle would have found mean and desolate, but for them were rich and fulfilling, had faith that answered his questions, and that all his logic could not provide.

This led Tolstoy back into the church and an intense effort to grasp its teachings and its practices. Along the way, he found the teaching of Jesus more meaningful than he had ever realized, but he also found that he could not leave his reason behind as he had hoped, that there was far too much in the belief and practice of the church that he could not accept and that actually appalled him.

---

53. Tolstoy, "A Confession," 34. In a short parody entitled "The Restoration of Hell," one of the devils tells of inventing sociology to teach people that all religion is superstition and that the sociologists will discover the laws by which people have previously lived (badly) so that they can conform to them. I very much doubt Weber ever read this. Leo Tolstoy, *On Life and Essays on Religion*, trans. Aylmer Maude (London: Oxford University Press, 1934), 326. "The Restoration of Hell" was first published in 1903.
54. Tolstoy, "A Confession," 49.

I cannot here begin to describe the radical simplicity of his solution, one that led to his excommunication by the Russian Orthodox Church in 1901, but, in spite of his claim to be teaching only what everyone at heart already knows, also led to the establishment of what can only be called a Tolstoyan sect, under the leadership of disciples, but not rejected by him.

His beliefs were the existence of God, which he knew from Kant he could not prove, but which was the necessary precondition for reason itself, and the teachings of the Gospel, especially the Sermon on the Mount, that is, the commandments to love and to not resist evil, radical non-violence. What appalled him most about the church was its betrayal of these teachings. When Russia was at war:

> In the name of Christian love, Russians were killing their fellow men . . . Prayers were said in the churches for the success of our armies, and our religious teachers acknowledged this killing as an outcome of faith. And this was not only applied to murder in time of war, but, during the troubled times that followed the war, I witnessed members of the Church, her teachers, monks, and ascetics condoning the killing of helpless, lost youths. As I turned my attention to all that is done by people who profess Christianity, I was horrified.[55]

It was not only the failure to uphold the obvious teachings of the Gospel that repelled Tolstoy from the church; it was also the plethora of beliefs that he found contrary to reason: the doctrines of the Trinity, the incarnation through the virgin birth, the resurrection, the real presence of the body and blood of Christ in the sacrament, the intercessions of Mary and the saints, and a great many others.

He came to reject the Orthodox Church, or any particular church, as being the one true Church. He found them equally true, or rather, equally false. He affirmed, nonetheless that there was truth to be found in all religions, not just in Christianity. Even if he thought Jesus's teaching was the most profound he believed there was truth in Judaism, Islam, Hinduism, Buddhism, Confucianism and others. He opposed any exclusive claim to truth. Tolstoy drew up his own version of the Gospels, without miracles or supernatural events, that is

---

55. Tolstoy, "A Confession," 76.

remarkably similar to what Thomas Jefferson undertook in what is known as the Jefferson Bible! Tolstoy turns out to be a highly unlikely combination of St. Francis of Assisi and an eighteenth century rationalist.

It is hard to overestimate Tolstoy's social radicalism, his rejection of the class structure and of the state itself as an instrument of violence. At one point he refers to "humanistic teachings that do not even call themselves Christian, for example: Socialism, Communism, Anarchism,—ideas that are really nothing other than partial manifestations of Christian consciousness in its true sense," though he always opposed the use of violence to bring about these ends. He was sure that violence in overturning a violent state would only lead to a new regime of violence, a prediction that the history of his own country sadly confirmed.

It is worth noting that though most of what he wrote after the age of fifty consisted of pamphlets that have little literary value and are now hard to find, though their moral value is still considerable in my opinion, he did write a third great novel, *Resurrection*, published in 1899, that combined his social concerns with his literary genius. It is a semi-autobiographical story of a young aristocrat who seduces a peasant girl who becomes pregnant after his departure, and turns to a life of prostitution. Consorting with lowlife, she is accused unjustly of murder, and is recognized by her seducer, considerably older now, in the courtroom. Through the course of the novel we see with sociological precision (Tolstoy visited prisons and interviewed prisoners) but with great narrative power, the corruption and horror of the Czarist state system of "justice," including the harshness of the way that convicts are treated during their journey to Siberia. Death is ever present in the prison and on the road; the prisoners are in no way treated as human beings. Max Weber noted it as a crushing reply to any doctrine of unchecked state power.

I must mention one other late work of fiction *The Kreutzer Sonata*, published in 1891, because it displays an appalling side of Tolstoy, his hatred of sex. Somehow for Tolstoy, and he is not alone in this, the rejection of sex goes along with the rejection of violence. This was particularly problematic for Tolstoy because he was by nature very sensual, and its most problematic result was what it did to his marriage. Tolstoy found his wife quite physically attractive—they had thirteen children, of whom seven survived. In his late religious phase he believed his physical attraction to Sophia, his wife, was sinful, and tried, and failed, to give up sexual intercourse with her. But part of him hated her for what he believed was her tempting him to evil. *The Kreutzer Sonata* is a story of an unreasonably jealous husband who kills his wife whom he suspects of committing adultery with a musician friend of hers. To me it is the most awful thing he ever wrote. Even worse, since the censor would not allow it to be printed, Tolstoy's wife Sophia, the object of this venomous novella, went to see the Czar (they were of sufficiently high nobility that that was not impossible) to ask him to override the censor's decision, which he did. There were also deep tensions between husband and wife over Tolstoy's wish to be radically consistent. The lands of the estate were given to the peasants who worked it, but when he wanted to hand over the royalties of his books, Sophia, with seven children to think of, fought hard to prevent him from doing so. That at the end this marriage, to which Sophia had contributed so much, copying the manuscript of *War and Peace* seven times, and running the estate because he was too busy writing, collapsed and Tolstoy, old and unwell, fled, dying in a railway station only a few days later. St. Francis gave away everything when he was just a boy, with no wife and seven children. Tolstoy's consistency was both admirable and insane.

Max Weber (1864–1920) was not only a founder of modern sociology; his thought about the meaning of modern society transcended any disciplinary boundary. Though a great champion of academic specialization, he was also a great example of going beyond it: he was a historian, an economist, a sociologist, a political scientist, and a student of antiquity and the world's great religions. No more than with the previous grand theorists can I deal with his work as a whole. It is with three late essays, two of which began as lectures, that reflect on central issues of modernity, that I will be concerned.

I consider Weber to be the greatest theorist of modernity. That is why he is the last figure in my gallery of theorists and poets in this Prologue. Not only did he study almost every aspect of modernity itself, he put it in the widest possible historical and comparative perspective. His lens was so wide that it has been difficult for his successors to see what he was doing. Here I want to give, briefly, my own understanding of his effort and an evaluation of the extent to which he succeeded in it.

Weber was the eldest son of a successful Prussian bureaucrat, descended from a family of cloth manufacturers, who had attained a significant post in the government in Berlin where he had moved his family from Erfurt where Max had been born. Max's mother, Helene, was an educated and thoughtful woman of different views from her husband: she was religious and idealistic whereas her husband was a realist and German nationalist. One can see aspects of both in

Max's development. We can note one more fact about his early childhood: he was diagnosed with meningitis at the age of four and was so sick that he wasn't expected to live. A lifetime of ill health, some of it psychological to be sure, and his early death at the age of 56 may be attributable to some degree to this serious early illness. In adolescence he was studious and rather solitary; he excelled in school though he wasn't much loved by his teachers as he tended to show his disagreements with them too readily.

He chose to go to Heidelberg, enrolling there in the course on law as had his father. Through his father's influence he joined his dueling fraternity and the skinny, studious boy put on weight, took up dueling and drinking, with a dueling scar on his face to show his commitment. Nonetheless, he continued to be an outstanding student, and, after a year of officer training in the army, where he again, after overcoming some physical problems, had a successful, if not entirely happy experience, he returned, this time to Berlin to complete his legal studies. After getting his doctoral degree in law and history at the age of 25, he alternately practiced law and began to teach as a *Privatdozent* at the University of Berlin. At the age of 29 he married Marrianne Schnitger, a highly educated and intelligent woman who would have a career of her own as a writer and lecturer, particularly about the woman question. The following year, when Weber was only 30, he was called to a full professorship at the distinguished University of Freiburg, which he commented later was a case of unusual good fortune when so many able older scholars were overlooked. But Weber had already published a good deal of important work and it was only with difficulty that he was able to get away from Berlin to go to Freiburg. His growing fame is evidenced from the fact that only two years later he was called to Heidelberg, the childhood home of his mother, who, together with his wife, had a continuing influence on him.

Weber was soon creating a circle of friends including Ersnt Troeltsch, Georg Jellinek, and others, and his work was making significant progress, when in the early months of 1897, he intervened in a conflict between his parents over his mother's wish to spend some weeks with Max and Marianne away from his father. Weber responded to his father's protests with a bitter denunciation, that showed his already sometimes ungovernable temper, but which preceded his father's death in May by only a few weeks and so led to enormous guilt on Max's part. Already by the end of the fall semester of 1897, Weber's own health showed signs of serious strain: fever, insomnia, depression, and overall weakness. By the end of 1899 he was no longer able to teach and took a leave of absence with pay.

There were periods when he could not even read and could not work at all. An extended trip to Italy helped him regain his spirits and he undertook in 1904 the intense study that led to the publication in two parts, in 1904 and 1905, of one of his most influential works, *The Protestant Ethic and the Spirit of Capitalism.* He could attend conferences and on occasion give talks, but he found he did not have the energy for giving a regular lecture course. He persuaded the university to give him a purely honorary position as he and his wife had inherited wealth from which to live.

In spurts of tremendous energy intermixed with periods of depression, Weber, in collaboration with other scholars, began research for an encyclopedic work in the social sciences, his portion of which would after quite a few years be published as his massive *Economy and Society.* It was also in the years before World War I that he began a second major project, a comparative study of the economic ethics of the world religions, some of which would only be published after his untimely death in 1920.

The war years pulled Weber into a variety of activities that expressed his belief in the right of Germany to respect as a major European power together with his contempt for the dilettante leadership of the Kaiser and the blind arrogance of the military high command that ultimately assured Germany's defeat. It is in the years between 1915 and his death in 1920 that he published the central essay of his comparative studies of religion, the "Intermediate Reflections," also known by the title of its most widely read English translation, "Religious Rejections of the World and their Directions," in November of 1915, and gave his great lectures, "Science as a Vocation" in November of 1917 and "Politics as a Vocation" in January of 1919.[56] It is on these that I will focus my attention.

In the "Intermediate Reflections" we can begin to see the grand evolutionary framework of Weber's understanding of world history.[57] Weber describes cultural history as the differentiation of six "value spheres" from an initially homogeneous whole into increasingly differentiated spheres, so that in the modern

---

56. The most convenient translation of these three essays remains H. H. Gerth and C. Wright Mills, *From Max Weber: Essays in Sociology* (New York: Oxford University Press, 1958), 194, hereafter cited as GM. I have discussed the "Intermediate Reflections" at some length in "Max Weber and World-Denying Love: A Look at the Historical Sociology of Religion," in *The Robert Bellah Reader,* ed. Robert N. Bellah and Steven M. Tipton (Durham, NC: Duke University Press, 2006), 123–49.

57. I am aware that Weber rejected the rather mechanical version of social evolution of the nineteenth century and did not use the term "evolution" himself. I am simply arguing that from a current understanding his views are evolutionary.

world we are faced with radically different cultural demands that are not easily united. Ground zero, so to speak, is the sphere of kinship and neighborhood, the world of "natural relations," "the matrimonial community," and magic, which permeates the earliest human societies. Its moral norms are based on in-group obligations of reciprocity and care, either without concern for out-groups or with active hostility toward them, and magical practices oriented mainly to this-worldly benefits of health, prosperity, children, success in war and the like.[58]

The religious sphere that breaks through and radically questions this ethic of in-groups of kin and neighbors is what Weber calls the ethic of brotherliness, taking a key term from kinship but giving it a radically universalistic turn, so that all men are brothers and there is to be no distinction between in-group and out-group.[59] From Weber's type examples of this ethic, the Buddha, Jesus, and Francis of Assisi, we learn that this does not happen until the axial age and involves elements unknown earlier. The Buddha is a central figure in the axial age and Jesus and St. Francis are examples of the Christian version of axial religion. What we know about the axial religions is that they are religions of religious virtuosi, that is, religiously gifted persons able to live beyond the expectations of ordinary daily life, and thus rare. We also know that the axial religions are religions of intellectuals, that is, persons who can rise above the given particularities of their social context and generalize to a universal level. Thus not only "love your parents," but "love all human beings." These are religions that promise not just worldly benefits, but salvation from the suffering that characterizes human existence.

> The more rational the conception of salvation became, the more it was sublimated into an ethic of conviction. Externally, such commands rose to a communion of loving brethren; internally they rose to the attitude of *caritas*, love for the sufferer *per se*, for one's neighbor, for man, and finally for the enemy.[60]

Weber does not mean that all followers of ostensibly axial religions actually practice this ethic of conviction; most people still live in the in-group ethic. Weber

---

58. GM 329.

59. GM 329–30.

60. GM 330. Following Wolfgang Schluchter and others, I translate *Gesinnungsethik* as "ethic of conviction" rather than, as in the original text of Gerth and Mills that I am quoting, as "ethic of absolute ends." See Wolfgang Schluchter, *Paradoxes of Modernity: Culture and Conduct in the Theory of Max Weber* (Stanford, CA: Stanford University Press, 1996), chapters 1 and 2.

develops the notion of "organic religion" to show how genuine salvation religions have developed compromise formations wherein some members of the community can embody an ethic of conviction but most people are not expected to. This is not our immediate concern here.

Weber is quite aware that for a long time the spheres that he finds so differentiated today, that is, the spheres of the aesthetic, the intellectual, and the erotic, even to more than a small extent the spheres of economics and politics, though these tend to differentiate relatively early, remain enmeshed in a totality in which religion, both in his sense as "rational," and what he called "organic," remains dominant. It took over two thousand years for these spheres to reach the degree of differentiation they have today. But the process by which they have differentiated is the process of rationalization, that is the same process that produced the salvation religions has now produced highly rational rival spheres.

At least three of these spheres have produced alternative forms of salvation, which from a religious perspective are ersatz, but which have for many moderns an effective claim: the political in the case of death in war, that is, death for a cause, death with a reason, not just death at the end; the aesthetic in which "experience," music without words is the most obvious case, is felt as having salvific meaning; and the erotic, where again a certain kind of experience is felt to have a mystical intensity. Weber feels only the economic and the intellectual spheres lack a rival claim to salvation, though perhaps his distinction between philosophy and religion doesn't take adequate account of antiquity, where philosophy does claim a salvific capacity.

But while the ethic of conviction (*Gesinnungsethik*) has a significant place in connection with religions of salvation in his sociology of religion generally, it has a somewhat narrower meaning in the great lectures on the Vocations of Science and of Politics. In the "Intermediate Reflections" the ethic of conviction is located in the religious realm, particularly the virtuoso religion of universal brotherliness. But in spite of the fact that the other realms described in that essay, including the intellectual within which science falls, are in radical competition with the ethic of universal brotherliness, one can still find the ethic of conviction within them. Here the key term for both science and politics is "vocation," and we need to glance, however briefly, at a central concern of Weber's sociology of religion in general to see what he means by vocation. Wherever we find it in the modern world, Weber implies that it comes from the Calvinist ethic of vocation, where this-worldly activism is seen as the only possible way for humans, guilty of original sin and with their fate sealed by predestination, to make sense of their situation. And this-worldly activism means not flight from the world into contemplation but to carry out your tasks, your work, your vocation, in the world with single-minded devotion, even long after the religious basis of this sense of vocation has disappeared.

Weber relentlessly emphasizes that the progress of science today means ever-increasing specialization, that specialization, where you know your results, however limited, are really valid, is what science as a vocation today requires. The alternatives, an intellectual concern with big issues of "meaning," or the brilliant guesses of the dilettante, are what are to be avoided. A scientist is not a "seer," and to pretend to be one is to betray one's vocation. The dilettante's insights may even be significant, but only if they are confirmed by specialists and dilletantism as an end in itself is "the end of science." Science involves the ethic of conviction when it is pursued, as Weber thinks it must be, as an end in itself, as having finally the value of increasing knowledge, and if it also increases some technology useful for other ends, that is still not its purpose.

All this is fine as far as it goes, yet one does wonder how Weber never manages to bring his own life and work into his discussion. The closest he comes raises more problems than it solves:

> All work that overlaps neighboring fields, such as we occasionally [!] undertake and which the sociologist must necessarily undertake again and again, is burdened with the resigned realization that at best one provides the specialist with useful questions upon which he would not so easily hit from his own specialized point of view. One's own work must inevitably remain highly imperfect. Only by strict specialization can the scientific worker become fully conscious, for once and perhaps never again in his lifetime, that he has achieved something that will endure. A really definitive and good accomplishment is today always a specialized accomplishment.[61]

Somewhat later in the essay Weber distinguishes science from art by saying that there is no progress in art: advance in technique does not mean advance in aesthetic value; an artwork that attains "fulfillment" can never be surpassed, no

---

61. GM 134–35.

matter how good subsequent work may be, whereas: "In science, each of us knows that what he has accomplished will be antiquated in ten, twenty, fifty years. That is the fate to which science is subjected; it is the very *meaning* of scientific work."[62] Hello, Max! It is well over a hundred years since you published *The Protestant Ethic and the Spirit of Capitalism* and it is still around, still in controversy. And where are those specialists upon whom you depended in this and all the rest of your work, and whose work was supposed to really "endure."? Nowhere! No one reads them, and if they try they are unreadable. Is it of you or of them that you wrote at the end of the *Protestant Ethic*, "Specialists without spirit, sensualists without heart; thus nullity imagines that it has attained a level of civilization never before achieved."[63] This leads to the question of whether, together with all the fields in which he was so deeply learned, Weber might also in some sense be considered a "philosopher," a matter already debated beginning right after his death. Weber never claimed to be or wanted to be a prophet, but it is just because his work is so much more than that of a "specialist" that it "endures."

But we have to be very clear about what Weber feared: that science would be expected to provide answers to questions with which it cannot and ought not deal. It is only the dilettante who would be a seer, and as Weber said in another essay, "He who yearns for seeing should go to the cinema."[64] It is here that he quotes Tolstoy's questions approvingly: "And if Tolstoi's question occurs to you: as science does not, who is to answer the question: "What shall we do, and, how shall we arrange our lives?" Weber answers that only a prophet or savior can give the answers, not a scientist. In the spheres of life that, like polytheistic gods, compete for our loyalty, we have to know where we are and what is possible within each sphere. To think that scientists, including even ones concerned with the most general history of culture as he was, could answer what are essentially religious questions was to Weber as it should be to us, a huge mistake. Scientists, whether in the natural or the social and cultural sciences, are not seers or prophets. But what I miss in Weber is a recognition of doubt that in any branch of science the specialist, in the incredibly narrow way he defines the specialist, should have the sole dignity of science. I think this was just plain wrong, for him and for us.

---

62. GM 138 (Weber's emphasis).

63. Max Weber, *The Protestant Ethic and the Spirit of Capitalism*, trans. Talcott Parsons (London: George Allen & Unwin, 1930), 182.

64. Weber, *Protestant Ethic*, 29.

We might note that the odd affinity we find between such opposite characters as Tolstoy and Weber is carried out by the fact that Tolstoy, similarly to Weber, made a survey of the major spheres of life in his day, found them incompatible, but, being a prophet and not a scientist, declared one and only one of them to be true and adequate to our needs, namely the religion of absolute brotherly love. He hardly takes the time to reject the economic and the political spheres in detail. For him only the peasants are capable of a real form of life, only on the land, in making one's living with animals and plants, do human beings live a human life. Needless to say, he hated cities and lived a much of his life as he could in the country—I think he is the only intellectual in this chapter of whom that could be said; all the rest were true city dwellers. And Tolstoy rejected the state, the political structure of his day, as a structure of pure violence and injustice. He argued that if every soldier and policeman, every judge and legislator, would just lay down his weapon or his pen and retire to the country where he could support himself by honest labor, all our political problems would be solved. He was acutely aware of the attractions of the erotic sphere and finds them wholly evil. He seldom misses a chance to comment on how disgusting is the revealing dress of dancers and actresses, or in general of the women of the upper classes, and how such dress tempts to sin.

Of Weber's five great spheres of life other than religion Tolstoy gave serious attention only to two: art, which was after all the sphere in which he became world famous, and science as his primary example of what Weber called the intellectual sphere. Tolstoy's *What Is Art?* is one of his longest and most discouraging tracts.[65] In it he actually carried out a lengthy literature review of all that had been written about aesthetics in the eighteenth and nineteenth centuries, which was about all there was as it was a new specialized field. He came to two conclusions after reviewing what he saw as, and which probably was, a largely disorganized and incoherent field: art is an expression of beauty; something is beautiful because it gives pleasure. Thus art is a form of hedonism. This "art" however, which includes most of the great classics of Western literature, including his own two greatest novels, is not really art, but only what the pampered and privileged elites especially of the modern world think is art. When Weber

---

65. Leo Tolstoy, *What Is Art?*, trans. Richard Pevear and Larissa Volokhonsky (London: Penguin, 1995). This book was written by Tolstoy in the 1890s but was prohibited from publication by the censors, so the first publication was in the English translation of Aylmer Maude in 1898.

noted the increasing importance of form over content in modern art, Tolstoy agreed. Even though he was very musical and a piano piece or a string quartet could reduce him to tears, he rejected all purely instrumental music as examples of pure form and so ultimately as examples of pure hedonism. Tolstoy developed a conception of real art as opposed to the false art which was then currently thought to be art.

Since the hedonistic art is collapsing because of its own complete vapidity, Tolstoy argued, there will be a return to true art which was always present among the people and all there was before elite art was created. The art of the future will return to that earlier art: "Those works alone will be considered works of art which convey feelings drawing people toward brotherly union, or such all-human feelings as will unite all people." Much that passes for art today will be entirely rejected:

> But art that conveys feelings coming from obsolete religious teachings, out-lived by the people—Church art, patriotic art, sensual art, art that conveys the feelings of superstitious fear, pride, vanity, the admiration of heroes, art that arouses sensuality or an exclusive love of one's own nation—will be regarded as bad, harmful art, and will be condemned and despised by public opinion.[66]

And how did Tolstoy know good art from bad art? He found out empirically: he read to the peasants and recorded their opinions. When he read them Shakespeare they understood nothing, and, presumably that was the case with his own great novels. He mentions two stories of his own that could be considered good art: "The Kingdom of God is within You," about an old man who helps several people in need and then realizes that he has helped Christ (Matthew 25), and "The Prisoner of the Caucasus," a simple but lovely story about a soldier who escapes capture with the help of a girl of the village where he had been held. The peasants certainly understood the Joseph story from Genesis, and this was a kind of model of good literature for Tolstoy.

In the last chapter of *What Is Art?* Tolstoy used the tools he had sharpened in order to attack the existing idea of art in order to attack contemporary science.

---

66. Tolstoy, *Art*, 151.

He says that the scientists "have invented a theory of science for science's sake, exactly like the theory of art for art's sake."[67] Just as in the case of art a great deal of money is wasted that could go to help people in need—improve primary education, for example—but is spent to please the "idle curiosity" of the scientist, as art is to entertain the wealthy. True science, like true art would concern itself with the ethical improvement of individuals and society. While science boasts of the good its technological achievements have created, Tolstoy says that the power derived from a waterfall is used in a factory "not for the benefit of the people, but for the enriching of capitalists, who produce objects of luxury or tools for destroying human beings [armaments]."[68] In another of his late tracts, *On Life*, he especially attacks the theory of evolution because the idea of "the survival of the fittest" is used for the exploitation of people. In short, if this is the best science can do we are better off without it.[69]

Such indeed is a prophet, and he is a kind of mirror image for Weber, reducing everything to one thing needful instead of realizing that our fate requires major indeterminate choices. But while Tolstoy is in a sense his opposite, Weber deeply respected him. His ethic of conviction is without reservation, involves his life, not just his thought. Weber was very critical of the "pacifism" of those who believed in the "one last violence" of revolution that would then lead to eternal peace. We know that Weber and his wife, Marianne, were attracted to socialism, but one reason that Weber did not become a socialist is because he felt he would have to give up his bourgeois form of life and live like a worker or he would be hypocritical.

There was another problem for Weber: the disenchantment of the world, which he felt had happened in the preceding 200 years meant that to be religious would require him to "sacrifice the intellect," to believe in the unbelievable, to give up modern rationalism. I am not sure how many of Tolstoy's late tracts Weber had actually read and whether he knew that Tolstoy was a radical rationalist who had definitely not sacrificed his intellect, for whom God was a kind of Kantian regulatory principle and all the dogma of the Church was nonsense.

---

67. Tolstoy, *Art*, 159.
68. Tolstoy, *Art*, 160.
69. Tolstoy, *On Life*, chapter 30.

So at the end of "Science as a Vocation" is a defense of science as disciplined inquiry, not to be confused with prophecy, nor with the current popularity of "religion" among the educated classes, about whom he spoke of "the need of some modern intellectuals to furnish their souls with, so to speak, guaranteed genuine antiques":

> In doing so they happen to remember that religion has belonged among such antiques, and above all things religion is what they do not possess. By way of substitute, however, they play at decorating a sort of domestic chapel with small sacred images from all over the world, or they produce surrogates through all sorts of psychic experiences to which they ascribe the dignity of mystic holiness, which they peddle in the book market.[70]

And yet, and yet . . . For all his rejection of prophecy and religious hypocrisy and his gentleness with those who "cannot bear the fate of the times like a man" and to whom "the doors of the old churches are widely opened," so that, if they are sincere and not too noisy about it, we can respect their decision to enter those doors, there is still something more.[71] Somehow the possibility of "genuine brotherliness," that was always at the heart of the religious choice, at least of the virtuoso, and that remains somehow implicit in the ethic of conviction with which the scientist carries on his work, however different the demands of science are, that possibility even in its religious form is not entirely gone, in spite of all the disenchantment. He finds it in "some of the youth groups" and the "religious"—and he is not sure that is quite the right word—sense they have given to their human community.

He ends on a strong note, somehow showing his Calvinist side: "We shall set to work and meet the 'demands of the day,' in human relations as well as in our vocation," but with one last gnomic remark that I shall leave uninterpreted: "This, however, is plain and simple, if each finds and obeys the demon [daemon?] who holds the fibers of his very life."[72]

Just before the end of "Science as a Vocation" and the lines I have just quoted, but after he spoke of the sense of community among some youth groups, Weber

---

70. GM 154.
71. GM 155.
72. GM 156.

made another statement that leads into a passage from the "Intermediate Reflections" that very much belongs in this context, the context of what Weber still wants to hold on to:

> The fate of our times is characterized by rationalization and intellectualization and, above all, by the "disenchantment of the world." Precisely the ultimate and most sublime values have retreated from public life either into the transcendental realm of mystic life or into the brotherliness of direct and personal human relations. It is not accidental that our greatest art is intimate and not monumental, nor is it accidental that today only within the smallest and intimate circles, in personal human situations, in *pianissimo*, that something is pulsating that corresponds to the prophetic *pneuma*, which in former times swept through the great communities like a firebrand, welding them together.[73]

He warns that this is something we cannot force, least of all with "academic prophecy." But then at the end of the erotic sphere in the "Intermediate reflections" another kind of *pianissimo*:

> From a purely inner-worldly point of view, only the linkage of marriage with the thought of ethical responsibility for one another—hence a category heterogeneous to the purely erotic sphere—can carry the sentiment that something unique and supreme might be embodied in marriage; that it might be the transformation of the feeling of love which is conscious of responsibility throughout all the nuances of the organic life process, "up to the *pianissimo* of old age," and a mutual granting of oneself to another and the becoming indebted to each other. Rarely does life grant such value in pure form. He to whom it is given may speak of fate's fortune and grace—not of his own "merit."[74]

It is interesting that Weber here uses the word "responsibility" for something almost identical with the ethic of "conviction." We need to look at one more, even less likely, place where they come together.

---

73. GM 155.
74. GM 350. It is worth remembering that Weber dedicated the first volume of his *Collected Essays on the Sociology of Religion* to Marianne with the words, "1893 [the year of their marriage] bis ins Pianissimo des höschsten Alters."

"Politics as a Vocation" is the essay in which Weber most clearly spells out what at first glance is a total opposition between two ethics, the ethic of conviction (*Gesinnungsethik*) and the ethic of responsibility (*Verantwortungsethik*). However we must look one more time at a passage in "Science as a Vocation" where the contrast between the two arises in a problematic way. Weber argues that in spite of, or perhaps because of, theology, "the tension between the value spheres of 'science' and the 'holy' is unbridgeable."[75] One would think from the beginning of the following passage that it is just that unbridgeable tension that he is discussing, but it takes an interestingly different direction:

> What man can take upon himself the attempt to "refute scientifically" the ethic of the Sermon on the Mount? For instance, the sentence, "resist no evil," or the image of turning the other cheek? And yet it is clear, in mundane perspective, that this is an ethic of undignified conduct; one has to choose between the religious dignity which this ethic confers and the dignity of manly conduct which preaches something quite different; "resist evil—lest you be co-responsible for an overpowering evil." According to our ultimate standpoint, the one is the devil and the other the God, and the individual has to decide which is God for him and which is the devil.[76]

So, after all, we don't have a conflict between science and the holy, but between the holy and "manly conduct." One thinks of the dueling society that Weber joined in his youth, and then one remembers that after the German revolution of November, 1918, Weber resigned from his old fraternity, whose exclusivity was based on the qualification for dueling, as incompatible with a democratic Germany.[77] And one has to ask if the manly code of honor that Weber came to find problematic, was really the same thing as "resist evil—lest

---

75. GM 154.

76. GM 148. The appearance of the devil here is interesting and is paralleled by Weber's injunction a bit later in the speech to the youth in his audience: "Mind you, the devil is old; grow old to understand him" (GM 152). Neither Weber nor Tolstoy believed literally in the devil, who has appeared often in this chapter, but they were aware of his symbolism. Let me add a couple of sentences from Tolstoy's parody of hell: "The devils encircled Beelzebub. At one end as they linked up was the devil in the cape—the inventor of the Church; at the other end was the devil in the mantle—the inventor of Science" (Tolstoy, *On Life*, 330).

77. For a discussion of Weber's resignation and criticism of the fraternity system, see Schluchter, *Paradoxes*, 23–24.

you be co-responsible for an overpowering evil" which seems to express exactly the ethic of responsibility, of a concern for consequences, and not an egoistic sense of personal honor.

But before getting into that, what about the idea that science can't refute the Sermon on the Mount? Of course, science can't prove it either. But why would one have to sacrifice one's intellect in order to follow teachings about which science has nothing to say? We have seen that Tolstoy, who among Weber's contemporaries was closer to the Buddha, Jesus, and St. Francis, especially not just in his words but in his conduct, than almost anyone alive that Weber knew of, did not sacrifice his intellect. And again when Weber said, "Under the technical and social conditions of rational culture, an imitation of the life of Buddha, Jesus, or Francis seems condemned to failure for purely external reasons,"[78] is Weber forgetting Tolstoy? And what he could not know, Tolstoy's later followers, such as Mohandas Gandhi and Martin Luther King, Jr.? With such thought in mind, one might question whether the great ethical commandments of the salvation religions are now entirely confined to the private and personal sphere, in *pianissimo*, so to speak.

It is with the other great vocation speech, "Politics as a Vocation," that I will try to clinch my argument. Following Schluchter we can see Weber coming close to ridiculing the ethic of conviction compared to the more grown-up ethic of responsibility at points late in "Politics as a Vocation." The politics of conviction is concerned with the good will alone, with doing the ethically right thing and leaving the consequences to God.[79] For Weber this can amount to something close to egocentric concern for one's own conscience rather than the possible human consequences of one's action. An example would be Tolstoy's concern with the consistent giving away of all his earthly goods, following the commandment of Jesus, without concern for the consequences for his children and his marriage. And it is an awful example, leading to hate, not love, and a marriage that did not meet Weber's extraordinary standard.

One has to see the context in which Weber criticized such an ethic, one that appealed to some of his own students, the consistent revolutionary ethic that

---

78. GM 357.

79. Weber was quite aware that the ethic of conviction, though historically located in the religions of salvation, had a modern version based on reason alone: Kant's practical (ethical) reason, which required one to treat others as ends in themselves and never as means, while not mentioning love. Schluchter, in *Paradoxes*, argues for the great influence of Kant on Weber.

absolutely ignored the consequences in the reality of German society, consequences that turned out to be just as awful as Weber predicted. But the temptation has been to misread the ethic of responsibility as a kind of success ethic, an ethic in which the means justified the end. But Weber clearly and explicitly never meant that. The ethic of power for its own sake was diabolical in Weber's mind—surely no good could come from it. So there are really three alternatives: the ethics of conviction, where the sense of right and wrong determines everything; the ethics of responsibility, where one starts from the question of right and wrong and then considers what is possible, given the actual situation; and the ethics of success, which is really not an ethic at all but the denial of all ethics. Thus, as Schluchter points out, insofar as they are ethical the ethics of conviction and the ethics of responsibility share the same fundamental assumption and the same starting point, and both of them oppose any sheer opportunism in the name of realism. The proof text of Schluchter's point comes late in "Politics as a Vocation." Weber has just been dismissing the "windbags" who "intoxicate themselves with romantic sensations" about how moral they are, when he writes:

> However, it is immensely moving when a *mature* man—no matter whether old or young in years—is aware of a responsibility for the consequences of his conduct and really feels such responsibility with heart and soul. He then acts by following an ethic of responsibility and somewhere he reaches the point where he says, "Here I stand; I can do no other." That is something genuinely human and moving. And every one of us who is not spiritually dead must realize the possibility of finding himself at some time in that position. In so far as this is true, an ethic of conviction and an ethic of responsibility are not absolute contrasts but rather supplements, which only in unison constitute a genuine man—a man who can have the "calling for politics."[80]

The words of Martin Luther add weight to this important statement, whatever Weber really thought of Luther.

---

80. GM 127. Schluchter, *Paradoxes*, 48–50, and throughout chapter 3, "Conviction and Responsibility," 48–101.

Schluchter, I think wisely, turns to Karl Jaspers in order to sum up who Weber was, in a debate that began almost as soon as Weber died:

> When Jaspers, immediately after Weber's death and subsequently, called Weber a philosopher, he identified him not as a member of an academic discipline but as a person who, like Nietzsche and Kierkegaard, advocated intellectual honesty and, unlike them, also lived up to its demands. To Jaspers, Weber was the embodiment of an idealized modern man who resolutely exposes himself to intellectual risks and lives through existential tensions passionately without accepting final resolutions. He saw Weber moved not so much by Nietzsche's dead God as by the God of the Old Testament, whom he experienced as both good and evil. According to Jaspers, Weber was dedicated to science and politics but with the awareness that even living for them could never be ultimately fulfilling. This tension explains why, Jaspers concludes, Weber posed the question of meaning in the modern world radically, that is, philosophically.[81]

Schluchter then points out that we need not accept Jaspers's idea of Weber completely to see that there was a philosophical dimension to Weber. However we want to phrase it, this seems to me absolutely right, in contrast to Weber's own idolization of the scientist as specialist. Early in "Science as a Vocation" Weber summarizes the "inner" requirements for becoming a scientist. His first point is a willingness to devote oneself with absolute rigor to a definite specialized accomplishment, but he must do it with a "strange intoxication" that outsiders will ridicule, such that finding out something definite is the most important thing in the world, and this attitude he does not hesitate to call "enthusiasm."

But enthusiasm is never enough: one must have an idea. Normally such ideas come from hard work, but not always. Dilettantes can have good ideas, though they must be validated to have any lasting value. But sometimes no idea comes and one must face the possibility that one has chosen the wrong calling. For all his stress on the scientist not as a "personality" but as someone with "an inner devotion to the task," as genuine as that of a real artist, there must still be the ideas.

---

81. Schluchter, *Paradoxes*, 1–2.

What I think makes Weber what he is to us, whether we call it philosophy or not doesn't really matter, is the virtual flood of ideas that came out of him, on almost every page he ever wrote. Some of these ideas have turned out to be completely wrong: Confucianism as a religion of absolute adjustment to the world, for example. But, and I think Darwin is not an unjust comparison, very many of his ideas are still stimulating, still give rise to new work and new reflection. In having to read quite a lot of biology for my last book, I was surprised to see how many times Darwin was cited, not as a revered icon, but as having ideas that are still being tested. That is what I would claim for Weber as well.

What Jaspers said about Weber as an archetypal modern man, one who lived and breathed the air of modern culture without ever idealizing it, often more in horror than in praise, surely gives him a special importance to us. But also, and this is what justifies his presence at the end of this long account of theorists and narrativists of the last two thousand years, he did not forget our past. He made us think of the whole story, or all of it that was known in his day, because, however different we moderns are, we are children of that past and indelibly marked by it. While many modern intellectuals carelessly or deliberately (try to) forget the past, Weber showed us that was a mistake, that we would move ahead knowing where we had come from if we would move ahead wisely at all, a question that he, wisely, left open.

I have wondered if I could find a theorist/poet pair later in the twentieth century or twenty-first century to complete my sequence. I thought of Wittgenstein and Wallace Stevens, who would have been great fun to write about. But they are both esoteric in ways that Tolstoy and Weber aren't. When I was young I knew many undergraduates who had memorized a lot of T. S. Eliot, not because they were nascent Christians, but because they loved the poetry. Not so many memorized Wallace Stevens, though for me his poetry gets at the heart of modernity in a way Eliot does only in the early poems, before the religious turn, and his greatest works, the Four Quartets, are in another world. So I will give Weber the last substantive word.

Yet Weber's world is not our world. He feared the worst, and surely the worst came, but not the worst we know: he could not know of the slow but now almost certain ecological catastrophe that we face, something whose consequences dwarf the worst crimes of World War II. So I have decided to close my Prologue with a very modern art form, a film.

Lars von Trier's film *Melancholia* is about the end of the world that actually ends with the end of the world, unlike so many where somehow humans manage at the last minute to avoid the final catastrophe. There is not even any suspense as we know from the beginning that a "rogue planet" will crash into the earth ending all life, as we have seen it happen even before the film proper begins. The rogue planet is appropriately named "Melancholia" and the film is certainly about depression and how depressed people, who expect the worst anyway, are more effective in comforting others in a real catastrophe than the congenital optimists.

Unlike most end-of-the-world films, von Trier's is not an action film, but rather quietly domestic, just with a great menace hanging over it. The most optimistic of the small group which awaits the end on a great and beautiful estate, can't even wait for the end and commits suicide before it comes. The person whom we have seen as clinically depressed faces the end with serenity and assures her sister and nephew who alone remain together near the end, that there is no life on any other planet so this will be the end of life in the universe. As to how she knows this, she alludes to occult powers that have been given her. The end, when it comes, is total, brief and not noisy. That, it seems, is that. Made in 2010 it is almost wistful, wanting an easy end rather than the long-drawn-out catastrophe that our planet seems to be facing, because the men in charge (most of them are men, but some are women) insist on not looking where they are going no matter how close we come to the edge.

I thought of saying after von Trier's quiet ending, "not with a bang but a whimper." (Eliot) But the end of life, even on this planet, is not a whimper. However quiet, it is a very Big Bang, one worthy to stand beside that other Big Bang 13.7 billion years ago. Let us hope we won't let it happen.

CHAPTER 5

CULTURE AND HOPE

Reflections on Bellah's Unfinished Project

ANA MARTA GONZÁLEZ

In both *Religion in Human Evolution* and in the long prologue to his unfinished and unpublished book, Robert Bellah quotes Merlin Donald as follows: "Narrative and theory are the two highest cultural capacities that humans have attained, making use of language to culminate a history of new cultural capacities that began with episodic culture, the capacity to know what kind of episode one is in, followed by mimetic culture, by which one enacts or embodies meaning non-linguistically." Then, complex narratives first emerged in the stage that he calls "mythic" and did not necessarily disappear with the onset of *theoretic* culture.[1]

How different are narrative and theory, though? How do they relate to one another?

1. On Argument and Narrative

In a highly stimulating book entitled *Número y logos*, the Italian mathematician Paolo Zellini reflects on how the Greek verb *legein*, from which we take the word "logos," was sometimes associated with *arithmos*, or "number." To this effect, he mentions a passage from the fourth Book of the *Odyssey*, in which Proteus "lekto arithmon" or says the numbers of the seals coming out of the sea "from five to five" (i.e., he counts them).

---

1. See Robert N. Bellah, *Religion in Human Evolution: From the Paleolithic to the Axial Age* (Cambridge, MA: Belknap Press of Harvard University Press, 2011), xviii–xix.

It is worth remembering that "counting" is used in various languages to designate the acts both of *narrating* and of *enumerating*. Thus, the German words for "number" and "enumerating," *Zähl* and *zählen*, are quite close to *erzählen*, which means "to narrate"—just like the English "count" and "recount," or the Spanish *contar*, which also mean both to enumerate and to narrate. In this case, the act of counting the seals that come out of the sea involves identifying *forms*, thus creating an order that contrasts with an otherwise chaotic and ambiguous nature, for numbering ultimately involves bringing to light and selecting by differentiating forms. Accordingly, in this account, "*logos* makes beings appear in the scenery of the world, through election, division, mediation, through the relations that the number defines."[2]

By calling our attention to these passages, Zellini recalls a world in which logos and number were not at all unrelated because both were tasked with bringing order to chaos. This world was so deeply fascinated by mathematics that it actually took mathematics as the model of reasoning; this was true not only for Pythagoreans, but also for Plato, Aristotle, and the Stoics[3]—suffice it to look at

---

2. Paolo Zellini, *Número y logos* (Barcelona: Acantilado, 2018), 22.

3. "El cálculo de las razones y de las operaciones entre razones constituye una ciencia que se llamó logismós o logistiké, un cálculo que también Platón utiliza en sus diálogos para toda clase de asuntos, desde la cosmología hasta la política, desde la ética hasta la geometría, desde la justicia hasta el análisis del placer y el dolor. Los estoicos siguieron en esta línea, uniendo la ética a la cosmología y la antropología. El par logos-nomos es recurrente en la filosofía estoica. Zenón de Citio afirma que 'la ley común, es decir, la recta razón, se difunde en el todo y es idéntica a Zeus, que rige el sentido de las cosas.' Crisipo afirmaba que hay una ley eterna que rige el mundo con sus normas, la cual coincide con la mente de Dios en la medida en que ordena y prohíbe las cosas. Y los esquemas de cálculo no eran extraños en absoluto a esta teología de la razón como providencia que rige el universo. En las interminables listas de las virtudes estoicas, transmitidas desde las fuentes, junto a la recta razón, está la *eulogistía*, el buen uso del cálculo y de la medida, la capacidad de sopesar sin perderse en los opuestos. Esta virtud era llamada *antanairetiké*, término que se refiere a un modo ya mencionado en que podía definirse la razón (logos como *antanairesis*)." "The calculation of the reasons and of the operations between reasons constitutes a science that was called *logismós* or *logistiké*, a calculation that Plato also uses in his dialogues for all kinds of subjects, from cosmology to politics, from ethics to geometry, from justice to the analysis of pleasure and pain. The Stoics continued in this line, linking ethics to cosmology and anthropology. The logos-nomos pair is recurrent in Stoic philosophy. Zeno de Citio affirms that 'the common law, that is, right reason, spreads throughout the whole and is identical to Zeus, who governs the meaning of things.' Chrysippus affirmed that there is an eternal law that governs the world with its norms, which coincides with the mind of God to the extent that it orders and prohibits things. And calculation schemes were not at all foreign to this theology of reason as providence that governs the universe. In the endless lists of Stoic virtues, transmitted from the sources, along with correct reason, there is *eulogistia*, the good use of calculation and measurement, the ability to weigh without getting lost in the opposites. This virtue was called *antanairetiké*, a term that refers to an already mentioned way in which reason could be defined (logos as *antanairesis*)." Zellini, *Número y logos*, 90–91 (my translation).

the role of calculus in Aristotle's approach to the nature of virtue and justice. In this world, however, counting was not merely a mathematical act; it was also capable of ritual meaning, as is apparent in the many censuses and lists of names that we find in the Old Testament.[4]

Indeed, numbers and names were supposed to bring order to the empirical world. But numbers were not merely thought of as having a deictic function, as is clearly seen in early Christian commentaries on the Scriptures. A particularly striking example of the latter are St. Augustine's reflections on the number 6 in his *Literal Commentary to Genesis*,[5] or on the numbers 40 and 50 in his *Commentary on St. John's Gospel*.[6] It is not by chance that in his *De libero arbitrio*, he explicitly related numbering and wisdom.[7] He was not alone in doing so: ancient writers frequently looked to numbers for a trace of the divine order that shapes the universe and presides over human history. Precisely because of this, they thought that numbers involved a deeper, symbolic meaning that can only be adequately understood through ritual and deciphered with myth;[8] if numbers were part of human culture, they were so on the assumption of an archaic connection between culture and cult.

Subsequent to the ancient deictic function involved in the act of counting and invested with transcendent significance, logos would come to incorporate, in philosophical writings, the meaning of "reason" and "definition."[9] "Giving reason" for something involved the idea of providing an *explanation* for what there is

---

4. See A. Seidenberg, "The Ritual Origin of Counting," *Archive for History of Exact Sciences* 2, no. 1 (1962): 1–40, quoted by Zellini, *Número y logos*, 45ff.

5. St. Augustine, *De Genessi ad Literam. Liber Duodecim* (*Patrologia Latina*, vol. 34), Liber II, Caput 2.

6. St. Augustine, *In Evangelium Ioannis Tractatus Centum Viginti Quatuor* (*Patrologia Latina*, vol. 35). Comm. Ioh, 5, 1–18. Tractatus 17, n.4.

7. St. Augustine, *De libero arbitrio* (*Patrologia Latina*, 32), Liber II, 8.20–11.32.

8. See Jürgen Habermas, "Versprachligung des Sakralen: Anstelle eines Vorworts," in *Nachmetaphysische Denken II: Aufsätze und Repliken* (Frankfurt, Germany: Suhrkamp, 2012), 14–15.

9. "La definición, o el logos, pertenecen al ser que se genera y aparece inscrito en una clase de seres semejantes a él. . . ." Pero "la forma actualizada que define la naturaleza del ser, depende, a su vez, de la existencia real y concreta de un conjunto o de una clase de individuos. . . . La existencia de la clase debe apoyarse en una selección o en una enumeración, que podrá ser finita o infinita. La forma inherente a la naturaleza según el logos depende, en última instancia, de la formación de categorías u órdenes a los que remite el significado primario de *legein*." "The definition, or the logos, belongs to the being that is generated and appears inscribed in a class of beings similar to it. . . ." But "the updated form that defines the nature of the being, depends, in turn, on the real and concrete existence of a set or a class of individuals. . . . The existence of the class must be supported by a selection or an enumeration, which may be finite or infinite. The inherent form of nature according to logos ultimately depends on the formation of categories or orders to which the primary meaning of *legein* refers." Zellini, *Número y logos*, 92–93 (my translation).

(i.e., for the forms identified through counting), and, in this way, logos came to mean "argument" or logic, language, and discourse.

Actually, whether numbering or logic represents the primary function of logos is a matter for debate that anticipates twentieth-century discussion on whether mathematics can be reduced to logic or not; by pointing to the existence of irrational numbers, as well as subtraction and addition, Zellini maintains that mathematics cannot as a whole be thought of merely as a part of logic.[10] On the contrary, he points to the influence that arithmetic exerted on the very logical structure of platonic dialogue.[11]

---

10. "El origen algorítmico de las ideas, primero, de razón y, después, de sección ha sido típicamente desestimado por las teorías logicistas. A lo largo del siglo XX estas han desarrollado la idea de Dedekind y de Cantor de expresar el concepto de 'número' en términos de conjuntos y de clases y de relaciones de clases. . . . Prototipo de las teorías logicistas son los Principia Mathematica de Whitehead y Russell, en los que se ha seguido viendo durante cierto tiempo—incluso después de los célebres resultados de incompletitud e indecidibilidad de los años 30—una prueba convincente de que toda la matemática puede traducirse en lógica. . . . Sin embargo, al definir el número mediante clase o conjuntos se acaba por perder la información más esencial. ¿Qué decir, por ejemplo, de los números que son raíces de una ecuación o que representan el punto de mínimo de una función real. . . ? No se trata de una exigencia de las ciencias aplicadas que puedan ignorar tranquilamente las matemáticas puras, sino de un aspecto irrenunciable de la ratio como cálculo que ha acompañado a las matemáticas en todas las épocas y en todos los lugares." "The algorithmic origin of the ideas, first, of reason and, later, of section, has typically been underestimated by logicist theories. Throughout the 20th century they have developed the idea of Dedekind and Cantor according to which the concept of 'number' can be expressed in terms of sets and classes and relations of classes. . . . Whitehead and Russell's Principia Mathematica represent a prototype of logicist theories, since these works have continued to be seen for some time—even after the famous results of incompleteness and undecidability in the 1930s— convincing proof that all mathematics can be translated into logic. . . . However, when defining the number by class or sets, you end up losing the most essential information. What to say, for example, of the numbers that are roots of an equation or that represent the minimum point of a real function . . .? It is not a requirement of applied sciences that pure mathematics can safely ignore, but rather an inalienable aspect of the ratio as calculation, which has accompanied mathematics at all times and in all places." Zellini, *Número y logos*, 83–85 (my translation).

11. "En el Teeteto (206 d) de Platón parece predominar el sentido de logos como explicación, como definición, pero el filósofo lo presenta en tres acepciones distintas. Como dice Sócrates, la primera 'es la manifestación del pensamiento por medio del sonido que se articula en verbos y nombres, revelando así la opinión en la corriente vocálica como si fuera un espejo o en el agua.' La segunda se refiere al número y a los procesos de análisis, como cuando Hesíodo habla de las 'cien piezas en un carro' y, con ello, de la posibilidad de definir la esencia de algo enumerando uno a uno los elementos que lo componen. La tercera acepción consiste en singularizar una diferencia específica, una señal que permita distinguir una cosa de todas las demás. . . . En el Sofista (218 c) vuelve a aparecer logos como 'explicación' o 'definición,' pero el método para comprender el concepto de 'sofista' consiste principalmente en una división sucesiva de géneros, recurriendo a un ejemplo relativamente sencillo, el de la caza. La explicación se basa esencialmente en una técnica diairética, mediante la progresiva distinción de géneros o rangos, gracias a la cual se espera atrapar el concepto como en una red. El procedimiento no es, pues, tan diferente del de la catalogación o el censo, salvo por el hecho de que no tiene lugar mediante una simple enumeración, sino según un recorrido laberíntico en el que domina una lógica binaria. . . . En este sentido la diaíresis del diálogo parece orientada a la construcción de

Interestingly, Aristotle's texts on logic had already made a central tension manifest, implicit in the very fact of conveying the universal laws of thought in a particular, historical language: to analyze the elements of enunciation (logos), he had to resort to the grammatical terminology *-onoma* (name) and *rhema* (verb). This was a source of confusion among medieval interpreters until St. Thomas Aquinas read *Peri hermeneias* in light of the entire Aristotelian corpus[12] and clarified the role of names and verbs within enunciations, implicitly distinguishing logic and rhetoric: unlike rhetoric, which incorporates optative or desiderative sentences, dealing with affective states, logic deals only with enunciations, which can be true or false. Hence, only enunciations are called "interpretations" because only they are meant to interpret what we have in our intellect.[13]

---

rangos, listas o matrices de palabras y significados, de acuerdo con un sentido del logos más cercano al espíritu de las matemáticas." "In Plato's Theaetetus (206 d), the sense of logos seems to predominate as an explanation, as a definition, but the philosopher presents it in three different meanings. As Socrates says, the first 'is the manifestation of thought by means of sound that is articulated in verbs and nouns, thus revealing opinion in the vowel stream as if it were in a mirror or in wáter.' The second refers to the number and the processes of analysis, as when Hesiod speaks of the 'hundred pieces in a cart' and, with it, the possibility of defining the essence of something by listing the elements that compose it one by one. The third meaning consists of singling out a specific difference, a sign that makes it possible to distinguish one thing from all the others. . . . In the Sophist (218 c) logos such as 'explanation' or 'definition' reappear, but the method for understanding the concept of 'sophist' consists mainly of a successive division of genres, resorting to a relatively simple example, that of hunting. The explanation is essentially based on a *diairetic* technique, through the progressive distinction of genres or ranks, thanks to which the concept is expected to be caught in a net. The procedure is not, therefore, so different from that of cataloging or census, except for the fact that it does not take place through a simple enumeration, but rather according to a labyrinthine path in which a binary logic dominates. . . . In this sense, the *diairesis* of the dialogue seems oriented to the construction of ranges, lists or matrices of words and meanings, in accordance with a sense of logos closer to the spirit of mathematics." Zellini, *Número y logos*, 72–73 (my translation).

12. See J. A. García Cuadrado, *La cultura de la palabra* (Pamplona, Spain: Eunsa, 2015), 19–21.

13. "Dicitur ergo liber iste, qui prae manibus habetur, perihermeneias, quasi de interpretatione. Dicitur autem interpretatio, secundum Boethium, vox significativa, quae per se aliquid significat, sive sit complexa sive incomplexa. Unde coniunctiones et praepositiones et alia huiusmodi non dicuntur interpretationes, quia non per se aliquid significant. Similiter etiam voces significantes naturaliter, non ex proposito aut cum imaginatione aliquid significandi, sicut sunt voces brutorum animalium, interpretationes dici non possunt. Qui enim interpretatur aliquid exponere intendit. Et ideo sola nomina et verba et orationes dicuntur interpretationes, de quibus in hoc libro determinatur. *Sed tamen nomen et verbum magis interpretationis principia esse videntur, quam interpretationes. Ille enim interpretari videtur, qui exponit aliquid esse verum vel falsum. Et ideo sola oratio enunciativa, in qua verum vel falsum invenitur, interpretatio vocatur. Caeterae vero orationes, ut optativa et imperativa, magis ordinantur ad exprimendum affectum, quam ad interpretandum id quod in intellectu habetur.* Intitulatur ergo liber iste de interpretatione, ac si diceretur de enunciativa oratione: in qua verum vel falsum invenitur. Non autem hic agitur de nomine et verbo, nisi in quantum sunt partes enunciationis. Est enim proprium uniuscuiusque scientiae partes subiecti tradere, sicut et passiones. Patet igitur ad quam partem philosophiae pertineat liber iste, et quae sit necessitas istius, et quem ordinem teneat inter logicae libros" (my emphasis). "This book, therefore, which is held before the hands, is called perihermeneias,

Yet the very tension between grammar and logic[14] implicit in the study of enunciations is significant when it comes to the distance between historical and scientific logos, which has marked the evolution of Western culture. Likewise, as Zellini writes, "the separation of mathematical logos—in the technical sense of measure or reason—from the sphere of language and word is one of the reasons for the modern separation between humanistic and scientific knowledge."[15]

That separation was particularly clear during the Renaissance, when grammar and rhetoric, praised above dialectic,[16] became the mark of cultural refinement, whereas logic and mathematics came to symbolize scientific knowledge. Academic culture was heading toward a stricter differentiation of disciplines that not only expelled numbers from their ancient metaphysical and theological contexts and confined them to the scientific realm, but also introduced an internal division between what Gottfried Wilhelm Leibniz would call *"vérités de raisonnement"* and *"vérités de fait,"*[17] somehow anticipating Lessing's later distinction

---

as if of interpretation. But interpretation, according to Boethius, is a significant word that means something by itself, whether it is complex or uncomplex. Hence conjunctions and prepositions and the like are not called interpretations, because they do not signify anything by themselves. In the same way, voices which signify naturally, not by design or by imagination, as the voices of brute animals, cannot be called interpretations. For he who interprets intends to explain something. And, therefore, only the names and words and enunciations are said to be interpretations, which are determined in this book. *But still the name and the verb seem to be principles of interpretation rather than interpretations. For he seems to be interpreted who declares that something is true or false. And, therefore, the only declarative speech in which truth or falsity is found is called interpretation. But the rest of the speech, such as optatives and imperatives, are more designed to express emotion than to interpret what is contained in the intellect.* Therefore, this book is entitled on interpretation, as if it were said about an enunciative speech: in which truth or falsity is found. But here we are not dealing with the name and the verb, except in so far as they are parts of enunciation. For it is the property of each science to deliver the parts of the subject, as well as the passions. It is therefore clear to what part of philosophy this book belongs, and what is its necessity, and what rank it holds among the books of logic" (my emphasis). St. Thomas Aquinas, *Expositio libri Peryermeneias*, Proemium (my translation).

14. See Eugenio Coseriu, *Introducción a la lingüística* (Madrid: Gredos, 1986), 54–55.

15. Zellini, *Número y logos*, 79 (my translation).

16. See García Cuadrado, *La cultura de la palabra*, 23–25.

17. "Il y a aussi deux sortes de vérités, celles de raisonnement et celles de fait. Les vérités de raisonnement sont nécessaires et leur opposé est impossible, et celles de fait sont contingentes et leur opposé est possible. Quand une vérité est nécessaire, on en peut trouver la raison par l'analyse, la résolvant en idées et en vérités plus simples, jusqu'à ce qu'on vienne aux primitives." "There are also two kinds of truths, those of reasoning and those of fact. The truths of reasoning are necessary and their opposite is impossible, and those of fact are contingent and their opposite is possible. When a truth is necessary, the reason for it can be found by analysis, resolving it into simpler ideas and truths, until one comes to the primitives." Gottfried Wilhelm Leibniz, *Monadologie* §§ 33 (Stuttgart, Germany: Finken & Bumiller, 2009) (my translation).

between "the contingent truths of history" and "the necessary truths of reason."[18] This conception of reason left no place for the ancient meaning of "logos," which embraced the two meanings of counting and had resonated for a long time in the work of philosophers and theologians.

Max Weber's famous words in his *Wissenschaft als Beruf* (1917) about the disenchantment of the world through science can be read against this background, as can Edmund Husserl's considerations of the fracture between scientific knowledge and the lifeworld.[19] Despite Husserl's own ambition to overcome that fracture through phenomenology, the role that he envisioned for philosophy in the contemporary world was not to recover the ancient synthesis, but rather to mediate between the meanings of science and the meanings experienced in the lifeworld. It was implicit that, under modern conditions, there seemed to be no more room for what Jürgen Habermas designates as "totalizing metaphysical constructs," adding: "Modern science has needed critical reason to clean nature and history of totalizing metaphysical constructs. This reflective impulse has placed nature and history in the hands of the empirical sciences and has left philosophy little more than those general competencies proper to subjects that know, speak and act."[20]

Contained in these words is the idea of a modern division of labor between philosophy and science, which would have left philosophy with no other mission than navigating through basic human competencies;[21] yet even someone prone to accept this view can easily recognize that scientific reason has not exhausted the human need for making sense of the world that we inhabit and of our own existence as intelligent beings. Even if we cannot describe the corresponding

---

18. Gotthold Ephraim Lessing, "On the Proof of the Spirit and of Power," in *Philosophical and Theological Writings*, ed. H. B. Nisbet (Cambridge: Cambridge University Press, 2005), 85. Also see Samuel A. Stoner, "Lessing and the Art of History," *Journal of the History of Philosophy* 59, no. 1 (January 2021): 93–112.

19. Husserl discussed this first in the speech "Die Philosophie in der Krisis der europäischen Menschheit" (1935), published in Belgrade in the journal *Philosophie* (1936) and later included in *Husserliana* (1954), as *Die Krisis der Europäischen Wissenschaften und die Transzendentale Phänomenologie*. Edmund Husserl, *Die Krisis der Europäischen Wissenschaften und die Transzendentale Phänomenologie. Ergänzungsband: Texte aus dem Nachlass (1934–1937)* (Husserliana XXIX), ed. von Reinhold N. Smid (Dordrecht: Kluwer Academic Publishers, 1993).

20. Jürgen Habermas, *Ein Bewusstsein von dem, was fehlt: Eine Diskussion mit Jürgen Habermas*, ed. Michael Reder and Joseph Schmidt (Frankfurt, Germany: Suhrkamp, 2008), 27–28 (my translation).

21. For a critique of the more controversial view that scientific reason exhausts the intelligibility that is discoverable in nature or history, see Vittorio Hösle, "Seine Geschichte der Philosophie—zum Alterswerk von Jürgen Habermas," *Philosophische Rundschau* 68, no. 2 (2021): 164–207.

intellectual effort as "metaphysical," we should recognize a metaphysical dimension in the aspiration to obtain a deeper understanding of existence.

At any rate, this is where Bellah's interest not just in argument or theory but in narratives, and not just in narratives but in *metanarratives*, comes into play. His last, unfinished project consisted precisely of using metanarrative to lay the groundwork for answering one big question: "Are the ethical traditions developed over centuries in the great religions and civilizations capable of meeting the ethical challenges of our rapidly escalating cultural condition?"

2. Bellah's Intellectual Ambition

Are the values developed in the Axial Age[22] still valid when facing the changes that the technological era has produced?[23] This is a big question indeed. Sometimes I have wondered whether we Westerners have perhaps grown incapable of confronting a question like this. Unlike Eastern peoples, who are trained in more synthetic mental habits and more ambitious horizons of meaning, Western thought—deeply influenced by its Roman roots—has developed more along analytical lines. Yet this is obviously not the case with Bellah.

Concern about our cultural heritage's capacity to deal with accelerated cultural change is not new. In a way, Georg Simmel's considerations about the tragedy of

---

22. Although the notion of Achsenzeit, as "a period of radical cultural transformations in several major civilizational centers, unfolding during four or five centuries around the middle of the last millennium BCE" is usually attributed to Jaspers (*Vom Ursprung und Ziel der Geschichte*, 1949) "it can be probably traced back to the eighteenth century. . . . The common constitutive features of Axial-Age world-views might be summed up in the following terms: They involve a broadening of horizons, or an opening up of potentially universal perspectives, in contrast to the particularism of more archaic modes of thought; an ontological distinction between higher and lower levels of reality; and a normative subordination of the lower level to the higher, with more or less overtly stated implications for human efforts to translate guiding principles into ongoing practices. All these innovations may be seen as signs of enhanced reflexivity, but the reflexive potential is channeled into specific contexts and directions." Johann P. Arnason, S. N. Eisenstadt, and Björn Wittrock, eds., *Axial Civilizations and World History* (Leiden, Netherlands, and Boston: Brill, 2005), 1–2.

23. "The Axial Age has established imaginary, narrative and normative frameworks that have more or less underwritten every major civilization up to now, they have become global consciousness. Two, with the birth of modern science and technology, the First Axial values have been under tremendous pressure to provide meanings for new species-development. Global acceptance of technology and AI is unavoidable for peoples who are to shape the future of the species. Those secular and religious cultures that remain agitated by outdated problems (conflicts among received axial values) will be bypassed if new Axial values become mainstream." Martin Beck Matuštík, "Which Axial Age, Whose Rituals? Habermas and Jaspers on the 'Spiritual' Situation of the Present Age," *Philosophy and Social Criticism* 47, no. 6 (2021): 758, DOI:10.1177/0191453720931903.

culture in 1911 anticipated this problem, although from a more individualistic perspective.[24] Bellah's concern, by contrast, is more a social one. In his view, it is not so much that we as individuals are increasingly incapable of making sense of objective culture, but rather that mankind, as a whole, seems to be lacking the cultural resources necessary to meaningfully govern the transformations it has introduced in nature and society. This concern was already present in Bellah's book *Religion in Human Evolution*, and it surfaces again in his last writings.[25]

Illustrating this big question in his Notre Dame lecture—namely, whether we have the cultural resources to deal with present cultural challenges—he picked a particular problem, which is in fact a global one.[26] Drawing on Ian Morris's "societal development index," he wondered "whether the kind of knowledge that has made it possible for our social development index to go from 43 to close to 1000 in 200 years is really able to cope with its own achievements."[27]

Bellah was convinced that the social development that we have experienced in the last two centuries cannot be accounted for in simplistic terms: it is not just a matter of technological or economic transformation, but rather a multifactorial process that we subsume under the word "modernity." Modernity, for Bellah, has at its core "*a* new understanding of the human person, the human individual, an understanding that is religious as well as ethical and political."[28] Both Athens and Jerusalem have contributed to that new understanding of the human being's place and destiny.

In his Notre Dame lecture, Bellah explicitly referred to Hans Joas's book *The Sacredness of the Person: A New Genealogy of Human Rights*, where Joas recalls the confluence of several religious traditions on this idea, while also noting that the sacredness of the human person "nowhere, outside private religious communities, became the standard of social and political practices and institutions."[29] This suggests an often-overlooked connection between religious conscience and cultural progress that, despite all its ambiguities and paradoxes, is necessary to underline.

---

24. Georg Simmel, *Die Philosophische Kultur* (Leipzig, Germany: Gesammelte Essais, 1911).
25. Bellah, *Religion in Human Evolution*, x.
26. Robert N. Bellah, "The Modern Project in the Light of Human Evolution," University of Notre Dame, South Bend, IN, March 19, 2013. Chapter 1 in this volume.
27. Bellah, "The Modern Project," 27.
28. Bellah, "The Modern Project," 31 (my emphasis).
29. Bellah, "The Modern Project," 32.

3. Religion and Culture

In Bellah's view, "Joas is very interested in institutionalization and practices rather than ideas alone."[30] Bellah, on the other hand, prefers to focus on the very *idea* of human rights, which accounts for the intrinsic limitedness of all institutionalization. Using terminology that he borrows from Paul Tillich, we could speak of human rights as a "prophetic" idea with the power to revolutionize existing practices and institutions.

Indeed, for Tillich, prophetism, with its tension about the future, involved a correction of institutionalized religion, which focused more on the questions of being and origin. Along these lines, Bellah observes, "It is prophetism that gave the Jews the capacity to survive a catastrophic history in which the land was lost and the survival of the group imperiled. Groups who live in the myth of origin alone do not survive such histories. It was the prophetic move from the world of space into the world of time that gave a people rooted in the idea of a promised land the capacity to maintain their faith in every corner of the world into which they have been driven after they lost the land."[31]

Yet the tension between "origin myth" and "prophetic word," as the key to avoiding accommodation and nourishing hope, is not restricted to Israel. It can also be recognized in the abovementioned contrasts between the two meanings of "logos": between saying numbers and telling stories; between articulating rational arguments through the identification of universal forms and recognizing the contingent dimension of historical languages; between metaphysics and narrative. All of this seems to be constitutive of modern culture as well.

Everything suggests that being human and preserving humanity consist of holding both extremes together, keeping that tension alive. It is not an easy task. Operating with his own theological categories, Tillich notes how even freedom and autonomy—the great "prophetic" principle of modernity, the seed of revolutionary changes—can eventually become domesticated in a bourgeois way of life, probably because the tension between origin and destiny, just like the tension

---

30. Bellah, "The Modern Project," 33.
31. Robert N. Bellah, "The Tillich Lecture: Paul Tillich and the Challenge of Modernity," 271. Chapter 8 in this volume.

between numbers and words and between metaphysics and narrative, is difficult to manage.[32]

Religious traditions, however, provide particularly clear examples of the two poles defining that tension and help us understand the ways in which it resurfaces in human history. Tillich's radiography of Christianity in terms of Protestant prophetism and Catholic sacramental religion can be viewed in this light, even if it runs the risk of oversimplifying their differences—there is prophetism in Catholicism and sacramentality in Protestantism—and of leaving out the important theological and cultural contributions of the Eastern Christian tradition. Nevertheless, Bellah considers that "the Protestant neglect of the sacraments" can be viewed as "part of the modern world's neglect of the natural as sacred," an aspect that also sheds light on the insufficiency of modern thought to counteract some of the unintended consequences of modernity.[33]

In this regard, Habermas has offered a complementary line of reflection. Just as philosophy can borrow from religious sources[34] some semantics that enrich philosophical discourse, without threatening its rational character,[35] he admits that postsecular society can find in religious traditions elements that can correct or rectify modernity where the latter is going off the rails. While he rejects Immanuel Kant's "postulates of practical reason"—specifically the immortality of the soul and the existence of God—as a legitimate continuation of Kant's own moral philosophy, Habermas nevertheless admits the possibility and necessity of translating some parts of religious traditions into secular terms, as Kant himself anticipated not only with the doctrine of the postulates—introduced as a requirement to make sense of the a priori duty to realize the highest good—but especially with his *Religion within the Boundaries of Reason Alone*. In so doing,

---

32. In other places, I have pointed to the notion of "natural law" as a privileged place from which to recognize that tension. Insofar as it is law, it should be regarded as an extrinsic principle; yet, insofar as it is natural, it should be regarded as an intrinsic principle. This tension is conceptually clarified in Aquinas's consideration of natural law in terms of rational creature's active participation in God's eternal law. See Ana Marta González, "Natural Law as a Limiting Concept: An Interpretation of Thomas Aquinas," in *Contemporary Perspectives on Natural Law: Natural Law as a Limiting Concept*, ed. Ana Marta González (Abingdon, UK, and New York: Routledge), 11–28.

33. Bellah, "The Tillich Lecture," 279.

34. See Jürgen Habermas, "Rückkehr zur Metaphysik?," in *Nachmetaphysisches Denken: Philosophische Aufsätze* (Frankfurt: Suhrkamp, 1988), 23.

35. See Jürgen Habermas, "Versprachligung des Sakralen: Anstelle eines Vorworts," in *Nachmetaphysische Denken II* (Frankfurt: Suhrkamp, 2012), 16–17.

Habermas recalls the inspiration that philosophical thinking has always found in religion and theology and wonders whether this could still be the case.

The answer to this question, however, does not merely entail a semantic dimension but a pragmatic one. Indeed, Habermas not only wonders whether religion and theology can still provide philosophy with a new impulse, orientation, and topics for reflection; he also asks whether religion can still motivate people enough to meet the requirements of reason. This question, however, asks for more than an adequate secular translation of religious content; it asks for access to the *performative* dimension of faith. Yet, as Habermas himself recognizes,[36] there are reasons to doubt that sociological or otherwise theoretical accounts of those dimensions are sufficient to mobilize human subjectivities, since such a transformative effect can be expected only from a *personal appropriation* of religious content.

Indeed, speaking of "personal appropriation" means that religious content must be regarded as something more than abstract logoi or logical enunciations; it needs to be approached as historical *events* that remain alive and relevant in the present. This possibility has to do with the sacramental dimension of faith, which is not entirely alien to its prophetic dimension.

Insofar as both Judaism and Christianity claim to be based on God's intervention in human history, they necessarily take history to be more than a contingent succession of facts whose meaning can be fixed and analyzed by an external observer. By claiming that the eternal God has *spoken* to humanity, Judaism and Christianity made it possible for human beings to read historical events, *once and again*, in light of God's words. They were able to recognize themselves as

---

36. "Theology would forfeit its identity if it attempted to detach itself from religion's dogmatic core—and with it from the religious language in which a religious community's practices of prayer, of confession, and of faith occur. These are the practices in which religious faith, which theology can only interpret, proves itself. From the beginning, theology has a certain parasitic or derivative status. It cannot hide the fact that its interpretive work can never entirely 'recover' or 'exhaust' the performative meaning of the living faith. . . . Theology cannot provide a substitute for religion, for the latter's truth is nourished from the revealed Word, which from the beginning appears in religious not in scholarly form. But philosophy has an entirely distinct relation to religion. It seeks to re-express what it learns from religion in a discourse that is independent of revealed truth. Thus, every philosophical translation, even Hegel's inevitably loses the performative meaning of the living faith. A philosophy that comes to depend on 'destinies,' or take solace from them, is no philosophy at all. The ambition of philosophy's 'translation program' is, if you like, to rescue the profane significance of interpersonal and existential experiences that have so far only been adequately articulated in religious language." Jürgen Habermas, "A Conversation about God and the World," in *Religion and Rationality: Essays on Reason, God, and Modernity* (Cambridge, MA: MIT Press, 2002), 163–64.

personally called, interpellated by these words, and ultimately by God's Word or logos. Here, in the very idea of a personal calling, we find the pragmatic dimension of faith in a nutshell.

4. Christianity and Logos

As we know, philosophical reflection on Logos played a crucial role in the religions of the Axial Age.[37] Philo of Alexandria's neo-Platonic reading of the Scriptures took Logos as an intermediary between God and the world, thus enmeshing philosophical reflection with Israel's faith in a Creator God. Taking this idea in the context of Christianity's faith in the Triune God, Augustine emphasized the divinity of Logos (i.e., its equal nature with the Father). Thus, he merged the first verse of Genesis, בְּרֵאשִׁית בָּרָא אֱלֹהִים אֵת הַשָּׁמַיִם וְאֵת הָאָרֶץ: (In the beginning God created the heavens and the earth), with that of St. John's Gospel,[38] in which the words about the creative power of God's wisdom resonate:[39] "Ἐν ἀρχῇ ἦν ὁ λόγος, καὶ ὁ λόγος ἦν πρὸς τὸν θεόν, καὶ θεός ἦν ὁ λόγος" (In principium erat Verbum, et Verbum erat apud Deum, et Deus erat Verbum; In the beginning was the Word, and the Word was with God, and the Word was God), thus underlining the identification between Word and Beginning. God created everything *through his Word*. With this exegetical move, Augustine not only incorporated the Stoic view of the cosmos' rationality in a theological framing that allows for the defense of Logos's personal condition; he also laid the ground for interpreting human history from an entirely new perspective. Indeed, as a Christian, Augustine believed that this divine Logos took on human nature and entered human history to fulfill God's promise of salvation.[40]

---

37. See Jürgen Habermas, "Eine Hypothese zum gattungsgeschichtlichen Sinn des Ritus," in *Nachmetaphysische Denken II* (Frankfurt: Suhrkamp, 2012), 94–95.

38. See St. Augustine, *In Evangelium Ioannis Tractatus centum viginti quatuor*, Tractatus I, n. 11.

39. See Wisdom of Solomon, 8, 1–6. See also Proverbs 8, 22–21. All biblical quotes from, *The Complete Parallel Bible with the Apocryphal/Deuterocanonical Books: New Revised Standard Version, Revised English Bible, New American Bible, New Jerusalem Bible* (Oxford: Oxford University Press, 1993).

40. In Origenes's words: "Multa sunt verba, sed non sicut verbum istud. Nullum enim verbum post verbum Moysi, post verbum prophetarum, multo autem amplius post verbum Iesum Christi et Apostolorum eius. Vide, si non clamavit sensus Dei, quod dictum est: legem enim in adiutorium dedit, ut dicant, qui acceperunt legem in aditorium: non est ut verbum istud, quomodo locutus est Moyses in lege lata per angelos in manu mediatoris. Multo autem dignius potest hoc ecclesia dicere: non est ut verbum istud, quod caro factum est, quod habitavit in nobis, cuius vidimus gloriam, non sicut Moyses velamine obtectam, sed gloriam tamquam unigeniti a patre, plenum gratiae et veritatis. Non et ut verbum istud, quod suscepit ecclesia, in quo credit, per quod et salvabitur, verbum, quod in

Tillich's reference to the sacramental dimension of Logos is relevant here. Christian faith in the Incarnation of the Word is actually what brought this idea to its ultimate conclusion. The Incarnation of the Word not only underlines the sacredness of the human being created in God's image, but it also imprints a definite, and yet inexhaustible, meaning on all human words, including of course the prophetic Word, which, in this context, points to Christ as the actual center of human history.

Here, we have *the biggest narrative*, whose historicity represents the core of Christian faith. Yet precisely this faith defies mere reason because, in contrast with the latter's abstract universality, it asserts that the eternal God has enmeshed himself in human history, always particular and contingent. In this way, it transforms the history of an "insignificant" people into something entirely unthinkable—into the universal history of salvation.

The Incarnation of Logos is the Event *par excellence* that shakes inherited cultural categories. Instead of merely subordinating human life and events to natural cycles, as was the case in ancient cultures, Christianity promotes the contextualization of natural and human events in light of the universal history of salvation. This has far-reaching cultural consequences that have been summarized in the idea of a transition "from mythic to linear" time, an expression taken from Maria Nikolajeva's studies of children's literature:

> In Greek, the eternal, mythic time is called *kairos*, to distinguish from the measurable, linear time, *chronos*. . . . In Latin, the counterpart is *"in illo tempore,"* and the closest everyday formula is that of the fairy tale: "once upon a time." Unlike *chronos*, *kairos* is reversible. It can be integrated with linear time through rituals, rites and festivals, human repetitions of primordial acts. . . .

---

principio erat apud Deum Deus, verbum, cui gloria et imperium in saecula saeculorum." "There are many words, but not like this word. For there is no word after the word of Moses, after the word of the prophets, but much more after the word of Jesus Christ and his apostles. Look, if the sense of God did not cry out, which was said: for he gave the law as a helper, so that those who received the law as a helper may say: there is no word like that word, as Moses spoke in the law given by the angels in the hand of the mediator. But the church can say this much more worthily: there is no word like that word which became flesh, which dwelt in us, whose glory we saw, not like Moses covered with a veil, but glory as the only begotten of the father, full of grace and truth. No word like that word, which the church received, in which it believes, and through which it will be saved, the word which was God in the beginning with God, the word to whom be glory and dominion for ever and ever." Orígenes, *In Isaiam Homilia*, VII, 4. See also *Die Griechischen Christlichen Shriftsteller der Ersten Drei Jahrhunderte*, Bd. VIII, ed. KirchenVäter-Commission der Preussischen Akadamie der Wissenschaften (Leipzig, Germany: J. C. Hinrichs'che Buchhandlung, 1925), 285.

It is quite essential to my study that contemporary Western children's fiction is written from a philosophical viewpoint based on linear time, which has a beginning and an end, and recognizes every event in history as unique. . . . The insight about the linearity of time invokes the problems of growing up, aging, and death. Since mythic time, *kairos*, is reversible, death in myth is transitory . . . the final formula of many fairy tales stresses that the linear progress of the plot is rounded into an everlasting, mythic time.[41]

Is Bellah's concern about our present ethical challenges perhaps related to a suspicion that contemporary culture leans toward reversing this Axial, specifically Christian, order? Are we perhaps abandoning linear time in favor of mythic time, or at least replacing meaningful narrative with "dataism," relying on numbers deprived of all formal and ritual significance, yet ultimately enmeshed in a repetitive version of mythic time? After all, a cyclical perception of time is coherent with a materialistic view of the circle of life: a generation is born, lives, perpetuates itself, and dies, and the next generation carries on the process without a significant event marking a beginning or an end, and thus meaningful direction or progress. Even if biological immortality might be conceived of as linear, it would not in itself provide us with meaningful narrative because, although we rather arbitrarily stipulate a beginning and a termination for life, this does not actually provide life with meaning. Τέλος (end or purpose) is more than περας (limit). In the Greek word Τέλος, the ideas of both "limit" and "meaning" are present, and it seems that the power of Τέλος to give meaning to human life has to do with its unavailable quality. Yet, in the absence of a beginning and an end, there would be no middle, something that Aristotle highlights as an essential feature of "plot," and thus of narrative.[42]

5. The Narrative and Christian Approach to History

It seems to me that Bellah's interest in metanarrative, as a cultural frame that provides meaning to otherwise undifferentiated natural events, is ultimately inspired by his reliance on the Christian approach to history. According to this approach, the immediate significance that particular events may have in light of

---

41. Maria Nikolajeva, *From Mythic to Linear: Time in Children's Literature* (London: Scarecrow, 2000), 5–6.
42. Aristotle, *Poetics*, I, 7, 1451 a25–a32.

short-term human interests is part of a deeper human interest that accounts for the largest history of salvation, as articulated by Christianity.

Since Kant's philosophy of history and religion was written to respond to reason's concern for the ultimate meaning of human life and history, and it represents in part a secularization of the Christian approach to time and eschatology, one might think that that is enough to account for the human need for meaning. Yet, in Kant's secular hermeneutics, there is no room for the Incarnation of the Word, and thus the pragmatic force of hope is severely weakened. We just need to consider the experiential way in which St. Paul conveys the content of Christian faith. For him, the ultimate signification of all things in heaven and on earth—thus nature, history, the individual, and society—is to be found directly and absolutely in the person of Christ,[43] as is also conveyed in the book of Revelation, where Christ is presented as το ‘Αλφα και το Ωμέγα" (the Beginning and the End).[44] Faith brings, for St. Paul, a new kind of knowledge that he explicitly describes in terms of *strength*.[45] It has a performative dimension that changes one's position in life. Paul's words are the words of a man whose subjectivity has been entirely *transformed* by that faith.[46] Yet he does not present this experience as an extraordinary or individualistic one: all believers are supposed to find here inspiration for a new life marked by a fraternal ethos.

As is well known, philosophical thought from previous centuries absorbed many elements of that vision in diverse ways. St. Augustine's *City of God* comes easily to mind, although modern philosophical appropriations of the Christian legacy are also indicative of various ways of dealing with Christianity's rational nucleus. Yet, as anticipated above, the mobilizing power of faith can never be completely subsumed by reason because it conjures up more forces than mere reason, even if those forces are awakened by the proclamation of kerygma, and thus through logos.

An early Christian philosopher like Justin could still refer to Christianity as "the true philosophy"[47] because at that time, as Habermas reminds us, logos and salvation were strongly connected in philosophical discourse.[48] Over history,

---

43. See Ephesians 1, 9–10.

44. Rev. 21, 6.

45. 1 Co, 1, 22–25.

46. Ga, 2, 20.

47. See Arthur J. Droge, "Justin Martyr and the Restoration of Philosophy," *Church History* 56, no. 3 (1987), 303–19, https://doi.org/10.2307/3166060.

48. See Jürgen Habermas, *Ein Bewusstsein von dem, was felht*, 28–29.

however, a division of labor between philosophy and religion gradually took place: philosophical focus on the permanent and universal essences sparked reflection on the historical contingency of individual existence, marked by individual responsibility. While the latter does not necessarily cancel out the individual sharing in a universal human nature, it certainly encourages a complementary, twofold approach to the human being. *Theory* and *narrative* emerge as two different approaches to one reality that we are unable to think of simultaneously under one and the same logos.

However, is this cultural division of labor between theory and narrative still valid when making sense of and facing the problems that lie ahead of us, many of them of our own making? Such concern is obviously related to Bellah's question about the capacity of our cultural and ethical practices to meet the challenges of our current condition, marked as it is by increasingly unsustainable development. The answer to this question will depend on how we conceive of culture.

6. Unsustainable Development and Work

Bellah's reference to Lars von Trier's film *Melancholia* does not anticipate a happy end to this problem. His fear resonates more with Christianity's eschatology than with Kant's secularized reading of it.

As suggested earlier, unlike the ancient view of time that ultimately integrated human life with natural cycles, Christianity upholds a lineal view of time, and thus of human history, which begins with creation and heads toward a transcendent goal. In the meantime (i.e., in historical time), humanity inhabits the earth, developing amid progress and conflict, the ultimate meaning of which cannot be judged merely from an intrahistorical perspective. Indeed, Christianity holds that the human world will experience a catastrophic, intrahistorical end that will be the prelude to Christ's intervention in history, on the "Last Day," representing the final judgment on human achievements and deeds.[49] Curiously, in Kant's reading of this doctrine, the catastrophic end is interpreted as a threatening mismatch between the "culture of ability," or worldly progress, and the "moral culture." However, Kant hopes that moral culture prevails in the end, so that the catastrophic end does not take place:

---

49. See St. Peter, second epistle 3, 10–13. See also St. Thomas Aquinas, *In Super Mattheum*, Caput 24, Lectio 3.

> In the progress of the human race the culture of talents, skill and taste (with
> their consequence, luxury) naturally runs ahead of the development of moral-
> ity; and this state is precisely the most burdensome and dangerous for moral-
> ity just as it is for physical wellbeing, because the needs grow stronger than
> the means to satisfy them. But the moral disposition of humanity, which . . .
> always limps behind, tripping itself up in its hasty course and often stum-
> bling, will (as, under a wise world governor, one may hope) one day overtake
> it; and thus, even according to the experimental proofs of the superior morals
> of our age as compared with all previous ones, one should nourish the hope
> that the last day might sooner come on the scene with Elijah's ascension than
> with the like descent of Korah's troops into hell, and bring with it the end of
> all things on earth.[50]

Thus, Kant replaces the catastrophic intrahistorical end with rational faith in
God's intervention, which would cause a final adjustment of natural and moral
progress, the only condition being our practical commitment to virtue.[51]

Interestingly, Christianity's certitude of a catastrophic end was not supposed
to nourish a passive moral stance on secular issues. As we know, St. Paul reacted
strongly when the Thessalonians began to abandon their worldly responsibilities: "We urged you when we were with you not to let anyone eat who refused
to work. Now we hear that there are some of you who are living lives without
any discipline, doing no work themselves but interfering with other people's. In
the Lord Jesus Christ, we urge and call on people of this kind to go on quietly
working and earning the food that they eat. My brothers, never slacken in doing
what is right."[52]

---

50. Immanuel Kant, "End of All Things," in *Religion and Rational Theology* (The Cambridge Edition of
the Works of Immanuel Kant), ed. A. Wood and G. Di Giovanni (Cambridge: Cambridge University
Press, 1996), 8: 332, doi:10.1017/CBO9780511814433.

51. While Kant complains that "this heroic faith in virtue does not seem, subjectively, to have such a
generally powerful influence for converting people's minds as a scene accompanied by terrors, which
is thought of as preceding the last things" ("End of All Things," 8: 332), he nevertheless thinks that
"however incredulous one may be, one must . . . believe in a practical way in a concurrence of divine
wisdom with the course of nature, unless one would rather just give up one's final end" (8: 337). Interestingly, Kant thinks that Christianity has a decisive role to play in nourishing that practical commitment insofar as "its founder" presents himself as "friend of humanity who appeals to the hearts
of his fellow human beings on behalf of their own well-understood will, i.e. of the way they would of
themselves voluntarily act if they examined themselves properly" (8: 338), for in this way, says Kant,
Christianity appears as "worthy of love."

52. 2 Thes, 3, 10–13.

Taking up one's own worldly responsibilities in a virtuous manner was part of the Christian calling, a way of incarnating the Gospel, a way of anticipating "the new heavens and the new earth, where uprightness will be at home."[53] Indeed, these words about the new heavens and the new earth can be taken as an indication that, despite the predicted intrahistorical catastrophic end,[54] all previous human efforts to anticipate and realize a better world, even those that currently seem frustrated, finally will bear fruit in a transfigured world; not even the most insignificant human effort to do good will be in vain.[55] In other words, while the catastrophic intrahistorical end leaves no room for naive optimism, God's final intervention, although of a transcendent nature, would not be entirely alien to prior human efforts.[56]

Interestingly, in the Christian account, as in Kant's secularized version of the Last Day, it is God's intervention that, by restoring the ultimate meaning of human deeds as well as the harmony of nature and freedom, has the last word on the progress and history of the world. This is entirely coherent with the human condition for, as we have noted, human beings' approach to reality is never simple: the multiple meanings of "logos" entertained in human culture suggest that the last word cannot be simply a human word.

Yet, in the final part of this chapter, I would rather focus on the fact that in both the Christian and the Kantian accounts, human agency still has a central role to play in the shaping of the new heaven and earth, provided that it is a virtuous, upright agency. The centrality of agency in Christianity is implicit in the very idea of a personal calling, which allows for seeing one's entire life in terms of response. That centrality is also clear in the Kantian account, with its emphasis on morality and freedom. However, in this context, I would like to draw attention specifically to the need to link this centrality of personal agency to an ethical approach to *human work*, to see it not just as a driver of ambivalent cultural progress, but also as a positive engine of true ethical progress, that is, as an engine of progress that is respectful of the natural environment and committed to social solidarity. That such hope can, and perhaps should, be inspired by religious faith

---

53. 2Pt, 3, 13; Rev, 21, 1–5.
54. See Josef Pieper, "Über das Ende der Zeit: Eine geschichtsphilosophische Betrachtung," in *Werke in acht Bänden*, Bd.6, ed. Berthold Wald (Hamburg: Felix Meiner, 1999), 286–374.
55. See St. Thomas Aquinas, *Super Ioannem*, Caput 6, Lectio 5.
56. This could perhaps be supported by the way that Paul speaks of Creation's anxious wait for the revelation of the children of God; such a revelation, however, is not merely a human endeavor, for it is inspired by God and is therefore God's own work. See Romans, 8, 14–31.

does not negate its intrinsically secular content. Habermas's reflection on contemporary threats to modern normative conscience is pertinent in this regard:[57]

> The division of labor between the integrative mechanisms of the market, bureaucracy, and social solidarity is out of kilter and has shifted in favor of economic imperatives that reward forms of social interaction oriented to individual success. In addition, the establishment of new technologies that deeply permeate substrates of the human person that used to be regarded as 'natural' promotes a naturalistic self-understanding among experiencing subjects in their interactions with one another. This disruption of normative consciousness also manifests itself in the dwindling sensitivity to social pathologies, indeed, to social deprivation and suffering in general. A sober post-metaphysical philosophy cannot compensate for this lack, which was already felt by Kant. It can no longer draw on the kind of reasons that could elevate a single motivating worldview above all others, specifically, one which satisfies existential expectations, provides binding orientations for life as a whole, or even offers consolation.[58]

In this context, appealing to the religious sources of ethical commitment is entirely relevant. It can certainly be argued that one of religion's most specific contributions to modernity consists precisely of nurturing an ethical commitment to secular affairs when almost all other human sources of hope have failed. From this perspective, Bellah's question—"Are the ethical traditions developed over centuries in the great religions and civilizations capable of meeting the ethical challenges of our rapidly escalating cultural condition?"—certainly deserves a positive answer, provided that we are able to prophetically actualize the meaning

---

57. "Hegel characterized the achievements of modernity with the concepts 'self-consciousness,' 'self-determination,' and 'self-realization.' Self-consciousness is a function of the growth in reflexivity in the context of a perpetual revision of dissolved traditions, self-determination is the result of the predominance egalitarian and individualistic universalism in law and morality, and self-realization the result of the pressure toward individuation and self-direction under conditions of a highly abstract ego-identity. This self-understanding of modernity is also a result of secularization, and thus of the liberation from the constraints of politically powerful religions. But today this normative consciousness is threatened not just from outside by the reactionary longing for a fundamentalist counter modernity, but also from within the uncontrolled process of modernization itself." Jürgen Habermas, "The Boundary between Faith and Knowledge," in *Between Naturalism and Religion: Philosophical Essays* (Cambridge and Malden, MA: Polity, 2012), 238.
58. Habermas, "The Boundary between Faith and Knowledge," 239.

buried in those civilizatory traditions. Ultimately, securing the positive response does not depend on tradition per se, but rather on human beings' capacity to actualize those meanings in their own lives.

Religious conscience can contribute to this response insofar as it infuses secular activities, and specifically human work, with that spirit, which, in St. Paul's words, could free "creation from its slavery to corruption" and bring it "into the same glorious freedom as the children of God."[59] Indeed, were we to follow the insights of early sociologists such as Émile Durkheim, the division of labor does not just have an economic meaning, but also a social and moral one that can be reinforced by religious faith. In his view, while the division of labor certainly enhanced production and objective culture, thereby increasing various forms of subjective alienation, it also fostered functional interdependence, which could constitute fertile ground for ethical solidarity, provided that work was well regulated and coordinated, as well as supported by an adequate social conscience. Seen in this way, the division of labor would not merely fulfill an economic function, but would also provide us with structural opportunities for developing social bonds and relational goods that are relevant for humanizing the economy and developing one's own personality. At any rate, the actual realization of these opportunities would not merely depend on structural conditions, but also require an ethical conscience that sustains solidarity on a daily basis.

It is clear, however, that in the present conditions of global interdependence and remote work, confronted with the challenges posited by unsustainable growth, such ethical conscience necessarily demands concretization at multiple levels. This occurs not just within organizations, securing meaningful work and time for genuine interaction among colleagues, but also across organizations, securing conditions for fair competition not just at the national level, but also at the international level, where we would do well to recall that while work is a condition of culture, there is no culture without nature. From this perspective, the humanization of work will not be complete until ethical conscience recalls the natural conditions of human existence.

On the whole, the present situation represents an invitation for economic agents to reconsider the organization of work on a larger scale, subordinating it to human ends—an invitation, perhaps, to be inspired by the role that

---

59. Rm 8, 19.

nature played in premodern cultures, when natural cycles defined feasts and other events that were socially shared. With that inspiration, we can articulate innovative solutions that increase social solidarity and are respectful of the environment. Reference to "nature" further makes sense if we consider that the acceleration proper to modern economics resembles what Aristotle once characterized as "non-natural chrematistics," an endless pursuit of production lacking any internal limitation whatsoever.[60] Aristotle thought this situation was ethically problematic, for it would potentially move human agents to subvert the order between the desire of acquiring what is necessary for living—the role of the economy—and the desire to conduct a meaningful life.

The fact that individual people can certainly conduct meaningful lives, even in the midst of disrupted societies, does not cancel out the fact that, with the ecological crisis, humanity is confronting the limits of a purely economic approach to the division of labor. In this context, Aristotle's reservation against nonnatural chrematistics is relevant because it reminds us of the ethical horizon of economic activity, even if thinking of that ethical order on a global scale represents an unprecedented ethical challenge.

Interestingly, addressing this challenge is now important for pragmatic reasons as well because, unless we deliberately subordinate economic competition to human goals (i.e., unless we explicitly frame economic development in ethical terms), we risk the sustainability of our planet. Such pragmatic motivation, however, does not represent the most adequate principle for changing economic practices, especially if we consider that the present state of affairs partly derives from unilateral reliance on the possibilities of pragmatic reason.

To reframe the economy ethically within human goals, we need to encourage the development of an ethical conscience within economic organizations and practices, and ultimately within human work. Grounding such conscience in

---

60. As Aristotle notes, along with a "natural art of acquisition, which has to be practiced by managers of households and statesmen" (*Politics*, I, 8, 1256 b37) and "aims at the accumulation not of currency but of true wealth—and therefore not at the infinite, but at the finite," (*Politics*, I, 9, 1256 b 40) there is another form of acquisition, which is "not natural, but is rather the product of a certain sort of experience and skill," (*Politics*, I, 9, 1256 b 40), which has to do with exchange: as long as exchange "simply serves to satisfy the natural requirements of sufficiency" (*Politics*, I, 9, 1257 a 19) it is in proper order; yet exchange easily goes beyond this, and becomes focused on money in a way that absorbs human desire because "the wealth produced by this second form of the art of acquisition is unlimited" (*Politics*, I, 9, 1257 b23). Aristotle, *Politics*, trans. Ernest Barker, revised by R. F. Stalley (Oxford: Oxford University Press, 1995).

religious faith is not a defect; rather, it constitutes an opportunity to recall the ancient—and perennial—connection between culture and cult. "Full of merit, yet poetically, man dwells on this earth."[61] Heidegger's reflections on Friedrich Hölderlin's words are relevant here.[62] To the extent that it confers on nature a transcendent meaning, to the extent that it anticipates a fully meaningful world, culture symbolically sets a limit on instrumental rationality and helps to make this world a suitable place for human beings.

61. Friedrich Hölderlin, "In Lieblicher Bläue," in *Sämtliche Werke, Bd. 2, Gedichte nach 1800*, ed. von Friedrich Beißner (Stuttgart: Cotta, 1953).
62. See Martin Heidegger, *Poetry, Language, Thought*, trans. Albert Hofstadter (New York: Harper and Row, 1971).

CHAPTER 6

AXIALITY AND THE CRITIQUE OF POWER

ALAN STRATHERN

Positively, he made the statement that Christ had been the first to proclaim the principle of equality and union, that the printing-press had propagated the doctrine, and that finally the French Revolution had elevated it into a law! All which our poor young friend found very muddling—he scarce knew why.

Thomas Mann, *The Magic Mountain*[1]

We answer to a higher authority. When there is a contradiction between the laws of the country and God's command, the Bible is very clear that God's command must win out.

A minister of an evangelical church in London,

defying COVID-19 lockdown regulations[2]

R obert Bellah's prologue does not seek to set out the principal theses of the book to follow; it is presented as a narrative in which the argument is largely implicit. Yet one preoccupation of the text concerns the capacity of Christianity, as the product of an Axial breakthrough, to offer a means of challenging the authority of rulers, as well as the way that this in turn

---

1. Thomas Mann, *The Magic Mountain*, trans. H. T. Lowe-Porter (London: Knopf, 1988 [1924]), 156t.
2. Harriet Sherwood, " 'Let Us Disobey': Churches Defy Lockdown with Secret Meetings," November 22, 2020, *Guardian*, https://www.theguardian.com/world/2020/nov/22/let-us-disobey-churches-defy-lockdown -with-secret-meetings.

yielded the modern principles of the autonomy of the individual and their right to political participation. Thus, what frequently has been taken as an achievement of the Enlightenment may be granted a longer history, reaching deep into the first millennium BCE. This is analogous to a tradition of interpretation that glimpses the intellectual preconditions of "the disenchantment of the world" in the teachings of the prophets and thinkers of that distant age.[3]

It is a valuable insight on the part of Bellah and the broader lineage of Axial theorists to have identified how political legitimacy became tied to the capacity to act in the name of higher principles that transcended politics and that established new means by which rulers may be called to account. It is sometimes argued that this was accompanied by a repudiation of divine kingship for a more human conception of the office. From the most long-term perspective, the prologue suggests, these may be seen as early steps along the road of establishing popular rights of arbitration over governing elites. This chapter interrogates the possible connections between axiality (or, more specifically, what I refer to as "transcendentalism") and the potential for kingship to become subject to disenchantment, critique, relativization, and even some expression of the popular will. Much of the discussion will develop criticisms and qualifications of any straightforward relationship, but ultimately, it preserves a sense of the continuing importance of the insight. Since a principal objective will be to place this narrative in a global context, many issues here have to be approached from the perspective of the nonspecialist, and with the intent of raising questions that others might take forward. As a historian of the premodern world, however, I do not attempt to offer any substantial analysis of the critical period of the eighteenth century and beyond.

From the perspective of some readers, this method may seem radically teleological. It is not teleological in the true sense of the word, of course: it does not posit some final telos or ultimate logic of history. With regard to the looser sense of the term, frequently deployed by historians to refer to an investigation of the long-term past to help explain features of the present, this chapter is indeed "teleological," and unapologetically so, for we are in a parlous state if

---

3. See José Casanova, "Religion, the Axial Age, and Secular Modernity in Bellah's Theory of Religious Evolution," in *The Axial Age and Its Consequences*, ed. Robert N. Bellah and Hans Joas (Cambridge, MA: Harvard University Press, 2012), 191–221; Charles Taylor, *A Secular Age* (Cambridge, MA: Harvard University Press, 2007); and others, influenced by Max Weber, as Philip Gorski's chapter notes (chapter 10 in this volume).

historians no longer feel able to contemplate such matters. The pejorative associations clinging to the loose usage derive from the anticipation that anachronism will result. That is evidently a risk and is where accusations of whiggishness, for example, have long derived their force. But less often observed are the errors that antiteleological critiques are liable to produce. One is to confuse claims about causes with claims about effects, when to argue that a cause or condition of *x* (say, "modernity") has emerged is not to claim that *x* itself has. Another is to imagine that etic concepts gain their utility by their proximity to emic ones, with more distantly etic terms being a corruption of the period sensibility in question, when there are all manner of explanatory tasks for which etic terms are indispensable.[4]

Throughout this chapter, I will be using a set of concepts that have been articulated much more fully elsewhere.[5] The most fundamental of these is a distinction between two forms of religiosity: immanentism and transcendentalism. To translate these into the terms used by Bellah and others, immanentism is broadly equivalent to that which characterizes pre-Axial or non-Axial religion, while transcendentalism captures the defining elements of the post-Axial "world religions."[6] Immanentist religiosity conceives the world as full of supernatural forces and beings with whom people must interact to flourish. Marshall Sahlins has described these beings as "metapersons": ghosts, spirits of place and thing, ancestors, gods.[7] The universalism of this phenomenon seems to reflect a profound orientation to the logic of the social in the development of the human mind: anything that bears upon our well-being is instinctively understood in terms of motivated agency. Indeed, achieving any worthwhile objective—to produce food, survive ill-health, become wealthy, give birth, wage war—depends on the

---

4. A related assumption is that the only proper goal of historical inquiry is to recreate a given slice of the past in a manner that comprehensively preserves its own proportions. But it is inherent to answering questions about long-term transformation that "disproportionate" attention will be given to certain elements over others. Writing a history of Christianity, one will give grossly "disproportionate" attention to the figure of Christ—from the perspective of Roman imperial religious life at the time, that is, in which this was a rather minor event. But from the perspective of the world today, it was a little more than that.

5. See Alan Strathern, *Unearthly Powers: Religious and Political Change in World History* (Cambridge: Cambridge University Press, 2019), chapter 1. An appendix to this chapter lists the ten features by which the former may be defined and the fifteen features characterizing the latter.

6. Or, even more loosely still, as Weber's distinction between world-affirming and world-rejecting religions, as discussed by Gorski in chapter 10 of this volume.

7. Marshall Sahlins, *The New Science of the Enchanted Universe: An Anthropology of Most of Humanity* (Princeton, NJ: Princeton University Press, 2022).

manipulation of supernatural power and the metapersons who wield it. Rituals, particularly gift exchanges or tributes effected through sacrifice, are the primary means by which these beings are guided into fruitful communication. There is no sphere of religious values that may be differentiated from the values of society per se; there is no emic concept of the "supernatural," of "religion," or of "a religion": these are the religions with no name.

The transcendentalist religions that emerge into view following the Axial Age are marked by a contrasting self-consciousness and capacity for identity creation. They may be seen as a response to various relativizing forces that have subjected the cognitive predicates, the sensed meaningfulness, and the social utility of immanentism to great strain. These traditions are defined by an entirely new guiding purpose: not the amelioration of the human condition but an escape from it. This is salvation, and in its purest form, it quite transcends the capacity of the human mind to comprehend it. Bellah refers to this clearly in his discussion of Aquinas's conception of God, a "situation where our highest knowing is a kind of unknowing,"[8] but the Buddhist concept of *Nibbāna* was in a sense even more profoundly ineffable. All worldly desiderata are relativized in this vision: power, status, wealth, family, even life itself, a message as vital to the *Vessantara Jātaka* as it is to the Gospels.

Bellah also refers us to the way in which cosmology is now entirely laced through with ethical preoccupations, and the way that ethics is reconfigured into the individualism-universalism of the golden rule. We might put it that the basic laws of the universe or the entire set of metapersons are now conceived in ethical-soteriological terms. The teachings of all transcendentalist traditions were textualized and canonized, and as such, they produced clerical elites, professional exegetes, and athletes of learning, who possessed an inherent moral autonomy that has tremendous implications for their relationship with the state. There is a great deal more that one could say in relation to its defining features (listed in the appendix to this chapter), but for our present purposes, perhaps we need only touch upon one final point insofar as it is echoed in the prologue. Bellah does not present it in this way, but his discussion of Goethe's *Faust* offers an illustration of what has happened, under this new, ethicized conception of the cosmos, to the immanentist notion of ritual exchange with metapersons to

---

8. Robert N. Bellah, "Prologue in Heaven (or Hell) to the Modern Project," 103. Chapter 4 in this volume.

secure worldly flourishing.[9] It has been reduced to a squalid transaction: a Faustian bargain that incurs fatal damage to one's salvific status.

"Nothing is ever lost," insisted Bellah, and similarly, it must be heavily underscored that transcendentalism only ever exists as an amalgam with immanentism (it is most important to appreciate that the reverse is not true).[10] Therefore, across the myriad forms of a tradition such as Christianity, one will find historically contingent processes of both immanentization and transcendentalization at work. Movements intent upon strengthening and clarifying the transcendentalist elements may be referred to as "reformist."[11]

CHRISTIANITY AND THE CRITIQUE OF MONARCHY

In his prologue, Bellah notes that he will not concern himself with the post-Axial traditions in general, but rather the Western tradition, beginning with the Old Testament, proceeding to Greek philosophy and then on to Aquinas and the Middle Ages. The first time that the theme of political critique emerges explicitly in the prologue is in a discussion of Jean Calvin, and his insistence on "the absolute sovereignty of God." Rather than conferring an equivalent status on His earthly representatives, this rather subjected them to the higher principle of His divine law. Thus "magistrates were justified in replacing a monarch who had become tyrannical."[12] Earthly sovereignty is upheld and respected—but has been relativized nonetheless. Calvin stands in here for the emergence of various genres of writing emerging out of the wars of religion in early modern Europe that agonized over and sometimes endorsed the right of religious communities to pass judgment on their rulers. As the narrative turns to the following century, the discussion of Milton allows the British Civil War to come into view as an early manifestation of the forces that might topple monarchism from its normative pedestal. Writing in defense of the Long Parliament and the Puritans and the

---

9. Bellah, "Prologue in Heaven," 123–24.
10. Robert N. Bellah, *Religion in Human Evolution* (Cambridge, MA: Harvard University Press, 2011), 267.
11. Compare with Bellah, "Prologue in Heaven," 108: "We could see Calvin as trying to return to and capture the essential breakthrough of the axial age"; and Taylor, *A Secular Age*, on the long-term impulse towards reform in Christianity.
12. Bellah, "Prologue in Heaven," 109. Compare Robert N. Bellah, "Religious Evolution," *American Sociological Review* 29 (1964): 370: "Where Calvinistic Protestantism was powerful, hereditary aristocracy and kingship were either greatly weakened or abandoned."

execution of Charles I, Milton's arguments can be taken as an ax blow to the neck of sacred kingship. Certainly, the king was humanized: "Milton declared human kings no better than any other humans, subject to the same laws and justly executed if they have committed crimes worthy of that punishment," according to Bellah.[13] Milton was also a voice for a circumscribed form of freedom of speech.

In Bellah's discussion of Kant, God remains aloft as the necessary transcendent principle but has been denuded of all else. If the self was always markedly autonomous in the Christian imagination (insofar as it may be contrasted with the relational self of immanentism as explored by Joel Robbins), now it has a sovereignty that not even God may transgress. Thus is formed a crucial link to the secular discourse of human rights. Bellah puts this most succinctly in his lecture on Paul Tillich: "In one sense the Enlightenment is a development out of Protestantism which had placed responsibility in the hands of every individual believer, with no intervening power before God other than the Bible; in another sense it calls in question everything that preceded it by proclaiming the absolute autonomy of individuals responsible only to their own reason."[14] And, like Calvin and Milton, we are told that Kant had a preference for republics over monarchies.

Finally, Tolstoy appears in this narrative as an heir to this legacy in the post-Kantian form. The fires of rationalism have burned off parts of the Christian heritage, while certain features of transcendentalism at their core are only hardened and pursued to their logical conclusion. Tolstoy is therefore appalled by both the immanentist element of Christianity and the inherently violent qualities of state power. This is a transcendentalist morality in concentrated form: at once filled with universal compassion and yet inhumanly idealistic and wildly undomestic. Indeed, Tolstoy himself makes the connection between the apparently secular, modern forms of political liberation and their religious origins most explicit, referring to socialism, communism, and anarchism as "ideas that are really nothing other than partial manifestations of Christian consciousness in its true sense."[15] He thus echoes the character of Ludovico Settembrini in Mann's *Magic Mountain*, whose words are paraphrased in the epigraph at the start of this chapter. (Later in the novel, Settembrini rather comically refers to Christmas as a celebration "of the birth of individualistic democracy.")

---

13. Bellah, "Prologue in Heaven," 114.
14. Robert N. Bellah, "The Tillich Lecture: Paul Tillich and the Challenge of Modernity," 272. Chapter 8 in this volume.
15. Bellah, "Prologue in Heaven," 140.

What can we make of this story? We might first want to flesh it out a little and begin it in the Axial Age. It has long been understood that the Christian potential for monarchical critique had its origins in the Jewish prophets.[16] Jan Assmann has provided an extremely clear account of the revolutionary nature of the covenental theology of the Hebrew Bible. Divine kingship is explicitly rejected in the figure of the hubristic pharaoh who claimed divinity but exercised tyranny. But in framing a new covenant between a people and God, the authors of Deuteronomy took as their template the insistence on absolute loyalty demanded by another towering emperor, the ruler of Assyria: "The loyalty oath that in 672 BCE King Essarhaddon had his subjects and vassals swear to his designated successor, Ashurbinpal, makes its influence felt right down to the wording of the biblical text."[17] The result was a "direct theocracy" that abolished any mediating institutions of representation. (Thus, both idolatry and kingship are attacked by this anathemization of mediation.)

If the divinized king is an axis that brings together Heaven and earth, what does that signify to a people like the Jews who have become the victims of such kings? Sans land and sans lords, the notion of an axis has been rendered obsolete by a single straight line that connects God to the whole people, thus sanctifying the collective—even yielding, according to Assmann, something like a " 'democratic' conception of the people." Kings, if they are necessary, are to be appointed by the people and considered "a danger rather than a blessing."[18]

But if this locates the story in Judaic and then Christian axiality, the prologue seems to be advancing a more specific argument, connecting attempts to challenge and limit monarchical agency with the more reformist movements within Western Christianity, which is to say those that derive their social energy from an insistent retranscendentalization.[19] One could identify further moments in European and American history that would amplify the series of stepping stones

16. Bellah has explored this line of thought in the Tillich lecture (chapter 8 in this volume), where he is also in dialogue with Hans Joas's work on human rights. Hans Joas, *The Sacredness of the Person: A New Genealogy of Human Rights* (Washington, DC: Georgetown University Press, 2013). See also Bellah, *Religion in Human Evolution*, 301–15, which has much in common with Assmann's account.

17. Jan Assmann, "Pharaonic Kingship and Its Biblical Deconstruction," in *Sacred Kingship in World History: Between Immanence and Transcendence*, ed. A. Azfar Moin and Alan Strathern (New York: Columbia University Press, 2022), 105.

18. Assmann, "Pharaonic Kingship," 106–7.

19. I leave out the Orthodox churches here.

leading from Hosea to the present day. We might alight on the Bohemian Hussites who gathered in the town of Tabor in 1420 and attempted to enact a communalist vision of a society without hierarchy or private property, or the similar vision of the Anabaptist revolutionaries of Münster in 1534.[20] The latter arose out of the German Peasants' War of 1524–1526. The drivers of this sprawling set of diverse revolts are much debated by historians, of course, some of whom underplay the significance of nascent Protestantism.[21] But this was the largest popular uprising in Western Europe before the French Revolution, and the chronological and geographical proximity to the eruption of Luther's teaching is unlikely to be a coincidence.

The peasants' aims, in many cases, may have been conservative, but if we are concerned less with the political vision itself than the implications of the discursive strategies and norms that may be invoked to defend it, we will notice how the Bible is used as the trump card against ecclesiastical, political, and aristocratic forms of privilege, or how the third of the twelve articles famously presented by the confederation of Swabian peasants referred to the fact that "Scripture establishes that we are and will be free."[22] Around 100,000 peasants died, and in the aftermath, more radical arguments circulated underlining "Jesus's critique of earthly power and violence."[23] Half a century later, the French wars of religion spurred both Huguenot and Catholic monarchomachs to theorize the popular right of rebellion against ungodly kings, contributing to the assassinations of both Henry III (1589) and Henry IV (1610). By this time, Calvinist rebels of the lowlands against the Catholic Habsburg monarchy had created a republican confederation appealing to principles of liberty.

---

20. Thomas Müntzer's movement has long been claimed as a precursor of communism; Müntzer was a preacher during the German Peasants' War. The Taborites and the Anabaptists were millenarian movements, which will be explored further later in this chapter.
21. Tom Scott, "The Peasants' War: A Historiographical Review, Part I," *Historical Journal* 22, no. 3 (1979): 693–720; and "The Peasants' War: A Historiographical Review, Part II," *Historical Journal* 22, no. 4 (1979): 953–74. See also Tom Scott, "Peasant Revolts in Early Modern Germany," *Historical Journal* 28, no. 2 (1985): 455ff.
22. Michael G. Baylor, *The Radical Reformation*, Cambridge Texts in the History of Political Thought (Cambridge: Cambridge University Press, 1991), 234; Michael Baylor, "Political Thought in the Age of the Reformation," in *The Oxford Handbook of the History of Political Philosophy*, ed. George Klosko (New York: Oxford University Press, 2011).
23. Sarah Mortimer, *Reformation, Resistance, and Reason of State (1517–1625)* (New York: Oxford University Press, 2021), 70.

We have already touched upon the English revolutionary period, but far more could be said about the political radicalism of the mid-seventeenth century and the association with reformist movements, of the Diggers and Gerrard Winstanley's claim that monarchy was a usurpation of the power of God, or the Levellers and the assertion of popular sovereignty articulated in their *A Remonstrance of a Thousand Citizens* (1646). If these were small minorities, the Parliamentary cause indicated the manner in which the godly self, and the godly community, might now pass judgment on the sacred king.[24] Long ago, Michael Walzer argued that Puritanism was the key to the radicalism of the English Revolution.[25] More recently, Eric Nelson has argued that the development in the mid-seventeenth century of arguments describing monarchy as inherently illegitimate "was provoked by the Protestant reception of a radical tradition of rabbinic Biblical exegesis, which understood the Israelite request for a king in I Samuel as an instance of the sin of idolatry."[26] Thus, it was through an encounter with the Deuteronomic logic laid out by Assmann that some of the fundamental features of the modern world began to take form. When Thomas Hobbes sought to construct a new basis for the absolute authority of the ruler during the chaos of the British Civil War, he was reacting to the consequences. He sought to found sovereignty upon a process of a priori reason, with a transcendentalist rationale quietly left to one side.[27] His own model of unified political and religious authority was surreptitiously symbolized, according to Robert Yelle, by none other than the figure of the Egyptian pharaoh—the archetype of immanentist rulership.[28] The threat of transcendentalism to central authority had been made all too bloodily real.

---

24. Paul Kleber Monod, *The Power of Kings: Monarchy and Religion in Europe, 1589–1715* (New Haven, CT: Yale University Press, 1999).

25. Michael Walzer, *The Revolution of the Saints: A Study in the Origins of Radical Politics* (Cambridge, MA: Harvard University Press, 1965).

26. Eric Nelson, *The Hebrew Republic: Jewish Sources and the Transformation of European Political Thought* (Cambridge, MA: Harvard University Press, 2011), 3.

27. Hobbes decapitated "the covenanting process. . . . The 'mortal God' of sovereignty was no longer bound, in an enforceable way, to his divine superior." Jeffrey Collins, "The Early Modern Foundations of Classic Liberalism," in *The Oxford Handbook of the History of Political Philosophy*, ed. George Klosko (New York: Oxford University Press, 2011), 263.

28. Robert Yelle argues that Hobbes set up a veiled association between his Leviathan (mortal God) and the pharaoh who had persecuted the Jews, for it was the Jews who had driven apart politics and religion. Robert A. Yelle, "Hobbes the Egyptian: The Return to Pharaoh, or the Ancient Roots of Secular Politics," in *Sacred Kingship in World History: Between Immanence and Transcendence*, ed. A. Azfar Moin and Alan Strathern (New York: Columbia University Press, 2022), 223–248.

Yet all of this is liable to arouse fears of a disinterred Whiggism.[29] Historians, naturally averse to the apparently teleological, will itch to supply a thousand qualifications and objections. The Taborites were a radical aberration. The German Peasants' War horrified Luther, who turned against the revolutionary interpretation of his teachings and helped stimulate the princely reformation. The establishment of a kingless commonwealth in England (1649) has been seen as a late and rather unforeseen development arising out of the chaos of civil war rather than the product of ideological transformation.[30] Democracy was generally a term of abuse in the period.[31] In any case, the Interregnum was quickly followed by the Restoration.[32] Protestant thinkers entertained diverse attitudes to the legitimacy of worldly authority; Catholic thinkers also developed theoretical justifications of resistance and tyrannicide. This last point matters less than it might seem, however, for the definition of reformism deployed here—an accentuation of the features that distinguish transcendentalism—may occur in any confession. Yet there is at least an irony, if not a hard contradiction, in the fact that confessionalization theory has long sought to connect Reformation and Counter-Reformation dynamics with enhanced forms of social discipline and centralization available to princes. Thus, a theme of this whole chapter: transcendentalism is both handmaiden and saboteur of state power.

Nevertheless, many objections of this kind lose much significance when placed in a truly long-term perspective. This is not quite the Hegelian story of Luther as the birth of the modern subject: it begins, after all, with Jewish

---

29. Glenn Burgess, "Political Obedience," in *The Oxford Handbook of the Protestant Reformations*, ed. Ulinka Rublack (New York: Oxford University Press, 2016), 98; Johannes Zachhuber, "Martin Luther and Modernity, Capitalism, and Liberalism," in *Oxford Research Encyclopedia of Religion* (New York: Oxford University Press, 2017), retrieved February 16, 2022, from https://oxfordre.com/religion/view/10.1093/acrefore/9780199340378.001.0001/acrefore-9780199340378-e-301. See chapter 7 of this volume on Otto von Gierke (1841–1921), for whom, "the idea of an inherent limitation of the powers of the state and of the duties of all subjects gained ascendancy" with Christianity's supersession of paganism, 238.

30. Jonathon Fitzgibbons, "Rethinking the English Revolution of 1649," *Historical Journal* 60, no. 4 (2017): 889–914, offers a corrective to this perspective. Whether or not republicanism per se was widely embraced, the authority of monarchy could now be seen as subject to the interests of the commonwealth.

31. Cesare Cuttica and Markku Peltonen, eds., *Democracy and Anti-Democracy in Early Modern England 1603–1689* (Leiden, Netherlands: Brill, 2019).

32. Still, if the thesis of the kingless period was met by the antithesis of the Restoration, we do not need to ignore the novelties of the synthesis, eventually expressed in the so-called glorious revolution of 1688. Steve Pincus, *1688: The First Modern Revolution* (New Haven, CT: Yale University Press, 2009), 480–82.

prophetism and encompasses all varieties of Christianity.[33] It is the story of a particular framework of meaning within which politics could be situated—but one that might become evident in action only in minor, discontinuous ways. Even at the level of ideas, we might have to imagine hidden transcripts that are only haphazardly brought to light, or chains of logic that connect actors separated by great expanses of time and space and working for quite different purposes. The muted proposition in the prologue that this frame of meaning began to have more radical consequences as reformist pressures mounted, as the perceived stakes of collective soteriological purity grew, and as arguments emerged that the laity could wrest from the church the authority to arbitrate the righteousness of kingship, is still worth contemplation.

PROBLEMS WITH THE EQUATION BETWEEN TRANSCENDENTALISM AND THE SUBORDINATION OF MONARCHY AT THE GLOBAL LEVEL

As for the crucial question of how this influenced secular theories of resistance and popular sovereignty in the eighteenth century and beyond (the Settembrini thesis), that is a task for others to take up.[34] Instead, we shall consider what happens if we place this story within the truly global scale summoned by the Axial literature. That is to say: What are the connections between transcendentalism more broadly and the authority or critique of monarchy?

The premise here is simply that the other Axial traditions, including Islamic, Buddhist, and Hindu forms, also yielded an equivalent framework of meaning for the political sphere.[35] To merely note a few points of comparability: the Indic traditions carved out a space for a more autonomous selfhood through their soteriological imperatives and introspective practices. These traditions also allowed "religion" to be sheared off from the rest of social life in certain ways. And, to

---

33. Hence Joas's depiction in this volume (chapter 7) of the organic social ethic of medieval Catholicism in which "Jesus Christ as the true king," 231; and see pages 242–48 on Troeltsch.

34. In his Notre Dame lecture (chapter 1 in this volume), Bellah discusses Hans Joas's work, referring to an alliance between nonestablished Christian groups such as the Baptists, Quakers, and Deist thinkers steeped in Enlightenment values, which lay behind the Declaration of Independence. E. P. Thompson, *The Making of the English Working Class* (New York: Vintage, 1966), put forth some classic reflections on the connections between dissent and political radicalism.

35. This point is explored in Bellah, *Religion in Human Evolution*.

follow, in Joel Robbins's elucidation of a Dumontian hierarchy of values, their "world-rejecting" qualities ensured that the field of politics could be subordinated to an ethical-soteriological field of value.[36] That field may be understood as cosmic law (dharma/dhamma) and the ultimate salvific reality (Brahman/Nibbāna) that it revealed. Rulers were also engaged in a dance of negotiation with the literati and virtuosi who gave voice to these higher principles.

In Islamic history, monarchs were clearly constrained by the revealed law in certain ways and the *ulema* and holy men who guarded and interpreted it.[37] According to Ibn Taymīya (1263–1328), "When the ruler is not sure about what to do, he should thus follow the advice of a religious scholar who knows what God and his Prophet would have done in his place."[38] The possible implications of this will be taken up later in this discussion, but before that, we must first register five highly important problems for any simple equation between transcendentalism and autocratic critique.

(1) The Disenchantment of Rulers?

Let us start by examining more closely how rulers are sacralized and distinguish two means by which this may be done. *Divinized kingship* is the mode afforded by immanentism, and it proceeds by regarding individuals as godlike, treating them as if they were gods. It is a less resonant but a more precise term than "divine kingship" because bald claims that kings are divine (as gods are divine) are rather rare in the historical record. One instead finds a multitude of ways of insinuating that the ruler is contiguous to the divine: related to the higher metapersons, identified with them, possessed by them, and so on. Crucially, this contiguity grants rulers the capacity to intercede with these metapersons to achieve success and flourishing in this world. Kings therefore embody, channel, and deploy immanent power.

---

36. See chapter 9 of this volume. What Robbins describes as "the Protestant principle," potentially allowing the individual to critique all social institutions from a transcendent point of view, is common to what I refer to "transcendentalism per se."

37. Chapter 7 in this volume refers to an early paper of Bellah's that emphasizes the egalitarianism-universalism of Islam under the early caliphs.

38. Albrecht Fuess, "A 'Medieval Islamist' Versus an 'Arab Machiavelli'? The Legacy of the Mamluk Scholars Ibn Taymīya (1263–1328) and Ibn Nubāta (1287–1366)," in *Order into Action: How Large-Scale Concepts of World-Order Determine Practices in the Premodern World*, ed. Christoph Mauntel and Klaus Oschema (Turnhout, Belgium: Brepols, 2021), 97–125 on Ibn Taymīya's (1263–1328), *Kitāb al-siyāsa al-sharia*.

It is one of the defining features of transcendentalist traditions that they never begin as cults of state—this is where their enduring power to relativize kingship came from. Yet this very alienation of the religious from the political generated an inevitable attraction between the two spheres. The transcendentalist traditions wielded an autonomous form of social power that ruling elites came to lust after or attempt to appropriate as soon as it was unleashed among their subjects. Therefore, as the transcendentalist traditions that emerged from the Axial Age spread, they did not give rise to some general secularization of rulership, as some theorists such as S. N. Eisenstadt suggested.[39] Instead, they gave rise to a different mode of sacralization: *righteous kingship*. This sacralizes the ruler by affording them a central place in the quest for salvation. Their sacredness lies not in their inherent being, but in their relationship to a transcendent principle. They embody and transmit righteousness. If it is the human mortality of kings that divinized kingship seeks to obscure, it is their human immorality that becomes unspeakable under the dictates of righteous kingship.[40]

But even this distinction is subject to a massive qualification, for this new mode did not displace the old but rather tended to combine with it in myriad ways. This follows, of course, quite naturally, from the more general principle that transcendentalism has found it impossible to exist without drawing upon immanentist forms of behavior and cognition. Examples of how this combination may be manifest have been conveyed elsewhere.[41] It is most fundamental to the Indic traditions, whereby kings may become bodhisattvas, merit-filled *cakravartins*, or incarnations of Vishnu. While the monotheistic traditions tended to provide stronger restrictions on explicit claims in this vein, both Christianity and (especially) Islam created many vehicles by which the divinized qualities of rulers could be acknowledged.[42] Across much of the world, the assemblages of

---

39. Bellah's prologue does not use these terms, but see S. N. Eisenstadt, "Introduction," in *The Origins and Diversity of Axial Civilizations*, ed. S. N. Eisenstadt (Albany: State University of New York Press, 1986), 8: "The King-God, the embodiment of the cosmic and earthly order alike, disappeared, and a secular ruler, in principle accountable to some higher order, appeared." Note also Hans Joas, *The Power of the Sacred: An Alternative to the Narrative of Disenchantment* (New York: Oxford University Press, 2021), 164.
40. The distinction made in this paragraph is fully in keeping with Hans Joas's reminder in *Power of the Sacred* not to confuse two aspects of Max Weber's concept of disenchantment: the demagification of the world, which in this case would imply the loss of divine kingship, and its desacralization, which would imply the erosion of righteous kingship too.
41. Strathern, *Unearthly Powers*, chapter 3.
42. Compare with Joas, *Power of the Sacred*, 262–65.

behavioral codes, ritual forms, discursive regimes, architectural contexts, genres of imagery, and popular practices that sustained these apprehensions of the ruler were not diminished until they met the forces of colonialism. Through the idiom of millennial sainthood, for example, the Mughal emperors stretched the capacity of Islam to concede the divinization of rulers further than it had ever gone before.[43] It is no coincidence that it was the great conquering king Akbar (1556–1605) who represented the apogee of Mughal ruler divinization. Feats of imperial expansion generated reservoirs of charismatic authority that could be used to sustain divinization claims which transgressed preexisting norms. Ambitious and successful rulers were also liable to challenge the autonomy of clerisies (such as the *ulema*) by attempting to unite religious and political authority in their own person.

To be sure, under certain conditions, these combinations could become tension-filled, and not only in ancient Israel or Reformation Europe. Akbar's claims invited internal critics in his own day, while the subsequent reign of Aurangzeb (1658–1707) evidently marked a turn to a more reformist religious policy that retreated from earlier millenarian claims. But most of the time, across the vast bulk of premodern history, the two modes of sacralization fitted smoothly together such that separating them remains a highly etic task with little emic resonance.

(2) The Immanentist Means of Constricting Royal Agency: The Ritualization Trap

A second qualification is that immanentist (or non-Axial) societies also found ways of constraining royal agency. The office of kingship in general is not simply a vehicle of autocracy; it is also a means by which a wider collective tames the will of the ruler. It may also be a means by which society secures for itself access to the fundamental sources of life. Two steps help us make sense of this. First, our European terms for "rulers," "monarchs," or "sovereigns" can serve us poorly in grasping figures who may be placed at the apex of society—both set apart from its main body and capable of representing it—but whose executive agency is secondary to their ritual functions. Second, we may appreciate the importance of these ritual functions if we give due regard to what Sahlins refers to as "determination

43. A. Azfar Moin, *Millennial Sovereign: Sacred Kingship and Sainthood in Islam* (New York: Columbia University Press, 2012).

by the religious basis."[44] In immanentist societies, the most fundamental forces of production are not conceived in mundane terms (as land and labor, say), but are located in the operations of supernatural power, the metapersons who wield such powers, and the ritual mechanisms by which humans may secure access to them. Indeed, it is these metapersons who are the true lords of the land and to whom tribute is due for its use. The social role that is normally rendered as "kingship" in English is an attempt to push solitary human beings into some sort of equivalence to these metapersons in order to deal with them from a position of something greater than abject subjection.

How does one do this to a human being; how does one blur the difference between person and metaperson? It may be assisted by the accumulation of charisma when rulers appear to achieve superhuman feats, as noted previously.[45] But more reliably, it is created by systematically denying the human, mortal, and mundane qualities of rulers through the performance of the office.[46] Rituals of divine propitiation may take up a portion of a ruler's time, but their whole lives may become ritualized to some extent, shielding them from normal interactions and stylizing their behavior in profound ways. This process might also concede some symbolic power to ritual officiants. In Babylonia, priests explicitly "tamed" the king through the explicit humiliations of the New Year festivals, pulling his ear, slapping him, and thus subordinating him to the responsibilities of his role.[47]

The point here is simply that the more this process of sacralization is relied upon—whether to achieve supernatural blessings or to legitimize the officeholder—the more that it can conflict with the capacity of the king to wield actual political power, to interact with subordinates, and to receive information. We should not want to push this point too far. It is perfectly possible for kings who have become subject to extreme forms of divinization to rule, not merely reign. An example from one of my own case studies would be that of King Narai of Ayutthaya (1656–1688), who appeared to his public only once a year and

---

44. Marshall Sahlins, "Kings before Kingship: The Politics of the Enchanted Universe," in *Sacred Kingship in World History: Between Immanence and Transcendence*, ed. A. Azfar Moin and Alan Strathern (New York: Columbia University Press, 2022), 48.

45. This is what I have referred to as "divinization in the heroic mode." Strathern, *Unearthly Powers*, 166–69.

46. This is "divinization in the cosmic mode."

47. Nicole Brisch, "Gods and Kings in Ancient Mesopotamia," in *Sacred Kingship in World History: Between Immanence and Transcendence*, ed. A. Azfar Moin and Alan Strathern (New York: Columbia University Press, 2022), 72–93.

appeared in his palace only in heavily orchestrated ways—but was still endowed with real political capacity.[48] Nevertheless, the immanentist logic of kingship certainly presents a means by which the agency and mobility of the ruler may be countered. David Graeber has referred to this as "adverse sacralization," placing the emphasis on a collective project, society moving against the state. I have referred to it as "the ritualization trap," placing a little more emphasis on strategic moves by officials and nobles beneath the ruler. Consider the way in which the kings of Benin and Kongo, conquering state builders in the fifteenth and sixteenth centuries, had become isolated figures dominated by their chiefs and confined to their palace or dwelling at times in the seventeenth and eighteenth centuries.[49] There is a power tussle here, then, but it is one that is fought through the structures of the immanentist imagination and the way that it makes sacredness a property of space, of being, of action, of performance. And it is precisely because there is indeed an actual and not merely theoretical tension between the ritual and political function of kingship that we find, in diverse cases worldwide, forms of diarchy that split the office into two distinct roles along these lines.[50]

(3) The Monarchy-Clerisy Dialogue—Not Equivalent to a Monarchy-People Dialogue

At the same time, it follows from the account of righteous kingship that there is a great difference between the subordination of rulership to the transcendentalist imperative and its subordination to notions of popular sovereignty. If we take the Theravada Buddhist world, for example, it is indeed important to note that rulers now stood in a relation to the sangha that R. A. L. H. Gunawardena described as "antagonistic symbiosis."[51] Let us return to the situation of King Narai of Ayutthaya, mentioned earlier as subject to a comprehensive project of divinization drawing particularly on Brahmanic traditions and the legacy of the Khmer court

---

48. This is explored and qualified in Strathern, *Unearthly Powers*.

49. See Strathern, *Unearthly Powers*, 186, for this and further examples.

50. It is true that the division of the office of kingship into executive and ceremonial functions appears to have its own logic, which is not reducible to that of immanentism per se (we see it in royal courts shaped by a transcendentalist tradition that is much less intent on royal divinization, as in the sultan-vizier role in Ottomans), nor even reducible to religion (we see it in the monarch–prime minister model).

51. Ranavīra A. L. H. Gunawardena, *Robe and Plough: Monasticism and Economic Interest in Early Medieval Sri Lanka* (Tuscon: University of Arizona Press, 1979), 344.

of Angkor. Formal meetings with Narai involved attendants inching toward his high window, face flat to the ground. But monks, alone of all people, were not to bow to the king (Narai tended to avoid their company as a result). Thus, this extraordinary edifice of royal divinization was contained within a larger frame which exalted the *sāsana* and the sangha still higher.[52] These tensions were not merely symbolic or ceremonial, for Narai had evidently waged a simmering campaign against recalcitrant elements of the monkhood throughout his reign and had even survived an assassination attempt issuing from that quarter. These signals of how "antagonistic" the symbiosis between ruler and clerisy could become were partly what encouraged the French court of Louis XIV in its conviction that Narai was becoming detached from the religion of his forefathers and could be won over for Catholicism. Hence two large and expensive embassies were dispatched to Siam in the 1680s to effect this glorious outcome. They were gravely mistaken. Narai had no such inclinations and understood all too well that his legitimacy depended on the support of the sangha. Even the mere rumor of his conversion when he was consigned to his sickbed triggered a coup in which the sangha was used to rouse the population of Lopburi and Ayutthaya. Missionaries and converts were persecuted, an opportunistic French colonial force was booted out, and a trenchant Theravada Buddhism was restored to the throne (never to depart it).[53] Some European commentators described this as the other great revolution of 1688—the British and the Thai versions both figuring the downfall of monarchies with French and Catholic leanings.

This was an intriguing event for the way in which popular participation and religious mobilization were involved in a decisive political eruption and may even signal the virtues in deploying "early modernity" as a global rather than merely European conjuncture. (Ayutthaya was a large, cosmopolitan city thriving on the seaborne commerce that had transformed much of maritime Southeast Asia.) It underlines the point that the monarchy was in some sense subject to a degree of moral arbitration by the sangha. But the Thai 1688 event was not in fact a revolution in any sense of the term with real sociological bite. Its aims were restorative: to preserve the Buddhist monarchy from European interference

---

52. Alan Strathern, "Sacred Kingship under King Narai of Ayutthaya: Divinisation and Righteousness," *Journal of Siam Society* 107, no. 1 (2019): 49–77.

53. Alan Strathern, "Thailand's First Revolution? The Role of Religious Mobilization and 'the People' in the Ayutthaya Rebellion of 1688," *Modern Asian Studies* 56, no. 4 (2022): 1295–1328.

rather than to introduce a new social distribution of power. In the following centuries, Thailand was one of the few societies in the world to preserve a semblance of autonomy, while most of the planet succumbed to various iterations of European imperial intrusion. It is also one of the few places in the world today where one can receive an inkling of what sacred kingship must have looked like before the forces of modernity ushered it from the stage.

(4) Transcendentalism: A Powerful Legitimator of Imperial Authority

A fourth qualification reminds us how much transcendentalist traditions came to buttress rulers' authority. How do we deal with the paradoxes of the transcendentalist legacy? Antipolitical or apolitical teachings come to saturate the political field; traditions of radical nonviolence are drafted in to endorse some of the most violent projects of imperial expansion. One option is to see these paradoxes as a consequence of the impossibility of transcendentalism to thrive on its own terms. Just as transcendentalism can exist only as an amalgam with immanentism in order to function as a living religious tradition, so these traditions had to form alliances with the state, with the family, with the market, in order to survive as viable social institutions. In short, transcendentalism must forfeit some part of itself as it makes peace with aristocratic cultures of violence-and-honor, nationalist codes of blood and soil, patriarchal norms of hierarchical kinship, bourgeois ethics of material comfort.[54] Transcendentalist norms are tamed as they are placed in uneasy dialogue with other realms of value. Hans Joas, in chapter 7 in this volume, has articulated this process in a highly sympathetic manner through the concept of the organic social ethic as applied to medieval Catholicism. By this means, "each individual is not morally overwhelmed by the ethos of love" but is instead held in place by a divinely ordained system of inequality.[55]

However, a second option is to see any apparently perverse outcomes as deriving more directly from some of the definitive features of transcendentalism itself.

---

54. Bellah's Notre Dame lecture (chapter 1 in this volume) seems to hold to something like this view in reflecting on a failure of institutionalization: "Rather, the very traditions that proclaimed the sacredness of the person lived side by side with and often validated harsh practices of inequality and violence.... The ideas were not meaningless and gave rise to prophetic criticism and social protests, but never were institutionalized even in a single society," 32.

55. The transcendent vision still retains a superordinate value in this type of organic social ethic, in Joas's account (chapter 7 in this volume). The resulting tensions explored in Joas's chapter bear comparison with the discussion in Strathern, *Unearthly Powers*, chapter 2.

From this perspective, for example, imperial ideologies do not simply emerge as corruptions of dominant transcendentalist traditions but as more natural consequences of them. There is no doubt that transcendentalisms lend themselves to strong notions of "civilizing mission." When set against the utopic state of salvation, any mundane suffering necessitated by the quest for its attainment must pale in significance.[56] (Even less utopic forms of progressivism such as liberalism may show this tendency, after all.) All such traditions are defined by their assertion of an unrivalled Truth over the dangerous illusions of less enlightened peoples. It was the monotheistic traditions, following the Mosaic distinction that set apart the Jewish people as the special beloved of God, that formulated hard-edged, exclusivist religious identities and generated the most explicit discourses of just war. But even Buddhist societies could, under certain circumstances, castigate the adherents of rival traditions as heretics or demonic threats.[57] I have suggested that the Janus-faced qualities of transcendentalist traditions served two conflicting imperatives of imperial expansion: on the one hand, they mobilized men to moralized war, and on the other hand, they helped to generate expansive zones of internal peace through their capacity to problematize violence, their association with literacy and education and legalism, their provision of nonmilitary forms of high-status masculinity, and their machinery of self-discipline. These all chimed with the reservation of the legitimate use of violence for an imperial elite.[58] There is, at a more elemental level, a deep affinity between the universal claims of the Axial traditions, their portability, their technologies of expansion, their capacity to overwrite local moral and religious orders, and the claim of imperial projects to transcend the political and cultural particularities of their constituent parts.[59]

The same might be said about the relationship between transcendentalism and monarchy in general. The social power of transcendentalism, its capacity to define and structure social groups, turned out to be formidable. Monarchs frequently took the lead in converting to these traditions, and by no means were

---

56. This theme is discussed in S. N. Eisenstadt, *Fundamentalism, Sectarianism, and Revolution: The Jacobin Dimension of Modernity*, Cambridge Cultural Social Studies (Cambridge: Cambridge University Press, 2000); for instance, at 29.

57. Strathern, *Unearthly Powers*.

58. Alan Strathern, "Religion and War: A Synthesis," *History and Anthropology* 34, no. 1 (2023): 145–74.

59. Compare with Joas, *Power of the Sacred*, 189. Jane Schneider [orig. 1991], "Spirits and the Spirit of Capitalism," in *Religious Orthodoxy and Popular Faith in European Society*, ed. Ellen Badone (Princeton, NJ: Princeton University Press, 2021), 24–54, makes an intriguing argument on the affinity between transcendentalism and the market, and indeed ecological exploitation.

they damaging the bases of their authority in the process.[60] In Anglo-Saxon England, no less than in the nineteenth-century Pacific, ambitious chiefs perceived Christianity as a glue of monarchical authority rather than its solvent. Did Christianity potentially redirect subject loyalties to the Lord above—or did it represent a remarkable model of lordship in general? When Japan reunified at the end of the sixteenth century after a long period of internecine strife, its new rulers were given to suspect the former. But those warlords who had converted in previous decades had rather attended to the latter. Jesuit missionaries had presented Christianity as modeling an idealized liege-vassal relationship based on total obedience—thereby recalling the origins of covenental theology in the loyalty oath to King Essarhaddon 2,000 years earlier.[61]

(5) Traditions of Broader Political Participation May Be Found in Many Diverse Settings

A fifth qualification is to remind ourselves that reformed transcendentalism is not a necessary precondition for political visions that deny or tame kingship. Monarchy is not some natural property of human social life in general that requires a one-off historical breakthrough to dislodge it.[62] There was a broad array of political systems in the premodern world that asserted more egalitarian principles. The republicanism of the Greco-Roman world is just one example, although I shall suggest that its Axial qualities were vital to its unusually enduring authority.[63] Furthermore, any such focus on ideology per se must be brought into dialogue with the development of more material factors and the dynamics of state formation.

Egalitarian societies are abundantly found in the historical and anthropological record. Of course, it is almost tautological to note that many small-scale societies, unencumbered by much of the apparatus of statehood, had no need for monarchy.[64] Yet the seriousness and consciousness with which these

---

60. Strathern, *Unearthly Powers*, chapters 4–6.
61. Alan Strathern, *Converting Kings: Kongo, Japan, Thailand, Hawaii and Global Patterns, 1450–1850* (Cambridge: Cambridge University Press, 2024).
62. Strathern, *Unearthly Powers*, 122, therefore notes that monarchy is an institution "fashioned through generations of symbolic labour" contra some antilegitimation theory arguments.
63. Greek philosophy may be understood as a member of the Axial family without representing a form of transcendentalism.
64. Indeed, it may be more striking that some such stateless societies have indeed generated forms of chiefhood and sacral kingship as ritual devices denuded of political power. See Sahlins, "Kings before Kingship," 31–52.

societies cultivated rough equality as a value must be recognized.[65] Pierre Clastres's *Society against the State* reminds us of this important expression of human creativity. More relevant, however, is that even as they did develop certain typical elements of statehood, some societies retained institutional means of either refusing monarchy or, more typically, preserving some counterweight to it. For example, the Tlaxcalans, who as allies to the Spanish played such an important role in the conquest of the Aztecs, were governed by a council of officeholders with a meritocratic element.[66] The point here is that such cases can be found in a variety of times and places rather than requiring legitimization from any one type of intellectual lineage. The political scientist David Stasavage recently deployed a perhaps overgenerous definition of "early democracy" including systems where councils and assemblies constrained the actions of rulers. He pointed out that in this form, it was more widespread across the world than is typically appreciated.[67]

However, Stasavage proposes that with the development of larger political orders, the growing capacity of states to monitor production (through intensive agriculture, literacy, and bureaucratic technologies), and the decline of exit options for potential subjects, ruling elites could dispense with these vehicles of popular consent.[68] We might conjecture that a Darwinian dynamic was at work here too, such that states that did not adopt forms of military fiscalism—and perhaps the strategic advantages of more autocratic decision-making—were liable to be devoured by those that had.[69] And as states grow in terms

---

65. See Joel Robbins, "Equality as a Value: Ideology in Dumont, Melanesia and the West," *Social Analysis* 36 (1994): 2–70, which therefore notes that it is reductive to see these societies as merely lacking the resources to achieve sociopolitical hierarchy.

66. Lane F. Fargher, Richard E. Blanton, and Verenice Y. Heredia Espinoza, "Egalitarian Ideology and Political Power in Prehispanic Central Mexico: The Case of Tlaxcallan," *Latin American Antiquity* 21, no. 3 (2010): 227–51. The case is discussed by both David Graeber and David Wengrow, *The Dawn of Everything: A New History of Humanity* (New York: Farrar, Straus and Giroux, 2021), and David Stasavage, *The Decline and Rise of Democracy: A Global History from Antiquity to Today* (Princeton, NJ: Princeton University Press, 2020).

67. Stasavage, *Decline and Rise*. This perhaps conflates too many disparate forms, including those that resist monarchy, as is the case with the Tlaxcala or in ancient Athens, and those that keep it in check in ways large or small (including the ritualization trap discussed previously).

68. Stasavage, *Decline and Rise*, 6–7; Graeber and Wengrow, *Dawn of Everything*; see also David Graeber and Marshall Sahlins, *On Kings* (Chicago: University of Chicago Press, 2017), which chimes with Stasavage's emphasis on the broad distribution of more egalitarian political forms but diverges from it insofar as their whole approach is to minimize any such loosely evolutionary model shaped by material dynamics.

of the scale and heterogeneity of their populations, the practical obstacles to incorporating popular representation surely increase. Therefore, while quasi-democratic systems do indeed have a much wider distribution across global premodern history, as states become larger in terms of both territorial extent and political capacity, the window of opportunity for nonautocratic systems seems to dwindle.

What is novel about *modern* democracy (i.e., from the eighteenth century), then, is that it emerged in expansive states that had developed such technologies of coercion and extraction—indeed, that it emerged when these technologies were vastly more developed than they had ever been before. Stasavage's argument as to why this developed in Western Europe and its offshoot in the United States is an ironic one: following the fall of Rome, these technologies of state were slow to develop in Europe, and thus they retained some archaic principles of popular participation, through assemblies and parliaments and ancient privileges, which laid out an enduring framework for subsequent innovations. (This is reminiscent of Ian Morris's historical principle of "the advantages of backwardness.")[70]

When Stasavage describes European statehood as slow to develop, he means in comparison with Asia, his main comparators being Chinese and Islamic empires. This contention can be illuminated by appealing to the geopolitical logic of the "exposed zone" of Eurasia, its lateral axis from the plains of Hungary to the Sea of Japan, as outlined by Victor Lieberman.[71] For various topological and climatological reasons, this area formed a great zone of communicability and circulation, which yielded civilizational precocity (this is the zone in which three of the four Axial breakthroughs emerged too) and would come to favor the rise and fall

---

69. This would allow us to make sense of the rise of the more autocratic monarchies across Eurasia in the last 2,000 years, for it is a weakness of Graeber and Wengrow, *Dawn of Everything*, that they do not properly account for the seemingly inexorable rise of monarchy across the Old World (although they do raise the question; see 443), which is what Stasavage is intent on explaining. Equally, while they celebrate the diversity of indigenous American political forms, it is astonishing how vulnerable these proved to be when exposed to Eurasian political systems (and not just diseases).

70. Ian Morris, *Why the West Rules—for Now: The Patterns of History, and What They Reveal about the Future* (New York: Picador, 2010). In Morris's case, this refers to the way in which relatively disadvantaged societies may leapfrog to the front of the pack by borrowing functional innovations from stronger neighbors without inheriting path dependencies that prove to be a hindrance in the coming conjuncture.

71. Victor Lieberman, *Strange Parallels: Southeast Asia in Global Context, c. 800–1830, Vol. 2, Mainland Mirrors: Europe, Japan, China, South Asia, and the Islands* (Cambridge: Cambridge University Press, 2009).

of huge territorial empires.[72] Thus, by 1600, a vast swath of the Old World was in the hands of just four ruling families: the Ottomans, Safavids, Mughals, and Ming. State-building at this scale was much harder to achieve in the "protected zone" of Europe, mainland Southeast Asia, and Japan. The point is that rapidly expanding imperial orders such as we find in the exposed zone are more likely to experiment with novel taxation-governance systems that dispense with the traditional rights of communities and local elites.[73] This may help to explain why Europe, with its squabbling medium-sized states, was allowed to maintain certain traditions of limited kingship. Not only was there greater long-term continuity here in aristocratic and dynastic terms, but also at the level of broader political-territorial communities.[74]

Stasavage is too quick to devalue the role played by ideas. Chapter 9 in this volume, by Robbins, reminds us that once formed, ideological systems may have transformative power in contexts that are utterly alien to the sociopolitical or material conditions that first created them.[75] Nevertheless, the opposite is also true: in other cases, ideas may ignite only in propitious material contexts.[76] And his work raises the possibility that what look like modern ideological critiques of modernity might owe something to archaic instincts that are much more widely found. To return to the British Civil War, a somewhat inchoate sense of old English traditions of political representation played a significant part in generating opposition to monarchical intransigence.[77] Turning our sights to more global horizons, elsewhere we also may be able to identify modern revolutionary moments that draw strength from persisting local egalitarianisms, from rebels in the Haitian revolution who may have been drawing on Central African traditions of tamed kingship, to Rammohan Roy's (1772/1833), arguments for reform

---

72. Ancient Greece lay outside that zone but was in dialogue with it.

73. See Stasavage, *Decline and Rise*, 16, 48, on the relationship between swift expansion and the erosion of early democracy.

74. See Mortimer, *Reform, Resistance, and Reason of State*, 271 (and also 133), on the way that European early modern political thought tended to conceive of "the common good of a specific and identifiable people." Clearly this was not only a result of the geopolitical situation, however, for mainland Southeast Asia also exhibited relatively late development of state technology in protected-zone, medium-size states but had few equivalent traditions to European assemblies. Thanks to Victor Lieberman for this point. (Indeed, this alerts us to the fact that while Stasavage's analysis involves serious comparison with China and West Asian Islam, a more comprehensive remit would cause problems.)

75. See chapter 9 of this volume. Also see chapter 3, by Rosa, on the material versus ideological.

76. Stasavage, *Decline and Rise*, 20, 122–23.

77. Jonathan Fitzgibbons, "Rethinking the English Revolution of 1649," *Historical Journal* 60, no. 4 (2017): 910.

of colonial governance in India that referred to local "forms of community self-government."[78]

But in the latter cases, the fact that such claims could be made within a larger framework of liberal discourse was surely vital. And in the case of the British Civil War, the fact that opposition to the king could find expression in more systematic critiques of kingship per se surely owes much to two Axial lineages of great coherence and power, which managed to subordinate monarchies to higher values: the role of Judeo-Christian prophetism now reconfigured by Protestantism, and the language of liberty and natural law inherited from the Greco-Roman world.[79] Classical Republicanism was not a random survival of archaic egalitarian instincts into much later periods of Western history; its authority derived from its place in a much larger field of philosophical achievement, which the subsequent supersession of Christianity and monarchism could never erase. Both the Judaic and classical lineages arose in the form of a conscious rejection of monarchical power at a time when quite powerful technologies of state were available. Indeed, the Axial literature often represents them as a moral reaction to the rise of the monarchical state and the legitimacy crisis that it precipitated, creating an ideological vision in which its claims and those of its divinized rulers found their limits.[80]

---

78. Such forms include the *panchayat* system; see Milinda Banerjee, " 'All This Is Indeed Brahman': Rammohun Roy and a 'Global' History of the Rights-Bearing Self," *Asian Review of World Histories* 3, no. 1 (2015): 99; John Thornton, "I Am the Subject of the King of Kongo: African Political Ideology and the Haitian Revolution," *Journal of World History* 4 (Fall 1993), examines the clues for the Haitian rebels. Graeber and Wengrow, *Dawn of Everything*, 27–77, present an extreme version of this argument, asserting that new conceptions of political liberty developing during the Enlightenment by thinkers such as Jean-Jacques Rousseau were primarily the result of exposure to arguments made by North American Indigenous peoples demonstrating the superiority of their ways of life. This claim would be convincing only if it came in the context of a much more thoroughgoing analysis of the development of the "Indigenous critique" trope and the myriad other streams in the confluence of thought that allowed Western thinkers to relativize their sociopolitical inheritance.

79. Enduring principles of political representation were frequently conceived in terms of a discourse of natural law that had its ultimate origin in classical philosophy. Mortimer, *Reform, Resistance, and Reason of State*, brings out strongly how often intimations of the importance of "the people" may be found in sixteenth- and early-seventeenth-century political thought. Contra moves to downplay the role of ideology in the revolution, see Quentin Skinner, "Rethinking Political Liberty," *History Workshop Journal* 61, no. 1 (Spring 2006): 158, on an "essentially Roman way of thinking about liberty."

80. S. N. Eisenstadt, ed., *The Origins and Diversity of Axial Age Civilizations* (Albany: State University of New York Press, 1986); David Graeber, *Debt: The First 5,000 Years* (New York: Melville House, 2011); Joas, *Power of the Sacred*, 183–84. See also Robert N. Bellah, "The Heritage of the Axial Age: Resource or Burden?," in *The Axial Age and Its Consequences*, ed. Robert N. Bellah and Hans Joas (Cambridge, MA: Harvard University Press, 2012), 451, on Jürgen Habermas and the "legitimation crisis."

ASIAN TRANSCENDENTALISMS AND
THE BUDS OF RADICAL POLITICS

But is it axiality in general, or the Judeo-Christian tradition per se, that provided the key potential for systematic antiautocratic thought? Bellah's prologue confines itself to the Western tradition, but his career, and the work of Axial thinkers in general, are marked by the urge to provincialize the West. This desire to take other traditions as seriously as those that emanated from Athens and Jerusalem should resonate among us now more than ever. If Bellah's book was going to explain the unusual path taken by the West toward modernity, it could hardly do so while ignoring the great outpouring of work debating the causes of the economic Great Divergence, and this has enshrined the principle that analyses need to be rigorously comparative in order to convince.[81] It no longer suffices to contrast the ascending path toward Western modernity against a static, traditional world beneath it. Instead, investigations of the transformations working through Asian societies in particular are called for, especially in the "early modern" period before industry-fueled European imperialism suddenly cut these other stories short.[82] Presumably, then, Bellah would have had to give some attention to these other "metanarratives" of intellectual development to distinguish what the key variables were in propelling Europe along its particular trajectory.

If Christianity contained within it some kind of tiny embryo of the modern, the inevitable question, from the perspective of Axial theory, is whether the other great post-Axial traditions were also pregnant with this possibility. Were they a fertile field from which the sprouts of "modern" principles (e.g., ideas around the individual self, political liberation) may have germinated if conditions had been somewhat different, especially if the forms of Western imperialism had not been unrolled across the global landscape?[83] Where, then, should we

---

81. This is a huge body of literature, but it obviously includes Kenneth Pomeranz, *The Great Divergence: China, Europe, and the Making of the Modern World Economy* (Princeton, NJ: Princeton University Press, 2000).

82. On global early modernity, see Alan Strathern, "Global Early Modernity and the Problem of What Came Before," *Past & Present* 238, suppl_13 (November 2018): 317–34.

83. Framing the question in this way may seem open to the charge of imposing "Western" concepts on other traditions (see Sebastian Conrad, "Enlightenment in Global History: A Historiographical Critique," *American Historical Review* 117, no. 4 (October 2012): 107–8), but this critique is open to a different charge of Eurocentrism—that of assuming an inherent incapacity of precolonial tradition to relate to contemporary progressive morality. As is so often the case, political instincts are a poor guide here.

place the accent in explaining the cultural revolutions that took hold before and during the Industrial Revolution?[84] On axiality? On monotheism? On Christianity? On broader, more conjunctural features of the early modern world? Or on industry-fueled economic growth itself? How teleological do we want to be?

In the premodern world, the great majority of movements that come close to producing revolutionary political visions were associated with millenarianism. This rendered the transcendent objective imminently immanent and thereby greatly enhanced the social power available to religious leaders. Bellah refers us to Tillich's insight into the way in which the Jewish prophets, cast out from a sacred landscape, found succor in a sacred time, allowing a novel focus on the "*the new in history*."[85] However, movements that are predicated on some approaching great transformation of the structure of reality are far more widespread in the historical and anthropological record. Indeed, partly in order to comprehend the full range of this phenomenon, I have suggested that a more general term, "supernatural utopianism," is preferable to "millenarianism."[86] This phenomenon can be found in all the transcendentalist traditions.[87] It is distinguished from secular utopianism insofar as the transition to the final state is conceived in supernatural terms.[88] However, in many cases, it spurred communities to emulate the heavenly order on earth through the profound reorganizations of worldly sociopolitical life too, as noted for the Taborites and Anabaptists of Münster.

The leagues assembled in the name of Jōdo Shinshū or True Pure Land Buddhism—especially the single-minded leagues or *Ikkō ikki*—in fourteenth-to-sixteenth-century Japan represent an intriguing non-Abrahamic example to consider. The galvanizing role of millenarian elements is more questionable here, and the literature is ambiguous about how much they may be associated with radical experiments in terms of daily life.[89] But as horizontal bandings of

---

84. Bellah raises such questions in his Notre Dame lecture.
85. Bellah, "The Tillich Lecture," 270. As quoted from Paul Tillich, *The Socialist Decision*, emphasis as per Tillich's original.
86. Strathern, *Unearthly Powers*, 83, 148–50.
87. They are notably present on the frontiers where an expanding transcendentalism such as Christianity meets the immanentist imagination. However, it is possible that versions of it may be found in entirely immanentist settings too. This complex matter is discussed in Strathern, *Unearthly Powers*, 148–50.
88. Hence my definition of supernatural utopianism: "visions of an imminent transformation of society through the agency of supernatural forces and beings such that it is lifted into a permanent, idealised, utopic state." See Strathern, *Unearthly Powers*, 327.
89. Carol Richmond Tsang, *War and Faith: Ikkō Ikki in Late Muromachi Japan* (Cambridge, MA: Harvard University Asia Center, 2007).

peasants, farmers, and others militating against the claims of temple complexes, warlords, and aristocrats, these leagues represented an entirely novel vision of societal order and a disturbing challenge to hierarchy of all kinds.[90] It is surely telling that their theology probably comes as close to monotheism as Buddhism has ever produced. In the later sixteenth century, aghast Japanese onlookers lumped the followers of the Jōdo Shinshū together with the Christian converts in terms of their subversive potential, their subordination of all earthly loyalties to an iron obedience to God/Amida. The Jesuit Alessandro Valignano (1539–1606), meanwhile, compared their radical lay energies and simplified soteriology to Lutheranism, as Max Weber, and Bellah himself in his *Tokugawa Religion*, would do.[91]

Another pertinent case study would be the early Sikh movement of Guru Nanak, which drew on potentials in the Hindu and Muslim traditions of the Punjab to found a new form of collective life at Kartarpur, characterized by certain features of egalitarianism, especially the rejection of caste.[92] The collective was understood as a vehicle for God's divine plan. A third case study would be the Taiping rebellion of mid-nineteenth-century China, in which East Asian transcendentalism merged with the teachings of Christian missionaries to produce a movement that tore through the land, plunging it into a civil war that killed staggering numbers of people. Their leader, Hong Xiuquan, founded a Heavenly Capital at Nanjing in the 1850s, which enacted a "peasant egalitarianism"

---

90. Pierre F. Souyri, *The World Turned Upside Down: Medieval Japanese Society* (New York: Columbia University Press, 2001), 193–95.

91. Galen Amstutz, "Materiality and Spiritual Economies in Premodern Japanese Buddhism: A Problem in Historical Change," *Journal of Religion in Japan* 1, no. 2 (2012): 142–67; Robert N. Bellah, *Tokugawa Religion* (Berkeley: University of California Press, 1957). Galen Amstutz criticizes the shortcomings of earlier comparisons while ultimately endorsing the comparability of Jōdo Shinshū with certain Protestant dynamics—most notably, for our purposes, in its assault on immanentism (or "animism/monism"), association with literacy, and strengths among urban communities of merchants and artisans. Also see Philippe Buc, "Sectarian Violence in Premodern Japan and Europe: Jōdo Shinshū and the Anabaptists," *Viator* 50, no. 2 (2019): 351–86, comparing the way in which both Jōdo Shinshū and Anabaptists moved, in a contextually determined way, between expressions of otherworldly quietism and worldly violence.

92. Pashaura Singh, "An Overview of Sikh History," in *The Oxford Handbook of Sikh Studies*, ed. Pashaura Singh and Louis E. Fenech (New York: Oxford University Press, 2014), https://doi.org/10.1093/oxfordhb/9780199699308.013.028. Compare, too, the revolt of the Satnamis against Aurangzeb in 1672, which brought together oppressed groups in a simplified puritanical monotheism (inspired by Kabir). They disdained caste and kings alike. See Irfan Habib, *Essays in Indian History: Towards a Marxist Perception* (London: Anthem, 2002); Irfan Habib, *The Economic History of Medieval India: A Survey* (London, Anthem, 2004), 244–46.

in which land was held in common and various social vices were banned.[93] In its comprehensive assault on Confucian hierarchy, its prophecies of sudden transformation, and its experiments in communalism, the Taiping Rebellion obviously prefigures the communist revolutions of the following century, a point to which we shall return shortly.[94]

In Asian early modernity too, then, there are signs that transcendentalist supernatural utopianism might generate radical politics. However, the revolutionary potential of supernatural utopianism was typically ephemeral, for two reasons. First, the sheer imminence of the salvific objective may have temporarily enhanced social power, but at the expense of conceptual control, for its failure to arrive would always prove a liability.[95] Second, as such movements mature, they tend to reproduce sacred kingship and the hierarchies that they had once risen up against. This was certainly what happened to the *Ikko ikki*, the Sikhs, and the Taiping rebels in various ways. (In a sense, communism would be subject to the same two vulnerabilities.) And, finally, we may speculate that the socioeconomic conditions were simply not yet propitious.

As we take the story into the modern period proper, once again the purpose of this chapter must be largely confined to raising questions for others to consider. The most difficult question raised by the Axial perspective is whether the Settembrini thesis has any Asian analogs. That is, do we find any movements toward conceptions of individual autonomy and political liberty arising out of Buddhism, Hinduism, and Islam?[96] There are some tantalizing prospects for research exploring intellectual transformations that occurred just before substantial European influence, as in the case of the "Ottoman Enlightenment," which may help to provide an answer.[97] Baki Tezcan recently argued that the

---

93. Thomas David DuBois, *Religion and the Making of Modern East Asia* (Cambridge: Cambridge University Press, 2011), 139–41.

94. Of course, Chinese Communist Party (CCP) ideologues have been enamored of this interpretation. Carl S. Kilcourse, Taiping Theology: The Localization of Christianity in China, 1843–64 (New York: Palgrave Macmillan, 2016), argues that in certain ways, the Taiping rebellion represented an attempt at an idealized Confucian vision of compassionate order.

95. See Strathern, *Unearthly Powers*, 253, on conceptual control, and Patrice Ladwig and James Mark Shields, "Introduction," *Politics, Religion & Ideology* 15, no. 2 (2014): 192, on charisma.

96. Bellah's discussion of Hans Joas's *The Sacredness of the Person* in "The Tillich Lecture" indicates that the fundamental ideological roots of human rights may indeed be found in all the Axial traditions, but other forces outside the history of ideas need to be accounted for to explain their institutional realization.

97. Marinos Sariyannis, "The Limits of Going Global: The Case of 'Ottoman Enlightenment(s),'" *History Compass* (2020), https://doi.org/10.1111/hic3.12623.

Kadizadeli movement in the mid-seventeenth-century Ottoman Empire may be seen as a kind of reformation, bringing to the fore an ascetic, legalistic, and epistemologically egalitarian idiom that helped to bring ruler and ruled together.[98] However, it must be noted that this was very far from a profound challenge to kingship altogether. Evidently, we are now encroaching on the field of "multiple modernities" and "multiple secularities."[99]

No less important is the question of how intellectual traditions originally issuing from the West, such as Enlightenment liberalism, were interpreted and deployed elsewhere. The new global intellectual history has underlined how quickly this happened and how actively non-Europeans participated in the development and reformulation of these traditions.[100] Thus the question of ideological origins is displaced from view as our attention is guided toward global networks of a much more diverse cast of characters, often using the evolving traditions to challenge Western forms of hegemony. Therefore, much work in this vein, such as David Armitage and Sanjay Subrahmanyam's edited volume, *The Age of Revolutions in Global Context*, has tended to focus on the question of non-Western agency rather than bringing to the surface the role played by *pre-existing*, non-Western intellectual traditions in driving revolutionary visions.[101]

---

98. Baki Tezcan, "Empires and Gods—Religions' Role in Imperial Histories," in *Empires and Gods: The Role of Religions in Imperial History*, ed. Jörg Rüpke, Michal Biran, and Yuri Pines (Berlin: De Gruyter, 2024); and also see Marinos Sariyannis, "The Kadizadeli Movement as a Social and Political Phenomenon: The Rise of a 'Mercantile Ethic?,'" in *Political Initiatives from the Bottom-up in the Ottoman Empire*, ed. Antonis Anastasopoulos (Rethymno, Greece: Crete University Press, 2012), 263–89. Baki Tezcan, *The Second Ottoman Empire: Political and Social Transformation in the Early Modern World* (New York: Cambridge University Press, 2010), refers to this period more generally as one in which the power of the imperial office was limited by a broader distribution of power.

99. S. N. Eisenstadt, "Multiple Modernities," *Daedalus* 129, no. 1 (Winter 2000): 1–29. Also note *Multiple Secularities—Beyond the West, Beyond Modernities*, a research project at the University of Leipzig, https://www.multiple-secularities.de/.

100. Conrad, "Enlightenment in Global History," 999–1027.

101. David Armitage and Sanjay Subrahmanyam, "Introduction: The Age of Revolutions, c. 1760–1840: Global Causation, Connection, and Comparison," in *The Age of Revolutions in Global Context, c. 1760–1840*, ed. David Armitage and Sanjay Subrahmanyam (Basingstoke, UK: Palgrave Macmillan, 2010), xvii, xxix. Sujit Sivasundaram, *Waves Across the South: A New History of Revolution and Empire* (Chicago: University of Chicago Press, 2020), sets out to underline non-European forms of resistance and revolution against European imperialism, but it works with a concept of revolution that is so capacious as to allow the formation of monarchy itself, as in the Pacific, to count as such. Priyamvada Gopal, *Insurgent Empire: Anticolonialism and the Making of British Dissent* (London: Verso, 2019), 18, rejects the "well-worn Caliban model" by which the British furnished the colonized with the intellectual tools that they could then use to escape their subjection. Again, however, the focus seems to be on non-European agency and creative engagement rather than on longer-term, non-European ideological origins.

We do find a pertinent suggestion in Armitage and Subrahmanyam's volume where Chris Bayly notes that ideas of human rights diffusing out of the European-Atlantic zone " 'bonded' with ideas in societies outside Europe with which they had an elective affinity."[102] Since the examples of very broadly revolutionary movements "infused with a sense of customary rights or of spiritual equality" given here are Sikh, neo-Buddhist, or Chinese millenarian, and perhaps Wahabism and Jihadism, the implication would be that reformist and millenarian forms of transcendentalism provided a kind of bridge to the predicates of Enlightenment liberalism. Elsewhere, Bayly referred to the influence on Indian liberals such as Rammohan Roy of *akhlaq*, "a kind of Indo-Islamic civic republicanism, which often reflected Sufi beliefs," valuing "the moral autonomy of the householder in a virtuous polity."[103] Indeed, Milinda Banerjee argued that Rammohan's ideas of equality and liberty, and the universalizing framework to which he appealed, were founded in a vision of the self with Vedic (and Perso-Islamic) foundations. We could infer that Indic transcendentalisms had already fashioned a discourse of "selves" all ultimately equal in their capacity to attain salvation, which might act as the foundation for more political claims.[104] Bayly goes on to mention various forms of Muslim rationalism, neo-Vedantism, and Unitarianism, among a number of "elective affinities between Indian and Western ideas at a subcanonical level."[105] For Islam, figures such as Syed Ahmad Khan, and modernist thinkers such as Muhammad Abduh, would heave into view.[106]

Note that adopting a broader perspective that foregrounds Asia creates problems with identifying religious toleration as an element of the modern watershed.

---

102. C. A. Bayly, "The Age of Revolutions in Global Context: An Afterword," in *The Age of Revolutions in Global Context, c. 1760–1840*, ed. David Armitage and Sanjay Subrahmanyam (Basingstoke, UK: Palgrave Macmillan, 2010), 214.

103. C. A. Bayly, *Recovering Liberties: Indian Thought in the Age of Liberalism and Empire* (Cambridge: Cambridge University Press, 2011), 36–40.

104. Banerjee, " 'All This Is Indeed Brahman,' " 88–94. This universalizing emphasis represented only one strand within the Vedic tradition. Milinda Banerjee, *The Mortal God: Imagining the Sovereign in Colonial India* (Cambridge: Cambridge University Press, 2018), chapter 5, argues that popular political movements in early-twentieth-century India had a certain agentive modernity in their utopian vision, but the premodern, Indigenous element at work here was really a form of messianic thinking revolving around divinized rulership.

105. No doubt as we move into the twentieth century, then the role of Hindu techniques of disciplined selfhood in animating Gandhi's *swaraj* (self-governance therefore had a double meaning here) would be relevant.

106. Albert Hourani, *Arabic Thought in the Liberal Age, 1798–1939* (Cambridge: Cambridge University Press, 1962). Thanks for the discussion here to Azfar Moin.

It becomes clear that the need to decisively overcome religious intolerance was unusually acute in Christian societies, particularly following the new significance of identity boundaries produced by the Reformation.[107] Therefore, when Bayly notes that Rammohan was influenced by the sensibility of religious tolerance enshrined in the principle of *Sulh-i Kull* (total peace) famously promoted by the Mughal emperor Akbar, it is probably better to see this principle as a revivification of an immanentist mode.[108]

As for the Buddhist world, Patrice Ladwig and James Mark Shields have called for an analysis of the way in which long-term elements of Buddhist tradition—including the sangha as leveling institution and the utopian promise of millenarianism—informed the formation of socialism and political radicalism in parts of Asia.[109] Indeed, Shields has noted that the *Ikkō ikki* referred to earlier in this chapter provided precedents for " 'righteous revolt' on the part of the common people against the secular authorities," which later Buddhist socialists and radicals in Japan looked to for inspiration.[110] From the late nineteenth century onward, some Indian thinkers found in Buddhism a means of legitimating socialist, pacifist and anticaste forms of progressive politics.[111] The key question remains of course, as to whether such Buddhist, Muslim, and Hindu "modernist" thinkers were merely ransacking ancient inheritances to provide an indigenizing legitimacy to projects that were fundamentally Western in origin, or whether these inheritances themselves played a more generative role. These notes are intended here to merely indicate the sort of analysis that might be required to establish the contribution of Asian Axiality to the political imagination of modernity.

---

107. I do not for a moment argue that nonmonotheistic states did not persecute religious groups—but the logic by which they did this was different in certain important ways. I leave to one side the question of Islam here.

108. *Sulh-i Kull* is rather the apogee of a profound immanentization of Islam arising out of Mongol hegemony, the preeminence of Sufism and Ibn 'Arabi thought, and the influence of a Neoplatonic tradition of monism, all of which allowed individual religions to be subordinated to the universal rule of a sacred king. See A. Azfar Moin "Sulh-i Kull as an Oath of Peace: Mughal Political Theology in History, Theory, and Comparison," *Modern Asian Studies* 56, no. 3 (2022): 721–48.

109. Ladwig and Shields, "Introduction."

110. J. M. Shields, "Peasant Revolts as Anti-Authoritarian Archetypes for Radical Buddhism in Modern Japan," *Journal of Religion in Japan* 5, no. 1 (2016): 3–21, 4, 9.

111. Dharmanand Kosambi [orig. 1910], "Ancient Indian Republics, the Buddhist Sangha, and Socialism," in *Dharmanand Kosambi: The Essential Writings*, ed. and trans. Meera Kosambi (Ranikhet, India: Permanent Black, 2010); Douglas Ober, "Translating the Buddha: Edwin Arnold's Light of Asia and Its Indian Publics," *Humanities (Basel)* 10, no. 1 (2020): 3.

CHINA

On the subject of Asian Axiality, the reader may have noticed that Confucianism has been excluded from the discussion thus far.[112] China has probably occasioned more debate about its place in the Axial Age paradigm than any other case, so it is perhaps not surprising that Confucianism does not fit readily into the concept of transcendentalism.[113] The principal reason for this is that Confucianism is not predicated on a principle of otherworldly salvation. Nevertheless, it did entail a profound ethicization of relations between persons, between persons and metapersons, and between both of these and the state. Remarkably, the crucial shift occurred very early, in the eleventh century BCE, when the Zhou empire justified its ascendance by reference to the Mandate of Heaven, a transcendent deity or principle that conferred the right to rule on the virtuous. But—and this is of vital significance in conceiving why the Chinese trajectory seems so different from the Indic or Abrahamic cases—that mandate was discernible only in the political fortunes of the realm and the Zhou dynasty itself: it was not tied to a concept of salvation or to a prophetic tradition.

Thus, when Zhou rule collapsed, giving way to ruthless competition between regional successor states, it engendered a skepticism about the possibility of discerning such Heavenly adjudication in the course of events. Confucianism was one among several responses. It claimed to reinstate the Zhou Mandate system, but it also quietly transformed the understanding of ritual—at least in the eyes of elite literati—from an activity designed to secure immanentist ends to one that was designed to remake the human subject and thereby generate social

---

112. At one point, it seems that Bellah intended to include China in his last project, but by the time of the prologue, that appears to have fallen away. The following section draws upon the discussion of China that will appear in Alan Strathern, *Converting Kings* (2024) and so does not include references to the literature, but the work of Michael Puett, "Humanizing the Divine and Divinizing the Human in Early China: Comparative Reflections on Ritual, Sacrifice, and Sovereignty," in *Sacred Kingship in World History: Between Immanence and Transcendence*, ed. A. Azfar Moin and Alan Strathern (New York: Columbia University Press, 2022), and Yuri Pines, *Foundations of Confucian Thought: Intellectual Life in the Chunqiu Period, 722–453 B.C.E.* (Honolulu: University of Hawai'i Press, 2002), were especially helpful. Note Strathern (2024) explores the ambiguities of Hinduism in the paradigm too.

113. Bellah, *Religion in Human Evolution*; also see Prasenjit Duara, *The Crisis of Global Modernity: Asian Traditions and a Sustainable Future* (Cambridge: Cambridge University Press, 2015), 131.

harmony.[114] So, Confucianism too, in its own way, relativized and ethicized ritual even as it retained it as the central form of action.

In contending with the judgment of a transcendent principle whose voice was entirely unified with the empirical world, an important strand of Confucian thought represented by Mencius and Xunxi argued that the virtue of a political regime, and therefore its accordance with Heaven's will, was most evident in the happiness and well-being of its subjects.[115] Indeed, what Yuri Pines describes as a "surprisingly democratic" principle, by which Heaven saw through the eyes of the people, already had a long history in China. Of course, nothing like democracy resulted: the cosmic king was still the linchpin of the whole edifice.[116] But this does represent a most significant king-taming maneuver—a certain sensibility of popular accountability, at least as interpreted by an official literati, that is highly relevant to our theme.[117]

Experimenting with the unusually long-term vision afforded by the Axial Age perspective, it may be possible to see two consequences of this that have shaped Chinese history and its encounter with the forces of modernity.[118] The first proceeds from the fact that this ethicized conception of rule, framed so early and reformulated so decisively by Confucianism, had tremendous enduring power, even folding incoming transcendentalisms such as Buddhism into its hegemony. The result was that, in one sense, it was not an afterlife but the state itself, or even the mortal condition, that remained the locus of idealization. In this light, apparently paradoxical terms used by Benjamin Schwarz, S. N. Eisenstadt, and others to describe the Confucian case as one of "this-worldly transcendence" come to make sense.[119] (A number of "Modern Confucian" Chinese philosophers working

---

114. The immanentist logic of ritual always remained in terms of both popular and elite practice, but Confucian discourse subtly transformed its raison d'être.

115. Bellah, *Religion in Human Evolution*, 460–71.

116. Yuri Pines, "Secular Theocracy? State and Religion in Early China Revisited," in *Empires and Gods: The Role of Religions in Imperial History*, ed. Jörg Rüpke, Michal Biran, and Yuri Pines (Berlin: De Gruyter, 2024).

117. Further, deBary has explicitly investigated the possible foundations for something like individualism and communitarianism in the Confucian tradition. Wm. Theodore deBary, "Individualism and Humanitarianism in Late Ming Thought," in *Self and Society in Ming Thought*, ed. Wm. Theodore deBary (New York: Columbia University Press, 1970). Also see Wm. Theodore deBary, *Asian Values and Human Rights: A Confucian Communitarian Perspective* (Cambridge, MA: Harvard University Press, 1998).

118. This perspective is liable to be misidentified as a form of cultural essentialism today. But a due regard for transformation and multiplicity within Chinese history is not incompatible with discerning certain structures of the long term. See, for example, Puett, "Humanizing the Divine."

in late-twentieth-century Taiwan and Hong Kong also explicitly drew upon Karl Jaspers to develop an account of Confucianism as "immanent transcendence.")[120] The question arises as to whether this is relevant to the way in which the Chinese Communist Party (CCP) has continued to maintain authoritarian control over a vast population, even as that population undergoes extremely rapid socioeconomic change and globalizing influences. The party's performance of a benign, people-oriented authoritarianism may register more authentically in the context of a state-centered morality that has persisted underneath adherence to communist and consumerist visions.[121] The fact that the CCP has signaled a return to Confucianism and its order-preserving values helps make the sense of continuity explicit.[122]

Second, however, Confucianism evidently paid a price for not configuring itself in the form of salvationism, for popular movements of the latter could generate social energies that the state struggled to coopt and instead must repress. In fact, in the form of Mohism and the Daoism of the Celestial Masters, ancient China witnessed movements that fit the transcendentalist paradigm in a more straightforward way. They never became dominant, but they remained part of the cultural landscape and fed into a legacy, joined also by Buddhism (particularly that of the Pure Land variety), that produced surges of millenarian enthusiasm.[123] Chinese history has been punctuated by popular movements of supernatural

---

119. S. N. Eisenstadt, "This Worldly Transcendentalism and the Structuring of the World: Weber's 'Religion of China' and the Format of Chinese History and Civilization," in *Comparative Civilizations and Multiple Modernities: A Collection of Essays*, ed. S. N. Eisenstadt (Leiden, Netherlands: Brill, 2003); Mingming Wang, "'All under Heaven' (Tianxia): Cosmological Perspectives and Political Ontologies in Pre-modern China," *HAU: Journal of Ethnographic Theory* 2, no. 1 (2012): 336; Benjamin I. Schwartz, "Transcendence in Ancient China," *Daedalus* 104 (1975): 57–68.

120. Jana S. Rošker, "The Philosophical Sinification of Modernity and the Modern Confucian Paradigm of Immanent Transcendence (內在超越性)," *Asian Studies* 2, no. 1 (2014): 67–81.

121. The reality of how the state rules may be closer to Legalism, however; Richard Madsen, "Introduction," in *The Sinicization of Chinese Religions: From Above and Below*, ed. Richard Madsen (Leiden, Netherlands, and Boston: Brill, 2021), 10.

122. See Vivienne Shue, "Regimes of Resonance: Cosmos, Empire, and Changing Technologies of CCP Rule," *Modern China* 48, no. 4 (January 2022): 25, which emphasizes Hu Jintao, and Yong Chen, "'Official Confucianism' as Newly Sanctioned by the Chinese Communist Party," in *The Sinicization of Chinese Religions: From Above and Below*, ed. Richard Madsen (Leiden, Netherlands, and Boston: Brill, 2021), 44–63. In "Official Confucianism" under Xi Jinping Shue dwells on enduring forms of (in effect) cosmic kingship shaping Chinese leadership; I focus here on the ethicized "Axial" element.

123. Dubois, *Religion and Making of Modern East Asia*; also see Lars Peter Laamann, "Christianity, Magic and Politics in Qing and Republican China," *Central Asiatic Journal* 58, no. 1–2 (2015): 94. More generally, Buddhism had at several points in Chinese history been ruthlessly suppressed. James A. Benn, "'Action Buddhism' in the Medieval Chinese Empire," in *Empires and Gods: The Role of Religions in Imperial History*, ed. Jörg Rüpke, Michal Biran, and Yuri Pines (Berlin: De Gruyter, 2024).

utopianism rising up against the state since the broadly Daoist Yellow Turban revolt of 184 CE. This is the long-term context in which to understand the Taiping rebellion of 1850–1864 mentioned previously, and then also, in a somewhat secularized form, the communist revolution and the Cultural Revolution. The paranoia that the CCP directs toward salvationist religious movements that might relativize its authority and belittle its worldly aims remains abundantly clear today.[124]

These comments relate to China's own distinctive iteration of modernity, but in other ways, its premodern past exhibits features associated with modern politics more generally. If we are willing to draw some kind of line between the modern condition and Jewish prophetism, then it is hardly less apposite to note that we find precursors to the following appearing startlingly early in Chinese history: bureaucracy, meritocracy, a certain disenchanted notion of ritual, a state subordination of transcendentalism, and a state structure that has suppressed its more parasitical tendencies to afford some genuine attention to the welfare of the people.[125] (Of course, welfare is not the same as liberty.) Does this reflect the precocious development of state power and affluence, or rather the fact that there was indeed, in an extremely abstract sense, a certain potential within the Chinese Axial Age that pointed the way to elements of the modern?

INTO MODERNITY AND THE CLIMATE CRISIS

This has largely been a discussion of the past, and the premodern past at that, leaving it to others who are better equipped to ponder the transition to modernity. But I would like to take up the editors' invitation to reflect a little on our contemporary predicament. This means turning our focus away from the critique of power via the emergent self and toward the need to transcend selfhood through collective action in the face of the climate crisis, for environmental catastrophe threatens to be the first and last apocalypse to materialize in human history: a grim and farcical telos indeed. In the Tillich lecture, Bellah suggests

---

124. To clarify, the CCP came to power on the back of an insurrectionary utopianism, but once in power, it inevitably had to tame its message and turn to techniques that resonated with Legalism and Confucianism. It thus replicated, again, the longer pattern in Chinese history. Note the move from a millennial countercultural mobilization to Confucian-Legalist authority undertaken by the founder of the Ming dynasty, Zhu Yuanzhang (1328–1398).

125. Alexander Woodside, *Lost Modernities: China, Vietnam, Korea, and the Hazards of World History* (Cambridge, MA: Harvard University Press, 2006) on bureaucracy-meritocracy. Also note Bellah, *Religion in Human Evolution*, 400, on the "hundred schools" of the warring states period "in their variety as well as in their content presaging modernity, differently but to the same degree as the classical Greeks."

that a sort of secular "instrumental individualism" combined with the exploitative potential of science may be the culprit.[126]

While a great mass of historical writing serves to undermine or qualify a grand narrative of secularization, I take some such version of it to be indispensable to understanding the long road leading to our present condition.[127] The Durkheimian functions of societal cohesion and organization were once served fundamentally through relations with metapersons.[128] This has left its imprint on our language of the "sacred," for the term conflates (1) that which conveys the presence of metapersons and the immanent power at their disposal, and (2) that which is held to be of supreme collective value. Yet, now, across many stretches of human life, particularly but not only in the West, the latter has become detached from the former.[129] Immanentist religious systems—that is, those without a transcendentalist dimension—have all but vanished from the face of the earth, for reasons that I have set out elsewhere.[130] Immanentist instincts, to be sure, remain: they are a function of universal cognitive tendencies and human needs, after all. They still find a ready home under the carapace of world religions: consider prosperity gospel preachers or Russian Orthodox priests blessing missiles in the war that has been launched upon Ukraine.[131] But their social significance has been reduced.

And those world religions or transcendentalist traditions endure too, partly because our need for ultimate meaning abides no less.[132] But their soteriologies no longer provide the unquestionable framework of thought and feeling by which society in general operates. When Charles Taylor refers to the modern condition as "the immanent frame," this helps capture the way in which the

---

126. Bellah, "The Tillich Lecture," 279.

127. I leave to one side the question of the global extent of this condition: a vital question obviously, but too large to be broached here. In observing that some powerful processes of secularization have occurred, I do not mean to endorse the thesis that "modernization necessarily leads to secularization" (Joas, *Power of the Sacred*, 199).

128. It was not quite his aim, but Marshall Sahlins's posthumously published work, *The New Science of the Enchanted Universe: An Anthropology of Most of Humanity* (Princeton, NJ: Princeton University Press, 2022), recently underlined this very eloquently.

129. See chapter 10 in this volume on the way in which religion has ceded jurisdiction over important regions of social life.

130. Strathern, *Unearthly Powers*.

131. In March 2022, the National Guard chief, Viktor Zolotov, spoke at a church service led by the Orthodox Patriarch Kirill, where he noted that "this icon will protect the Russian army and accelerate our victory." Sravasti Dasgupta, "Top Putin Ally Says Russia's Military Operation in Ukraine Had Been Slower Than Expected," March 15, 2022, *Independent*, https://www.independent.co.uk/news/world/europe/putin-viktor-zolotov-ukraine-invasion-b2035891.html. Thanks to Ana Marta González for a discussion of this topic.

132. In dialogue with Joas and Gorski, one might say that the desire for self-transcendence persists no less.

ontological breach pushed to center stage by transcendentalism has now been ushered into the wings. Modern life, for many in the West at least, once again dances to the rhythms of "ordinary human flourishing." But what Taylor means by "the immanent frame" is very far from a return to what I described as immanentism; indeed, it is the product of transcendentalism's drive toward a buffered, disciplined, interiorized self, moving among a relatively disenchanted landscape.

In the more secularized societies of the world, communities still form by fashioning a common psychology of the "sacred," even if this no longer needs to proceed in a "religious" manner—that is to say, as dependent on either immanentist or transcendentalist predicates. Philip Gorski refers to the current totems of political sacrality as being "the nation" for the populist right and "social justice" for the progressive left. We have had many recent examples of how profoundly people may be swept up into such secular moral communities fighting for their sacred values above and beyond their own self-interest. If Durkheimian sensations of the sacred have fragmented into multiple and optional forms, the same problem has always applied to the competing world religions, at least on a global scale.[133] And one such secular moral community, one based around the discourse of human rights, is coterminous with humanity itself.

In what way, then, might religious forms of the sacred become indispensable to solving the collective action demands of the climate crisis? The popular imagery associated with the environmentalist movements would suggest that this is most naturally achieved by a return to immanentism, untouched by the incipient disenchantment of Axial creeds. To the extent that the transcendentalisms denied the attribution of personhood to the natural world, they also removed it from the moral sphere of reciprocal relations. Hence, ecological strategies have responded with a renewed anthropomorphism, as in the growing movement to grant legal personhood to rivers and mountains. The Brazilian philosopher Déborah Danowski and the anthropologist Eduardo Viveiros de Castro, in a densely thoughtful piece, say that "the concept of the Anthropocene reveals the terminal obsolescence of the theological-philosophical equipment bequeathed by the Axial Age."[134] (It would seem in fact that their target is really monotheism or

---

133. See chapter 10 of this volume on the fragmentation of the sacred. Indeed, there is at least one sense in which it was ever thus, if we consider the way that salvific religion always had to jostle for supremacy (to again invoke Robbins's discussion, chapter 9 in this volume) with other collective values—as this chapter does.

134. Eduardo Viveiros de Castro and Déborah Danowski, "The Past Is Yet to Come," *e-flux Journal* 114 (December 2020), https://www.e-flux.com/journal/114/364412/the-past-is-yet-to-come/.

Christianity per se.) This equipment, the transcendentalist-immanentist binary, was secularized into the "modern ideologeme of Nature and Culture," albeit not in any stable fashion, for which of this pair was equivalent to the transcendent, and which to the immanent, could flip from context to context.

We must be careful not to assume that the ecocritique of transcendentalism entails the ecovalidation of immanentism, for the latter category encompasses much more variety than the set of small-scale societies that tend to be associated with a more harmonious means of engaging the natural world.[135] If immanentism is sometimes seen as the virtuous counter to the imperialistic claims of monotheism and the imperialistic claims of science, it is not remotely antagonistic to imperialism tout court. We only have to think of the Egyptian pharaoh, the Roman emperor, or the Aztec tlatoani to grasp that immanentism may be pressed into the service of forceful attempts to totally dominate and transform the wider world. The natural sphere may indeed be conceived in terms of teeming metapersons, but metapersons can be corralled into imperial hierarchies too.

The role of science in ecological critique is deeply ambiguous. On the one hand, it is subject to blame, as humanity's ultimate hubris. On the other hand, it is only because of science that we have any sense that there is a problem, why it happened, and what we have to do about it. Believing in the science is the sine qua non of all subsequent action. In recent decades, the strongest impulses to relativize science within academia often appeared to come from the left, drawing deeply on the intuition that knowledge is a mere creature of power. These tendencies include the postcolonial desire to consider all forms of knowledge originating in the West as suspect and as bound up with imperialism; the more general supposition issuing ultimately from Marx that knowledge is a superstructure maintaining inequality; a poststructuralist destabilization of grand narratives; a historicized understanding of the production of scientific knowledge as an all-too-human affair; and a sociological understanding of it in terms of contingent social relations and networks of things and people.[136]

The climate crisis and the COVID-19 pandemic should present a massive obstacle to that tendency. Perhaps if these twin threats had demanded a response that challenged the sacred values of the left, then the relativistic framing of

---

135. Further, from a trenchantly etic perspective at least, is not the anthropomorphization of nature only another way, ultimately, of establishing the moral centrality of humanlike personhood?

136. Bellah remarks of metanarratives: "They have come into bad odor of late because, it is claimed, they are forms of power, openly or tacitly trying to convince people that some particular story is true when it actually is an apology for the status quo." Bellah, "Prologue in Heaven," 92. Note also Joas, *Power of the Sacred*, 130.

science may have been further energized. But instead, the necessary responses chimed with the left's appreciation of collective action, state direction, and global cooperation.[137] For whatever reason, the more centrist and left-inclined have been happy to consider science as the arbiter of truth on such matters, indeed even as giving us something like the Truth: objective facts about a reality that exists regardless of how we think or feel about it, and on which the fate of all creation depends—a revelation no less freighted with ultimate significance than a biblical prophecy. Instead, it has been the sacred values of the right that were challenged—the prerogatives of individual and national liberty—and it is those in the populist right, most strikingly but not only in the United States, which have reacted by removing themselves from reality-based discussion, questioning not just science but any expert knowledge—about elections, laws, viruses, vaccines, and weather patterns. In short, any move to reenchant the world that further diminishes the authority of science will not help us in the long run.

Nevertheless, it is more reasonable to suggest that if science can be regarded as an oracle, it cannot quite play the role of the prophet in galvanizing us into action. It might be surmised that the flaws of human psychology are such that only the social machinery of religion will help to overcome them in producing collective action as swift and unified as it needs to be. By far, the most powerful such machinery operative in the world today comes in the form of the regnant transcendentalisms, the world religions. But transcendentalism's otherworldly conception of salvation is a treacherous principle upon which to rely. In the Tillich lecture, Bellah has already hinted that transcendentalism may be to blame: "The Protestant neglect of the sacraments is part of the modern world's neglect of the natural as sacred."[138]

Eugene Halton has put the point much more strongly in asserting that the Axial Age teachings amounted to "a philosophy of escape from the earth," which has incurred "an unacknowledged tragic cost, the forgetting of the earth."[139] Millenarian groups have most explicitly regarded the destruction of the world as a

---

137. In the United Kingdom, Brexit would be another example where the left's trust in economics remained supreme while the populist right questioned "experts."

138. Bellah, "The Tillich Lecture," 279. See also the introduction to this volume.

139. Eugene Halton does note that thinkers such as John Stuart-Glennie and Lewis Mumford found ways of perceiving how Axial revolutions might be brought into harmony with the wisdom of immanentism or "relational consciousness." Eugene Halton, "The Forgotten Earth: Nature, World Religions, and Worldlessness in the Legacy of the Axial Age/Moral Revolution," in *From World Religions to Axial Civilizations and Beyond*, ed. Said Amir Arjomand and Stephen Kalberg (Albany, NY: SUNY Press, 2021), 209–38. (Stuart-Glennie uses the term "panzooninism" around the time that E. B. Tylor referred to animism.)

necessary prelude to a higher reality.[140] But all transcendentalisms erect a sense of cosmic time and reality that far exceeds the bounds of our little planet. Perhaps the Asian transcendentalisms, which in some versions locate ultimate reality within the human self, present a less stark logic. Certainly, Prasenjit Duara has argued that such traditions of "dialogical transcendence" may be the surest route to forming all encompassing "networks of hope" that might elevate the quest for sustainability.[141]

As for returning to immanentism, Danowski and Viveiros de Castro raise the question of whether this is possible, but they cannot do so unequivocally. Can we attempt "an intensive reanimation of the local cosmos (the earth) by means of a counter-axial re-enchantment of the world, necessarily secondary and somewhat strained?" they ask. Can we wish religious movements into being from a sense of their social utility? For those of us who are religiously unmusical, a return to either immanentism or transcendentalism seems a remote possibility. Of all the Axial Age models, perhaps it was only the Chinese thinkers and their almost Durkheimian appreciation of ritual as a means of closing the gap between the individual and society that indicates something like an historical example of how this may be done.

CONCLUSION

Much of this chapter has proceeded by problematizing the equation of axiality and the critique of power. I spent a great deal of time establishing that: egalitarian principles are not the sole legacy of any one type of intellectual tradition; immanentist societies found various means of neutering the agency of chiefs and princes; if transcendentalist traditions found new ways of doing this by setting

---

140. Shortly before I began drafting this chapter, a handwritten letter from local Jehovah's Witnesses was dropped through my door. It began in the style of green ethics: "*Who will Save the Earth?*" it underlined. "Will humans ruin the earth? Or will they ever be able to live closer in harmony with nature?" The answer, apparently is no, for "deep-seated greed, selfishness, and shortsightedness" will rule the day. At this point, one imagines where the argument is leading: only through faith will these fallen instincts be submerged in a cause for the greater good. But again, the letter takes an unexpected turn. Our reason for hope, it says, is not in our hands: "We all need to look and wait for our Creator, the one who made the heavens and earth . . . he will make all things new." The answer is not to join collective action but to wait for our imminent salvation. This is escape from planet earth in a very literal fashion.

141. Duara, *Crisis of Global Modernity*.

up a dialogue with a clerisy, this is quite different to setting up an institutionalized dialogue with the broader population. Transcendentalism did not give rise to the secular ruler so much as the righteous one, and as such, it provided powerful new forms of legitimation of monarchy and empire. But these points do not undermine the central insight of Bellah and the Axial literature more generally regarding the rise of new moral frameworks for the political sphere. The more significant question is to consider what would happen if we were to take Bellah's metanarrative and show how it may be compared with Asian analogs, and also how it intertwined with them, following Asian axiality beyond the germinal period of antiquity, into the centuries of empire building in the first millennium, on into the interconnected world of early modernity, and then the encounter with European ideological and material forces in modernity. This is called for not only out of a necessary anti-Eurocentrism, but also to refine when and how exactly the European trajectory ever marked itself out as distinct. Only some starting points for an answer have been sketched here.

As for our contemporary predicament, can transcendentalism provide a means of overriding forms of individualism that, in some highly distant sense, it first set in motion? Flip the coin of Axial selfhood and one finds on the other side an emblem of the universal. The traditions that emerged did indeed have the great merit of encompassing all mankind, or, even better, all living beings—theoretically. But practically, historically, they did so in the form of competing versions that leave us divided. Some kind of minimal grounds for a shared vision are provided instead by the rather different and smaller-scale truths offered by the scientific method. To speak so simply of science and truth may once have seemed slightly gauche in a scholarly context. But the climate crisis demands that we are more serious about such things. Planet earth needs neither to be rejected nor affirmed only as a mirror to our own personhood in order for us to comprehend and protect it.

Acknowledgment

Many thanks to Vic Lieberman for comments on a draft of this paper, and to the editors for their helpful advice.

APPENDIX

THE ATTRIBUTES OF IMMANENTISM AND TRANSCENDENTALISM[142]

IMMANENTISM IS CHARACTERIZED BY:

(1) The rampant generation of metapersons

(2) A monistic cosmology

(3) An undifferentiated afterlife

(4) A focus on power

(5) An unsystematized and community-focused morality

(6) Amoral metapersons

(7) An empirical understanding of the function of ritual

(8) The free incorporation of new revelation

(9) No equivalent to the concept of religious identity

(10) Translatability or de facto universalism

TRANSCENDENTALISM IS CHARACTERIZED BY:

(1) An ontological division between transcendent and mundane spheres

(2) An orientation toward the objective of salvation

(3) An ethicization of values and metapersons

(4) Otherworldly or utopian values

(5) An emphasis on individual interiority

(6) Ideological 'offensiveness'

---

142. The contents of this appendix are adapted from Strathern, *Unearthly Powers*, chapter 1.

(7)   Attempts to control and textualize revelation

(8)   Intellectualization

(9)   Self-conscious identity formation

(10) Universalist reach and proselytising tendencies

(11) The field of metapersons is monopolized or inferiorized

(12) The deprecation of magic

(13) The development of autonomous clerisies

(14) Emergence outside the state

(15) The dynamic of reform

An immanentist tradition	immamentism
A transcendentalist tradition	transcendentalism
(e.g., Buddhism, Christianity)	immamentism

CHAPTER 7

ORGANIC SOCIAL ETHICS

Universalism Without Egalitarianism

HANS JOAS

W hen Robert N. Bellah retired at the age of seventy in 1997 as the most important historically oriented sociologist of religion of the second half of the twentieth century, he formulated a plan to pull together the threads of his decades of research into one great work. To be called *Religious Evolution*, it was to bear the same title as the attention-grabbing essay published by the young Bellah in 1964.[1] The structure of the planned work, as set out in 1998, reveals the full extent of the author's ambitions at that point in time.[2] What he envisaged was nothing less than a world history of religion from the early stages of the human species to the present, through an approach theoretically informed and permeated by both sociology and biology. When it came to interdisciplinary knowledge, nobody was better prepared for such a project than Bellah. As we now know, he was granted time enough only to tackle the period from the Paleolithic to the end of the so-called Axial Age, that is, from the beginning of human cultural history about 2.5 million years ago to around 200 BC, in a book published in 2011 with the modified title *Religion in Human Evolution*.[3] When Bellah died unexpectedly in 2013, he had started to work energetically on the next phase of his colossal project. It had become clear to him, however, that his lifetime would be insufficient to produce an account as exhaustive as his 2011

---

1. Robert N. Bellah, "Religious Evolution," *American Sociological Review* 29 (1964): 358–74.
2. Robert N. Bellah, "Religious Evolution," Table of Contents, unpublished manuscript, July 1998, in author's files.
3. Robert N. Bellah, *Religion in Human Evolution: From the Paleolithic to the Axial Age* (Cambridge, MA: Harvard University Press, 2011).

book. He thus decided to write the new volume in more essayistic form and to limit comparison of world religions and cultures to the "West" and China. This meant, above all, saying little about India and Islam, jumping from the end of the Axial Age to the sixteenth century, and starting at the real or supposed beginning of "modernity" in the Reformation era.

Bellah's outline from 1998, however, reveals how he originally intended to proceed. The historical developments between the end of the Axial Age and the Reformation era that he was now poised to forgo entirely were to be titled "Secondary Formations." While this term exists in other disciplines and contexts as well, it clearly marked Bellah's attempt to convey the fact that two religions of particular importance today (namely, Christianity and Islam) are not themselves products of the Axial Age, but only emerged after it. Without the Axial Age breakthroughs in ancient Judaism and in Greece, they would have been inconceivable. But Christianity grew out of Judaism as a secondary formation and soon began to interpret itself through the categories of Greek philosophy. Islam emerged in constitutive engagement with Judaism and Byzantine Christianity. This interaction was so profound that some have been tempted to see Islam as a kind of reformed Christianity.

It was not just Christianity and Islam, however, that Bellah wished to analyze as "secondary formations," but also religious developments in India and East Asia after the Axial Age. With respect to all these developments, Bellah introduced a further and crucial term in his outline that indicates the tenor of his analyses: "organic social ethics." In what follows, I elaborate on this term and the issues that it highlights. I focus mainly on the history of scholarship that has given rise to this concept. This focus may seem too historical and narrow to some readers, but others may agree with me that it helps us understand an important phase in the history of moral universalism between the "Axial Age" and "Modernity." It may also sensitize us to certain problematic features of "modernity" and provide potential resources for our contemporary attempts to cope with them.

MAX WEBER AS BELLAH'S SOURCE

There is little in Bellah's publications to suggest what he himself would have contributed to the topic. But it is entirely clear where he got this term: Max Weber's writings, especially his famous "Intermediate Reflection," to whose "close reading" Bellah dedicated an acute interpretive essay.[4] As is well known, Weber's text ends with admiring remarks on the "extraordinary metaphysical achievement" of the concept of theodicy in the religiosity of Indian intellectuals, which, he tells us, brings together radically opposing elements within a unified framework, including "the strictest rejection of the world with organic social ethics."[5] Bellah was also aware that, besides India, Weber had identified another case to which it seemed appropriate to apply the term "organic vocational ethic"—namely, medieval "Catholic" Christianity, as articulated in representative form in the social philosophy of St. Thomas Aquinas. In this case too, according to Weber, a natural inequality among human beings is assumed, but then a conception of vocations—like the castes in India—is developed in the following way:

> The various vocations or castes have been providentially ordained, and each of them has been assigned some specific, indispensable task desired by god or determined by the impersonal world order, so that different ethical obligations devolve upon each. The diverse occupations and castes are compared to the constituent portions of an organism in this type of theory. The various relationships of power which emerge in this manner must therefore be regarded as divinely ordained relationships of authority. Accordingly, any revolt or rebellion against them, or even the raising of vital claims other than those corresponding to one's status in society, is reprehensible to god because they are destructive of sacred tradition and are expressions of creaturely self-arrogance and pride.[6]

For Weber, this *organic* vocational ethic is *the* alternative to the *ascetic* vocational ethic, and thus to ascetic Protestantism, to which he ascribed such a crucial role in the emergence of the spirit of modern capitalism.[7] Under the

---

4. Robert N. Bellah, "Max Weber and World-Denying Love," in *The Robert Bellah Reader*, ed. Robert N. Bellah and Steven M. Tipton (Durham, NC: Duke University Press, 2006), 123–49. On page 137, he ascribes the term to Weber and interprets it as a "compromise formation" between Axial Age ideals and real-world conditions.
5. Max Weber, "Intermediate Reflection" retitled as "Religious Rejections of the World and Their Directions," in *From Max Weber: Essays in Sociology*, trans. and ed. H. H. Gerth and C. Wright Mills (New York: Oxford University Press, 1958), 323–359, 359.
6. Max Weber, *Economy and Society: An Outline of Interpretive Sociology*, ed. Guenther Roth and Claus Wittich (Berkeley: University of California Press, 1978), 598.
7. Weber, *Economy and Society*, 551.

conditions of the organic social or vocational ethic (*Sozialethik, Berufsethik*)—the terminology fluctuates, and occasionally Weber also refers to an organic *Gesellschaftsethik*, social teaching or social theory[8]—individuals do not strive for social advancement and economic success for themselves. Rather, they seek the complete fulfillment of their duties, which may be of a contemplative character, in the particular position in which they find themselves in life. They do not strive for the accumulation of earthly goods but for the creation of a collective treasure trove of good works. In return for adding to this trove, as individuals they can expect to be rewarded in the beyond or (in India) to enjoy future happiness in this world.

Bellah stays very close to Weber in his remarks. He says nothing about the origin or intellectual history of the concept of the organic social ethic, nor about the backgrounds to Weber's view of the Middle Ages and Catholicism or his understanding of India. This would presumably have changed had Bellah had the chance to continue his work. However, I do not want to speculate here about what he is likely to have written; the few pages in his "Prologue in Heaven (or Hell)"[9] on Thomas Aquinas and Dante show his continuing interest in the study of medieval Europe but mostly address questions of theology and cosmology and not the topic of the organic social ethic. I will rather set out a stand-alone argument explaining why the conception of organic social ethics seems to me of key importance. This will also require me to go into the problematic features of Weber's thinking and to at least hint at an alternative understanding of medieval Catholicism. I will also have to briefly address a problem with Weber's understanding of India, as well as a crucial weakness in his interpretation of Islam. Weber (unlike Bellah, evidently) denied the presence of such an organic conception in Islam.[10] But the point that I wish to make in this regard will make sense only once I have brought out the deeper meaning of the medieval Christian notion of "organism." This was in fact far from being a simple, organicist legitimization of political and social inequality.

Such legitimization was at large in antiquity without any Christianity whatsoever. The metaphor of the single body as a means of understanding the state and the social division of labor has in fact been common in Europe since

---

8. Occurrences are few and far between (about twelve in total). At times, it is impossible to clearly distinguish this from other ways of using the term "organic," which of course appear far more often.

9. Robert N. Bellah, "Prologue in Heaven (or Hell) to the Modern Project," 102–105. Chapter 4 in this volume.

10. Weber, *Economy and Society*, 599.

Greco-Roman antiquity.[11] This metaphor is most famously expressed in the fable of the belly and the members delivered to posterity by the Roman historian Livy. The Roman senator Agrippa Menenius Lanatus is said to have alluded to this tale in an attempt "to persuade the plebeians who had congregated on the Mons Sacer to return to Rome."[12] This fable pervades Western intellectual history in multiple variations. William Shakespeare gave it immortal linguistic expression in the opening scene of his Roman drama *Coriolanus*:

> There was a time when all the body's members
> Rebell'd against the belly, thus accused it:
> That only like a gulf it did remain
> I' the midst o' the body, idle and unactive,
> Still cupboarding the viand, never bearing
> Like labour with the rest, where the other instruments
> Did see and hear, devise, instruct, walk, feel,
> And, mutually participate, did minister
> Unto the appetite and affection common
> Of the whole body.[13]

In the fable, the belly replies in a deliberate and detailed way that it never keeps anything for itself, and when asked by the puzzled citizens what relevance all this talk might have to the rebellion, its answer is:

> The senators of Rome are this good belly,
> And you the mutinous members; . . . you shall find
> No public benefit which you receive
> But it proceeds or comes from them to you
> And no way from yourselves.[14]

The intent to justify an unequal distribution of power and goods is palpable here. Strikingly, the rebellion is directed against the "stomach" rather than

---

11. For a very good overview, see Tilman Struve, *Die Entwicklung der organologischen Staatsauffassung im Mittelalter* (Stuttgart: Anton Hiersemann Verlag, 1978), 10–43.
12. Struve, *Die Entwicklung der organologischen Staatsauffassung*, 31.
13. William Shakespeare, *Coriolanus*, Act I.
14. Shakespeare, *Coriolanus*, Act I.

the "head," which has been taken to indicate a particularly ancient view of the metaphor of organism.[15] When Bertolt Brecht composed his socialist-communist adaptation of Shakespeare's play, this entire scene was grist to his mill.

It is not my intention to counter the exposure of the crude ideology of legitimation found in this fable. But I do want to sensitize readers to the fact that the use of the organism metaphor was changed in an epoch-making way by Christianity. This does not instantly neutralize the suspicion that, even in this modified form, we are dealing with a mere attempt to bolster legitimacy. But we must first appreciate the change wrought by the Christianization of the organism metaphor in terms of politics and social teaching, before we can critically examine the extent to which the Christian version lends itself to rhetorics of legitimization.

What exactly did this radical change consist of? To put it in a nutshell: it is no longer the Roman Senate or a king or another ruler who serves as point of reference or head, but Jesus Christ. Certain passages in the First Letter of Paul to the Corinthians, in chapter 12 in particular, are fundamental to this turning point:

> [12] For as the body is one, and hath many members, and all the members of that one body, being many, are one body: so also is Christ. [13] For by one Spirit are we all baptized into one body, whether we be Jews or Gentiles, whether we be bond or free; and have been all made to drink into one.[16]

Paul then continues, fully in the style of the older fable, to interpret the body metaphor with a view to a division of labor and functional differentiation, linking this with an exhortation to unity in the Christian community—in line with his impassioned question at the start of the letter with reference to disputes within it: "Is Christ divided?"[17] This is why he ends this passage with the important sentence: "Now ye are the body of Christ, and members in particular."[18] It is this that is followed by his famous remarks on believers' various charisms, their different talents for mission or teaching, administration, healing, help, and ecstasy.

This idea of the community of Christians as the body of Christ exercised a profound effect on Christian thought. Today, this notion causes many people

---

15. See Struve, *Die Entwicklung der organologischen Staatsauffassung*, 31.
16. 1 Cor. 12: 12–13.
17. 1 Cor. 1:13.
18. 1 Cor 12:27.

to shake their heads in incomprehension. If at all, they relate it to the church, although here too, the more it is perceived as a mere form of justification (now of clerical power), the more suspicion it arouses. But historically, in the Christian world, the church was not generally perceived as sharply distinct from the secular realm, so this reference was by no means limited to the church as such, but rather was a key principle of all social order. Here, then, we have continuity with the ancient metaphor of the organism, but now it is no longer worldly power that stands center stage but Jesus Christ as the true king: a shift from the mundane to the transcendent, from the particular to the universal.[19]

It would, of course, be rash to assert close proximity between the remarks of Paul the apostle and medieval Latin Christianity. Paul clearly sees only the community of Christians as the body of Christ. It is thus a completely different question how Christians understand the polity and how they should relate to it. This may perhaps also be thought of as an organism, but certainly not as one that is identical with Christ or whose head is Christ. This delimited the prevailing conceptual framework as long as the state order itself was not influenced by Christianity or even anti-Christian—as in the Roman Empire before the conversion of the emperor Constantine or the adoption of Christianity as state religion under the emperor Theodosius. Only when the entire polity is conceptualized as Christian can the fully realized notion of the body of Christ offer itself as a model for social and political thinking. Only then can Christian salvific universalism be linked with a decidedly nonegalitarian concept, as with the organic social ethic of the Latin Middle Ages.

Since, under modern conditions, egalitarianism seems to follow necessarily from universalism, and thus universalism without egalitarian consequences is not considered true universalism at all, considerable obstacles to understanding must be overcome at this point. It is probably helpful, therefore, to briefly recall that the famous typology of possible relations between gospel and culture developed by H. Richard Niebuhr identifies Thomas Aquinas—the greatest representative of an organic social ethic, including in the eyes of Max Weber—as the epitome of one of these types—namely, that which Niebuhr calls "Christ

---

19. Here, I leave to one side the difference between the metaphors of the body of Christ and of Christ as the head of the body, as evident in the contrast between Corinthians and the pseudo-Pauline letters. On the emergence of the concept of the "mystical body" see the classical study by Henri de Lubac, *Corpus Mysticum: The Eucharist and the Church in the Middle Ages* (1949) (Notre Dame: University of Notre Dame Press, 2007).

above Culture."[20] This means a position that takes the salvific universalism of Christianity and the demands of the gospel deeply seriously, but eschews a sharp opposition between the gospel and worldly culture.

For Christians in this camp, it is not only the moral demands that can be traced back to Christ that hold validity, but the other rules of morality and law, which, although not originating with Christ, can also be traced back to God in a sense that requires further clarification. This involves sincere respect for worldly authority and not just for the church, for natural law and not just the divine commandments, for philosophical and not just theological thinking. This respect, however, should not be perceived as a lessening of the demands of the gospel, but arises from the insight into how incredibly demanding, indeed super-human, are the demands of the Christian ethos of love. These are *not* reduced to a mere harmless ethic of amicability. But from this point of view, a social whole can be organized only if, while everything is correlated with the gospel in a rea-sonable hierarchical order, each individual is not morally overwhelmed by the ethos of love. Such an understanding view of the organic social ethic expounded by Thomas, of the kind I am hinting at here, should not be equated with the can-onization of his teachings in nineteenth-century Catholicism. The latter, it seems fair to say, entailed not so much an attempt to achieve a new, creative synthesis of Christianity and modern culture as to recommend for the present the old synthesis put forward by Thomas, which was creative in its time.[21] Even in retro-spect, there is a risk of idealizing this past synthesis as such and of dehistoricizing it.[22] But we have to understand it as a time-bound attempt at a solution, which nonetheless remains instructive for all moral universalists, whether Christians or others. This is my focus here. An adequate understanding of organic social ethics is necessary if our goal is to explore viable forms of moral universalism.

It is, therefore, crucial to grasp the difference between a this-worldly and particularist organic social ethic, as found historically in many systems of domi-nation, and the Christian organic social ethic, which foregrounds transcendence and universalism. It is very doubtful that Max Weber perceived this difference or gave it enough consideration. It is thus useful to go back to his sources because

---

20. H. Richard Niebuhr, *Christ and Culture* (1951) (New York: Harper & Row, 2001), 116–48. For a recent and in-depth analysis, see Hans Joas, *Under the Spell of Freedom: Theory of Religion after Hegel and Nietzsche* (New York: Oxford University Press, 2024), 256–76, esp. 263–67.

21. Niebuhr, *Christ and Culture*, 139.

22. Niebuhr, *Christ and Culture*, 146.

they allow us to relativize his point of view. But we also have to ask exactly how institutional consequences could be drawn in the here and now on the basis of a transcendence-focused and universalist organic social ethic.

It is from this vantage point that one would have to recall two institutional complexes as they appear differently in Thomas Aquinas and Dante. Both these great thinkers thought and wrote in the field of tension between two institutional complexes, both of which embodied universalist claims—namely, imperial rule and papacy. These two institutional complexes did not simply negate one another. Their relationship was, however, subject to vehement dispute, not just in historical reality but also at the level of social theory. Once these points have been cleared up and we have critically evaluated Weber, we can then, as adumbrated previously, briefly examine how we might conceptualize the relationship between universalism and worldly order in the Indian and Islamic traditions.

The immediate and main source for Weber's use of the term "organic social ethics" in relation to the Latin Middle Ages seems to be Ernst Troeltsch.[23] Time and again, Weber acknowledged that the Protestant theologian had a superior knowledge of the history of Christianity, and by no means only of the Reformation and Protestantism. Yet this superiority applies to the Middle Ages as well, although Protestant theologians often paid little attention to them and neglected them in their research. Superior knowledge is one thing, however, analytical perspective another. As often as the former was later recognized, the analytical difference between Weber and Troeltsch was seldom noticed. Above all, Troeltsch's great work of 1912, *The Social Teachings of the Christian Churches and Groups* (to translate its original German title) contains a large number of passages that make reference to an organic social ethic or the like. I will discuss his views in more detail in a moment. But Troeltsch too makes recourse to certain predecessors. Before him, in his 1883 history of medieval metaphysics—part of his reflections on the origins and foundations of the humanities—Wilhelm Dilthey had already set out how the idea of the organism "was transferred from the mystical body of the church . . . to the state in a new sense that went beyond Aristotle."[24]

---

23. This view was also held by the editors of Weber's "Sociology of Religion" in the German *Max-Weber-Gesamtausgabe*, vol. I/22-2, 397n53. Strangely enough, however, they refer to a text by Troeltsch in which Thomas Aquinas is mentioned, but not an "organic social ethic." Yet the term often appears in his *Social Teachings*, as discussed later in this chapter.

24. Wilhelm Dilthey, *Einleitung in die Geisteswissenschaften: Versuch einer Grundlegung für das Studium der Gesellschaft und der Geschichte*, vol. 1 (1883), in Wilhelm Dilthey, *Gesammelte Schriften*, vol. 1 (Göttingen, Germany: Vandenhoeck & Ruprecht, 1973), 346.

But informing the writings of Dilthey and Troeltsch—and Troeltsch for his part clearly acknowledges this—there is another figure who shed light on the developmental processes of the medieval "social ethic" more than any of his predecessors: Otto von Gierke. Particularly in the third, 1881 volume of his monumental work *Das deutsche Genossenschaftsrecht* (*The German Law of Associations*), he reconstructed theories of the state and corporations in antiquity and the Middle Ages with reference to a wide range of sources. Since the title of this text is unlikely to attract many readers today, it should be added that Gierke's interest in the associative realm was due to his belief that it could help construct an alternative or at least supplement to a purely domination-oriented understanding of the state and associations. I am not the first to see this as a basis for relativizing what Max Weber wrote about state and church.[25] In chronological order let's briefly run through the figures who anticipated and laid the ground for Weber's influential concept.

IDEAL OF HUMANITY AND WORLDLY POLITY: OTTO VON GIERKE

Beginning in the Romantic era, and with the emergence of the Historical School of Jurisprudence, both characterized by their resistance to the rationalism of the Enlightenment and rejection of an abstract understanding of natural law, the concept of the organic became increasingly saturated with connotations. It became the antithesis of the mechanical, artificial, or even the merely individual, and was thus often disdained as reactionary by opponents of Romanticism and defenders of rationalism. Yet the text that provides the broadest historical account of the development of the "organological" conception of state and society cannot be accused of a backward-looking idealization of German or Germanic realities or of simple dependence on the organism metaphor. I am referring to the history of the German law of associations produced by the legal historian Otto von Gierke in four volumes from

---

25. This is clearly apparent in Otto Hintze, "Max Webers Soziologie" (1926), in Otto Hintze, *Soziologie und Geschichte: Gesammelte Abhandlungen*, vol. 2 (Göttingen, Germany: Vandenhoeck & Ruprecht, 1964), 142.

26. Otto von Gierke, *Das deutsche Genossenschaftsrecht*, 4 vols. (1868ff) (Graz, Austria: Akademische Druck- und Verlagsanstalt, 1954), 135–47.

1868 onward.[26] It was greatly admired by contemporaries. Max Weber called it "magnificent"[27] in his "Sociology of Law," while Wilhelm Dilthey mentioned Gierke in the same breath as Comte and Spencer as "leading exponents of a social orientation in the conception of society"[28] and Ernst Troeltsch leaned heavily on him in his account of the Middle Ages (more on this below). In our context, the key point is that in his reconstruction of the history of Christianity and the Middle Ages, Gierke laid the ground for a *universalist* understanding of the idea of an organic social doctrine. For him, the prototype was not the ancient Roman, but the Christian use of this metaphor. His account of the effect of Christianity on the ancient concept of the association thus begins with the following powerful sentences:

> Christianity destroyed the foundations of ancient social theory by transferring man's conception of the ideal state from the temporal sphere to the Empire of God. The state no longer appeared as the universal expression of the human community. There was a higher and more thoroughly integrated society that encompassed both heaven and earth. As a living entity, society linked its members with the personality of God. The individual did not find his end merely as a part of the state who found his fulfilment in the life of the total community. Rather, by virtue of his immortal soul, man was endowed with an absolute value and a transcendental purpose.[29]

The political thought of the Middle Ages is evidently of particular interest to Gierke precisely because it defies a simple, dichotomous distinction between individualism and holism. Although, as Gierke believed, it shares with ancient thought the prioritizing of the social whole, it is in accord with modern natural

---

27. Weber, *Economy and Society*, 717. Elsewhere, admittedly, he inveighs against the ideas inherent in the "organic theory of the state" as a contemporary theory of the state, but even here, he concedes that this body of thought "has been of the greatest heuristic value" to Gierke and historical research. See Max Weber, "Roscher and Knies and the Logical Problems of Historical Economics," in Max Weber, *Collected Methodological Writings* (London: Routledge, 2012), 24n1.

28. Wilhelm Dilthey, "Thomas Carlyle," in Wilhelm Dilthey, *Die Jugendgeschichte Hegels und andere Abhandlungen zur Geschichte des deutschen Idealismus: Gesammelte Schriften*, vol. 4 (Göttingen, Germany: Vandenhoeck & Ruprecht, 1974), 525n1.

29. There are several partial translations of Gierke's work into English. Here and in the following notes I give the reference to the German original and the respective translation. Gierke, *Genossenschaftsrecht*, vol. 3, 106f; Otto Gierke, *Associations and Law: The Classical and Early Christian Stages* (Toronto and Buffalo: University of Toronto Press, 1977), 143.

law in its proclamation of "the intrinsic and aboriginal rights of the individual."[30] In this way of thinking, on the one hand, every human polity will be part of "that ordering of the world which exists because God exists, and every earthly group must appear as a member of that Civitas Dei, that God-State, which comprehends the heavens and the earth. Then, on the other hand, the eternal and other-worldly aim and object of every individual man must, in a more direct or more indirect fashion, determine the aim and object of every group into which he enters."[31] Gierke, however, takes good care not to construct historical developments solely at a conceptual level, painstakingly examining the extent to which the shift evident within theological speculation did in fact exercise a formative influence on the law. As long as Christians were persecuted or merely tolerated, such an influence could in any case not emanate from them; in law, their communities were at best "collegia illicita."[32]

But even later, initially the church, this completely new entity that the Christians had created, was merely allocated a place among the unchanged institutions. To be more specific, this means that on the one hand, the idea of the kingdom of God itself, which is opposed to the kingdom of this world in the gospel, had to be transformed in such a way that an institution existing in the world, known as the church, could be thought of as at least a partial realization of an ideal that transcends all that is worldly. On the other hand, a place had to be found in the law for this novel, transcendence-focused entity, which differs from all known forms of association.

This search for the right place took place at two levels, which are clearly distinguishable, although the associated developments naturally occurred in relation to one another and we can identify all kinds of interactions. The converted Emperor Constantine thought it would be a solution to incorporate the church into law by conceptualizing it as a state institution in continuity with the tradition of the empire. Hence, nothing was more obvious than to view the emperor himself as "the living source and active representative of the unity of the church," so that "he could assemble the ecumenical council that was dependent on him. Only under his rule and with his collaboration could the church give the impression of unity. Consequently, the emperor qua emperor could rule over its

---

30. Gierke, *Genossenschaftsrecht*, 514; Otto Gierke, *Political Theories of the Middle Age* (Cambridge: Cambridge University Press, 1900), 7.
31. Gierke, *Genossenschaftsrecht*, 514; Gierke, *Political Theories of the Middle Age*, 7f.
32. Gierke, *Genossenschaftsrecht*, 114; Gierke, *Associations and Law*, 149.

dogma and its constitution."[33] This did not preclude the relative autonomy of the church's subunits. In theological thought, however, this simple integration of the new entity of the church into the state had a charged relationship with the church's universalist self-understanding. In other words, what Gierke describes as the "profound Pauline allegory"[34] of the body of Christ transfers the ancient organism metaphor both to this new entity of the "church" and to all of human-ity, because of course, Paul regards the whole of humanity, now or potentially, as unified in Christ. Through Paul and in his effective history (*Wirkungsgeschichte*), in a way that goes far beyond the approaches of the Stoics, the whole of humanity is thought of as "a united spiritual and ethical organism,"[35] and the church itself is imagined as a worldly representative of what is still to be realized on earth through the preaching of the good news. The tension between "humanity" and "church" could remain concealed as long as the associated political aspiration was also universal; this was the case in the empire. It was bound to become acute as soon as the empire was threatened with disintegration or collapsed.

This tension between imperial political and ecclesiastical moral-religious uni-versalism was also reflected in the church's internal structure. We can think of the church as the community of believers in Christ, but right from the start, this community featured a gap engendered because some could claim to have been called by Jesus himself, spawning a charisma of closeness to Jesus and close-ness to those close to him. Within what we might describe as the social move-ment of Christians, as in most social movements, stabilized structures quickly developed, such as the fixed roles of priests and bishops. Precisely because of the church's transformation into a state institution, the community of believ-ers was increasingly interpreted as involving mere membership and, according to Gierke, "Its active side was transferred to the healing task represented in its spiritual function. The church as a whole still encompassed the totality of the faithful and unified them. But this subjective unity of the association, and its personality, survived and acted exclusively in the church's healing apparatus that was derived from its transcendental origin. The conception of the church, insofar as it appeared as a living legal entity, a fellowship, yielded entirely to the idea of a transcendental institutional church."[36] The more the church endeavored to assert

---

33. Gierke, *Genossenschaftsrecht*, 114; Gierke, *Associations and Law*, 149.
34. Gierke, *Genossenschaftsrecht*, 108; Gierke, *Associations and Law*, 145.
35. Gierke, *Genossenschaftsrecht*, 109; Gierke, *Associations and Law*, 146.
36. Gierke, *Genossenschaftsrecht*, 110; Gierke, *Associations and Law*, 147.

itself in the sphere of political power, the more it itself developed a hierarchical structure. In structural analogy, next to the "bureaucratically articulated temporal state" stood a "hierarchic spiritual state" in the shape of the papal church.[37]

But despite all the structural analogies and all the legal and de facto involvement of the church—as an institution of salvation—in the state, associative structures were retained, in the monasteries for example. Most important, however, despite all the deficiencies in the new set-up in a *positive* sense, the ground was laid for "basic negations of ancient views of the state and the law":[38] "Man's existence was not exhausted in his citizenship nor was the community identical with the state. The influential idea that obedience was due to God rather than to men began its victorious career. The pagan state's omnipotence vanished before it. The idea of an inherent limitation of the powers of the state and of the duties of all subjects gained ascendancy. The right and duty to resist the coercion of the state were sealed with the martyrs' blood."[39]

What we discern here in incipient form could have an institution-forming effect beyond the framework of the church only under the radically changed conditions of the Middle Ages. Because the whole of creation was thought of as one organism, this gave rise directly to the "postulate of an External, Visible Community comprehending All Mankind."[40] This conception had always been inherent in the idea of the church, as well as the idea of the empire, which gained new vigor as a result of the *translatio imperii* from Rome or Constantinople to the Frankish Empire. But now two institutional complexes existed, both of which made universalist claims: empire and papacy, worldly and spiritual order, with their this-worldly and otherworldly goals. Of course, this does not inevitably mean that the two were mutually antagonistic. No one doubted that they depended on each other and together formed a higher unity. The leading intellects and the institutions, however, differed on what this unity involved and whether it was to be achieved by "theocratic" means (that is, through the supremacy of pope and church), or through a "monarchical" approach (in other

---

37. Gierke, *Genossenschaftsrecht*, 114f, n8; Gierke, *Associations and Law*, 150f.

38. Gierke, *Genossenschaftsrecht*, 123; Gierke, *Associations and Law*, 155.

39. Gierke, *Genossenschaftsrecht*, 123; Gierke, *Associations and Law*, 156. It is noteworthy that here, Gierke only emphasizes the contrast between the church and the ancient state, not the difference between ancient Roman and Christian religion, as did Fustel de Coulanges, Émile Durkheim's teacher. See Numa Denis Fustel de Coulanges, *The Ancient City: A Study on the Religion, Laws, and Institutions of Greece and Rome* (orig. 1864) (New York: Doubleday Anchor, 1956), 389–96.

40. Gierke, *Genossenschaftsrecht*, 517; Gierke, *Political Theories of the Middle Age*, 10.

words, by pope and church renouncing worldly jurisdiction and enforcement of authority).

Gierke, meanwhile, provides an overview of the range of views. In the first instance, the most important point that he makes is that all sides used the Pauline metaphor not just for the church, but for all associations, ecclesiastical or worldly, for the state as such, and for humanity as a whole, with the latter supposedly finding institutional expression in the universal church and empire.[41] But it would be quite wrong to use the organism metaphor as deployed in this Christian tradition founded by Paul to describe a single state or a single society as distinct from others or even as struggling with others in a state of nature.

THE MEDIEVAL METAPHYSICS OF HISTORY AND SOCIETY: WILHELM DILTHEY

The first to continue Gierke's line of argument in a way of relevance to us here was Wilhelm Dilthey: in his historical stock-taking of Occidental metaphysics, he turned to the question of where medieval thinking went beyond that of antiquity. For him, the creative character of medieval thought came to the fore when a metaphysics of history and society "was added to the metaphysics of nature as the creation of the Greek spirit."[42] As he sees it, this applies to theocratic ideas, but also to the specific power of the idea of the emperor and notions of the unity of Christianity. Dilthey is particularly interested in the development of a form of historical thinking that is guided by the idea that humanity is a unity, "an individual, so to speak, that has to pass along a developmental path but, as a pupil, is taught the laws governing this development chiefly by his methodically operating teacher."[43] Dilthey finds this idea

---

41. Otto von Gierke, *Johannes Althusius und die Entwicklung der naturrechtlichen Staatstheorien* (orig. 1880) (Aalen, Germany: Scientia 1981), 61, 133.

42. Dilthey, *Einleitung in die Geisteswissenschaften*, 329. It should be noted at this point that Dilthey's book was the subject of an extensive and well-disposed review by Gierke. Otto von Gierke, "Eine Grundlegung für die Geisteswissenschaften," *Preußische Jahrbücher* 53 (1884): 105–44. This text also shows beyond doubt that Gierke was no naive advocate of the organism metaphor. He writes (137): "Every hypothesis that posits an entity living and operating outside of individuals, using terms such as 'soul of the people' (*Volksseele*), 'spirit of the people' (*Volksgeist*) or 'organism,' goes beyond the limits of experience."

43. Dilthey, *Einleitung in die Geisteswissenschaften*, 336. The English translation of Dilthey's work does not contain the part on the Middle Ages to which I am referring here.

prefigured in the work of the Church Fathers, and especially that of Augustine, but then sees it developed further in the Middle Ages in the form of a doctrine of two historical ideational spheres, church and empire. Particularly original here is the "view of the church," whose "creative nucleus" lies in Paul's teaching on the body of Christ: "In the church, the spiritual substances of all hierarchies are bound together to form a mystical body, which extends down from the Trinity and the angels that stand beside it to the beggar at the church doors and the man in bondage who, kneeling humbly in the furthest corner of the church, shares in the offering of the mass."[44] Dilthey sets great store by *not* viewing this metaphor—this "trope," as he puts it[45]—as an idea that applies to every political whole. In the first instance, we are told, it applies only to Christian communities animated by a common spirit ("pneuma"), but then in medieval thought, emanating from the church as a whole, this idea comes to guide the understanding of the entire universal order encompassing the church or ruled by it ("theocratically").

In the details of his historical account, Dilthey quite obviously relies on Gierke and refers to him several times.[46] Just how much he, like Gierke, is influenced by the issue of universalism is apparent in the fact that he identified a backward step in the "valorization of the state as such" in the writings of Marsilius of Padua, the notion of the "sacerdotium" as a component and function of the state, which could be interpreted as an important step in a history of secularization. According to Dilthey, Marsilius was "at bottom [fighting against] the *progress* entailed in Christ's claims about the law of the emperor and the law of God."[47] He expressly mentions that the concept of the organism with its roots in Paul went beyond that of Aristotle,[48] and that its application to the state did not represent a return to Aristotle. Dilthey acknowledges the emergence of natural law ideas, in which, as in ancient times, the "unity of political will" and the right to rule are derived "from the individual will of the persons bound together to form an organization."[49] But this does not prompt him to see in the "theocratic metaphysics of society" a medieval step backward from the

44. Dilthey, *Einleitung in die Geisteswissenschaften*, 337.
45. Dilthey, *Einleitung in die Geisteswissenschaften*, 338.
46. Dilthey, *Einleitung in die Geisteswissenschaften*, 344n3, 348n1.
47. Dilthey, *Einleitung in die Geisteswissenschaften*, 345 (my emphasis).
48. Dilthey, *Einleitung in die Geisteswissenschaften*, 346.
49. Dilthey, *Einleitung in die Geisteswissenschaften*, 346f.

understanding of the political already achieved in antiquity. On the contrary, for him, the medieval organological theory was "superior to all earlier versions in that its starting point was the encompassing context of the social life of humanity and every statement about the powers of a political authority as well as every assertion about the concept of a virtue or duty was conditioned by this context."[50]

Hence, while he defends this universalistic orientation, he criticizes the inability of medieval thinkers to truly analyze historical facts rather than merely integrating them into a predetermined teleological interpretation. The main feature of the medieval metaphysics of society, as Dilthey saw it, was the new conceptual framework that it constructed to convey "what tradition and profound religious insight" always already possessed.[51] For Dilthey, in medieval metaphysics, the ancient search for eternal truths collides with the idea inherent in Christianity of God's historical plan, of a God who is himself active historically. In Dilthey's view, there is an irresolvable contradiction here—not, as neo-Scholasticism would have it, a harmonious synthesis.[52] Acting human beings' experience of freedom and the idea of an order that is a once-and-for-all given, one encompassing political-social reality, Dilthey states, are mutually exclusive: "The vibrant personal experience of the will, which includes needs and change, cannot be reconciled with the immutable world of eternal ideas, through which the intellect possesses the necessary and universally valid truth."[53] Although for Dilthey, this form of thinking inevitably had to perish because it overestimated its potential to resolve contentious issues such as the relationship between "state and church, between world monarchy and individual state" by means of syllogisms,[54] these issues still required resolution. For Dilthey, this task is handed to the postmetaphysical humanities, which, however, he believed must not forget what the Christian Middle Ages bequeathed to them with its vision of a single human nexus.

---

50. Dilthey, *Einleitung in die Geisteswissenschaften*, 348.
51. Dilthey, *Einleitung in die Geisteswissenschaften*, 348.
52. Dilthey, *Einleitung in die Geisteswissenschaften*, 349. On this passage, see also Matthias Jung, *Dilthey zur Einführung* (Hamburg, Germany: Junius Verlag, 1996), 82f.
53. Dilthey, *Einleitung in die Geisteswissenschaften*, 349.
54. Dilthey, *Einleitung in die Geisteswissenschaften*, 350.

THE UNIVERSALISM OF MEDIEVAL CHRISTIANITY:
ERNST TROELTSCH

We turn now to Ernst Troeltsch, who drew on the work of Gierke and Dilthey when he set about addressing "medieval Catholicism" in the context of his lengthy account of the history of Christianity and its "social teachings." A contemporary review of his book by a leading Protestant church historian, which was highly critical overall, declared "the account and evaluation of Thomism, in its enduring significance to Catholicism, one of the outstanding features of Troeltsch's work." The review continued, "He has projected himself into Thomist thought with a sympathy that is rare among Protestants, while perceiving as well as acknowledging what is truly impressive about this leading form of Christian social philosophy."[55] Considering Troeltsch's scholarly oeuvre and his diverse journalistic writings in the politics of religion, it is almost surplus to requirements to mention that his sensitive interpretation of Thomas Aquinas does not reveal a sympathy for neo-Thomism or neo-Scholasticism. It is quite obvious that, when it comes to contemporary Catholicism, his sympathies lie with the so-called modernists, whom the pope condemned in a 1907 encyclical.[56] In their endeavors, he saw exciting parallels to his own efforts within Protestantism, which also met with strong resistance from the official church. Although Troeltsch drew partly on the research literature on the Middle Ages produced by neo-Thomist authors (Victor Cathrein, Max Maurenbrecher, Joseph Mausbach, and Theodor Meyer, S. J.), to accuse him of being dependent on them, it seems to me, is to succumb to an unduly foreshortened perspective.[57] If he was dependent

---

55. Paul Wernle, "Vorläufige Anmerkungen zu den Soziallehren der christlichen Kirchen und Gruppen von Ernst Troeltsch," *Zeitschrift für Theologie und Kirche* 22 (1912): 355.
56. See the impressive article that this event prompted Troeltsch to write. Ernst Troeltsch, "Katholizismus und Reformismus" (1908), in Ernst Troeltsch, *Schriften zur Religionswissenschaft und Ethik* (1903–1912) (Berlin: De Gruyter, 2014), 643–56, in *Kritische Gesamtausgabe*, vol. 6.1, ed. Trutz Rendtorff.
57. This is the view taken by the authors of the only two extended attempts that I know of to get to grips with Troeltsch's view of the Middle Ages. Ulrich Köpf, "Die Idee der 'Einheitskultur' des Mittelalters," in *Ernst Troeltschs Soziallehren: Studien zu ihrer Interpretation*, ed. Friedrich Wilhelm Graf and Trutz Rendtorff (Gütersloh, Germany: Gütersloher Verlagshaus Gerd Mohn, 1993), 120; and Ludger Honnefelder, "Die ethische Rationalität des mittelalterlichen Naturrechts und die Bedeutung der Lehre vom natürlichen Gesetz bei Thomas von Aquin," in *Max Webers Sicht des okzidentalen Christentums: Interpretation und Kritik*, ed. Wolfgang Schluchter (Frankfurt, Germany: Suhrkamp Verlag, 1988), 254–75, esp. 263–68.

on predecessors—and he could in fact draw on the sources himself only to a limited degree—then in my opinion, they were Gierke and Dilthey.

But what motivated this intense engagement and empathy and an interpretation that ascribed to Thomas a greater closeness to life than "the biological naturalistic constructions of modern sociology, with their collectivism, which represses the individual, and with their relativism, which finally tends to Monism"?[58] If we simply take Troeltsch at his word, then the reason is that for him, Christianity features a notion of moral universalism that goes beyond any particular social form; for this very reason, it requires both an institution of its own and an idea about its relationship to other institutions—and to a way of life that distances the individual from exclusive enmeshment in particular social forms and leads them beyond these forms. In Troeltsch's own language, this means that the contradictions and tensions addressed by Thomas inevitably arise and demand resolution

> since alongside of the ordinary secular institutions an idea has arisen, an idea which will certainly never be allowed to die out, a universal, ethical, religious idea, the idea, namely, of personality united with God, and of human society united with God, and this idea is struggling to create a society which will accord with its point of view, and it must aspire to carry out these ideas into the life of the whole, far beyond the circle of the particular religious community.[59]

We would be missing the point of Troeltsch's remarks if we were to emphasize the religious dimension here rather than the universal one. Troeltsch certainly saw the moral universalism of Christianity as the highest form of such an orientation and perceived in the religious inspiration of the ethos of love the soundest basis for intense motivation to realize this universalism. But his concern is not with religion per se versus secularism per se, but with universalism versus particularism. In his historical account of Christianity, its ideational core is characterized by universalism and individualism. The Middle Ages thus posed a new challenge for Christianity because now an ideal that had assumed its

---

58. Ernst Troeltsch, *The Social Teachings of the Christian Churches and Groups* (1912) (London: Allen & Unwin, 1931), 277.
59. Troeltsch, *Social Teachings*, 277.

concrete form under the conditions of the Roman Empire was transplanted into conditions under which it could not have arisen. This is true, at least, if the idea is correct that moral universalism would never have got off the ground without the challenge of the empire's "political universalism."[60] Under the conditions into which it was transplanted, this ideal could neither be simply abandoned nor sufficiently realized by those seized by it. The church, then, represents nothing less than the bridge between the past and the present. Yet this is the source of the tension that medieval Catholicism sought to overcome and that persisted even under the radically changed conditions of later eras. This is what drove Troeltsch's intensive engagement with an organic social ethic.

This is the term that he used for this solution in countless passages of his oeuvre, in multiple variations. I will not be going into these or his similarly frequent references to Gierke in detail here,[61] but rather limit myself to the way in which Troeltsch aspires to supplement Gierke. Troeltsch emphasized more than the latter that besides the organism idea, there was another source for medieval social teaching, without which we cannot understand this specific form of Christianity. This second source arises from the fact that, despite all the disregarding of "worldly" differences in the cultic community, and for all the universalism inherent in the notion of Christians as the children of God, "the community itself is affected by the various differentiations and hindrances as well as advantages which result from the connection with social institutions outside the Church, and from natural differences."[62] To this, however, Christians responded by breaking in a quite specific way with the patriarchalism that was already culturally available to embrace what Troeltsch calls the "patriarchalism of love," that is, "the voluntary acceptance of, and submission to,

60. I am unable to elaborate this thesis further here. It is crucially developed in the literature on the so-called Axial Age, especially the work of Robert Bellah. See Hans Joas, *The Power of the Sacred: An Alternative to the Narrative of Disenchantment* (New York: Oxford University Press, 2021), 154–94, and Joas, *Under the Spell of Freedom*, 317–30.

61. Troeltsch repeatedly uses the predicate "magnificent" in referring to Gierke's work, as did Weber (see, e.g., *Social Teachings*, 198n77). It is also evident here how much Troeltsch considers himself emancipated by Gierke and the Catholic authors from a specific blindness typical of the Protestant theologians of his time: "They regard the Christian nature of the State and of Society as something which is so obvious that they have no idea of or eye for the toiled and devious ways along which the Early Church, the Mediaeval Church, and their own Protestant forefathers had to travel before they could secure these ideas on a firm basis." Especially with regard to his interpretation of Augustine, Troeltsch was in fact accused of being too close to Gierke, an idea that he rejected.

62. Troeltsch, *Social Teachings*, 285.

these differences, which were to be utilized by some as an opportunity for the exercise of charity and devotion towards their less fortunate brethren, and by others as occasions for displaying the virtues of trust, patience, and humility to those above them; by this means the voluntary relationships of submission and authority produced the peculiar ethical values of mutual personal relationships."[63]

This patriarchalism of love affects relations of social inequality, but also those between men and women, adults and children, and even affects the subjective sense of having been favored or disadvantaged with respect to one's lot in life.[64] Without patriarchalism, the organism metaphor would very quickly become a conception of the division of labor and functional differentiation, though, unlike in antiquity, with a focus on transcendence and universalism. But in the concrete form of Thomist social philosophy, the organic idea, with its roots in the church, is joined by another idea, that of the patriarchalism of the family, though this is softened and humanized by the ethos of love: "The sociological ideal of the Family as the original ideal of human relationships is applied to all the conditions of rule and subordination in general. Repeatedly we are reminded that Christendom is a great family, in which the virtues of the family ethically hallow and glorify all the infinitely varied mutual relationships of humanity."[65]

By assuming a basic schema rooted in the merging of two components—"church" and "family," "organism" and "patriarchalism"—Troeltsch provides himself with an analytical tool capable of explaining what seems at first glance the contradictory character of Catholicism in political and social terms. For him, the organic idea of the Christian Middle Ages entails more than just an ideological patina on existing conditions of inequality. It also has the implication "that whenever this harmony, in actual fact, has been disturbed, it ought to be restored" and the endowment of every member of the order, that is, every individual, with the status of "end in itself" and with her or his own dignity and "the obligation to assist every other member into his spiritual inheritance where it is necessary."[66]

---

63. Troeltsch, *Social Teachings*, 285.
64. Troeltsch, *Social Teachings*, 288.
65. Troeltsch, *Social Teachings*, 287.
66. Troeltsch, *Social Teachings*, 288.

Troeltsch goes so far as to claim a kind of revolutionary potential for Catholicism, because for him, the "organic idea" is

> the active, formative critical principle of Christian sociology, which on occasion can even become revolutionary. Unjust institutions, which are not obedient to the Law of God, may and must be altered; godless rulers must be deposed or warned, and taught to amend their ways. The "right of resistance" and of rebellion is a right of the Christian conscience for the sake of love and of organic harmony—that is to say, if it can be exercised without causing still greater general disorder.[67]

In particular, the church itself claims a kind of right to revolution, but it refuses, despite impulses that well up time and again, to apply the organic idea to itself in the sense of greater synodalization of church governance.

Troeltsch, meanwhile, associates "the conservative, stabilizing aspect of the system, which accepts actual conditions as it finds them" and, indeed, its often quietist character, with the patriarchal idea.[68] Medieval, but for Troeltsch, all later Catholicism as well now represents a hybrid entity. It is "that peculiar mixture of active and militant, passive and quietistic elements, of legitimist and absolutist, and of democratic and individualist points of view, of revolution from above and from below, of optimistic rationalism and of a pessimistic sense of sin, which dominate the sociology of Catholic thought down to the present day."[69] From this vantage point, individualist and secular liberalism, as well as the absolutist doctrine of sovereignty, merely represent different varieties of one-sidedness. As a result, it is mostly impossible to shoehorn Catholicism into the schemas of left and right.

In this view, to preserve the "masterpiece of reconciliation"[70] and prevent any form of one-sidedness, what is required is an authority with the final say—namely, the papacy. Troeltsch traces in detail the consequences of this way of thinking for the understanding of law and the state, family and vocation, while seeking to take stock, on an empirically sound basis, of the ascertainable effects of these

---

67. Troeltsch, *Social Teachings*, 288f.
68. Troeltsch, *Social Teachings*, 291.
69. Troeltsch, *Social Teachings*, 291f.
70. Troeltsch, *Social Teachings*, 293.

ideas and of the church's actions in the different spheres of society. There is no room to explore any of this in the present text. In any case, what emerges here is a picture of an impressively cohesive social doctrine, which is also anchored in a specific metaphysics.

Neither in the work of Troeltsch nor that of Gierke and Dilthey, however, did intensive efforts at historical reconstruction aim to revive this form of Christian social philosophy—quite the opposite. In fact, this historicization was intended to act as an antidote to the idealization of this way of thinking, to any tendency to make it into a timeless principle—to its "eternalization," so to speak. After the hegemony of this thinking had waned in the late Middle Ages and in the Enlightenment era, the Catholic Church fell back on it in the Counter-Reformation and in the nineteenth century, adapting it to new problems but also declaring it a binding authoritative source of orientation. As Troeltsch saw it, a large part of Protestant thought remained dependent on this thinking as well.[71] The clear distinction between the "organic social ethic" of the Middle Ages and that of the nineteenth century—"reactive organicism," as the British sociologist David Martin called the latter in his attempt at a general theory of secularization[72]—is for Troeltsch a prerequisite for the creation of a new Christian social philosophy appropriate to modern conditions, one that his entire oeuvre is dedicated to constructing.

A particularly nice example of Troeltsch's facility for combining historical reconstruction and contemporaneity can be seen in his examination, in the situation of extreme crisis that pertained in the aftermath of World War I, of Dante's medieval vision of empire and papacy: "the empire as the supreme and just arbitrating authority for the European family of nations, with members of equal status, and this empire closely allied with a papacy that guarantees and preserves Europe's spiritual unity and foundation."[73] Troeltsch regards the idea of the League of Nations as the equivalent of this vision in his day—one just as threatened by individual powers' pursuit of hegemony and by imperialism as in the Middle Ages. Troeltsch sees in this idea "the imperishable Christian-European

---

71. Troeltsch, *Social Teachings*, 323.

72. David Martin, "The Pattern of Reactive Organicism," in *A General Theory of Secularization* (New York: Harper & Row, 1978), 244–77. Similar comments are made by Franz-Xaver Kaufmann, *Soziologie und Sozialethik* (Fribourg, Switzerland: Academic Press, 2013), 321–53.

73. Ernst Troeltsch, *Der Berg der Läuterung: Zur Erinnerung an den 600jährigen Todestag Dantes* (Berlin: E. S. Mittel & Sohn, 1921), 9.

idea as distinct from the empires of antiquity,"[74] moral universalism in contrast to the merely political universalism of the empires,[75] an organic social ethic in the Christian sense.

THE ASCETIC VOCATIONAL ETHIC VERSUS ORGANIC SOCIAL ETHICS: MAX WEBER

But neither Gierke, Dilthey, nor Troeltsch made the term "organic social ethics" world-renowned and part of the conceptual apparatus of sociology. It was Max Weber who did so. The purpose of my lengthy reconstruction of the work of Weber's predecessors was to develop a yardstick to assess what Weber made of his forerunners' ideas. We now have two standards by which to evaluate him. The first question is whether Weber took sufficient account of the topic of universalism—so central to the work of Gierke, Dilthey, and Troeltsch—and thus of the difference between pre-Christian and Christian organic social ethics. The second is whether Gierke's emphasis on the associative realm, which forms a counterweight to a domination-focused analysis, is retained by Weber. This was undoubtedly the case in Ernst Troeltsch's understanding of the church. It is true that he sometimes referred to the (Catholic) church—as Weber did—as an "institution of salvation"[76] but he never forgot that it always claimed to be a "community of believers" as well. His view of the church is thus complex: "Thus from within the church appears as an organism which is partly an institution for faith, partly a fellowship of believers, while from without she appears to be the ruler of a sphere of law which is independent of the State and cannot be touched by the State."[77] Here, Troeltsch referred directly to Gierke, who reacted highly critically to attempts within the church to repress the associative dimension.[78] But what about Weber?

---

74. Troeltsch, *Der Berg der Läuterung*, 9f.
75. For my view of the current situation in this regard, see Hans Joas, *Friedensprojekt Europa?* (Munich: Kösel-Verlag, 2020).
76. For a useful text on the history of this term, see Andreas Anter, "Charisma und Anstaltsordnung: Max Weber und das Staatskirchenrecht seiner Zeit," in *Max Webers Religionssoziologie in interkultureller Perspektive*, ed. Hartmut Lehmann and Jean Martin Ouédraogo (Göttingen, Germany: Vandenhoeck & Ruprecht, 2003), 29–49, esp. 40ff.
77. Troeltsch, *Social Teachings*, 98.
78. See, for example, Gierke, *Das deutsche Genossenschaftsrecht*, vol. 1, 144.

I contend that Weber's understanding of the church and of organic social ethics was inadequate in both respects. In some of his most influential texts, he paid insufficient attention to the emphasis on Christianity as universalism, while also neglecting the stress on the associative dimension, even regarding the church as an institution of salvation. Comparison with Troeltsch and Gierke makes this contrast unmissable. Moreover, this comparison is not an artificial one since Weber relied in large part on the writings of these two scholars. He repeatedly mentioned his familiarity with Troeltsch's *Social Teachings*; for a time, the pair were such close colleagues that their families moved into the same house. The only thing that generally prevents comparison here is the myth that Troeltsch was one-sidedly influenced by Weber and had no ideas truly independent of the latter.[79] Gierke, meanwhile, as has only been appreciated fully in recent years, was one of Weber's most important academic teachers, an examiner of his PhD and postdoctoral qualifications, and a key source for the typology in Weber's sociology of domination.[80]

In the introduction to this chapter, I already pointed out that the most famous passage in which Weber refers to "organic social ethics" is to be found in the last sentence of his "Intermediate Reflection," in the context of his treatment of Indian intellectual religiosity, whose examination this text was intended to introduce. It is, therefore, not surprising that the same idea occurs in his India study itself, now under the guise of an " 'organicist' social ethics" or " 'organic' societal doctrine."[81] But the most detailed account appears in Weber's so-called "Religionssystematik" ("systematics of religion"), that is, the text known as the sociology-of-religion chapter of *Economy and Society*, in a section titled "Religious Ethics and the World."[82] There, explicitly drawing on Troeltsch's investigations,

---

79. For a crucial rebuttal of this myth, see Friedrich Wilhelm Graf, *Fachmenschenfreundschaft: Studien zu Troeltsch und Weber* (Berlin: De Gruyter, 2014).

80. The excellent studies by Gerhard Dilcher have played a key role in uncovering these connections. See, for example, Gerhard Dilcher, "Historische Sozialwissenschaft als Mittel zur Bewältigung der Moderne—Max Weber und Otto von Gierke im Vergleich," in Gerhard Dilcher, *Die Germanisten und die Historische Rechtsschule: Bürgerliche Wissenschaft zwischen Romantik, Realismus und Rationalisierung* (Frankfurt, Germany: Klostermann, 2017), 415–42 and his introduction to the re-publication of Weber's doctoral dissertation, "Zur Geschichte der Handelsgesellschaften im Mittelalter," "Max-Weber-Gesamtausgabe," vol. 1, Schriften 1889–1894 (Tübingen, Germany, 2008), 1–105. The references to Dilthey in Weber's writings are extremely rare and do not address the problem of interest here.

81. Max Weber, *The Religion of India: The Sociology of Hinduism and Buddhism* (Glencoe, IL: Free Press 1958), 122, 147.

82. Weber, *Economy and Society*, 597–602.

which "have brilliantly demonstrated"[83] Christianity's changed position vis-à-vis the state in the medieval church, Weber refers to the "general schema according to which religion customarily solves the problem of the tension between religious ethics and the non-ethical or unethical requirements of life in the political and economic structures of power within the world" by relativizing and differentiating ethics into "organic" (as contrasted to "ascetic") ethics of vocation. This solution, we are told, "holds true whenever a religion is dominant within a political organization or occupies a privileged status, and particularly when it is a religion of institutional grace."[84] At this point, Weber promptly mentions Thomas Aquinas and the Indian caste-centered ethic, to which he once again attributes a more consistent implementation of the "organic traditionalist ethics of vocation" than medieval Catholic teaching or Luther's doctrine of the three estates.

Since Weber associates the organic vocational ethic with strict traditionalism, the medieval Christian form seems to him "a much less secure foundation for the traditional stratification of vocations than did the steel-like anchorage of caste to the altogether different religious promises contained in the doctrine of metempsychosis."[85] By way of contrast, Weber denies any proximity between the organic conception and Islam, which, according to him, "rejected universalism, regarding the ideal status order as consisting of believers and unbelievers or pariah peoples, with the former dominating the latter."[86] Within this framework, unbelievers only had to make subsistence payments to believers; as "pariah peoples," how to regulate their own lives was left entirely up to them.[87]

These passages are bound to confuse the reader in several ways. First, against the background of Gierke, Dilthey, and Troeltsch, it is striking that in Weber's characterization of medieval Christianity, there is no mention of its universalism. Yet it was this that the abovementioned thinkers and scholars saw as the fulcrum of specifically Christian organological thinking. The motif of universalism, however, which at first glance seems to be simply missing from Weber's account of Christianity, suddenly appears in his characterization of Islam, if only in a negative sense as something that this religion renounced, in favor of economic motives, in its confrontation with other religions. Meanwhile, as expressed in the "Intermediate

---

83. Weber, *Economy and Society*, 597.
84. Weber, *Economy and Society*, 598.
85. Weber, *Economy and Society*, 600.
86. Weber, *Economy and Society*, 599.
87. Weber, *Economy and Society*, 599.

Reflection" and in Weber's major study dedicated to Indian religion, the latter is explicitly ascribed a "universal accessibility of salvation,"[88] so in this context at least, universalism seems to form part of an organic social ethic. Amid this confusion, it makes sense to consult other texts by Weber for purposes of clarification. His remarks on the "Church" must surely be a particularly apt source for clarifying whether he took enough account of medieval Catholicism's universalist ideal. Some of these can be found in his "Sociology of Religion," others in his "Sociology of Domination," especially the section titled "State and Hierocracy."[89]

In his "Sociology of Religion," it is the typological distinction between "church" and "sect" that is relevant to us here. This distinction makes sense only if, in line to some extent with Gierke's ideas on associations, one distinguishes, as in Troeltsch's work, between various forms of organization of believers (namely, believers of a religion whose universalism makes it impossible for it to fit neatly into the existing forms of political and social organization characteristic of a particular polity).[90] Weber's "Sociology of Religion" thus includes its own section on "congregation," but this expressly omits "the relationships between political authority and religious community, from which the concept of religious denomination derived" because these are tackled in his "Sociology of Domination."[91] In the latter, however, the difference between "Axial-universalist" and "pre-Axial, particularist" religions is systematically lost or is leveled off in general statements about the power of priests and hierocratic associations. Here, Weber proceeds without taking into account the specific organizational problems of a universalist religion. In this regard, then, Weber's "Sociology of Religion" and "Sociology of Domination" certainly do not form a logically consistent, and in this sense harmonious, whole.[92] Some claim to see signs that Weber would have remedied the inadequate integration of the two dimensions had he been able to continue his work.[93] But this is highly speculative. The problem lies deeper—in the

88. Weber, "Intermediate Reflection," 359.

89. Weber, Economy and Society, 1158–1212.

90. For a very clear understanding of these matters in connection with the analyses of the Bellah group, see the appendix "Ecclesiology in Action," in Steven M. Tipton, Public Pulpits: Methodists and Mainline Churches in the Moral Argument of Public Life (Chicago: University of Chicago Press, 2007), 425–42.

91. Weber, Economy and Society, 455.

92. Even a heavily Weber-oriented sociologist like Hartmann Tyrell concedes this. See Hartmann Tyrell, "Katholizismus und katholische Kirche," in Max Webers Religionssoziologie in interkultureller Perspective, ed. Hartmut Lehmann and Jean Martin Ouédraogo (Göttingen, Germany: Vandenhoeck & Ruprecht, 2003), 193–228.

93. Tyrell, 209, with reference to §17 of Weber's "Soziologische Grundbegriffe," one of his late texts.

one-sidedness of his sociology of domination as such, which fails to take account of the "associative" dimension. This is a shortcoming even of Weber's understanding of the state,[94] but it represents a far greater problem when it comes to an organization, such as the universal church, which aspires to transcend the state and all specific orders.

A mere sociology-of-domination perspective is one that "places the hierocratic case on the same level as political parties and associations, commercial enterprises, criminal groups, military organizations and so on in a 'levelling' way, and then seeks to identify the structures of 'superordination and subordination' *without distinction.*"[95] This leveling perspective is not good *"verstehend"* sociology, since the latter's core purpose is to take actors' self-understanding seriously, in this case the church's claim to universalism. Unfortunately, many believe that a sociology-of-domination framework in itself inevitably entails a critical perspective, although it is only a notion of freedom from domination that enables us to perceive specific structures of domination and the alternatives to them.

Before making a definitive assessment, however, it remains to consider whether Weber's comparative remarks on the lack of an organic social ethic in Islam and on India's organic social ethic in the caste system are well founded. As for Islam, the answer seems to be unambiguously negative. The originally universalist orientation of Islam is indisputable and also undisputed by Weber. The whole world ought to be and is to be pervaded by Islam. The military conquest of other peoples served as one of the means for this, especially in the early days. This holds true even if the proportion of peaceful expansion in the success of Islam is traditionally underestimated in those parts of the world with a Christian heritage.[96]

---

94. I have already indicated this with reference to Otto Hintze and Otto von Gierke (footnotes 23 and 78). I am unable to go into detail on this point here. Key evidence of Weber's "new approach" after 1918, which consists in not reducing the sociology of the state to the sociology of domination, can be found especially in studies by Stefan Breuer, such as, "Max Webers Staatssoziologie," *Kölner Zeitschrift für Soziologie und Sozialpsychologie* 45 (1993): 199–219. Also important is the edited volume of written notes and transcripts of Max Weber's last lecture (given immediately before his death) and the introduction by the editor, Gangolf Hübinger: Max Weber, *Allgemeine Staatslehre und Politik (Staatssoziologie)* (Tübingen, Germany: Mohr Siebeck, 2009) (=Max-Weber-Gesamtausgabe III-7) (Introduction, 1–41).

95. Tyrell, *Katholizismus und katholische Kirche,* 210 (my emphasis).

96. Of epoch-making importance to achieving a change of perspective is Marshall G. S. Hodgson, *The Venture of Islam: Conscience and History in a World Civilization,* 3 vols. (Chicago: University of Chicago Press, 1974). For a recent, brilliant account of the emergence of Islam in the field of tension between religious and political universalism, see Glen W. Bowersock, *The Crucible of Islam* (Cambridge, MA: Harvard University Press, 2017).

Weber went so far as to call the "religious war for the Muslim" essentially an enterprise directed toward the acquisition of large holdings of real estate because it was primarily oriented toward securing feudal revenue."[97] And—in his discussion of the "economic relationships of organized groups"—he also emphasized that "the Islamic missionary ardor, originally a religious obligation, found its limits in the conquering warriors' desire to have a non-Islamic, and hence underprivileged, population that could provide for the maintenance of the privileged believers.[98] But Weber underestimated two things. First, during the Islamic expansion, the attitude toward Jews and Christians and the tolerance shown toward them were shaped to a significant extent by respect for these older monotheistic "religions of the book" and were not simply a matter of foregoing religious conversion for economic reasons. Conversion was pursued in an unbridled form when it came to "heathen" Arabs, but not "non-Arabs," let alone Christians and Jews. An Arab ethnic particularism, in which conversion to Islam partly aimed to overcome tribalism, and Islamic religious universalism, were locked in constant struggle.

Weber is largely right about the Arab tribal warriors. But he underestimated—and this is my second criticism—the inner-Islamic religious opposition to their way of thinking, which pushed for equal treatment of all Muslims, regardless of their ethnicity. Weber's analyses are thus valid only to a very limited extent. In reality, regarding the period after the first conquests, one can say: "Rather than a regression, as implied by Weber, Islamic universalism was on the ascent. This paved the way for the acceleration of the process of Islamization, first under Muslim rule, and then far beyond the frontiers of the military expansion of the Muslims."[99] Universalism, however, impels the development of an organic social ethic; this has held true historically, up to and including present-day Islamic fundamentalism.

As far as India is concerned, again, Weber's conceptual ambiguity sounds a jarring note. In his "Intermediate Reflection," he ascribes to the Indian religious tradition the idea of the "universal accessibility of salvation," and yet he begins his study of India with a detailed discussion of Hinduism as a "birth-religion,"

---

97. Weber, *Economy and Society*, 474.
98. Weber, *Economy and Society*, 344.
99. Nehemia Levitzion, "Aspects of Islamization: Weber's Observations on Islam Reconsidered," in *Max Weber and Islam*, ed. Toby E. Huff and Wolfgang Schluchter (New Brunswick, NJ: Routledge, 1999), 154.

to which one belongs by being born of Hindu parents and that is exclusive in the sense that there is in fact no other way to be admitted into this religious community. "Hinduism does not wish to encompass mankind. No matter what his belief or way of life, anyone not born a Hindu remains an outsider, a barbarian to whom the sacred values of Hinduism are in principle denied."[100] Here, we come up against the fact that universalism may mean the ultimate goal of encompassing all of humanity, or it may denote only the accessibility of salvation to all members of a specific culture, into which one must be born in order to belong to it.

It is true that moral universalism as such does not in any logically compelling way imply a missionary mindset, that is, the tendency to disseminate inherent in the universalist religion. In his study of ancient Judaism, Weber was particularly interested in why the universalism of the Old Testament prophets was fractured in such a way that it did not give rise to a missionary world religion, but rather to a ritually self-segregating congregational community (*Konfessionsverband*) that, however, ascribed to itself a world-historical mission as the chosen people.[101] It is surprising that Weber fails to pay similar attention to whether we can ascribe moral universalism to "Hinduism" in the first place. In no way do I deny that there have been multiple universalist (in the sophisticated sense of the term) upheavals within the Indian tradition, such as the emergence of Buddhism; the reign of Emperor Ashoka, the Buddhist ruler of the Indian Maurya Empire; the numerous *bhakti* movements; and Mahatma Gandhi's ingenious practice and theory.[102] But in light of these efforts to depart or establish distance from the prevailing, power-backed tradition (which illuminate its character), the fate of Buddhism on the subcontinent and the background to present-day Hindu nationalism, it is difficult to call "Hinduism" universalist. If this is so, Weber's thesis that the Indian caste system is the most

---

100. Weber, *Religion of India*, 6. Here, Weber goes on to make nuanced remarks on Hinduism's nonetheless existing missionary practice.

101. Max Weber, *Ancient Judaism* (New York: Simon and Schuster, 1967). See Joas, *The Power of the Sacred*, 146–50 and 345n100, which refers to the distinction between "covenanted" and "missionary peoples" in Anthony D. Smith, *Chosen Peoples* (Oxford: Oxford University Press, 2003), 95.

102. On the emergence of Buddhism and on Emperor Ashoka, see Bellah, *Religion in Human Evolution*, 527–66; on *bhakti*, see the studies by Martin Fuchs, esp. Martin Fuchs, "Indian Imbroglios: Bhakti Neglected; Or, the Missed Opportunities for a New Approach to a Comparative Analysis of Civilizational Diversity," in *Anthropology and Civilizational Analysis: Eurasian Explorations*, ed. Johann P. Arnason and Chris Hann (Albany: SUNY Press, 2018), 121–54 (on Weber and Dumont, see esp. 126–29).

consistent example of organic social ethics loses some of its plausibility; rather than putting forward a rationale for social and political inequality under the conditions of a universalist religion, as in medieval Christianity, this system simply seeks to legitimize such inequality in a way common in European antiquity prior to Christianity, without reference to moral universalism. Weber's assessments of the universalist character of the Islamic and Indian traditions thus both seem problematic.

BELLAH OR WEBER? ORGANIC SOCIAL ETHICS AS AN OBSTACLE TO RATIONALIZATION OR INSPIRATION FOR REFORM

Instead of discussing Islam and India here in greater detail, let us return to our starting point—namely, Robert Bellah's unfinished oeuvre and the role within it of organic social ethics, especially as envisaged by Max Weber. If, in the absence of the originally planned chapters, we search through Bellah's other writings for traces of the arguments that he intended to make, we will find only a few helpful passages.[103] As far as Islam is concerned, in essence all we have is one article from 1970 on the relationship between Islamic tradition and modernization.[104] Here, early Islam is presented—in a way reminiscent of Bellah's work on the Axial Age—as remarkably modern. While it did not emerge from an empire, Bellah underlines that it took on clear traits of an egalitarian-universalist project under the early caliphs. He describes the subsequent history of Islam as a constant struggle over the distinction between religion and politics, one that is implied by this universalist religious vision but is also repeatedly called into question. At this point, the terms in which Bellah describes these processes are still borrowed entirely from modernization theory. Less than two pages are devoted to medieval Islam. In

---

103. I would like to thank Matteo Bortolini and Steven Tipton for valuable pointers here.
104. Robert N. Bellah, "Islamic Tradition and the Problem of Modernization," in Robert N. Bellah, *Beyond Belief: Essays on Religion in a Post-Traditional World* (Berkeley: University of California Press, 1970), 146–67; see also Robert N. Bellah, "Religious Aspects of Modernization in Turkey and Japan," *American Journal of Sociology* 64 (1958): 1–5. Bellah himself states in *Beyond Belief*, 146, that these are his only publications with a focus on Islam.

its Sufi forms, it is portrayed as a return to magical practices. Otherwise, it is presented as stagnant (within the framework of a sacralization of political power), and subsequently as a victim of Western interventions. We have no way of knowing to what extent Bellah would later have come to more nuanced conclusions.

Bellah's view of India after the Axial Age is somewhat clearer. This is because we can infer a close proximity between his ideas and those of the great French Indologist Louis Dumont. He mentions his name frequently and even calls him "my old friend" in his magnum opus.[105] Now, in the present context—namely, a discussion, informed by the history of ideas, of an appropriate understanding of organic social ethics—Dumont is a particularly interesting case. Wherever this Indologist turned to the history of Christianity for comparative purposes, Ernst Troeltsch, whose *Social Teachings* he described as a "masterpiece,"[106] was his mainstay. He referred to him constantly.

In his earliest text on the emergence of "individualism" (1965), meanwhile, it was not the work of Troeltsch but that of Otto von Gierke that was the key source of ideas,[107] which—as shown previously—also applied to Troeltsch himself with regard to the Middle Ages and the processes of intellectual transformation culminating in modern natural law. When Dumont was accused of deviating from Max Weber's project, which sought to analyze the tensions between differentiated value spheres and the ethos of brotherliness, he went on the offensive: his investigation was indeed located "quite outside the Weberian paradigm."[108] We might surmise that Dumont had already taken the path that I have been guiding us along here. But this impression is deceptive. Overall, what we find is an ambiguous picture. If, as I argue, it is of crucial importance to understanding the history of moral universalism to distinguish between an understanding of social orders with a universalist value system and those

---

105. Bellah, *Religion in Human Evolution*, 484. See also Bellah, "Response to Dumont," *Religion* 12 (1982): 83f.

106. Louis Dumont, "A Modified View of Our Origins: The Christian Beginnings of Modern Individualism," *Religion* 12 (1982): 5. See also Louis Dumont, *Essays on Individualism: Modern Ideology in Anthropological Perspective* (Chicago: University of Chicago Press, 1986), 29.

107. Dumont, "A Modified View," 73–117. On page 81 he refers to his "classic treatise."

108. The criticism was made by Roland Robertson in a debate in which Robert Bellah also took part (see fn. 101): Roland Robertson, "Response," *Religion* 12 (1982): 87. The quote from Dumont is in Dumont, *Essays on Individualism*, 12n7.

without one (in other words, to overcome the ambiguity in the concept of the organic—as Gierke, Dilthey, and Troeltsch managed to do), then the dichotomous distinction between "holism" and "individualism," for which Dumont has become famous, is inadequate. Then we are dealing here with two different forms of holism, both of which must be distinguished from the modern individualism of natural law.

If this is so, Dumont's deviation from Weber means something different from the argument that I am developing here. This difference is highly instructive when it comes to one's understanding of India. As is well known, the key concept in Dumont's analysis is that of hierarchy; the "homo hierarchicus" of India and other "holistic" cultures is contrasted dichotomously with the "homo aequalis" of Western modernity and all individualistic cultures. Dumont vehemently rejects the "modern" misunderstanding of hierarchy as a military-style "chain of super-imposed commands," "a ladder of command," and "a progressive subordination from commander-in-chief to private soldier."[109] What is more important to him is the originally religious element in the word "hierarchy" (i.e., the reference to the sacred in the first syllable); this reflects the ranking of those who serve the sacred and only in this respect exercise authority over subordinates and laity. As in Weber's analysis of "State and Hierocracy," however, in his discussion of "hierarchy" Dumont fails to make a sufficient distinction between universalist and particularist forms of the sacred or of religion. This is quite evident when he compares India and the Catholic Middle Ages. Common to both, we are told, is that the limits of society are determined by its highest values, while views of the relationship between spiritual and worldly power differ. It is true, Dumont contends, that by placing the Brahmins above secular rulers, ancient Hinduism approaches the aspirations of the Christian church vis-à-vis the holders of power. But, he goes on, no more than a slight resemblance is in evidence here, since in the Indian case religious supremacy was not associated with any claim to political power.[110]

109. Louis Dumont, *Homo Hierarchicus: The Caste System and Its Implications* (rev. ed.) (Chicago: University of Chicago Press, 1980), 239, 65. The contrasting term "homo aequalis" is found in the original French title of Dumont's book on the rise of the "idéologie économique." English translation: Louis Dumont, *From Mandeville to Marx: The Genesis and Triumph of Economic Ideology* (Chicago: University of Chicago Press, 1977).
110. Dumont, *Essays on Individualism*, 67. See especially the appendix ("The Conception of Kingship in Ancient India") in Dumont, *Homo Hierarchicus*, 287–313.

Again, it is striking that what Dumont sees as the universalist aspiration that distinguishes the Christian church of the Middle Ages from other hierocratic entities does not prompt him to critically relativize the Indian case. Hence, while his differences from Weber are numerous insofar as they relate to his understanding of caste and power and the whole conception of a world-historical process of Occidental rationalization,[111] Dumont never goes beyond the holism/individualism dichotomy.

This is not a criticism that can be made of Robert Bellah's portrayal of ancient India. More clearly than Weber and Dumont before him, he brings out the tensions between moral universalism and ethnic-cultural particularism in India. One element of Dumont's analysis of India is particularly important to Bellah—namely, the role of what Weber would have called world rejection, especially among individuals who refuse to comply with cultural expectations (the "sannyasin," or in Dumont's case, the "renonçants").[112] Bellah continually returns to Dumont with respect to this point. Insofar as there is an institutionalization of renunciation in Indian culture, a kind of expectable role that individuals may take on, we will have a far-from-adequate picture of this culture if we regard the caste system as our only guide to understanding it—while ignoring the highly individualized forms of world rejection and renunciation that would appear at first glance to radically contradict this system. Without them, the caste system could not have existed for long.[113] These elements also make it clear that there has always been "individualism" in India, not just in the "West." If it can also be shown which forms were taken by "holism" in the West, then we have overcome the idea that this conceptual distinction can simply be transferred to a typology of cultures. But this changes nothing about the need to differentiate between universalist and particularist forms within holism.

In the introduction to this chapter, I pointed out that Bellah acquired the concept of "organic social ethics" from Max Weber's "Intermediate Reflection" in

---

111. See Dumont, *Homo Hierarchicus*, 249–251, for his highly critical remarks on Weber's understanding of caste; see pages 76–78 (implicitly) on the emphasis on the dimension of power. This is not intended to detract from his (justified) admiration for the power of Weber's analysis of India. Dumont calls it "a miracle of empathy and sociological imagination" (*Homo Hierarchicus*, 30).

112. Dumont, Appendix B, "World Renunciation in Indian Religions," in *Homo Hierarchicus*, 266–86.

113. Dumont, "World Renunciation in Indian Religions," 184–86.

particular.[114] It is clear that Bellah took a sympathetic view of the compromises struck in an attempt to balance the far-reaching demands of moral universalism with the conditions and requirements of particular polities. Yet Bellah advocated radical social reforms, while Weber claimed that "the organic ethic of society is everywhere an eminently conservative power and hostile to revolution."[115] This, of course, completely contradicts Troeltsch's view: he had traced conservatism in Catholic Christianity back to its "patriarchalism of love" while, as mentioned already, ascribing considerable critical, even revolutionary potential to the organic idea.[116] Bellah, however, chafed mainly at the fact that Weber could find no place, beyond private convictions, for an ethos of universal brotherhood, not just in history but especially in the present of modern societies. Weber saw more danger than hope in the restraining of economy and state by means of such an ethos. For Weber, unlike Troeltsch, the organic social ethic was merely an impediment to the rationalization of economics and politics—rather than a vehicle for amending these processes, a counterweight to their dominance.

Weber's political writings contain a whole number of polemical passages railing against contemporary attempts to build on an "organic theory of the state." For him, ideas centered on a "communal economy," or a stronger role for cooperatives were an expression of the "profound ignorance of the nature of capitalism" on the side of the contemporary "litterateurs," while the vision of an organic state structure reminded him of ancient Egypt which would now be dominated by the rational machine of bureaucracy.[117] In retrospect, this certainly fails to do justice,

---

114. Bellah, "Max Weber and World-Denying Love," esp. 138f and 146. I would like to add at this point that Bellah planned to deal with developments in China as well under the heading of "organic social ethics." Weber himself did not do so, however. He explained the reasons for this in his study of India, where he asserted that China was at bottom the "appropriate basis for a social ethic of pure utilitarianism." He interpreted China as a welfare state, in which ideas "approaching 'organic' theories of state and society" had come about solely due to the opposition between educated officials and uneducated masses, though these theories, we are told, were never fully developed: "Not the organic status group structure, but the patriarchal family provided the dominant image for social stratification. The patrimonial bureaucracy could recognize no other autonomous force." Weber admits, however, that this picture reflects more the self-image of the bureaucracy than the social reality, in which there were vibrant organizations such as guilds and kin-based associations. See Weber, *The Religion of India*, 142f. Of course, the question also arises of whether Confucianism and Buddhism entailed the potential for universalism when it comes to the treatment of China and East Asia as a whole. Bellah's answer with respect to the Axial Age was clearly affirmative in both cases.
115. Weber, "Intermediate Reflection," 340.
116. Troeltsch, *Social Teachings*, 288.
117. See Max Weber, "Wahlrecht und Demokratie in Deutschland" (1917) and "Parlament und Regierung im neugeordneten Deutschland" (1918), in Max Weber, *Gesammelte politische Schriften* (Tübingen, Germany: J. C. B. Mohr [Paul Siebeck], 1973), 253, 333.

for example, to the role of Catholic social teaching, inspired by neo-Thomism, in the development of the European welfare state.

The tension between moral universalism and egalitarianism will stay with us. Egalitarianism is not a logical implication of moral universalism, but certainly under universalist preconditions, inequality can be justified only if it serves the common good. In a highly individualist approach like John Rawls, *A Theory of Justice*, the so-called Difference Principle allows inequality if it makes the least advantaged in society materially better off than they would be under strict equality. The reform discussions in the communist countries in the late 1980s moved in a similar direction. For all contemporary attempts to deal with challenges like climate change, this is a reminder to pay constant attention to what are the consequences of measures with regard to social equality.

But this is not the main message of this study. Elsewhere, I have tried to show that while Weber devoted a superb passage in the "Intermediate Reflection" to the genesis of moral universalism,[118] he failed to pursue further how this universalist ethic of brotherhood developed historically. Instead, he constructs a schema of tensions between moral universalism and cultural value spheres featuring numerous elements that are unclear and unsatisfying.[119] In his writings, the issue of the global history of moral universalism is repeatedly eclipsed and crowded out by his other great concern—namely, with the emergence of modern capitalism or (alleged) Occidental rationalism. Because Weber was so focused on the contrast with the ascetic vocational ethic of Protestantism, the difference between a universalist and particularist social ethic was less important to him.

There is good reason to believe that had Robert Bellah managed to bring his great later-years project fully to fruition, he would have remedied this marginalization of the history of moral universalism in Weber's work. Unlike Weber, in his account of the Axial Age, Bellah did not analyze India and China from the perspective of their "shortcomings"—as cultures that failed to spawn the same developments as in the West—but rather as impressive sources of religious and moral development in their own right. I see Bellah as gradually liberating himself from the constraints of the Weberian project, with its focus on the emergence of modern capitalism and the history of "occidental rationalism" and moving in the

118. Weber, "Intermediate Reflection," 328–30.
119. I have attempted to explain this point in detail in Joas, *The Power of the Sacred*, 195–233.

direction of a global history of moral universalism. Had he been granted more time, he would likely have done the same in an analysis of "secondary formations" and of "organic social ethics" from the Axial Age to the modern era.

Acknowledgments

With special thanks to Alex Skinner for his superb translation of this text from German to English, and to Steven Tipton for his advice and helpful bibliographic suggestions.

PART III

THE CHALLENGE OF MODERNITY

CHAPTER 8

THE TILLICH LECTURE

Paul Tillich and the Challenge of Modernity

ROBERT N. BELLAH

Harvard Memorial Church   May 6, 2013

O ver the last few weeks in preparing for this lecture, I have reread
books I thought I knew and read quite a few I had never read
before. What I have found is that my lecture title, given months
ago, was even more apt than I initially thought; Tillich not only was concerned
with modernity, dealing with modernity was at the heart of all his work. This is
in part because of what he called his correlation theology: theology can't just tell
us what has been handed down; it must answer the questions of the present age,
and to know what those questions are we need to understand quite deeply the
world in which we live. In all his work he is thinking about what his theological
and philosophical traditions have to say with respect to the quite new and problematic society in which we live. But he also saw that he needed history as well: if
we don't know where we came from how can we know where we are now?

His concern for modern society and where it came from was more than a
methodological choice on Tillich's part. It was brought home to him by his life,
not just his thought. The Twentieth Century was the most violent and catastrophic century in human history, and Tillich's life exposed him personally to
two of its worst horrors. He was born in a small town in rural Brandenburg,
a province whose capital was Berlin. His father was a Lutheran pastor whose
career progressed until he held a position in Berlin. Tillich grew up loving the

countryside, but also loved Berlin when they moved there and he completed his secondary education. During these years he largely accepted his father's conservative worldview including his politics. Soon after he completed his education for the ministry and was ordained, World War I broke out. Tillich responded as most young men did throughout Europe, with nationalist enthusiasm, foreseeing a rapid German victory as had occurred in 1871, and enlisted as a chaplain.

Instead of a quick victory Tillich experienced four terrible years, much of the time at or near the front lines, including his presence at the Battle of Verdun, the greatest of the war, where over 850,000 men on both sides were killed, but no one was victorious. For Tillich it was a quick education from a sheltered childhood and youth into the reality of Germans of all social classes subjected to relentless horror. Besides preaching to the troops his duties entailed care of the wounded and endless funerals. He was given an Iron Cross for bravery, but at two points he suffered a nervous collapse under the appalling conditions to which he was subjected and had to be given time to recover before returning to the front lines.

One can say that this experience initiated Tillich into modernity with a vengeance. It led to his political and cultural awakening. He experienced the end of the war, the brief revolution in 1918 and the founding of the Weimar Republic in 1919 as a dramatic new beginning. For him it was a moment of hope; the old order was gone and a new one was beginning. His immediate response was to join a circle of intellectuals concerned with what they called "religious socialism." This group came to be known as the *Kairos* Group. "*Kairos*" is a New Testament term for a time when the transcendent breaks into the immanent; the continuity of ordinary time is broken by the appearance of a "new time." The archetype of *kairos* is the appearance of Jesus as the Christ, but there have been many *kairoi* in history and the *Kairos* Group thought that the immediate Post-World War I period might be such a time.

The group saw this new time in terms of socialism, but not the socialism of any existing party. Rather they were trying to formulate a religious socialism and to stimulate a movement centered on such an idea. Tillich's group rejected both the new Communist Party as too close to the Russian Communist Party that was, they believed, too continuous with Russian absolutism. On the other hand they thought the German Social Democratic Party (SPD) was too reformist, too beholden to the society it was supposed to be replacing. They sponsored lectures and discussions and published a journal of small circulation, hoping their criticism of both capitalism and the main existing socialist parties would stimulate a new birth of creative social thought and action.

It is important to remember that Tillich's writing and speaking in the first part of his academic life, culminating in his book *The Socialist Decision* of 1933, and in terms of his career moving from being a *Privatdozent* at the University of Berlin to finally a full professorship at Frankfurt University from 1929 to 1933, was deeply influenced by the religious socialist movement and focused on the meaning of socialism as a possible "new beginning" for modern societies. It is sometimes said that Tillich's intellectual life moved from a social and political concern when he was in Germany to a private and psychological concern after his emigration to the United States. That assertion, however, needs serious qualification which I will give below. Tillich's political concerns were further stimulated by his early awareness of the existence of the National Socialist German Workers Party, the Nazis, and his sense of the dangers that party represented. Even so, Tillich probably underestimated the Nazi threat for a long time, in part because he had actually heard Hitler speak and believed the German people could never support someone of so little culture who spoke such bad German. Even his deep exposure to ordinary, less educated, Germans in WWI did not prepare him for what his people might come to believe.

The second great crisis of Tillich's life came when that group that once seemed so marginal grew strong enough to actually take power. Frankfurt was a new university, founded only after WWI, with an unusually high percentage of Jewish professors. In 1932 some of the Nazi students staged an attack on Jewish and leftist students that left some of the latter seriously injured. Professors intervened and, as Tillich attended to the wounded, he remembered his duties as a chaplain in WWI. A large group of Frankfurt professors, of which Tillich was a member, called for the expulsion of the Nazi provocateurs. As Tillich's fears of the Nazis grew, he finally became a member of the Social Democratic Party, not because he had abandoned his old criticism of it, but because he saw it as the only realistic alternative to the Nazis.

Also in 1932 Tillich finally decided to write a major book about the current political situation, situating it in a rich historical, philosophical and theological context, showing why the Nazis would lead to disaster and religious socialism would offer a positive alternative. It was called *The Socialist Decision* and was published in early 1933. But it was too late. Hitler had come to power in January of 1933 and one of the first acts of the new government was to ban Tillich's book. Also early in 1933 the ministry of education issued the first list of German professors who were no longer allowed to teach. The list contained mostly Jews, but Paul Tillich was also on that list and led to the claim that he was the first non-Jew fired by the Nazis, which may have to be softened to "one of the first non-Jews."

Tillich was reasonably well known in the United States—in 1932 H. Richard Niebuhr had translated his *The Religious Situation*, first published in Germany in 1926—and his friends in the United States moved quickly to offer him a position at Union Theological Seminary in New York after he could no longer teach in Germany. But what they had to offer was a one year temporary appointment. So on top of the terrible shock of having his worst fears for Germany confirmed—he didn't want to leave, but when a high official at the Nazi Education Ministry offered him a full professorship in theology at the University of Berlin in exchange for disavowing *The Socialist Decision*, he knew he had to go—he had to deal with the shock of moving at the age of 47 to an entirely new country, about whose cultural level he had his doubts, and beginning all over again at the lowest academic level, lecturing and writing in a language not his own. In fact it took him eight years to again attain the status of full professor.

I want to begin by giving serious attention to *The Socialist Decision*. John R. Stumme, the translator, in the Introduction to the English translation described it: "None of his books so clearly and forcefully spoke to the historical and social crisis confronting his society," which made it a key text for this lecture on how modernity challenged Paul Tillich. Tillich told his friend James Luther Adams (who was also my friend during my Harvard years) that of all his books he was proudest of *The Socialist Decision*. And Alfred Lowe an old German friend of Tillich's, said of the book that it was his "most prophetic book" and his "most Jewish book."

It was not, however, the first book of Tillich's that I ever read—it is close to being the last as I only read it in preparation for this lecture. Like so many others, the first book I read was *The Courage to Be*. I had grown up in a mainline Protestant church and in my high school church had been given the great Hebrew prophets to read by our high school minister, a young ministerial student devoted to the social gospel. That in turn led me directly to Marxism and atheism as a Harvard undergraduate, but when that went sour I was left wondering what I believed or could believe. By chance I read in the *New York Times* a one paragraph review of Tillich's *The Courage to Be*, by C. Wright Mills. Mills highly recommended the book, which, since Mills was a founder of the "New Left" and a strong opponent of my teacher, Talcott Parsons, astounded me. How could such a left-winger recommend a book of theology, I thought, which led me to buy it as soon as I could. I had actually never heard of Tillich before, but *The Courage to Be* changed my life. Tillich told me that faith is not "belief in the unbelievable" when I had come to think it was. For me as for so many others of my generation and younger Tillich opened a closed door to the possibility that an educated person could be a Christian.

The Socialist Decision is not an easy book to read: it has never been one of his more popular books, whether in Germany where it was finally made available in a new edition in 1948 nor in America where the English translation was published in 1977, well after Tillich's death in 1965. But for those with a little background its analysis is grandly structured and compellingly argued. It involves a double criticism of capitalism, not just as an economy but as a way of life, which he sums up as the Bourgeois Principle, and socialism, again as a total cultural and social system, not just an economic system, which he characterizes as the Socialist Principle. Tillich was advocating socialism as against capitalism, but not socialism as it was currently formulated because he thought it had preserved too much of the capitalist heritage, in particular a lack of a religious dimension, depriving it both of persuasive power and the possibility of self-criticism. Tillich did not see the religious dimension he was formulating in either the Protestant or the Catholic churches of his day, so it was not church religion he was advocating. Tillich spoke of religious socialism, not Christian socialism, in order not to be identified with the existing churches, which at the time were becoming more and more attracted to Nazism (the Protestants) or more concerned with being left alone than criticizing the Nazis (the Catholics).

Yet Tillich, and this is what to me gives the book its great power, located this basic contrast between the Bourgeois and the Socialist Principles in the context of a sweepingly large framework from the history of religion. Very schematically, Tillich describes the starting point of human religiosity in what he calls "the mythical powers of origin," which characterize all religions earlier than the axial age, the first millennium BCE, when what we have come to call the world religions emerged, but which he sees as still active in the world of today. I should note also that from the beginning of the book, as we will see, there is a clear borrowing from psychoanalysis, reminding us that Tillich had been interested in Freud and "depth psychology" since the end of WWI, not, as some have argued, only after he came to America.

Tillich describes what he calls "the primordial human situation" as follows: "The myth of origin envisions the beginning of humankind in elemental, super-human figures of various kinds. Common to them all is the fact that they are expressions of the human tie to father and mother, and that by the power of this tie they want to hold consciousness fast." (13) The religion of origin is always particularistic; it has no capacity for universalism. It is rooted in such things as the particular soil on which people live, the blood they share, and they are often divided by lineage between noble blood and commoner blood, and finally the group to which they belong in contrast to all other groups which are seen as barely human. Such a religion, according to Tillich, can produce sacraments and priests, but not prophets. For it time is cyclical, nothing new can ever happen, and time is always dominated by space, since where you are is always more important than where you are going. "And yet it is," he writes, "the demanding character of the father-origin that makes it at all possible to break through the myth of origin." But as long as the "the origin still rules" this is only a possibility. "Liberation from the origin becomes real only in prophetism." (15)

Tillich sums up the religion of origin by saying, "The new can only be accepted in terms of the original. Ontologically speaking this means: *being is holy*. For being is the origin of everything that exists and being provides the criterion of everything that exists: the power of being is the highest standard . . . Ontology is the final and most abstract version of the myth of origin." (17–18) Now this sounds very like the Being of Tillich's *Systematic Theology*, and there clearly is a connection, but here "being" is never capitalized. The religion of origin is the first glimpse of being, one that can never be forgotten, but it is still an inadequate version. Its greatest failure is its attempt to deny time, and it is above all time that concerns Judaism and Christianity.

The next step in Tillich's schematic account of the history of religion is Jewish prophetism. Tillich writes, "It is the significance of *Jewish prophetism* to have fought explicitly against the myth of origin and the attachment to space and to have conquered them. On the basis of a powerful social myth of origin, Jewish prophetism radicalized the social imperative to the point of freeing itself from the bond of origin." (20) For the prophets the command comes not from the father who demands only that one repeat the same thing, but from a righteous God who gives universal ethical commands that go beyond the origin and take those to whom the commands are given "into the phase of *the new in history*." Breaking the myth of origin does not mean the abandonment of soil, blood, and group membership, but deprives them of ultimacy and places them under commands that surpass them. It is prophetism that gave the Jews the capacity to survive a catastrophic history in which the land was lost and the survival of the group imperiled. Groups who live in the myth of origin alone do not survive such histories. It was the prophetic move from the world of space into the world of time that gave a people rooted in the idea of a promised land the capacity to maintain their faith in every corner of the world into which they have been driven after they lost the land. It also gives a particular poignancy to recent history where the land has been recovered and all the ambiguities of the myth of origin emerge once again, though never without the prophetic criticism. But it is part of Tillich's to me profound narrative that the Jewish myth of origin with its inevitable link to soil, blood and group membership, was never lost, but was never without the prophetic criticism, a dialectic that continues today as ever.

Tillich then argues that Christianity is caught in the same dialectic. It made the spirit of Judaism its foundation by keeping what Christians called the Old Testament as essential to their own scriptural self-definition. (We must remember that many of the "German Christians" gaining power as Tillich was writing this book, wanted Christians to exclude the Hebrew Scriptures from their Bible, proving to Tillich that they were returning in their nationalism to a myth of origin unbroken by a prophetic ethic.) Of course the myth of origin had long before returned in Christianity in other forms. Tillich in this book sees the development of Catholicism out of early Christianity as largely the return to the myth of origin in the emergence of the priesthood and the centrality of the sacraments. Still Tillich insists "It remains the *function of the Jewish spirit* to raise the prophetic protest, both in Judaism and Christianity, against every attempt to revive such bondage to the myth of origin, and to help time, the unconditional demand, and the "Whither" to be victorious over space, mere being, and the "Whence." To publish such a book in early 1933 was an expression of an overwhelming opposition to the central Nazi teaching of anti-Semitism.

Tillich does not identify prophetism as such with Judaism or Christianity, both of which have been compromise formations with the older myth of origin. Here we must understand Tillich as in the best sense a dialectical thinker, always aware of the ambiguity and ambivalence of history. The prophetic protest which has time and again broken out in the history of Judaism and Christianity is essential to their identity, yet protest alone cannot create a viable way of life. Even as it breaks the myth of origin, it must come to terms with it because it, too, is a part of human life. Thus Tillich, with his deep concern for his own Protestant tradition, must deal with the ways various forms of Protestantism have come to terms with the world of daily life, with the repetitiousness without which we could not live. For him Lutheranism made its compromise by giving its own leadership to the state, and identifying itself with the state through most of its history. Calvinism he sees as more dynamic, in a sense more open to the prophetic than his own Lutheranism, but it compromises by becoming identified with its environing society, above all with its bourgeois, merchant-class, membership. Max Weber and Ernst Troeltsch hover over all that Tillich has to say about the Reformation and its consequences.

The history of Western prophetism took another big step beyond Protestantism, a step that begins in the Seventeenth Century but becomes fully developed in the Eighteenth Century: The Enlightenment. In one sense the Enlightenment is a development out of Protestantism which had placed responsibility in the hands of every individual believer, with no intervening power before God other than the Bible; in another sense it calls in question everything that preceded it by proclaiming the absolute autonomy of individuals responsible only to their own reason.

I will have more to say about autonomy as a philosophical understanding of the human condition, particularly and enormously influentially, by Immanuel Kant, but also autonomy as a looser term which in common usage meant independence from the powerful network of religious and political constraints that bound most people in pre-modern societies. Autonomy in both of these senses was expressed already in the democratic revolutions of the eighteenth century leading very unevenly and with many lapses to be sure, to the institutionalization of human rights that had been implied by all the world religions but never begun to be institutionalized in actual societies until recently.

I must pause here to emphasize some important points that Tillich and almost everyone else until quite recently, failed to see. Tillich and most others see the Enlightenment and the revolutionary efforts to put its beliefs into political practice as an expression of what he calls, parallel to the Protestant Principle, the Bourgeois Principle, and that he also, as we shall see even more problematically, calls the spirit of industrial society. The dynamic of modern society in this understanding is capitalism. What I want to do is question the whole idea that revolutionary modernity from the eighteenth century on can be explained holistically as due to the rise of bourgeois capitalism. This was Marx's idea, picked up with qualifications by Weber and others, including Tillich, and was accepted by scholars of all ideological persuasions because of the prevailing belief in economic determinism.

Let me give you my reasons for doubting this dominant story, even though I don't have time to spell them out. The economy of the eighteenth century cannot explain the revolutionary changes in thought and action that began in that century because it was no different than the vigorous commercial economy that preceded it by several centuries in the West, and, even more tellingly, was actually surpassed by the more highly developed commercial society of China, which Adam Smith noted was larger than the economy of Europe, and which goes back almost a thousand years to the Song Dynasty that also had a commercial economy quite as developed as eighteenth century Europe. Industrial capitalism did not exist in the eighteenth century; it only began in England (and nowhere else) in the early nineteenth century and very gradually and unevenly spread to other parts of Europe and to the rest of the world, Japan first of all, in the second half of the nineteenth century. Industrial capitalism was the greatest revolutionary change in technology and the economy that the world has ever seen and it continues to revolutionize our relation to the global environment as we speak, but it simply did not cause the ideological and political revolutions of the eighteenth century when nobody, not Adam Smith, not Thomas Jefferson, not Robespierre, had the slightest idea it was coming. If Jean-Jacques Rousseau had known the industrial revolution was coming he would have had a heart attack; he was upset enough with the modest commercial society in which he lived.

The great changes in ideas and politics of the eighteenth century occurred in largely traditional, heavily agrarian, societies with a vigorous commercial sector not different from similar economies in earlier Europe or China and Japan at the time. None of these similar economies led to the radical changes that modern historians attribute to economic causes in eighteenth century Europe. We don't have controlled experiments in history, but this is as close as one can get. Causes are attributed to events in one case but extremely similar causes elsewhere had no such consequences. What did cause the extraordinary changes of that time? I don't want to substitute an idealistic for a materialistic explanation, as Marxists would say. What I think is necessary is what Weber preached sometimes more than he practiced: we have to have a multicausal explanation; no one cause is enough. Political, economic, social, cultural, religious factors are all part of the story. We need to take them all into account however difficult that turns out to be.

Immanuel Kant (1724–1804), the most important thinker of the modern age, was born and educated in Königsberg, Prussia, where he grew up in a strict Pietist Lutheran family. He went to the University of Königsberg and eventually became a professor there. He never in his life ventured more than a few miles from his home town. A lifelong bachelor, he was a highly disciplined scholar with an enormous production even before he wrote the three Critiques, of Pure Reason, of Practical Reason, and of the Power of Judgment, which made him famous. Everything of importance that he wrote was published in the eighteenth century. His interests were wide and his reading extensive, but he lived his quiet but sociable life in a backward part of a backward country, far from the centers of European life, though the French Revolution made a great impression on him as it did on most educated Europeans. Still, it is hard to see a man who devoted himself to the life of the mind as much as any human who has ever lived as busily at work promoting "the Bourgeois Spirit," much less the spirit of industrial society, which didn't yet exist. He lived in the world and cared about the world; all I am arguing is that he wasn't determined by it.

So why is Kant important? It would take a long time to answer that, but, as noted above, he is important as having given the most influential definition of a key word in the Enlightenment vocabulary, "autonomy." We might think autonomy means you can do whatever you like, that it is a synonym for individualism. It is not unrelated to a serious ethical form of individualism, but it definitely does not mean you can do whatever you like. Tillich reminds us that the word comes from the Greek, "auto" for the self, and "nomos" for law. So it means you are responsible for the law of your life. Its opposite is heteronomy from "hetero" meaning other, and "nomos" meaning law, that is, if you are heteronomous you are under a law given by another. Kant takes the law part of autonomy very seriously; an autonomous person lives under the law of reason which is the determining characteristic of human beings. And what your own law tells you to do is to obey the categorical imperative, that is, act so that the maxim for your action could be applied to everyone in the world, or more simply, act toward yourself and others as though you and they are ends in themselves, never means to anything else. So why does autonomy not mean you can do whatever you want? Because a lot of the things you want, indeed most of them, arise not from your reason but from your desires and your inclinations. But your desires and inclinations, so far as they do not arise from reason, are not really you but are external forces, that is, heteronomous as far as the real you is concerned. One can draw an example from Plato who said that a tyrant is the most abject slave in the world because with his great power he is most at the mercy of his passions and so least able to determine his own self. To us Kant's notion of autonomy might seem to limit our freedom, as it says we must give ourselves laws that are very hard to live up to. But for Kant autonomy and freedom are virtually identical. Only a free person can be autonomous and only a society of autonomous persons can be a free society.

For Tillich, Kant represents a great moral advance, another step forward in the history that begins with Jewish prophecy, but it also runs a great risk. It is all too easily perverted into its opposite. Freedom and autonomy can indeed become the Bourgeois Principle if they are interpreted as did Jeremy Bentham (1748–1832) in his philosophy of utilitarianism: "it is the greatest happiness of the greatest number that is the measure of right and wrong," with happiness defined as the predominance of pleasure over pain, which for Kant would mean it had no connection with right and wrong at all. Its connection with capitalism, where the measure of success is the increase in profit, is clear enough. For Tillich, Bentham's utilitarianism would represent a major step away from the prophetic tradition and toward an ideology that vindicated an exploitative economic system. Of course I am using Bentham to stand in for classical economics, Thomas Malthus, Herbert Spencer, and a whole phalanx of the defenders of what by the middle of the nineteenth century had finally become a reality, modern industrial capitalism.

For Tillich there is a third alternative beyond autonomy and heteronomy, that is, theonomy, the law of God, not a word used by Kant. For Tillich heteronomy is the great enemy of the prophetic tradition, but the autonomy that comes out of that tradition needs the model of divine self-giving to keep it from falling into the idolatry of the self. Tillich's conception of God is not one who desires to control us from without, but one who wants to be with us as we realize our God-given selfhood. Tillich saw Christianity during the Enlightenment and afterward as continuing to play that role, but as continually threatened by a this-worldly sense of the self, lacking a dimension of transcendence and so tempted into an amoral idolatry of the self. Since the Enlightenment was so much a movement for human freedom, it stressed self-affirmation and self-assertion, good in themselves as alternatives to the constraints of traditional forms of social control, but vulnerable to losing any ethical dimension at all. We have seen such a downward slide with Bentham's utilitarianism; then the appearance of Social Darwinism in the late nineteenth century, preaching the survival of the fittest, often defined as the richest; and reaching a kind of culmination in the late twentieth century in the teaching of Ayn Rand and her philosophy of what she called Objectivism, but which consists of the idea that selfishness is the highest good and that the only valuable people in the world are those who think only of themselves. It is remarkable that a candidate for vice-president in the 2012 US election [Paul Ryan], for whom Ayn Rand was his favorite philosopher, claimed not to know that she was an extreme atheist, although one needs only to read one page of hers to see that her teaching is the exact opposite of the teaching of the Gospel.

Tillich was interested not only in the rise of an ideology that justified the most radical form of capitalism, but with the powerful waves of opposition to industrial capitalism that were already emerging in the mid-nineteenth century, the most influential of which was Marxism. Tillich's reading of Marx, based on his early philosophical manuscripts, was of Marx as a kind of existentialist philosopher, revolting against a form of life that was turning people into commodities and emptying life of any meaning beyond economic accumulation. Tillich was so sympathetic with this reaction against capitalism that after World War I he became a lifelong religious socialist. Yet Tillich feared that both the Communist and the Social Democratic forms of Marxism accepted an economic understanding of humanity, that is, of humans as motivated above all by self-interest, so that Marxism lost its leverage for a genuine criticism of modern capitalism. For Marx the interest of the proletariat was identical with the interest of all humans and so the dictatorship of the proletariat would bring the good society. Tillich doubted that the proletariat, like humanity in general, or its self-designated leaders, could be trusted to work for the interest of everyone and would be much more likely to end up working only for their own interests. He saw religious socialism as bringing in the theonomous dimension that would link pursuit of one's own ends together with the pursuit of the good life for all seen as ends in themselves, as a necessary corrective.

So, as was his wont, Tillich had an ambivalent attitude toward the enormous changes in human society coming out of the Enlightenment and the later industrial revolution. He was aware of the ethical and material achievements of modernity but also of what he called the demonic side of modernity. Hans Joas has a new book, *The Sacredness of the Person: A New Genealogy of Human Rights*, that, without referring to Tillich, helps us understand Tillich's concerns. Joas sees the modern movement for human rights, beginning with the American and

French Revolutions of the late eighteenth century, as making human rights no longer simply ideals of religious or humanistic groups but as demands for actual implementation in existing societies. Joas, like Tillich, is fully aware of the fact that human rights, though they have been extended in many societies to some degree, are violated every day in every society, so this is not a process that is completed, but one that is a continuing demand and a continuing process. This is very close to Tillich's notion of the prophetic tradition, and also of the Protestant Principle, though Joas, as a Catholic, cannot see it as in any way exclusively Protestant. Instead Joas turns for his fundamental definition of human rights to Émile Durkheim, a secular Jew.

Durkheim, who first clearly formulated the idea of the sacredness of the person, did so in 1898 in an essay in which he defended individualism, but what we have to call an ethical individualism, concerned with the rights of all, not only of the self, and so very far from sheer egoism. About the ethical individualism which he saw as essential for French society insofar as France itself stood for the Enlightenment and a genuinely modern ethic, he wrote: "Here we have come a long way from that apotheosis of well-being and private interest, from that egoistic cult of the self for which utilitarian individualism has been rightly criticized. Quite the contrary, duty consists in disregarding all that concerns us personally, all that derives from our empirical individuality, in order to seek out only that which our humanity requires and which we share with all our fellowmen. This ideal so far surpasses the level of utilitarian goals that it seems to those minds who aspire to it to be completely stamped with religiosity. This human person (*personne humaine*), the definition of which is like the touchstone, which distinguishes good from evil, is considered sacred in the ritual sense of the word . . . And the respect which is given it comes precisely from this source." Such respect for the human person leads us to believe any attack on a person's life, liberty, or honor must be seen as a profanation. So Durkheim, in language that is close to that of Kant, goes beyond Kant in bringing in the idea of the sacredness, the religiosity, of the idea of human rights, thus showing that he saw the necessity of what Tillich called theonomy if the idea of human rights was not to fall back into a concern for purely private well-being.

I know that I have taken us on a long road from Tillich's idea of the myth of origin where human consciousness began, an ideal of original being, sufficient unto itself so that it need only be repeated, and if it had ever really existed would have kept humans in a permanent state of what Tillich called "dreaming innocence." But now as I near the end of my talk I must return to the prophetic and Protestant efforts to break through that self-sufficient original being, so that we can understand true ethical responsibility and face the task, in spite of our profound inadequacies, of realizing our God-given ethical capacities. But I must follow Tillich in arguing that in spite of prophetic criticism, that original being never goes away but is only more deeply understood in the course of human history. I want to do this by returning to one of Tillich's characterizations of original being: it is sacramental; it shows the presence of the divine in everything finite. And we find that Tillich is just as concerned with what he calls sacramental substance, which he sees as finding the infinite as a dimension of the finite, as he is with Judaic prophecy; they belong together, they need each other.

Perhaps surprisingly for someone who all his life spoke as a Protestant, Tillich believed the Protestant Principle alone was self-destructive. He affirmed that the Protestant Principle only made sense in relation to Catholic substance, and Catholic substance is above all sacramental. Tillich believed that the history of Protestantism was the history of its abandonment of the sacraments. At first he said the great Reformers spoke of the Word and the Sacrament. Then their followers spoke of the Sacraments through the Word. And finally they spoke only of the Word. The Word itself is sacramental, says Tillich, but without any embodiment in physical reality it is greatly diminished. Protestantism reduced the seven Catholic sacraments to two, and then neglected those two, especially the most important, Communion or Eucharist, which became infrequent and marginal, its profound symbolic meaning as the real presence of Christ in the sacraments dismissed as a magical idea. "In the course of its history," wrote Tillich, Protestantism has become so indifferent to sacramental thinking that even the two remaining sacraments have lost their significance . . . The phenomenal growth of secularism in Protestant countries can be explained partly as a result of the weakening of the sacramental power within Protestantism." (Protestant Era, 111–112) But what is worse than secularism is when Protestantism replaces the missing embodiment of the sacraments with something demonic, as for example nationalism among the majority of Protestant "German Christians" under Hitler, or the fusion of Evangelical Christianity with American nationalism in the United States today.

Long before Vatican II Tillich published in 1941 a remarkable article entitled "The Permanent Significance of the Catholic Church for Protestantism." Here is what he says:

> Protestantism needs the permanent corrective of Catholicism and the continuous influx of sacramental elements from it in order to live. Catholicism, by its very existence, reminds Protestantism of the sacramental foundation without which the prophetic-eschatological attitude has no basis, substance and creative power. Catholicism represents the truth that the "holy of being" must precede the "holy of what ought to be," that without the "mother," the priestly-sacramental Church, the "father," the prophetic-eschatological movement has no roots. It becomes cultural activism and moral utopianism. (25)

Tillich did not live long enough to see the final and longest document of Vatican II, *Gaudium et Spes*, a ringing affirmation of human rights and centrally the right of religious freedom in a way the church had never explicitly done before. One can see Vatican II as the rediscovery of Catholicism's own inherent Protestant Principle (which may be why it is under a shadow in some Catholic quarters today) but which is part of any genuine Christianity. But Tillich was also calling on Protestants to affirm their own inherent claim to Catholic substance.

Tillich makes another point that ties everything I have been trying to say together as it points to our most central problem in the world today. The Protestant neglect of the sacraments is part of the modern world's neglect of the natural as sacred. Individualism in some form or other is at the heart of the modern project. An ethical kind of individualism which sees the human person as sacred can also see God's natural creation as sacred. But an instrumental individualism that uses others as means for one's own aggrandizement, and ends up even seeing one's self as a means in an endless and meaningless series of means, also sees the natural world as something only to be manipulated and exploited, not as in its own way also sacred. Tillich was aware of the ethically destructive consequences of what he called the Bourgeois Principle or the Capitalist Principle, and of the dangers in it for the release of demonic powers such as Nazism and fascism even in America. But he did not see, or only glimpsed, the possibility that an exploitative attitude toward nature would end up being physically suicidal, would lead to the destruction not only of genuine human community but of the biosphere upon which all life depends. What he did not see is what the modern project, in spite of its enormous achievements, was actually bringing. If I may borrow some words from Terry Eagleton:

> The Apocalypse, if it ever happens, is far more likely to be the upshot of technology than the work of the Almighty. In the long apocalyptic tradition of cosmic portents, fiery signs in the skies and the impending planetary doom, it was never envisaged that we might prove capable of bringing this about all by ourselves, without the slightest help from a wrathful deity. This, surely, should be a source of pride to cheerleaders for the human species like [Dawkins and Hitchens]. Who needs an angry God to burn up the planet when as mature, self-sufficient human beings we are perfectly capable of doing the job ourselves? (*Reason, Faith, and Revolution*, Yale, 2009, 134)

Eagleton, a Marxist but also a practicing Catholic who teaches part time at Notre Dame, fuses the Protestant Principle and Catholic substance to unveil the demonic reality that "mature, self-sufficient human beings" are perfectly capable of bringing about the end of the world as we know it.

But I don't want to leave you only with the idea of doom. Preaching doom leads to cynicism and despair, not corrective action. Tillich would remind us of the theological virtue of hope, which is not sentimental optimism, but a transcendent command to look for a better future "in spite of" (*trotzdem*, one of Tillich's favorite words) the terrible things happening in the world. When I first began to teach at Harvard the faculty and graduate students of my department, the then department of social relations, invited Tillich to speak at an afternoon tea and me to be the respondent. Tillich was at his rhetorical best, but he focused on the dark forces of modernity, on the meaninglessness of modern life, in a compelling lecture. In my short remarks I thanked Tillich but suggested there were some positive things going on as well. Tillich, as was his wont, not only agreed with me, he apologized for talking only about demonic structures and forgetting to stress what he called "the structure of grace in history," which makes it possible for us to hope.

So let me close by returning to one of Tillich's earliest ideas, the *kairos*, the possibility of something new in history. One of his first essays, published in 1922, was called, simply, "Kairos," and he republished it in 1948 in *The Protestant Era*. At the end of the essay he asks if we could be wrong about the *kairos*. His reply is pure Tillich: He said the message of the *kairos* is always wrong because it is always too late or too early. And yet (*trotzdem* again), the message is never wrong, because where the *kairos* is proclaimed it is already present. Don't worry about too late or too early, the *kairos* is now, always now. It is now that we are called to hope and to act.

CHAPTER 9

ON THE SEARCH FOR "A SERIOUS ETHICAL FORM OF INDIVIDUALISM"

Bellah, Tillich, and the Anthropology of Christian Individualism

JOEL ROBBINS

I n his recent biography, Matteo Bortolini ends his account of the intellectual side of Robert Bellah's life with the sociologist's work on his Paul
Tillich Lecture of 2013 and his trip to Harvard to deliver it.[1] This return
to Harvard gives the book a nice inclusio pattern, as Harvard also figures centrally in the account of Bellah's early intellectual development. Moreover, Tillich
himself runs like a bit of a red thread throughout the biography, as is appropriate
for someone who Bellah tells us in the Tillich Lecture wrote a book—*The Courage
to Be*—that "changed . . . [his] . . . life" by showing him that "an educated person
could be a Christian." So there is a certain valedictory sense that attaches to the
lecture—a chance to go back to where Bellah first became a scholar, taught, and
met Tillich and to settle up a number of accounts. In the lecture itself, Bellah
manages, in a light, unobtrusive way that does not interfere with his main goal
of discussing the challenge of modernity in relation to Tillich's work, to make of
the piece something of a final pass at themes that had preoccupied him for much
of his academic life: religion and its profound cultural and social influence, individualism and its discontents, and even, by reading early Tillich as "Jasperian"
avant le lettre, the world historical importance of the transformations of the
Axial Age. Superbly crafted, the essay touches on many themes. But it is arguably

---

1. Matteo Bortolini, *A Joyfully Serious Man: The Life of Robert Bellah* (Princeton, NJ: Princeton University
Press, 2021).

most centrally about individualism—a phenomenon that Bellah tells us "in some form or other is at the heart of the modern project." Individualism is for Bellah born of the prophetic drive of what Tillich calls the "Protestant principle," and in discussing individualism in the lecture, Bellah looks to Tillich to discover how a moral, rather than a "demonic" form of this protean cultural complex might arise from complementing this principle with what Tillich calls "Catholic substance." Working with the Tillich Lecture and several of Bellah's other writings, and putting them in dialogue with my own anthropological work on Christianity and individualism, it is the entanglement of individualism, religion, and ethics that I want to explore in this chapter.

The idea that individualism can often take something less than a "serious ethical form" is, of course, an important theme that runs throughout the history of sociology. Ulrich Beck and Elisabeth Beck-Gernshiem go so far as to refer to sociology as "an institutionalized rejection of individualism."[2] The brilliant sociologist and philosopher Lucien Goldmann attests to the plausibility of this observation in a sharp attack on what he sees as the specifically moral vacuity of individualism, arguing that "there is no room in any consistently individualistic mode of thought . . . for any system of genuine morality."[3] In terms that will find an echo in *Habits of the Heart*, Goldmann goes on to add that while individualism, like any "world vision," will offer "rules of conduct" that it might refer to as moral or ethical, these codes will not, to borrow Bellah's term, be "serious" candidates for the status that they claim for themselves. This is so because "whether its ideal is one of power or one of prudence or wisdom, any thorough-going individualism will still need to deduce these rules either from the individual's mind or from his heart, since by very definition individualism has abolished any supra-individual reality capable of guiding man and offering him genuinely transcendent norms."[4] From here, it is not a big step to Bellah's account in the Tillich Lecture of the contemporary understanding of autonomy as doing whatever you like, which he takes to be "a synonym for individualism" of a morally impotent form.[5]

---

2. Ulrich Beck and Elisabeth Beck-Gernsheim, *Individualization* (London: SAGE, 2001), xxii.
3. Lucien Goldmann, *The Hidden God: A Study of Tragic Vision in the Pensees of Pascal and the Tragedies of Racine*, trans. Philip Thody (London: Routledge & Kegan Paul, 1964), 30.
4. Goldmann, *The Hidden God*, 30.
5. Robert N. Bellah, "The Tillich Lecture: Paul Tillich and the Challenge of Modernity," 274. Chapter 8 in this volume.

So Bellah is far from alone among sociologists (nor among anthropologists, with whom he was in dialogue from the start of his career) in having his doubts about the moral depth of at least some forms of individualism. But the crowd thins out when you send home those who stop with that critical observation, most of its members showing no interest in going on to explore whether other, moral forms of individualism might be developed. And even among the small remaining group of scholars that does search for a moral individualism, Bellah stands out not only for the breadth and quality of his work, but also by virtue of the way that he guides his quest for a moral individualism by consulting treasure maps provided by the history of the Protestant and Catholic strands of the Christian tradition. It is true, as he discusses in the lecture, that Durkheim is his closest ally when it comes to turning to religion in the effort to morally improve individualism, since the great French sociologist stakes so much moral hope on the modern sacralization of the individual. But Durkheim's sacred is generic, as characteristic of Australian Aboriginal totemism as it is of the French Revolution, while Bellah's is not, or at least not in his work on individualism. When discussing individualism, Bellah's sacred is rather Protestant in the first instance, and in the second, it is Protestant reaching back for some Catholic qualities. It is Bellah's profound engagement with these Christian traditions that renders his prophetic attempt to find a moral individualism so distinct from other social scientific considerations of this topic.

Over the course of Bellah's career, there is a trajectory to his exploration of the entanglement of Christianity and individualism, and particularly to his reading of Protestantism's role in this process. Although I have not read nearly all of Bellah's work, I can point out that in *Habits of the Heart* (originally published in 1985), he and his coauthors present the traditions of biblical religion and civic republicanism as potential brakes on the runaway development of an American individualism that was by then most fully shaped by what they call America's utilitarian and expressive traditions.[6] It is true that the authors sometimes hold up Catholicism in passing in the book as having greater resources than Protestantism for counterbalancing individualism's slide into amorality, but they more often discuss churches in general, and the biblical tradition in general, as

---

6. Robert N. Bellah, Richard Madsen, William M. Sullivan, Ann Swidler, and Steven M. Tipton, *Habits of the Heart: Individualism and Commitment in American Life*, 3rd ed. (Berkeley: University of California Press, 2007).

repositories of some hope for America's future. By the time we get to the Tillich Lecture, however, and even by 2000, when Bellah first publishes the essay "Flaws in the Protestant Code,"[7] he has come to see Protestantism as a primary driver of American individualism, leaving it to stand less as a possible corrective to that cultural complex and more as needing to answer for its faults. This is why he is at such pains in the Tillich Lecture to argue away any assertion that the Industrial Revolution is the primary cause of modern individualism, defining such claims as anachronistic. Since individualism comes after the Reformation but before the Industrial Revolution, he suggests, Protestantism deserves at least some causal pride of place in its advent, and more than a little responsibility for how it has ended up. As Jeffrey Guhin succinctly puts the trend of Bellah's thought in this regard, as his work progressed, Bellah "came to blame Protestantism more and more for America's radical individualism."[8]

Having made this point, Guhin goes on to add that Bellah "sought within Catholicism the resources for a communitarian answer to America's atomism."[9] If Christianity were to be part of the solution to the moral woes brought about by individualism, in this new framework, it was not going to do so in its most usual contemporary Protestant forms alone. And it is here that Tillich becomes crucial for Bellah's story, for the great theologian influentially argued that both Protestantism and Catholicism have a Protestant principle within them, allowing the individual to find God for themselves and to critique all social institutions from a transcendent point of view, and a Catholic substance that respects sacraments, institutions, communities, and, harking back to Goldmann, moral sources beyond the self.[10] It is the balance between the Protestant principle and the Catholic substance that matters for either kind of Christianity, and this means that Protestantism in its American guises might eventually be able to give birth to its own ethical individualism, though not without modifying its current expressions. It is on this basis that Bellah can end the Tillich Lecture with a call to hope and action in which Christianity can have a role to play, and this on the basis of the work of a decidedly Protestant theologian.[11]

7. Robert N. Bellah, "Flaws in the Protestant Code," in *The Robert Bellah Reader*, ed. Robert Bellah and Steven Tipton (Durham, NC: Duke University Press, 2006), chapter 15.

8. Jeffrey Guhin, "Robert Bellah's Catholic Imagination," in *The Anthem Companion to Robert N. Bellah*, ed. Matteo Bortolini (New York: Anthem, 2019), 144.

9. Guhin, "Robert Bellah's Catholic Imagination," 144.

10. Paul Tillich, *The Protestant Era*, abridged ed. (Chicago: University of Chicago Press, 1957).

11. Paul Tillich, *On the Boundary: An Autobiographical Sketch* (New York: Charles Scribner's Sons, 1966), 39.

Bellah's breathtaking telling of this story in his Tillich Lecture opens up many questions for further exploration. I want to follow up on two of them here. The first is to ask if it is correct to say that Protestantism virtually on its own can lead to a kind of radical individualism that can develop in ways that thin out crucial aspects of moral concern. This is a question that I will approach ethnographically rather than historically, drawing on my own research among the Urapmin people of Papua New Guinea. The second is whether there might be a theoretical approach that will allow us to add some analytic precision to the kinds of relationships between individualism and other cultural forces that somewhat escapes their framing in Tillich's terms of a principle complemented by a substance, and Bellah and his coauthors' use of the notion of first and second languages to describe the interactions between the four American traditions on which they focus in *Habits*.

The theoretical approach that I will draw on derives from the anthropologist Louis Dumont's theory of the way that values, and most importantly the relations between different values, influence both the structure and the ethos of any given culture. I will ultimately argue that this way of coming at the Urapmin ethnography and, in very broad terms in this chapter, the American material discussed in *Habits* as well, allows us to consider in a bit more detail what at least some forms of moral individualism might look like. In the next section, I will discuss the Urapmin encounter with Christian individualism. Following that, I will say a bit more about Dumont's theoretical outlook before then turning in the conclusion to consider what these ethnographic and theoretical discussions can contribute to the search for a moral individualism.

PROTESTANTISM AND INDIVIDUALISM AMONG THE URAPMIN

At that point in the Tillich Lecture at which Bellah wants to argue that religion more than economics played a key early role in the rise of individualism, he notes that it emerged in the eighteenth century in traditional, predominantly agricultural and commercial societies that were not radically different in economic terms from those of earlier times in Europe, or from then-contemporary societies in Japan and China, none of which generated this value in the form in which we recognize it today. Pointing out that this is bad news for economic determinists, since from their point of view similar economies should produce similar effects, he goes on to note that we "don't have controlled experiments in history, but this is as close as one can get."[12] It probably goes without saying that we do not have controlled experiments in anthropology either, but nonetheless the Urapmin case may similarly be as close as one can get when it comes to documenting in some ethnographic detail the ability of Protestantism alone to install individualism as a high-level value in a society in which it had not held anything like that position before.

The Urapmin are a language group of about 400 speakers living in the mountains of the Sandaun Province of Papua New Guinea. I carried out twenty-seven months of fieldwork with them in the early 1990s. With their community perched on a ridge that juts out of the central mountain range that runs down the spine of the island, the Urapmin live at least a six-hour, vigorous walk from their neighbors in any direction, all of whom speak languages different from theirs. With no road or airstrip connecting them to anywhere else, the Urapmin had in the early 1990s almost no involvement in the cash economy and only a slightly less marginal connection with the government of independent Papua New Guinea, nor had they had much more of one with the preceding colonial government that was set up in their region after World War II. During the period of my fieldwork, they still lived as subsistence gardeners and bow-and-arrow hunters, made their houses from bush materials, and had no access to electricity. Even today, the national media occasionally makes its way to Urapmin to report on how the country's government is failing its least "developed" citizens, ones who are remote even by the standards of the province in which they live, itself not so long ago declared the most remote and least developed in all of Papua New Guinea. At a glance, then, Urapmin looks very much like the Western primitivist stereotype of a highly traditional fourth-world community. But if you look a little closer, this initial interpretation proves wrong in one crucial respect: since 1977, all Urapmin people who are old enough to do so are converts to a Protestant, charismatic form of Christianity. Indeed, living a successful Christian life is the paramount collective (and in most cases, individual) project for the Urapmin people, and Christian ideas and themes dominate both public and private discussions at most times of the day and night.

---

12. Bellah, "The Tillich Lecture," 273.

I have told the story of how the Urapmin came to convert to Christianity in detail elsewhere and will not dwell on it at much length here.[13] The most surprising aspect of the process is that the Australian Baptist missionaries who came to their region in the early 1950s played only a limited role in it. The missionaries settled in two more populous communities to the east and the west of Urapmin that had airstrips, but given the arduous nature of the trek to Urapmin and the fact that the population was so small and spoke a distinct language, they did not visit Urapmin very regularly. Yet in the 1960s, the Urapmin, realizing that many among their neighbors were embracing the new religion, sent a large number of their older teenagers, mostly boys but also some girls, to study at the main school that the missionaries had set up and report back about the nature of Christianity. Traditional Urapmin religion had centered around extensive stocks of secret/ sacred (which is one word in the Urap language) knowledge that everyone knew was passed on to boys slowly through elaborate stages of ritual initiation in a series that could last more than fifteen years. The Urapmin students therefore understood the pedagogical setup of the mission school, and they were eager learners. They were so eager and successful, in fact, that as some began to graduate, the Australian Baptists hired several of them to act as what the missionaries called "evangelists" to groups even more remote than their own. But the majority of the young people came home to Urapmin when they finished school and began teaching everyone in the community the Baptist version of the Christian faith that they had learned. They also, quite remarkably, taught everyone up to about age forty how to read the lingua franca of Papua New Guinea (Tok Pisin), which allowed many members of the community to develop a habit of regular Bible study that they carry on today. By 1977, then, most Urapmin children and adults knew a good deal about many Christian doctrines, as well as having the kind of firm grasp on biblical stories that one would expect of people living until very recently in an exclusively oral culture.

Despite having a sophisticated understanding of many key elements of the faith, however, up to the early 1970s, no one in Urapmin except the former mission students had converted. Urapmin religion was under strict gerontocratic control, and even as its leaders were willing to learn about the new religion that was emerging as so central to the recently installed colonial order, they were

---

13. Joel Robbins, *Becoming Sinners: Christianity and Moral Torment in a Papua New Guinea Society* (Berkeley: University of California Press, 2004).

not inclined to adopt it in favor of their own. This was the situation in 1975, when Papua New Guinea became independent of Australia, causing a great deal of apprehension among small, remote groups such as the Urapmin that had no political or economic foothold in the new country. Around that time, and perhaps in part in response to the major changes going on around them, Christianity's fortunes among the Urapmin began to change. Two rising political leaders, too old to have gone to the mission schools, converted. Then, in 1977, a charismatic revival movement that had begun in New Zealand swept through Papua New Guinea, brought from place to place by local people who had encountered it in their travels. When it reached the Urapmin community, many people became possessed by the Holy Spirit. Their bodies shook, they felt intensely hot, and, as they say, they came to know that God truly exists and that they were sinners in profound need of salvation. Within a year, everyone in the community had converted. They tore down their old ritual structures, burned or otherwise disposed of the ancestral bones and other sacred objects that had filled them, and built a second church so everyone would live near one or the other and could easily attend often twice-daily services. Some of the most able among the returned students became lead pastors. Very quickly, Christianity became a major focus of Urapmin life.

It is difficult in a short chapter to convey either the sophistication of Urapmin Christianity or the extent of the changes it rang on traditional Urapmin life. But one point that I need mostly to tell rather than show here is that Urapmin Christianity is not the kind of lightly held, heavily syncretized, traditional-at-its-core amalgam that many anthropologists and others used to imagine was the normal product that emerged when remote people converted to world religions. The kind of charismatic faith that the Urapmin adopted thoroughly demonizes traditional religious beings and practices and demands that people reject all allegiance to them. It is, as anthropologists sometimes say, "antisyncretic." Very much according to type, Urapmin charismatic Christianity strongly rejects traditional religion and for the most part looks and sounds like charismatic and Pentecostal Christianity elsewhere in the world, and this similarity extends to many of the ways that the Urapmin and other Christians of this type understand the key theological tenets of the faith. Given the topic at hand, the one area in which I want to go beyond assertion to make this point in detail regards Urapmin understanding of the individualistic aspects of the Protestant message.

In the course of making an argument that his church is not as bereft of community-building resources as it is sometimes thought to be, the Baptist theologian Stephen Holmes finds that he nonetheless has to admit that it is critical to the Baptist faith that "God deals directly with each particular human person."[14] The Urapmin fully understand this point and hold fast to the idea that people are saved as individuals, not as members of churches or families or any other groups to which they might belong.

To demonstrate this, let me give you an admittedly unusually eloquent example of what this claim sounds like in Urapmin terms. Rom is an important figure in Urapmin. Extremely intelligent, and with a Bible school background (though from a time when the mission was withdrawing and the school was being run by a man from the region, not by the missionaries), Rom is one of the political leaders of the Urapmin community. One night, I came across him reading the Bible by firelight in his house. He was, he explained, studying what is often called "The Parable of the Wise and Foolish Virgins" from Matthew: 25. In this parable, ten virgins are waiting one night for the arrival of a bridegroom. Hearing that the bridegroom is approaching, the five wise virgins light their lamps to go to meet him. But the five foolish virgins have not brought enough oil for their lamps. They ask the wise ones who did bring oil to give them some, but the wise virgins refuse and tell them to go out to buy some oil of their own. While the foolish virgins are away on their errand, the bridegroom comes and takes the wise virgins into the wedding and the doors to the hall are closed. When the foolish virgins return, they ask the bridegroom to let them in, but he refuses, saying he does not know them.

When I learned that this was the passage that Rom was studying, I immediately assumed that I knew why he found this chapter of Matthew worth pondering, for the parable ends with a line that seemingly all Urapmin know and often repeat: "Watch therefore, for you know neither the day nor the hour in which the Son of Man is coming." The phrase "no one knows the day nor the hour" is a staple expression of the intense millennial concern that marks Urapmin Christianity, and I imagined that this was the point upon which Rom was focused. But even though I thought I knew why he was interested in this chapter, I decided to ask him anyway what the parable meant. This was a bit of field-workers' luck, as his answer did not go in the direction that I expected. This passage, Rom explained,

---

14. Stephen R. Holmes, *Baptist Theology* (London: Continuum, 2012), 6.

tells us that "belief is a big thing." Everyone, he went on, has to have belief for themselves; they cannot share someone else's. "My wife," he added, "cannot break off part of her belief and give it to me, and I cannot break off part of my belief and give it to her. Everyone has to have their own."

Even without much further discussion, it is clear that Rom's Protestantism has taught him the shape of individualism as a major value by making it clear to him that people can only be saved on their own, one by one. But it is worth dwelling for a moment on the question of why Rom found this point so worthy of close study. He was drawn to dwell on it, and so ready to explain it with great clarity, I want to suggest, because it ran directly counter to the traditional Urapmin way of thinking about things with which he had been raised and which still governed his conduct in many domains of his life. If we can say in analytic terms that individualism is the highest value in Urapmin Christianity, such that producing the saved individual is the most important thing that the Urapmin can accomplish by its lights, then we can add that a different value, one we can call "relationalism," is the highest value in their traditional understanding, an understanding that still in the early 1990s organized much of their productive, political, and, more broadly, civic life. In those contexts in which the value of relationalism is dominant, the most important thing that people can do is successfully maintain the relationships that they have and strive to make new ones. People do this primarily by giving gifts of foodstuffs, other items, and sometimes labor, and they give and receive many such gifts every day. To illustrate this quickly, I can note that Urapmin have two verbs for eating. One translates as "eating for nothing," which means eating food that you yourself have grown or hunted. The other, much more highly valued form, translates simply as "eating" and refers to eating food that someone else has given you while giving your own harvest to others. Almost all of the eating that Urapmin do is of this second type. Husbands and wives sometimes go so far as to split their shared gardens into his and hers halves, so that even food that one gives to the other can count as a relation-enhancing gift. With this background in mind, it is not hard to understand why Rom finds it a "big thing" worthy of study that his wife cannot give him any of her Christian belief, nor can he give her any of his. This point does not hold true for any other important features of his world.

Since my concern in this chapter is ultimately with the prospects for a moral individualism, the best way for me to further develop an account of Urapmin Protestant individualism, and to consider more closely its relationship to relationalism, is to look at its moral aspects, and I can most easily do this by discussing a conflict between traditional Urapmin morality and their Christian one that was central to Urapmin life in the early 1990s (and may well still be today). This conflict is evident when we turn to a discussion of Urapmin moral psychology.

In traditional Urapmin moral psychology, there are two parts of the "heart" (the seat of all thought, feeling, and intention) that people must mobilize correctly to succeed in creating and maintaining relationships. The first of these they call the "will." This is the part of the heart that leads a person to push others to enter into relations with himself/herself, such as by insisting that the two garden together, share food together, hunt together, build their houses close together, or engage with each other in any other way. The other part of the heart, they call "good thinking," which leads people to act in lawful ways. Behavior is defined as "lawful" if it recognizes the demands of relations that people already have so it leads them, for example, to garden with people they have already gardened with, to share food with people they have already shared food with, etc. Ideally, as the Urapmin see things in traditional terms, willfulness and lawfulness work together, such that people use their wills to create new relationships and follow the promptings of their good thinking to ensure that all their relationships remain in good order. In a more anthropologically detailed discussion, one that would honor the fact that Bellah's first book focused on Apache kinship, I could link the appeal of relational values for the Urapmin to technical details of their social structure. Put simply, the point of such an argument would be that Urapmin social-structural norms allow a great deal of choice about which potential relationships to participate in, and therefore people do not imagine that relationships or broader social orders are timeless, or, as it were, come of themselves. Instead, the Urapmin assert that such orders must be made, maintained, and remade, and for these things to happen, people have to put relational values at the top of their hierarchy. But for present purposes, I do not have to go further into the niceties of Urapmin social organization. It is enough to have indicated that relational values held an extremely high place in traditional Urapmin life, and they gave shape to a moral system that saw the correct balancing of willful, expansive relational impulses with lawful ones aimed at maintaining existing relations as the key task that dominated their ethical life.

The coming of Christianity to Urapmin has, as we have seen, introduced individualism as a new high-level value that, at least during the period of my fieldwork, was fundamentally incompatible with relationalism. At the heart of this individualism, to make in a bit more detail another point that I have made before, is the conviction that one's ultimate salvational fate depends upon the moral state of one's own heart at the time of Jesus's return, rather than on the moral state of any relations that one might have to others. Given the millenarian tenor of Urapmin Christianity that I also mentioned earlier, Urapmin are preoccupied with their moral status, knowing that at any moment, it could be subject to a final judgment.

Urapmin efforts to realize the Christian individualist value of having a good moral heart has led to a profound change in their moral psychology. The interior state that the person now aims to achieve is not one based on a careful balancing of willful and lawful impulses, but rather one that is marked by an "easy" feeling that signals that one is free of willful drives and able to avoid the sinful practices of pushing others, arguing, fighting, and other actions to which they can lead. In Christian terms, having only lawful feelings is the route to having an easy heart and realizing the value of lawful living that one needs to be saved, and the will is now condemned as sinful by nature. One sees this new emphasis on the need to act on the basis of lawful impulses alone playing out in many central areas of Urapmin life. For example, in the name of the value of Christian individualism, some otherwise highly skilled and well-liked Urapmin men who appeared qualified to take leadership roles have withdrawn fairly extensively from social life so as to avoid the kinds of willful behavior that the occupation of such positions requires, or, as they put it, to avoid "ruining" their "Christian lives." Others have withdrawn from the will-driven, contentious, but politically important exchanges that surround marriage (perhaps the ultimate willful act of relation creation). More generally, the pursuit of an easy heart has attenuated for many the appeal of participation in public life, a picture of the effects of individualism that fits neatly with Bellah's expectation for the effects of a morally nonserious version of this value, one that, in his article "Flaws in the Protestant Code," he describes as being unable to support "solidarity, a sense of being members of the same body."[15]

But even as Urapmin individualism has led to some withdrawal from social life, its success has been far from complete. Even people like those I have just

---

15. Bellah, "Flaws in the Protestant Code," 344.

discussed, those who forgo some of the key relation-making practices of tra-ditional Urapmin life, do need, just like all other Urapmin, to work toward creating and maintaining at least some relationships to survive in the local social and economic conditions that they still inhabit, and to do this, they need to exercise their will to some extent, regardless of the inevitability of this leading them into sin. It should not be surprising, then, to learn that the Christian model of humanity as fallen and a correlated fixation on issues of moral difficulty are central to Urapmin life: from the point of view of their highest Christian value, the Urapmin are moral failures whenever they engage in the willful relation-making work that their social life depends upon, while from the point of their highest traditional values, they are moral fail-ures whenever they succeed as Christians in cultivating the consistently easy, lawful heart, devoid of the willful, relation-promoting impulses upon which their salvation depends. As expressed in the title of my monograph about the Urapmin, the clash between the values of an individualism developed virtually from whole cloth out of an encounter with Protestantism and a relationalism rooted in tradition has led them to lead lives marked by a significant degree of "moral torment."[16] They are committed to being hopeful about the future—it is important to recognize that they do not feel themselves to be defeated in any sense—but they often express how difficult they find it to live good lives in the present.[17]

I hope by now that it is clear that the recent history of the Urapmin speaks to the strength of Bellah's account of the way that Protestantism, working vir-tually on its own, can introduce the value of individualism in a place where it had little standing before. It is also not hard to conclude that Protestant indi-vidualism as it is currently understood in Urapmin has the morality-inhibiting features that Bellah, Tillich, and Goldmann worry about. It provides very little by way of support for aspects of morality that are based on regard for others or for social institutions. It is, to borrow a term that Karl Polanyi famously applied to the market economy, a socially "disembedded" form of ethics.[18] This is so because, from a transcendent point of view, the social aspects of one's life

16. Robbins, *Becoming Sinners*.

17. Joel Robbins, "Beyond the Suffering Subject: Toward an Anthropology of the Good," *Journal of the Royal Anthropological Institute* 19 (2013):447–62.

18. Karl Polanyi, *The Great Transformation: The Political and Economic Origins of Our Time* (Boston: Beacon, 2001 [orig. 1994]).

will not bear heavily on one's salvation.[19] Thus the question arises of whether there is any prospect for a "seriously ethical form of individualism" to develop in Urapmin. In the next section, I want to consider this question by reframing it in terms of the emphasis on the relations between values that I draw from the work of Dumont.

LOUIS DUMONT'S ANTHROPOLOGICAL APPROACH TO VALUES

As Hans Joas notes in his contribution to this volume (chapter 7), Bellah engaged with Dumont's work in a number of places.[20] It is true that Dumont is not featured much in *Habits*, certainly not as much as he would have been in most anthropological discussions of individualism, in which his 1986 collection *Essays on Individualism* is treated as a key source. But he does come up from time to time in the book, and in one of those instances, he is discussed alongside Alasdair MacIntyre and Jürgen Habermas as constituting a small group of interdisciplinary scholars concerned with the social who, like the major founders of the social sciences such as Marx, Weber, and Durkheim, take "conscious responsibility for their philosophical positions in a way that most social scientists today do not."[21] This is heady company, and Dumont does not at present enjoy the status, or at least the broad readership, of these other two thinkers, though at one time his standing reached these heights in anthropology, and he is having

---

19. Joel Robbins, "When Did It Become Hard to Be Good? Axial Dynamics and the Problem of the Moral Self," in *Society and Morality in Eurasia: From Prehistory to the Present Day*, ed. Chris Hann (Halle-Wittenberg, Germany: Max Planck Institute for Social Anthropology, 2021), 27–38.

20. For this discussion, I draw on a wide range of Dumont's works, in particular, *From Mandeville to Marx: The Genesis and Triumph of Economic Ideology* (Chicago: University of Chicago Press, 1977); *Homo Hierarchicus: The Caste System and Its Implications*, Complete Revised English Edition, trans. M. Sainsbury, L. Dumont, and B. Gulati (Chicago: University of Chicago Press, 1980); and *Essays on Individualism: Modern Ideology in Anthropological Perspective* (Chicago: University of Chicago Press, 1986). I have laid out my understanding of Dumont's theoretical approach to values in more detail in a number of places and provided extensive references to his work there. Joel Robbins, "Equality as a Value: Ideology in Dumont, Melanesia and the West," *Social Analysis* 36 (1994): 21–70; "Monism, Pluralism and the Structure of Value Relations: A Dumontian Contribution to the Contemporary Study of Value," *Hau: Journal of Ethnographic Theory* 3, no. 1 (2013): 99–115; and "Dumont's Hierarchical Dynamism: Christianity and Individualism Revisited," *Hau: Journal of Ethnographic Theory* 5, no. 1 (2015): 173–95. For that reason, I have not cluttered this text with detailed references.

21. Bellah et al., *Habits of the Heart*, 301.

something of a minor revival in the discipline today. His declining influence in anthropology and beyond is surely in part due to an effect that afflicts the vast majority of scholars, for whom death tends to dampen their influence, at least for a time. In this regard, it is worth noting that Dumont was born eighteen years before both Habermas and MacIntyre and that he died in 1998. But even before he died, his fate was largely sealed by the scholarly tendency to read him as an ethnographer of India, or as a scholar of the history of Western thought, which he approached by reading the great works of that tradition through an ethnographic lens.

What is lost in these approaches to his work is an appreciation for his impressive social theoretical ambition, an ambition that made him easily the most important anthropological theorist of values in the discipline's history. Too often, scholars who ignore this ambition dismiss his oeuvre on the basis of disagreements with one or another of his specific ethnographic arguments rather than by critically engaging with his broader theoretical claims. This is a shame. Imagine the social sciences today if Durkheim had been read mostly as someone who was not quite right about Australian Aboriginal religion, or Weber as a scholar who missed important aspects of the empirical cases that he discusses (many of which have been subject to extensive critique and reanalysis, of course). Like Bellah, but unlike most other French anthropologists (or American ones for that matter), Dumont knew the German as well as the French sociological traditions. It is out of their conjunction that he fashioned his theory of values. It is that theory—rather than his ethnographic and historical work (even his well-known historical account of the Christian origins of Western individualism, which would of course be worth discussing in detail in a longer or different version of this chapter)—that I am going to draw on in considering both Urapmin individualism and the prospects for Bellah's search for moral individualism.

For Dumont, individualism is first and foremost a value. It is a value that defines the development of the individual as the most important goal of any cultural formation in which it is dominant. To fully understand what Dumont means by this, it is necessary to make two points about how he understands values more generally. The first is that, in good structuralist fashion, values never exist on their own for Dumont. They are defined in relation to other values. And crucially, their definition through differentiation is not based only on oppositions at the level of meaning (as in classic structural linguistics and anthropology), but also on oppositions of rank in what Dumont calls not a "binary" but a "hierarchical opposition."[22] Values are thus always arrayed in hierarchies vis-à-vis one another.[23] Moreover, other cultural phenomena, such as practices, social institutions, or even whole domains or fields of social life, are in turn ranked vis-à-vis one another on the basis of how much or how little they contribute to the realization of high level values. In the U.S. case, this would mean that various cultural elements are ranked in relation to each other with regard to how much they contribute to the development of individuals.

The second feature of Dumont's theory of values that I will draw on here is his claim that higher-ranking values relate to lower-ranking ones in some predictable ways. The most well known of these in anthropology is a relation that Dumont calls "encompassment," but since I will not draw on this concept in what follows, I will set this kind of relation aside here. More important for present purposes are two further kinds of relationships between values that Dumont models in his work. One is a relationship in which higher-level values set limits on the social contexts in which lower-level values can express themselves, relegating their most fulsome expression to contexts that are themselves lower ranked. We can call this relationship one of relegation. The other is a relationship in which higher-level values restrict the extent to which lower-level values can express themselves even in the contexts where they are allowed to do so. This relationship can be called one of restricted elaboration.

Dumont was profoundly influenced by the English anthropologist E. E. Evans-Pritchard, who famously defined anthropology as the study of relations and "relations between relations."[24] As the previous paragraph attests, this kind of theory building can become dizzyingly abstract very quickly. To put at least a little flesh on this skeletal account of how higher-level values relate to lower-ranked ones, let me give an all-too-quick example of the kinds of concrete analyses that Dumont carries out by means of his understanding of value relations. I will do

---

22. Dumont, *Essays on Individualism*, 227.

23. As Joas notes in chapter 7 of this volume, Dumont does not adopt Weber's notion of value spheres. Instead, he gets at something similar, an understanding of the tendency of social formations to be marked by divisions between domains or fields, through his use of the term "levels." It is noteworthy that this phrasing implies ranking between such divisions in a way that spheres, domains, and fields do not. This is because the values that hold sway on various levels are themselves ranked in relation to one another. This goes some way toward addressing the weakness that Gorski (in chapter 10 of this volume) finds in Weber's account of spheres because the latter does not take into account the relations between spheres, "their relative size and power."

24. E. E. Evans-Prtichard, *The Nuer: A Description of the Modes of Livelihood and Political Institutions of a Nilotic People* (Oxford: Oxford University Press, 1940), 266.

this using material likely to be familiar to all readers of this chapter, having to do with the relation of liberty and equality in what the late Marshall Sahlins used to like to call "standard average" U.S. culture.

If we define liberty as the ability to guide one's own life as one sees fit—to choose one's own goods and become the unique person that one is—then it clearly provides a major part of the substance of the value of individualism in the United States and is therefore very highly ranked. It finds very well elaborated expression in the highest-ranked social fields that constitute what is defined as the public sphere: the market, the political arena, the legal domain, etc. Equality is also a prominent value in U.S. culture, although anyone with even a modicum of social critical inclination can point out that it is most often honored in the breach. This follows from the way that it is subordinated to liberty. This subordination means first that equality's most developed expressions are relegated to lower-ranked domains of social life such as the family (where many hold that children should be treated equally) and the school (where many people at least assert that, as much as possible, everyone should be given equal chances). In demonstrating the lower rank of these domains, it is worth noting that their ultimate success is judged by their production of adults who can leave them and fully realize their liberty in the more highly ranked domains, particularly that of the market. Their telos is beyond and above themselves. Along with its relegation to lower-ranked domains, the value of equality is also restricted in its elaboration. Those aspects of equality that accord with liberty, particularly equality of opportunity, get a lot of public play. But those that do not, such as equality of outcome figured as some kind of leveling, get less and are less well worked out in both thought and practice. One of the ways that equality as a value is restricted in its elaboration is evidenced in the way that the logical requirement for some kind of equality of outcome to provide the baseline for equality of opportunity is not nearly so deeply or creatively reflected upon in thought as is equality of opportunity itself, and it finds very little expression in practice.

The payoff for all of this detailed analysis of how values are shaped by their hierarchical relations with other values and the relations between these relations is an understanding of values that does not consider them one at a time, but rather recognizes that the forms that they take depend on the complex value structures in which they exist. The discussion of the four traditions that play into American culture in *Habits*, as well as the sorting of them into first and second languages, are moving toward a picture like this. One sees evidence of this when the authors write that "even the most secure, happily married of our respondents had difficulty when they sought a language in which to articulate their reasons for commitments that went beyond the self."[25] Being a second language, in Bellah et al.'s terms, is like, in Dumont's scheme, being a lower-ranked value that is restricted in elaborating itself past the point where it begins to contradict higher-ranked values. This understanding of values will, in the conclusion of this chapter, lead me to reframe the question of the nature of a moral individualism into one about what kinds of relations individualism needs to contract with other values to create an overall gestalt that makes ethical life possible, even when individualism plays a key role in its organization.

CONCLUSION: ON MORALITY AND VALUE RELATIONS

The pioneering popular culture scholar John G. Cawelti gets a quick mention in a footnote in *Habits* for his portrait of the individualism of those mythic heroes of American masculinity: the Western gunslinger and the hard-boiled private detective.[26] In one of his writings on this topic, Cawelti argues that for Americans,

> the individual who can mold society and the law to his own ends is as much admired as condemned. There is a slight edge of contempt in our attitude toward the conscientious and law-abiding citizen, as if some weakness or impotence prevented him from acting aggressively for himself. On the other hand, Americans are clearly not prepared to extend this view of individualism to its logical conclusion of a war of all against all, for there are other, different values that are also important to us, in particular the ideals of equality and community.[27]

Cawelti's essay "Myths of Violence in American Popular Culture," quoted here, was originally published in 1975.[28] If he had written a decade later, after reading *Habits*, he might not have been so confident about the ability of other

---

25. Bellah et al., *Habits of the Heart*, 109.
26. Bellah et al., *Habits of the Heart*, 319.
27. John G. Cawelti, *Mystery, Violence, and Popular Culture* (Madison: University of Wisconsin Press/Popular Press, 2004), 175.
28. Cawelti, *Mystery, Violence, and Popular Culture*, 152–72.

values to place some limits on the expression of individualism in the United States. Nonetheless, I think he was on the right track in theoretical if not empirical terms, as was Tillich in proposing the need for Catholic substance to counterbalance the Protestant principle in all versions of Christianity, and as were the authors of *Habits* in their discussion of the moral potential that America's second language has to complement and modify the utilitarian and expressive individualism of its first. What all these arguments share is a claim that the moral tenor of a culture should never follow from the demands of a single value, no matter how highly ranked. The question of the nature of a moral individualism is thus not a question about individualism alone, regardless of how we understand it, but is rather about how individualism can be related to other values in ways that allow people to live moral lives in which they can respect their own needs and potentials, as well as those of their society. I think that this is at least part of what Tillich means by his elusive but also attractive notion of "theonomy," the ideal state that he opposes to both autonomy and heteronomy.[29]

I have suggested that Dumont's theoretical approach to value relations can help us cash out this vision in some analytic detail. To conclude this argument, let me return to the Urapmin case and consider again why their lives were so morally fraught during the period of my fieldwork. The key to understanding their moral difficulty is recognizing that among them, the relationship between the values of individualism and relationalism was not at all settled; instead, both made strong claims to the position of highest value. In Dumont's terms, this meant that neither had managed to relegate the other to less-valued contexts or restrict its elaboration. For the Urapmin, to borrow Weber's image, these gods were at war on all fronts within Urapmin social life.

My guess is that in the early 1990s, the Urapmin would have plumped for Christian individualism as their highest value if they could have found a way of making any kind of viable society out of it. If they had not, to put this otherwise, been stymied from going all in on individualism by the flaws in the Protestant code, that meant that they could not make a social world out of its resources alone (and without the social resources, such as they are, provided by a capitalist market economy). Over time, one imagines that they will find a way of bringing individualism and relationalism into cooperation, dividing between them the

29. Paul Tillich, *On the Boundary: An Autobiographical Sketch* (New York: Charles Scribner's Sons, 1966).

various domains of Urapmin social life and letting one of them in some ways control and restrict the other. This is what it would take, I think, to make their individualism morally livable.

Bellah had an enviable ability to speak about society in big picture terms without losing his feel for the details. I want to close by trying to borrow just a tiny bit of his gift here, using it to illuminate our present situation in the terms that I have laid out in this discussion. It is probably as good a definition of neoliberalism as any other to say that it is a cultural formation in which the value of individualism, here understood primarily in its utilitarian sense, has not only risen to the top of the hierarchy of values, but has also colonized domain after domain of social life, leaving precious little space for other values to express themselves except in the most restricted ways. This outcome was the threat that hung over the argument of *Habits*, and the book has sadly turned out to be one of those few works of social science that has proved highly reliable in its predictions, and this despite its best efforts to make a course correction in the direction of travel that it diagnosed. A call for some attention to restoring a balance between values—a balance that allows them together to foster the conditions for living well-rounded moral lives—is clearly even more necessary now than when that book was first published.

CODA

Even at the height of Dumont's influence, many anthropologists had a sense that he might be a bit too conservative, or at least too traditionalist, for their tastes. That is, they worried that as a political project, he may have meant to promote the value that he called "holism," a primary concern for the state of the social whole that he argued was the highest value in India, as the best value for any society to rank most highly. In political terms, this was not true—he was, for example, apparently quite far to the left of Claude Levi-Strauss, the only more prominent French anthropologist of his era. But in theoretical terms, too, he was adamant that any attempt to turn to holism in a society that had already fully elaborated the value of individualism led down a dark path. This is so because holism, as Dumont understands it, values social difference because, in an organic-solidarity sense, it claims that different kinds of people are needed to create a flourishing whole. Such a holist conceptualization involves what Joas (in chapter 7) calls an "organic social ethic" (though in Dumont's case, he took no position on the relative merits of the universalist versus particularist holism that is important to Joas's discussion). Dumont argues that individualism, by contrast, ultimately promotes sameness—a right to differ that everyone possesses in equal measure. If individualists try to make a whole, the only way they can do so is by making the substance of their bond a kind of mechanical solidarity—one based on the ways that they are all the same. Dumont calls this a pseudo-holism. In his terms, with the rise of Christian nationalism in the United States, we might well say that pseudo-holism is in the streets. This makes the project of finding a pattern of values in which individualism can contribute to, rather than preclude, a moral way forward urgent in just the ways that Bellah always recognized.

CHAPTER 10

"DISENCHANTMENT OF THE WORLD" OR FRAGMENTATION OF THE SACRED?

PHILIP GORSKI

Just as God, founder of the universe, has constituted two large luminaries in the firmament of Heaven . . . so he has established in the firmament of the Universal Church . . . two great dignities, a major one to preside . . . over the days of the souls, and a minor one to preside over the nights of the bodies.

—Pope Innocent III, 1198

On the marble floor of a collapsed building in the ruined temple of an ancient city, a group of archaeologists discover a trove of pottery shards. They appear to be the remains of a collection of vases. Some of the shards are large enough that one can still imagine the shape and pattern of the original. Others are so small that they resemble specks of dust. Judging by the style, some of the shards appear to be from the region around the capital city. But others look to be of foreign origin. The archaeologists set about cataloguing and classifying the remains. The archaeologists argue endlessly about the vases—their number, provenance, and demise.

In the meantime, a group of artists enters the temple. Some of them patiently try to piece together one of the vases in its original form. Others gleefully assemble motley fragments into something new. Still others quietly pocket their favorite fragments, whether as a personal talisman or as raw materials for a future project. They, too, begin to wonder if and how the pieces should be put together again.

The image of the shattered vases captures something fundamental about the religious, spiritual, and cultural situation of the present moment—something that the dominant imagery of "disenchantment" and "differentiation" and "rationalization" and "secularization" does not. What follows is a brief sketch of what might be called "fragmentation theory."

This chapter has five parts. It begins with a critical discussion of differentiation theory in the work of Max Weber. Then, it sketches an alternative approach built around the concepts of "sacralization," "monopolization," "fragmentation," and "hybridity." The approach taken is broadly Durkheimian, although it draws on other traditions as well. This is followed by an effort to reintegrate the two theories via the concept of "weak fields." The final, concluding section uses the resulting framework to make sense of some of the more puzzling aspects of the present situation.

DIFFERENTIATION THEORY: A PARTIAL AND PRELIMINARY CRITIQUE

Differentiation theory comes in many forms and from various sources. Here, for reasons of space, I focus on just one of them: Max Weber's. Also, for reasons of influence: within contemporary American sociology, and especially the sociology of religion, by far the most influential theory of differentiation is Weber's theory of "value spheres" or "life orders." As readers of Weber will recall, he argued that the social order of the "modern West" consists of neatly differentiated and internally rationalized "value spheres" or "life orders."

This argument first appears in one of the two "intermediate reflections" sandwiched between Weber's "essays on the world religions." The original title of the essay in question was "Theory of the Degrees and Directions of Religious Rejections of the World."[1] There, and elsewhere, Weber distinguished between "world rejecting" and "world affirming" religions. The former postulated a

---

1. Max Weber, "Religious Rejections of the World and Their Directions," in *From Max Weber: Essays in Sociology*, trans. and ed. H. H. Gerth and C. Wright Mills (New York: Oxford University Press, 1958); Max Weber, *The Sociology of Religion* (Boston: Beacon, 1993); Max Weber, *The Protestant Ethic and the "Spirit" of Capitalism and Other Writings*, Penguin Twentieth-Century Classics, trans. and ed. P. R. Baehr and Gordon C. Wells (New York: Penguin, 2002).

"supramundane order" that was ontologically discontinuous with, and also ethically superior to, "the world" of everyday experience. Think of "heaven and earth" in the Christian tradition. World-affirming religions did not posit any such discontinuity between higher and lower orders, nor any notion of the good beyond what we would nowadays call ordinary human flourishing (i.e., progeny, prosperity, and health). Think of Mt. Olympus in the Ancient Greek imagination.[2]

This initial differentiation between mundane and supramundane orders, Weber argued, gradually catalyzed further differentiations within the mundane order, at first between religious and nonreligious forms of community, such as the family and the polity, and then between religious and nonreligious systems of value, such as charity versus interest, or truth versus beauty.

Recall Jesus's warning that he came to bring not peace, but a sword or his teachings regarding God and Caesar. The result of these tensions, Weber argues, was the gradual emergence of at least seven distinct "value spheres" or "life orders," each oriented toward one "ultimate value," and each dominated by its own elite of "intellectuals" and "virtuosi," to wit: "religion," "family," "polity," "economy," "art," "science," and "eroticism."

The Western version of Weber's narrative of social differentiation stretches across three millennia and may be divided into three chapters. The protagonists of the first chapter are the Hebrew prophets; they drive the transition from a world-affirming monolatry to a world-rejecting monotheism, from a protector god who is first among equals to a righteous God who reigns alone. The protagonists of the second chapter are Jesus and Paul, who preach otherworldly salvation first to the Jews, and then to the Gentiles. In this way, ethical monotheism becomes a "world religion." The third and final chapter features an ensemble cast: the "ascetic Protestants" of the Reformation era, who break down the monastery walls and loose an ethos of "innerworldly asceticism" on an unsuspecting world. The first chapter opens the chasm between mundane and supramundane spheres within ancient Israel; the second extends the chasm to the Gentile world; and the third opens new cracks within the mundane order.

Where do "disenchantment," "rationalization," and "secularization" fit into this story? The German term for "disenchantment"—*Entzauberung*—is more

---

2. For a brilliant elaboration of this distinction, within and beyond the Christian West, see Alan Strathern, *Unearthly Powers: Religious and Political Change in World History* (Cambridge: Cambridge University Press, 2019).

literally—if less poetically—translated as "demagification." For Weber, it should be noted, the initial impetus toward disenchantment comes not from science but from religion itself, specifically from the ethical monotheism of the Hebrew prophets, for they vehemently rejected the magical worldview in which the actions of a god can be conjured or influenced by words or rituals performed by a human. The only thing that pleases God, the prophets insisted, is obedience to His laws or charity toward others. Ironically, then—and Weber's narrative is laden with ironies—it is the prophets who begin building the path for God's "exit" from "the world" and clearing the ground for a naturalistic view of that world qua inanimate mechanism.

What about "rationalization"? Here, the crucial development is the institutional differentiation of the "value spheres" and the crystallization of "virtuoso" elites within them. In Weber's sociology, elite competition is most often the "locomotive" of historical development; no less so in rationalization processes. They arise from competition (1) between elites from different spheres as they seek to defend their jurisdiction against encroachment from neighboring spheres; (2) within the elites of each sphere, as they seek to distinguish themselves from internal rivals by their virtuosity; and finally (3) over control of "lay" followers. As a result of this ceaseless struggle, the "ultimate value" that defines each sphere is ever more clearly articulated, as are the most efficient means to achieving it, and the domination of the elites over "the masses" is reproduced in the process. Rationality is formal, instrumental, and oriented toward power.

Weber is often counted as one of the foremost theorists of "secularization." However, he himself only rarely used the term, and then only in his writings on the history of law.[3] But if "secularization" means the differentiation of religious and nonreligious values and elites, then Weber is rightly characterized as a secularization theorist. The same applies if "secularization" refers to the decline of religious belief. While there is no indication that Weber thought such beliefs would disappear altogether, it is quite clear that he thought they were declining, a view that he shared with many European intellectuals of his era.[4] Taken

---

3. Max Weber, *Economy and Society: An Outline of Interpretive Sociology* (Berkeley: University of California Press, 1978).
4. Max Weber, "Science as a Vocation," in *From Max Weber: Essays in Sociology*, trans. and ed. H. H. Gerth and C. Wright Mills (New York: Oxford University Press, 1958).

together, Weber's conceptual triad of "differentiation," "disenchantment," and "rationalization" adds up to a form of secularization theory.

There is, by now, a vast literature on this theory, which is far too vast to digest here.[5] In this context, two features of Weber's theory of value spheres bear underlining. The first is its ontological parsimony. In Weber's typology, the core of any value sphere has only two components: a "carrier class" of "virtuosos" or "intellectuals," and an "ultimate value" that can be stated in univocal terms (e.g., "salvation," "wealth," "power," or "pleasure"). The periphery of each sphere presumably consists of the less devoted or talented, the fellow-travelers and also-rans.

Note, too, that Weber does not explicitly address the issue of the spheres' boundaries.[6] Presumably, he would conceptualize them as a form of "social closure," through which the carrier class and their followers seek to monopolize jurisdiction over their ultimate value and police the boundaries of their value sphere. Nor does Weber adequately clarify the relations among the value spheres—their relative size and power. Certainly, the aesthetic or erotic spheres were not, and are not, on quite the same footing as the economic or political spheres. In short, Weber's theory of value spheres is conceptually underdeveloped at best.

The second feature of Weber's theory that warrants examination is his account of historical dynamics. One of the signal attractions of Weber's narrative is its millennial depth, its magisterial sweep. But this is also one of its central weaknesses. Are we really to believe that the seeds of the seven value spheres that Weber identifies were already planted three millennia ago in ancient Israel? And was it really the case that they first sprang forth only two-and-a-half millennia later, in Calvinist Europe during the Protestant Reformation? Why not earlier or later? Why not in Catholic or Lutheran regions?

Of course, theorization always involves simplification, an attempt to isolate those aspects of social reality that are causally significant in a given context and in relation to a specific question.[7] Placing Weber's theory in its historical context sheds considerable light on some of his simplifications. In retrospect, it is evident

5. For a brief overview, see Philip S. Gorski and Ateş Altınordu, "After Secularization?," *Annual Review of Sociology* 34, no. 1 (2008), https://doi.org/doi:10.1146/annurev.soc.34.040507.134740.

6. Today, the concept of "social boundaries" is a central element of much social theorizing. The seminal analysis is by Michèle Lamont and Virag Molnar, "The Study of Boundaries in the Social Sciences," *Annual Review of Sociology* 28 (2002): 167–95.

7. On Weber's understanding of, and solution to, this problem, see Thomas Bürger, *Max Weber's Theory of Concept Formation: History, Laws, and Ideal Types*, expanded ed. (Durham, NC: Duke University Press, 1987).

that Weber's life coincided with the historical highwater marks of (1) the European nation-state, (2) European church-state conflict, and (3) Western and especially British colonialism. So perhaps we should not be so surprised that Weber's theory of value spheres presumed that (1) value spheres, social organizations, and cultural communities were equivalent terms, given that they were largely coterminous with one another in the national states and national churches of most of Europe; (2) the boundaries of value spheres were relatively clear cut and well policed, given that church-state relations were increasingly codified and enforced during this period; and (3) the power of Protestantism in general, and Calvinism in particular, as being superior to other types of religion, at least in their capacity to transform the world.

Weber would not have been surprised by this critique; on the contrary, he would have expected and even welcomed it. As an interpretivist and a historicist, Weber was only too aware that his research questions arose out of the cultural questions of his own era and his ideal types would have an expiration date. This is why he prophesied "eternal youth" for the "cultural and historical sciences."[8] This is not to say that Weber's theory of value spheres—or differentiation theory more generally—has outlived its usefulness. It has not. But such theories do miss important aspects of the present moment. Something more is needed: a theory of sacralization processes to supplement the theory of secularization processes.

MERE SACRALITY: A PRELIMINARY OUTLINE

One of the most ubiquitous icons of the Internet age is the heart symbol. One can "heart" or "love" most anything: a photo or video, a joke or a song, an object or a recipe, and, of course, another person. The heart icon is an exaggerated expression of personal affinity, a "like" elevated into a "love." Of course, the heart symbol figured prominently in Christian iconography as well.[9] It still does so for some devout Catholics. Its roots can be traced to one of the noncanonical gospels, the Gospel of Nicodemus, which claims that a Roman soldier pierced a crucified Christ's heart with his lance as he hung on the cross. Medieval iconography

---

8. Max Weber, *The Methodology of the Social Sciences*, trans. and ed. Edward A. Shils and Henry A. Finch (New York: Free Press, 1949).
9. Timothy Terrance O'Donnell, *Heart of the Redeemer* (San Francisco: Ignatius, 2018).

depicted a bleeding heart as one of the five wounds of Christ, alongside those inflicted to his feet and hands when he was nailed to the cross. Beginning in the fifteenth and sixteenth centuries, the latter wounds fell away as objects of veneration and the bleeding heart became a freestanding symbol. Perhaps the most familiar variant of this icon today is the "sacred heart," adorned with a small cross, flame, or crown of thorns. It is apparently due to Saint Margaret Mary, a female saint of the late seventeenth century, who had a mystical vision of Jesus's heart. The sacred heart subsequently became a powerful symbol of Catholic resistance to Protestantism, and later to secularism. The Church of the Sacred Heart (Sacré-Coeur) in Paris was built to atone for the sins of France following its defeat by Prussia in 1871. French soldiers carried images of the sacred heart into battle during World War I.[10]

One could easily fit this potted history of the sacred heart icon into an orthodox narrative of secularization: what was once an object of collective veneration of the divine has now become nothing more than a cultural means of expressing an emotional response to the mundane. But that would be too simple, for as neo-Augustinian theologians such as James K. A. Smith like to remind us: "you are what you love"—or just "like."[11] For Smith, of course, as for believing Christians in his lineage, the heart symbol of today represents a manifestation of "disordered loves," which puts divine things below worldly ones, or omits them altogether, a sign that God is no longer the central focus of human veneration. For workaday sociologists, on the other hand, the dizzying proliferation of hearts in the contemporary world could also be construed as a manifestation of something else: the fragmentation of the sacred. Love now comes from within the human heart, rather than emanating from the god-man's heart, and its objects are many and different, rather than one and unified. The sacred, in short, is no longer the monopoly of religion, and narratives that blithely equate the decline of Christianity with the triumph of science and the evaporation of the sacred assume far too much.

For Émile Durkheim, of course, religion originates not out of a historic rejection of magic, as for Weber, but rather out of collective experiences of the sacred. While Weber broke his bold promise to define religion, Durkheim did not. He

---

10. Raymond Anthony Jonas, *France and the Cult of the Sacred Heart: An Epic Tale for Modern Times* (Berkeley: University of California Press, 2000).

11. James K. A. Smith, *You Are What You Love: The Spiritual Power of Habit* (Grand Rapids, MI: Brazos, 2016).

offered the following: "A religion is a unified system of beliefs and practices relative to sacred things, that is to say, things set apart and forbidden—beliefs and practices which unite into one single moral community called a Church, all those who adhere to them."[12] What Durkheim does not do is explain how experiences of the sacred lead to the formation of religions, that is, to "unified systems" and "moral communities." Nor does he tell us how we might distinguish religious systems and communities from nonreligious ones. Such a distinction might have seemed unnecessary in Durkheim's France, when the Catholic Church and the French Republic were the only real competitors for love and "likes." But it is imperative in our era. As anyone who has ever taught Durkheim's *Elementary Forms* to undergraduate students well knows, the most "relatable" examples of "collective effervescence"—that font of the sacred—come from the realm of pop culture—from sports, music, and art—rather than from religion, as Durkheim defines it.

But how do experiences of the sacred lead to the formation—and reformation—of religion? Religion differs from mere sacrality in its postulation of ontological transcendence and ethical ideals or, in Durkheim's terms, a "unified system of beliefs and practices." But how is such unity attained?

To address this question, we might return to Weber—not to his sociology of religion, however, but to his sociology of domination. There, Weber famously defines the state as an organization that claims a monopoly on the legitimate means of violence within a particular territory.[13] State formation, for Weber, is best understood as a process of monopoly formation in which a ruler and his or her "administrative staff" progressively and successfully disarm and/or delegitimate their potential rivals within a given territory. "Church" formation, in Durkheim's sense, that is, the formation of religious institutions, might be conceptualized in an analogous way: as the gradual monopolization of legitimate forms of the sacred by a religious leader and his or her clerical staff. Of course, not all religious institutions take a churchlike form *strictu sensu*, and even those that do rarely (if ever) achieve a perfect monopoly. "Churchness" is a variable property of a religious community. Further, there are various types of religious leaders, clerical staffs, and religious communities, as Weber himself made clear.

---

12. Émile Durkheim, *The Elementary Forms of Religious Life*, Oxford World Classics, abridged ed., trans. Carol Cosman and ed. Mark S. Cladis (Oxford and New York: Oxford University Press, 2001), 46.

13. Max Weber, "Politics as a Vocation," in *From Max Weber: Essays in Sociology*, trans. and ed. H. H. Gerth and C. Wright Mills (New York: Oxford University Press, 1958), 78.

One of the central tasks of a theory of church formation qua religious monopolization would be to distinguish and explain these variations.

While Weber's sociology of domination is helpful in conceptualizing the monopolization of the sacred, it gives us less purchase over the ensuing process of fragmentation. Here, Hartmut Rosa's theory of "resonance" provides a useful starting point.[14] By "resonance," he roughly means those moments in which we feel deeply attuned with, and connected to, the world. Resonance is a social relation, not an internal emotion. Rosa distinguishes three types of resonance: with other humans, with material objects, or with a sensed totality. He refers to these as "horizontal," "diagonal," and "vertical" resonance, respectively. The role of objects in experiences of sacrality is captured in the "diagonal" dimension of resonance.

Rosa's framework also has another advantage over neo-Durkheimian and neo-Weberian theories: it allows us to distinguish different degrees or levels of "effervescence" and "transcendence." Processes of sacralization do not always involve a sense of "losing oneself" or being "shattered," as they do in neo-Durkheimian accounts. Often, they involve something less dramatic, a sense of "flow" in which one is fully absorbed in an interaction, task, or experience: a lively conversation, a physical challenge, or a beautiful landscape. The same is true of many experiences that people describe as "transcendent": they may be large, as in a religious conversion, but they may also be small, as in a momentary epiphany of the sort that James Joyce wrote about. If sacralization processes are the starting point for church formation, then resonant experiences might be understood as the elementary form of sacralization processes. Seen in this way, resonance is the ur-form of sacrality, just as sacrality is the ur-form of religion—not just the elementary form of religion, but the elementary particle, as it were.

But while Rosa's theory of resonance describes the world that we live in more adequately and fully than orthodox theories of secularization, it does not fully explain how that world came to be. Why do we even need a theory of resonance? Why are resonant experiences more common than religious ones, at least in some modern Western milieux? Why, in other words, has religion lost its monopoly on the sacred? And why has the sacred itself become so fragmented?

---

14. Hartmut Rosa, *Resonance: A Sociology of Our Relationship to the World* (Cambridge: Polity, 2019).

SUPERNOVAS AND IMMANENT FRAMES: HISTORICAL MECHANISMS OF DE-MONOPOLIZATION AND FRAGMENTATION

Charles Taylor's work is replete with arresting images and memorable conceptualizations. And his most recent magnum opus, *A Secular Age*, is no exception to this rule.[15] The big bang that initiated the secular age in the Christian West, he argues, was the rapid proliferation of competing worldviews that began during the Enlightenment era. For the better part of two millennia, the Western Church was the metaphysical sun at the center of the social systems of Europe. The Church's gravitational pull was so powerful that it drew all forms of the sacred into itself and kept the systems of the world in its orbit. Its gravitational force grew so powerful, in fact, that it eventually imploded in on itself, first within elite circles, during the Enlightenment, and later, among the popular classes, during the nineteenth century. Taylor analogizes this development to a "nova" or "supernova." In truth, however, the present constellation is more akin to a "gas giant." Instead of the "nova effect," we might speak of the "Saturn effect."

Taylor's description of the secular age has a second component: the "immanent frame." By the twentieth century at the latest, he argues, the churchly monopoly had been displaced by the "immanent frame." Religion did not disappear, but it did become just one "option" among many. For most, at least in Europe, and among educated elites worldwide, the "default option" was now the "immanent frame." In this view, "ordinary human flourishing"—family and friends, pleasure and prosperity, honor and fame—were the most that one could or should aspire to in this life. Of course, hints of transcendence continued to intrude into the everyday in the form of what Taylor calls "fullness," the sense that there might be, *must* be, "something more" than just "flourishing." But these were typically something less than the "shattering experiences" of which Hans Joas speaks. To put it in Rosa's terms, inhabitants of the immanent frame focused their sights and their lives on horizontal and diagonal forms of resonance. But they, too, occasionally experienced moments of vertical resonance, though more often of an aesthetic or mystical rather than a conventionally religious type.

---

15. Charles Taylor, *A Secular Age* (Cambridge, MA: Belknap Press of Harvard University Press, 2007), http://www.loc.gov/catdir/toc/ecip0712/2007008005.html.

Attentive readers may have noted a subtle but significant misapplication of, and tension between, the two images in Taylor's narrative: the nova effect and the immanent frame. A supernova is the cataclysmic explosion of an aging star. The progenitor star either disappears altogether or contracts into a black hole. The explosion produces heat as well as light, as well as new and heavier elements; but it does not produce new large-scale structures, only the raw material for them. If the cultural history of the modern era were analogous to a supernova, then the Christian churches would disappear altogether or form black holes incapable of producing light. What's more, the remnants of the churches would be nothing but diffuse particles, the dying embers of fused hydrogen. They would hardly coalesce into a coherent "frame." But that is clearly not Taylor's view. The churches may have become weaker, but they have not disappeared. They may produce less heat than before, but they have not ceased to emit some light. And the result of that weakening is not a diffuse collection of heavy particles. It contains some structure or coherence. But not the kind of unity implied by the concept of the "immanent frame."

This is not to deny that Taylor's account represents a major advance, not only over orthodox theories of secularization, but also over the Weberian narrative of "disenchantment." The decline of Western Christianity has not gone with the rise of scientific materialism, nor even of rationalism broadly conceived, except perhaps in the self-contained social milieu inhabited by secular intellectuals, and even they have never been as disenchanted as Weber's narrative implied. Neither can the dominant "social imaginary" of today's "secular age" be understood as just "the world minus religion," nor its genesis as a simple "subtraction story" in which the artificial patina of religious superstition is stripped away by the solvent of reason to reveal bare nature. Instead, it involved a complex set of shifts in the dominant conceptions of self, society, and cosmos. About all this Taylor is quite right.

And yet Taylor's image of traditional religion plus immanent frame does not quite capture the macrostructure of modern sacrality. In astronomical terms, it more nearly resembles a gas giant than a supernova. Think of the planet Saturn. At the core of the system is a large but diffuse body, which appears solid only when viewed from afar. Call it "religion." Its gravitational field is comparatively weak, but still strong enough to hold various objects in its orbit: moons that are smaller but also far denser; multiple rings, each consisting of small, dustlike particles; and finally, on the outer periphery, asteroid belts that are not visible to the naked eye. One might read the moons as nation-states, the rings as so many forms of sacrality, and the debris as the mundane and profane. Of course, the contemporary world consists not of one such gas giant but several of them, situated close enough to each other that their gravitational fields overlap to some degree, leading to the formation of loose, hybrid structures that bridge across the systems. Call them "civilizations." The Western system—call it Saturn—can no longer be understood in isolation from its non-Western neighbors.

Of course, one should not press this metaphor too far. It is only meant to capture certain aspects of the contemporary situation that remain obscured in Taylor's imagery of supernovas and immanent frames. Among other things, the existence of (1) multiple, competing, loosely bounded, and overlapping religious fields (i.e., "world religions"); (2) multiple, competing, clearly bounded, and nonoverlapping political fields ("nation-states"); and (3) forms and structures of sacrality and resonance of various scales and sizes, some contained within a specific religiopolitical field and others that span multiple fields. In the present context, the third point is by far the most important.

MODERN RELIGION AS A WEAK FIELD

Pierre Bourdieu's theory of "social fields" was based explicitly on Weber's sociology of religion.[16] The starting point, of course, was Weber's theory of value spheres. But it drew as well on Weber's typology of "religious leaders." In this way, Bourdieu recast Weber's theory in relational terms. Weber had tacitly assumed that each value sphere was dominated by a unitary elite oriented toward a single value. Bourdieu conceived of social fields as constituted by an ongoing struggle between elite factions—dominant and dominated—over competing interpretations of value—orthodox and heterodox.[17] Bourdieu also spoke of a "field of power," a sort of second-order field where the dominant elites from each field—especially the economic, cultural, and political fields—vied with one another, but in which the economic elites were generally hegemonic. Here, Bourdieu nods to Marx rather than Weber.

16. Pierre Bourdieu, "Legitimation and Structured Interests in Weber's Sociology of Religion," in *Max Weber, Rationality, and Modernity*, ed. Sam Whimster and Scott Lash (London: Allen and Unwin, 1987).

17. For a relatively accessible introduction to Bourdieu's (difficult) theory, see Pierre Bourdieu and Loïc J. D. Wacquant, *An Invitation to Reflexive Sociology* (Chicago: University of Chicago Press, 1992).

Bourdieu's theory is an important advance over Weber's in several respects. First, as Weber himself clearly recognizes in his typology of religious leaders, authority within a value sphere or social field is always and continually contested: priests versus prophets, regular clergy versus secular clergy, settled versus itinerant clergy, and so on. What is more, that contestation is never solely about power or position, but also about values or ideas. A sociology of religion that does not take theology seriously is no sociology at all because practical and symbolic struggle are simply two sides of the same coin. Second, values and ideas must be understood semiotically or relationally. Christians versus Jews, Christians versus Muslims, Catholics versus Protestants, and beneath these broader identity categories, there is a veritable sea of binary oppositions.[18] These are "principles of vision and di-vision" that were, and still are, at the heart of "class-ification struggles."[19] Or, put differently, systems of classification that classify the classifier—and conjure certain classes into being. Third, unlike Weber, Bourdieu explicitly attends to interfield relations as well as intrafield relations. Weber assumes (or at least implies) that there is some sort of rough parity between the value spheres. Bourdieu explicitly rejects such a view, arguing that the economic sphere is predominant in the modern world and perhaps the political sphere qua early state.

But what of the epoch in between? One could make the case that there were periods in European history when the religious field was hegemonic, or when it at least vied for supremacy, as in the Middle Ages. In this view, the great shift that occurred in the centuries between, say, 1500 and 1900 was not the decline of religion so much as the transfer of the sacred from Catholic Church to nation-state. And the nova effect was not so much the implosion of religion as the proliferation of sacrality, or, in Bourdieu's terms, of new cultural fields out of the religious field.

Bourdieu himself does not advance a theory of weak fields, however. Instead, he speaks of "heteronomous fields." By this, he means fields that are strongly influenced by actors and ideas from other fields. In authoritarian states, for example, cultural fields may be "synchronized" with the political field. Thus, a work of art or literature or scholarship is evaluated not in relationship to the

---

18. Bourdieu discusses this point at the greatest length in Pierre Bourdieu, *Masculine Domination* (Stanford, CA: Stanford University Press, 2001).

19. On "class-ification struggles," see especially Pierre Bourdieu, "Conclusion," in *Distinction: A Social Critique of the Judgement of Taste* (London: Routledge & Kegan Paul, 1984), 481–86.

internal standards of a particular cultural field, but rather to a particular political ideology. Synchronization is the limiting case of heteronomy.[20] More common are instances in which the "logic" of a field is distorted by that of another, as when MBAs specializing in finance supplant seasoned journalists in newsrooms or television stations, and return on investment swamps informing the public as the main goal of the organization.[21]

Developing a theory of weak fields requires that we develop two underdeveloped aspects of Bourdieu's theory.[22] First, we need to supplement field theory with boundary theory. Bourdieu himself avoids this terminology, arguing that the boundaries of a field are simply the limits of its effects. But this is too simple. His own work on cultural capital and cultural fields presumes that a certain price must be paid to enter a field, and this price increasingly takes the form of an educational credential. Of course, this is much more the case in, say, the academic or legal fields, where a specific degree is generally required, than it is in the artistic or literary fields, where formal education can be helpful but is not mandatory. All else being equal, fields that have relatively permeable boundaries are weaker than ones that have highly impermeable ones because they can easily be invaded and colonized by outside elites.

Second, we need some way of conceptualizing the relative size of a social field. Three metrics come to mind: (1) population, (2) resources, and (3) practices. Consider the religious field. If attending religious services is the litmus test, then the religious field in most Western European countries now only encompasses a small minority of the general population. Even in the United States, the fastest-growing so-called religious group is the "nones," that is, those who claim no religious affiliation when queried by survey researchers. The material resources monopolized by the religious field are steady at best, and more often are shrinking. In nineteenth-century America, the "net worth" of the Christian churches was similar to that of the federal government. This is certainly not the case today. In Europe, meanwhile, the churches increasingly

<hr>

20. On the dynamics of "synchronization," see Gisele Sapiro, *Les écrivains et la politique en France—De l'affaire Dreyfus à la guerre d'Algérie* (Paris: Le Seuil, 2018).
21. Rodney Dean Benson and Erik Neveu, *Bourdieu and the Journalistic Field* (Cambridge and Malden, MA: Polity, 2005).
22. I elaborate on this and other revisions to field theory in Philip S. Gorski, "Maps, Mechanisms and Methods: Towards a Bourdieusian Analysis of Historical Change," in *Bourdieu and Historical Analysis*, ed. Philip S. Gorski (Durham, NC: Duke University Press, 2013), 327–66.

live off of the state. In the past, it was often the other way around, prior to the great "secularization" of church properties following the Protestant Reformation. The effective jurisdictions covered by the religious field have also shrunk. In many European countries, the churches continue to play an official role in the provision of various social services. But their role in other areas, such as education or jurisprudence, is much diminished. In the United States, this shrinkage has been greater in some respects, less in others. Some government social services are now channeled through "faith-based community organizations," but these organizations are tiny when compared to their European cousins. By contrast, religious communities play an enormous role in the educational field and at every level, from preschool through university. By all these metrics, the religious field in Western nation-states has become smaller, and therefore also weaker, over time.

This weakening can also be expressed via the language of boundaries. The boundaries of the religious field have retreated, and in two distinct ways. On the one hand, the religious field has ceded territory to neighboring fields. It has ceded jurisdiction over important regions of social life to the political field (i.e., the nation-state). And it has lost authority over important aspects of cultural life to the faction of the secular clergy (i.e., nonclerical intellectuals). On the other hand, it has lost control over a large segment of the population who are no longer subject to its authority. In these anarchist jurisdictions, individuals and groups are free to fashion their own forms of sacrality or seek resonance on their own. The parish and the mystic have given way to the subculture and the seeker.

The subcultures are themselves miniature fields. At the apex are elite practitioners—of sports or sex or travel or whatever—the inner-worldly ascetics of the modern era who devote their lives to a particular practice, however mundane or trivial it appears to outsiders, from which the insiders and virtuosos derive a sense of meaning or purpose. They set themselves apart with adjectives such as "extreme" or "ultimate" or simply "elite." They exercise authority over a mass public of hobbyists and enthusiasts, and that authority is challenged by purists and innovators who claim to pursue a more "authentic" or "extreme" version of the practice. This basic logic holds across a wide range of subcultures: the monolatrous worship of small gods. Then, there are the seekers who refuse such single-minded devotion, hopping from one subculture to the next or piecing together scraps into a personalized "brand." They make their homes in the spaces between fields, some by moving from one subculture to the next, others by assembling a hybrid lifestyle out of various practices. Again, the basic logic of modern seekerdom is simple enough: a principled polytheism.

The emergence of anarchist jurisdictions beyond all religious authority is one aspect of the changing boundaries of the religious field. The other is the weakening of the boundaries themselves. They have become more permeable. This renders the religious field vulnerable to invasions from without. This is particularly the case in the United States. Just as newsrooms there were invaded by "finance bros" who focused on "the bottom line," so the religious field has been invaded by people without religious credentials and metrics not rooted in theology. Churches hire or employ "church growth" specialists, whose mission is to increase church membership—and donations. Laypeople without any theological training feel "called" to occupy pulpits and "plant" churches. Even ordained ministers often prefer to style themselves after successful businesspeople, as "CEO-pastors." In Europe, of course, the religious field is not a free market. Established churches often receive state subsidies, upstart religions face various barriers to entry, and ministers are trained and licensed by universities. In sum, the American religious field is relatively larger, but its boundaries are more permeable, while the religious fields of Western Europe are more strongly bounded, but also much smaller. Both are weak, but in different ways—weakly bounded in one case, weakly populated in the other.

The weakening of religious fields and the increasing fragmentation of the sacred in Western societies are really just two sides of the same coin. As Christian churches have gradually lost their monopoly over the legitimate forms of the sacred, the sacred has not disappeared; it has simply become more scattered and diffuse. Today's churches are more akin to gas giants than supernovas. They still emit light and exert force. But they are no longer the suns at the center of the system. They are mere fragments of their former selves.

In trying to understand how churches lost this monopoly in the modern era, we might first ask how they gained it in the first place. There was nothing inevitable about this. That much becomes immediately clear once we place Western religious history within a comparative historical frame. Asian civilizations gave rise to various forms of religious community—monasteries, millenarianism, sectarianism, and others—but churchlike monopolies were the exception rather than the rule. If we take the year 0 BCE as our starting point rather than 1500

BCE, then the formation of churches is as much in need of explaining as the fragmentation of the sacred.[23]

If we examine the present through the optic of de-monopolization and fragmentation, rather than of differentiation and secularization (or, to shift metaphors, if we envision the modern world as a gas giant rather than a supernova), then several important aspects of the contemporary situation come into view. The first pertains to scale. The "religious sphere" has not disappeared; churches still exist. But they are surrounded by formations of the sacred of all shapes and sizes, just as Saturn has its rings, moons, and asteroid belts.

At the macro scale, the most important form of sacrality today is arguably "the political." For the populist right, the sacred is most often "the nation," or sometimes a "civilization," often with a religious adjective affixed, as in "Christian nation" or "Hindu civilization."[24] For the progressive left, the sacred is more often democracy or social justice. Some conservative observers worry about "the return of political religion"; others denounce the "cult of wokeness." Progressive critics, meanwhile, decry political "cults of personality" and partisan "tribalism." And they are not wrong to do so: nation and state, party and ideology, race and identity, have become sacred objects of devotion for many. This is why the language borrowed from religion often seems to apply.

At the micro scale, the most important form of sacrality is surely "the individual."[25] The individual, in this sense, is, among other things, a bearer of "autonomy" and "rights" who can and should be "self-determining." The individual has become, to a remarkable degree, the elementary particle in the social imaginary of the modern West, the raw material out of which states, economies, and churches, among other things, are to be constructed, be it via "social contracts," "free markets," or "personal convictions." As Charles Taylor has shown at length,

---

23. Much of the recent, revisionist work by historians of late antiquity can be viewed through this lens. For a survey and synthesis of this scholarship, see especially Peter Brown, *The Rise of Western Christendom: Triumph and Diversity, A.D. 200–1000*, 10th anniversary revised ed. (Oxford and Malden, MA: Wiley-Blackwell, 2013).

24. On white Christian nationalism, see Philip Gorski and Samuel Perry, *The Flag and the Cross: White Christian Nationalism and the Threat to American Democracy* (New York: Oxford University Press, 2022). On Hindu nationalism, see Jyotirmaya Sharma, *Hindutva: Exploring the Idea of Hindu Nationalism* (New Delhi: Penguin India, 2011).

25. Dick Houtman and Stef Aupers, "The Spiritual Turn and the Decline of Tradition: The Spread of Post-Christian Spirituality in 14 Western Countries, 1981–2000," *Journal for the Scientific Study of Religion* 46, no. 3 (2007): 305–20.

the individual in this specific sense is neither a biological datum nor a cultural universal, but rather a social construct within Western history. Like the sacralization of the political, the sacralization of the individual comes in many forms and covers the entire political spectrum, from pro-life defenders of the unborn through libertarian advocates of personal freedom to progressive champions of human rights.

But it is perhaps at the meso-level—at scales between individuals and states—that the most interesting forms of sacrality have emerged.[26] Religious and quasi-religious bodies such as confraternities and lodges have been increasingly displaced by small groups that devote themselves to a particular passion or pursuit. Also, there are the loose networks of the "spiritual but not religious," bound together by yoga studios, health food stores, and meditation classes, among other things.

What, if anything, holds this weak field together? What, to return to our metaphor, are the sources of gravity? The so-called old religions have not entirely lost their pull. Even those outside the fold can feel it, if only as a yearning for unity, meaning, or order. Nation-states also exert a powerful attraction for some, and for much the same reasons, especially for the less privileged classes who derive a sense of status from collective belonging rather than individual achievement. For still others, the entrepreneurial strivers and the credentialed meritocrats, it is the world of work that often centers their orbit. To some degree, the old monopoly on legitimate forms of the sacred exercised by the Roman Church has been replaced by a new oligopoly of the sacred shared by church, state, and religion.

But this planetary system is not as stable as it first appears. It is being buffeted by powerful forces from within and without. On the one hand, centrifugal forces threaten further fragmentation via processes of disruption via start-up enterprises that threaten the hold of the oligopoly. On the other, centripetal forces press toward a reconsolidation via de-differentiation and remonopolization led by a renewed alliance between thrones and altars.

The political and religious futures of contemporary societies hang in the balance.

---

26. Paul Heelas and Linda Woodhead, *The Spiritual Revolution: Why Religion Is Giving Way to Spirituality* (Oxford: Oxford University Press, 2005).

CONCLUSION: TRANSCENDENCES AND
IMMANENCES IN A WORLD OF FRAGMENTS

In the beginning, the world was one. There was no heaven and earth, just one single cosmos. Nor were there states or economies, just so many societies. Then, heaven and earth were split apart, and society was divided into various spheres, and all the magic in the world rose into heaven, and all that was left on earth was bare rationality. That, in simplified form, is the basic narrative of Weber's theory of the "disenchantment of the world," the historical narrative on which most contemporary theories of secularization are built.

This account is flawed for at least three reasons. First, as many of Weber's critics have rightly noted, contemporary culture is not really that disenchanted; it is fairly bursting with magic, myth, gods, and heroes. Second, because contemporary society is not so neatly differentiated, not only do the spheres intersect and interact, they are surrounded with mix-and-match fragments and hybrids of all shapes and sizes. Third, and finally, because rationality—however defined—has never really won the day, not even among its would-be contemporary carriers, the global class of educated meritocrats.

Fragmentation theory suggests a different metanarrative, consisting of five chapters: pre-Axial, Axial, medieval, early modern, and late modern.[27] In the beginning (which is to say, early antiquity), the world is one, but the sacred is plural and cannot be monopolized.[28] Later, in the Axial Age, the world becomes two, but the sacred becomes one and monopoly becomes possible, at least in theory.[29] In some places, such as Latin Christendom, a de jure monopoly is eventually achieved. In Western Europe and its settler colonies, monopoly gives way first to oligopoly, following the Reformations, and then, following the revolutions and revivals of the eighteenth and nineteenth centuries, to a free trade zone, in which "religious firms" openly compete with one another.[30] Today, these

---

27. This schema, of course, draws on Robert N. Bellah, "Religious Evolution" (1964), in *The Robert Bellah Reader*, ed. Robert N. Bellah and Steven M. Tipton (Durham, NC: Duke University Press, 2006), 23–50.
28. On this point, see especially Strathern, *Unearthly Powers*.
29. S. N. Eisenstadt, *The Origins and Diversity of Axial Age Civilizations*, SUNY Series in Near Eastern Studies (Albany: State University of New York Press, 1986); Robert N. Bellah and Hans Joas, eds., *The Axial Age and Its Consequences* (Cambridge, MA: Harvard University Press, 2012).
30. Rodney Stark and Laurence R. Iannaccone, "A Supply-Side Reinterpretation of the 'Secularization' of Europe," *Journal for the Scientific Study of Religion* 33, no. 3 (1994): 230–52.

legacy firms compete with other purveyors of the sacred from around the globe, some religious, some secular, others spiritual.

The language of political economy captures the broad arc of the fragmentation process. But an architectural metaphor is more adequate to its inner dynamics. Imagine a temple in the pre-Christian era, such as the Parthenon. It was just one of many such temples. And the sacred was not confined to these temples. The gods could be addressed in many different ways, at many different sites, at many different times, and about the most "worldly" of concerns. Now imagine the Second Temple in Jerusalem. It was erected to the one, true God. It could, and sometimes did, claim a monopoly on the sacred, at least among the Israelites, who fought fiercely with one another to control it. Next, think of St. Peter's Basilica in Rome. Above it, the "heavenly Jerusalem"; inside it, the cult of the saints and its totems; around it, the secular territory of Vatican City. It is Christendom *en miniature*: a temple that provides access to a transcendent God and eternal salvation; within it, a "magic garden"[31] of superhuman intermediaries; outside it, the "secular city"[32] of everyday life; beyond it, barbarian wastelands. The achievement of monopoly involves the drawing of boundaries: between heaven and earth, religion and magic, and church and state. Of course, this monopoly is never complete. It is a claim rather than a fact. Fragmentation presses in the other direction. It erases boundaries, constructs new temples, and scavenges from old ones. Now, Gothic cathedrals compete with suburban megachurches resembling shopping malls, and also with wellness spas, sports fandoms, video games, and yoga mats, to name just a few of the sacred sites of late Western modernity. Fragmentation does not destroy the aspiration to unity. But it does create the imperative to individuate. In so doing, fragmentation generates conflicts and dilemmas around pluralism and unity not imagined in any political theology since Augustine's time (which was, after all, a late imperial age very much like our own).

Weber's theory of disenchantment also included an existential diagnosis of the times—two diagnoses to be precise, each captured in a single phrase: "the warring gods" and "the iron cage."[33] In the conclusion to his lecture on "Science as

---

31. Max Weber, *The Religion of China*, trans. H. H. Gerth (New York: Free Press, 1968), 200.

32. Harvey Cox, *The Secular City: Secularization and Urbanization in Theological Perspective* (Princeton, NJ: Princeton University Press, 2013).

33. These metaphors appear at the end of Weber, "Science as a Vocation" and Weber, *The Protestant Ethic and the "Spirit" of Capitalism*, respectively.

a Vocation," he drew a parallel between the polytheistic culture of the pre-Axial era and the cultural pluralism of his own time. Like the gods of old, he mused, the value spheres of the present day vie with one another for our allegiance, and we must ultimately choose among them, or at least the strong among us must. The discussion of the "iron cage" comes at the end of Weber's essay on "the Protestant ethic." In this diagnosis, the problem is not the plurality of ultimate ends, but their paucity or absence. These two diagnoses seem very much at odds with one another: How does a plurality of values lead to an absence of meaning?

Fragmentation theory suggests a very different diagnosis. Weber implies that the only possible response to a polytheistic world—the only "manly" one, anyway—is some form of monolatry: devoting oneself to just one god, be it salvation, power, wealth, truth, or whatever. But this is simply not the case! Confronted with such an existential either/or, many late moderns respond with "Both/and/and, please!" That is, they choose hybridity over monolatry, as in "religion and spirituality and secularity." Perhaps the most fundamental existential decision that late moderns confront in "a secular age" is not between "the sacred and the secular," but between exclusivity and unity, on the one hand, or plurality and hybridity, on the other. Is the choice for the latter a choice for "meaninglessness," for Weber's "iron cage"? Not at all! The problem of late modernity, if it is one, is not a "deficit of meaning" so much as a *surfeit* of meanings. Never before has humanity had so many religious and cultural meaning systems—so many competing visions of the sacred—quite literally at their fingertips. Of course, this surfeit of meanings may well involve a loss of "ultimate significance" of a unitary sort. But the reverse is also true, of course: the choice of ultimate significance and unity also implies the renunciation of multiple meanings and sacred plurality.

Differentiation theory also leads to a certain political diagnosis of the times. From this perspective, the fundamental problem of modern politics is the relationship between "church and state," or more broadly, "religion and politics," or, more broadly still, among different "comprehensive worldviews."[34] The usual solution to this problem is some sort of liberalism, be it "disestablishment,"

---

34. See, for example, Robert Audi and Nicholas Wolterstorff, *Religion in the Public Square: The Place of Religious Convictions in Political Debate*, Point/Counterpoint (Lanham, MD, and London: Rowman & Littlefield, 1997); John Rawls, "The Idea of Public Reason Revisited," *University of Chicago Law Review* 64, no. 3 (1997), http://www.jstor.org/stable/1600311; Jürgen Habermas, "Religion in the Public Sphere," *European Journal of Philosophy* 14, no. 1 (2006), http://search.ebscohost.com/login.aspx?direct=true&db=aph&AN=20069227&site=ehost-live.

"freedom of conscience," or "public reason." Perhaps this diagnosis was correct in Weber's time, or even in John Rawls's time. But it is certainly inadequate for ours. In the United States, the religious field is no longer very autonomous; it is largely governed by the logics of partisan politics and consumer capitalism. In much of Western Europe, it is so weak as to be almost irrelevant.

The great political dilemmas of the late modern era derive from the deep cultural tension between moral universalism and cultural individualism that is itself a result of the monopolization and then fragmentation of the sacred. It was the religious universalisms of the Axial Age, after all, that eventually, if haltingly, gave rise to the moral universalisms of our own, in aspiration if not in reality. But it was religious freedom that eventually, if haltingly, gave rise to the moral individualism of the present day. Cultural diversity is the inevitable result of individual autonomy.

Today, humanity confronts a political problem for which individual freedom is not a complete solution: climate change. Science and technology will be important. But solidarity and sacrifice will also be required. And they are not readily forthcoming in cultures that prize freedom and individualism. That much should be clear from the political battles that erupted over anti-COVID-19 measures in liberal democracies around the world. If COVID was a test run for dealing with climate change, then liberal democracies may have scored very well on the science portion of the test, but they also did rather poorly on the politics section. COVID, a biological virus, mutated into QAnon, a cultural one. One shudders to think about the cultural viruses that will be spawned by the economic disruptions and population movements that will result from—indeed, are already resulting from—climate change.

Today, at least, Weber's diagnosis of the modern condition (cultural disenchantment and bureaucratic ossification) feels much less prescient than Durkheim's (egoism and anomie). Durkheim's diagnosis was also Robert Bellah's. Much as he prized his own California freedom, he worried that American individualism was undermining American democracy, and with it all forms of social solidarity. And skeptical as he was of how religion is understood by many of its purported friends and declared enemies, he, like Durkheim, never lost his faith in its importance as a source of individual wholeness and social solidarity. Pessimistic as he eventually became about the future of America, and even of humanity, he never gave up hope for either, or hope that the role of what we call "religion" would evolve yet again, and humanity with it. Nor should we.

CONCLUSION

RICHARD MADSEN, WILLIAM M. SULLIVAN, ANN SWIDLER, AND STEVEN M. TIPTON

R obert Bellah's *Religion in Human Evolution* is a "deep history," as he put it, a grand narrative, a "history of histories," and a "story of stories," all situated within the "primary metanarrative" of cosmic and biological evolution accepted by modern physicists and biologists. He accepts this primary scientific metanarrative because "as a social scientist I really have no other alternative if I am to be true to my calling, and, practically speaking, this is the only metanarrative that will allow me adequately to describe and compare all the other narratives and metanarratives that comprise human history."[1] But he frames the primary scientific metanarrative, where "disengagement is an absolute methodological requirement," within a history and story about the multiple forms of human agency that have led to our world today and will continue to shape it, for better or for worse, into the future. This scientific narrative posits universal laws of physics and biology that lead via random mutations to diverse biological species, with some species more complex than others. At the apex is the human species, with a level of complexity that enables it to use symbols to learn to control its environment. This learning is driven not by random mutation but by purposeful agency, always in the context of what has been learned before. It leads, often in ways that the actors could not foresee, to the diverse cultural communities that inhabit the earth today. But in the long run, human evolution has not necessarily led to successful adaptation. In fact, the capacities that humans have developed to control their environment may be leading to a

---

1. Robert N. Bellah, *Religion in Human Evolution: From the Paleolithic to the Axial Age* (Cambridge, MA: Belknap Press of Harvard University Press, 2011), 45.

destruction of that environment, which threatens the flourishing and even the survival of the human species. One-celled bacteria may outlive us all.

In envisioning his project to pick up the story and see how modernity fits into it, Robert Bellah rehearsed major themes from that book in his final papers. In his "Prologue," Bellah unfolds this story of stories—always open to contestation and correction—throughout the past two millennia of Western history, which build on one another but then lead to new stories beyond the purview of their original authors, all of which are intertwined with the practices that shape social life in different eras. The end of this story could be a bleak one: "In the late twentieth and early twenty-first centuries we know a great deal more about the universe than anyone did in the nineteenth century, and we are, if anything, more at sea than ever about how that relates to who we are as human beings and why life is so very difficult."[2] We live in an interdependent world driven by overwhelmingly powerful technological capacities but, as Bellah stressed in the Notre Dame lecture, without a moral "thermostat" to regulate our use of energy and prevent catastrophic destruction of our environment. None of this is inevitable, however. In the Tillich Lecture, Bellah notes that the kind of narrative that natural and social science offers (driven by the kind of time that the Greeks called *Chronos*, where one thing follows another in relentless quantitative progression) must be supplemented by *Kairos*, the sacred time that opens up the moment as the right time for human choice. We have agency and time enough, if we use it responsibly, to make a better history.

In concluding his major work with this challenge to contemporary readers, Bellah was reworking Karl Jaspers's original formulation of the idea of the Axial Age.[3] In his conception of an axial age as revealing the source and goal of history, Jaspers was concerned, as Bellah noted, not only to articulate an empirical historical description of evolving societies, but even more, to pose an existential question: "Where are we in history?"[4] That is, Jaspers wrote from a standpoint that accepted the biological and sociohistorical conditioning of thought, a detached and external view. But he emphasized that this viewpoint stood in tension with the demands of living an actual human existence, which can make sense and be motivated only from an internal point of view that has to be lived out rather than simply observed.

---

2. Robert N. Bellah, "Prelude in the Theater," unpublished manuscript, August 2012, 1.
3. Karl Jaspers, *The Origin and Goal of History* (New Haven, CT: Yale University Press, 1953).
4. Bellah, *Religion in Human Evolution*, 268.

Jaspers learned a great deal about social change and the history of religion from his academic colleague Max Weber. He inherited from earlier philosophers, especially Immanuel Kant and Søren Kierkegaard, an acute awareness that agency entails responsibility for actions taken or not taken. Reason, for Jaspers, therefore means more than logic or empirical investigation. It necessarily poses questions that have no theoretical answer, but nonetheless define human consciousness, existential questions about who we are and what we should do.

For Jaspers, the novelty of the Axial Age is summed up by the appearance of a new type of human figure that he called "philosophers," who engage in a new kind of social practice that poses radical questions about previously taken-for-granted conditions of human life. While these figures emerged in the radically different cultural worlds of ancient India, China, Israel, and Greece, Jaspers sought to show that they all explored the limits of human existence within horizons far broader than those previously explored.

Historically considered, the Axial opening of universal horizons was a tremendous leap. But for Jaspers, it also holds a continuing relevance that has to be consciously evoked as a living reality. "Philosophy," in Jaspers's understanding, is not a specific intellectual field among others. It has a history in both East and West, as he showed, but its traditions need to be understood in the service of a deeper cultural aim: philosophy describes an attitude of radical openness and will to communicate. This distinguishes it both from science, whose methods make possible a description of reality as a system of objects and laws, though only from an external point of view, and from religion, which shares with philosophy the awareness of a horizon beyond the scientific world of objects and forces, but which Jaspers feared tended too easily to mistake the symbols of ultimacy for ultimacy itself.

Jaspers contrasts philosophy to science and technology, which embody an objective and abstract universalism, and also to the particularized universalisms of the world religions. He proposes philosophy as a mediating cultural practice that can make possible further development in both domains. This practice of reason, which he thought to be the continuing legacy of the Axial "breakthroughs," embodies an even more inclusive universalism. It arises from an unlimited effort to communicate disparate understandings of self and world, in dialogues between the religious and the secular and among religions, to find ways to better understand one another, learn from one another, and ultimately to cooperate in fuller forms of human life. Jaspers consciously sought to provide a means toward such a mediating dialogue through his philosophically informed history, as Hans Joas has elsewhere reminded us.[5] But for Jaspers, the immediate task was to awaken awe at the horizon before us and stir commitment to sharing the full experience of humanity. This is the call to responsibility that Jaspers offers through his work, including his account of the Axial Age as a powerful illustration and an inspiration for modern endeavor. This is very much what Robert Bellah aimed to do in *Religion in Human Evolution*, even though his historical account of the cultural developments of the first millennium BCE is much more theoretically and empirically nuanced than that of Jaspers. This aim continues in Bellah's final papers and his intended book on modernity.

HISTORICAL TENSIONS FROM THE AXIAL AGE

The Axial religious visions all direct us to transcendent ultimate principles that posit a fundamental unity of humanity. As the neo-Confucian philosopher Zhang Zai put it: "All people are my brothers and sisters and all things are my companions."[6] No longer could one's family, tribe, or small community claim to be the exclusive focus of moral responsibility. All humans are interconnected through a universal ethic. The great gap between these transcendent principles and the concrete commitments of everyday life leads to never-ending tensions. Over the course of history, these tensions have been extremely generative, setting in motion centuries of reflection on how to connect the transcendent and mundane, and centuries of human practices striving to reach beyond the demands of everyday life.

The chapters in this volume all reflect such tensions, and they resolve the tensions each in their own way, coming down on different sides. Articulating these tensions gives us tools for thinking through our common predicament. One set of tensions might be called *cultural*: the tension between the theoretical universalism that social science, qua science, aspires to achieve and the lived particularisms that history produces. Along with evolutionary biologists, modern

5. Hans Joas, "The Axial Age Debate as Religious Discourse," in *The Axial Age and Its Consequences*, ed. Robert N. Bellah and Hans Joas (Cambridge, MA: Belknap Press of Harvard University Press, 2012), 23.

6. Zhang Zai, "The Western Inscription," in Wing-Tsit Chan, *A Sourcebook in Chinese Philosophy* (Princeton, NJ: Princeton University Press, 1963), 497.

social scientists look for general principles that drive social development. All our authors use such principles to explain where we have come from and to forecast where we are going. In chapter 2, Kyle Harper writes about the pressures on human populations produced by population growth and microbial infection. Modern medicine has reduced some of the threat from microbes, and modern science and technology have produced enough food to sustain greatly expanded and long-lived populations, but these threats are by no means over. In chapter 3, Hartmut Rosa argues that modern "progress" is imposing limits on the modern quest for individual autonomy. The narratives that these authors have written describe powerful, universal forces that are shaping our futures. But Harper also shows us how societies at different times have for periods defied these tendencies so as to produce more flourishing than would have been expected. Rosa ends by invoking the idea of "resonance" as a way of being in the world that connects us to society and nature and engenders a creative mutual response—a form of lived connection that has been found among some members of most religions of the world throughout deep history.

These tensions also become *political*. In his comparative historical essay (chapter 6), Alan Strathern tells a story as broad as that detailed in Bellah's *Religion in Human Evolution*, but more expansive than Bellah could develop in his "Prologue to the Modern Project." The Axial traditions differ in the substance of their cosmology, philosophy, and theology, but they share a fundamental commonality. They all introduce a tension between this world and an ideal world, which leads to the possibility of universal ethics regulating the powerful as well as the weak. Strathern shows in great detail how over the past two millennia, these universal visions of transcendence are always amalgamated with immanent institutions and meanings, leading to widely divergent social practices. Although common processes of ritual development and myth construction can be found among all Axial traditions, these all lead through the contingencies of history to particular immanent outcomes. Often enough, this results in transcendent ideas strengthening and legitimating immanent structures of power. Universalistic Axial visions have made possible the large-scale, collective action of empires and helped provide the elaborate rationales needed to justify such empires and the administrative techniques needed to manage and expand them. But these visions have not necessarily led to human moral solidarity.

Religiously justified monarchs conquer territory to expand the reach of the one true faith, carry out crusades to destroy enemies of the faith, and call on teachings of the faith to legitimize their rulership. Yet transcendent Axial visions always sit uneasily with immanent structures of power. They always contain the critical possibility of judging those particular structures in universalistic terms and pushing beyond the orthodox systems of thought used to justify them. One gets a particularly vivid account of what this tension looks and feels like in Joel Robbins's ethnography (chapter 9) of the effects that a sudden conversion to Christianity had upon the isolated community of Urapmin in the highlands of Papua New Guinea as Christian individualism leads to conflicts with their customary relational life.

Robbins shows how these tensions permeate the Urapmin's collective moral imaginations, as indeed they permeate the moral imaginations of all societies that are heirs to Axial traditions. Thus a final set of tensions is *sociological* and *moral*. All these traditions proclaim a universal humanism but live within a world of social hierarchy, sustained by time-honored ritual and myth. Chinese Confucians proclaim that "all people are my brothers and sisters." But in the Chinese family, brothers are ranked higher than sisters, elder siblings higher than younger, husbands higher than wives, and parents higher than children. If, as Weber argued, universal brotherhood is fundamental to all the axial religions,[7] then hierarchical relations and both spiritual and material inequalities are also given deeply religious meanings.

The Christian version of the tension between universal humanism and social hierarchy is articulated most fully in Hans Joas's discussion of the moral principles underlying medieval Christianity in chapter 7. Only a transcendent anchor for the sacredness of each person and the mutuality of redemptive love among them, he argues, can reconcile the unequal interdependence of an organic social ethic with moral universalism. Those tensions and their possible resolutions preoccupied medieval theological debates and, as Ana Marta González notes in chapter 5, they remain fundamental to our thinking about the modern division of labor.

Indeed, we live in a world where equality is increasingly seen as the bedrock moral principle inhering in the equal dignity of each and every human person and justifying "universal human rights." Yet, as Robbins reminds us at the end of his chapter, the social orders that modern people inhabit, based on a

---

7. Max Weber, "Religious Rejections of the World and Their Directions," in *From Max Weber: Essays in Sociology*, trans. and ed. H. H. Gerth and C. Wright Mills (New York: Oxford University Press, 1958), 323–59.

moral individualism inspired by Christianity in the West, have led to grotesque inequalities of wealth and power, unchecked by any binding moral narrative. The reified ideal of "free markets" implicitly justifies whatever inequalities those markets produce as natural and necessary, if not entirely fair. Even the language of human rights offers little leverage for shaping a just set of economic or social arrangements to realize our equal rights to adequate food, housing, health care, education, and employment.

Finally, there is the tension between scientific reason and humanistic narrative, whose deep history within Western Christian thought is explored by González. Today, these are realized in tensions felt between the so-called hard constraints on human social development, such as those created by climate change and disease, versus the unpredictable emergence or reanimation of cultural and institutional capacities. On the one hand, there is the absolute impossibility that Bellah stressed of sustaining the "thermostatless growth" that has defined the modern era. On the other hand, there are new possibilities arising from the role of contingency in human history. We see the importance of such contingency in Ukraine's heroic resistance to Russia's 2022 invasion, and how the narrative of sacrifice and solidarity that it generated came to rally broader global action than anyone had thought possible. The definition of AIDS and Ebola as global crises likewise led to the coordination of transnational action on a massive scale, even if the COVID-19 epidemic also prompted short-sighted hoarding of vaccines and other medicines by rich countries, especially the United States.

In addition to unexpected possibilities created by crises, emergent social possibilities arise through the gradual development of new practices and experiences. Hartmut Rosa points to possibilities of what he calls "resonance"—ways of experiencing commonality with others, of listening, of being aware—that counter preoccupation with individual autonomy. Some are simply a matter of universalized consumerism, some are linked to notions of universal human rights, and others involve heightened awareness of human and natural interdependence. In these ways, new forms of social imagination and moral consciousness can begin to develop that are not articulated as conscious ideologies or worldviews. While none of these yet counterbalances the relentless growth of global finance capital and resurgent authoritarian nationalisms, under the surface new institutional possibilities may be arising at the level of shifts in sensibilities, practices, and forms of valuing. These may not themselves appear to change the world, but when contingent developments make structural change possible, they may provide the ingredients for new kinds of social ordering.

Bellah's larger project sought to shape a grand narrative arc, in which the whole evolution of life unfolds as a story of which we ourselves are part and for which we are responsible. How responsible can we be? At the end of his Prologue, Bellah dwells on Max Weber: "What Jaspers said about Weber as an archetypal modern man, one who lived and breathed the air of modern culture without ever idealizing it, often more in horror than in praise, surely gives him a special importance to us." Is our modern world really one in which we live torn by tensions between the "warring gods" of differentiated value spheres, all driven by a relentless rationalization that traps us within an "iron cage" in a dismal process that will continue "until the last ton of fossilized coal is burnt"?[8] (Actually, given the pace of global warming, the end will come well before that.) In late modernity, the Euro-American moral universe (as Philip Gorski describes it in chapter 10) is even more completely fragmented than Weber considered. This yields a surfeit of meanings, but it multiplies and divides moral consensus and commitment. Yet within this surfeit of meanings, resources may emerge for people to combine an ethic of responsibility with an ethic of conviction to build new forms of social solidarity to confront the challenges of a truly troubled modern world.

LEGACIES OF THE AXIAL AGE FOR THE FUTURE

How can we build such solidarities? Robert Bellah traced our modern crises to permutations in and betrayals of the legacies of the Axial Age—to the contingent ways that universalistic Axial legacies have always been amalgamated with particularistic meanings and institutions. He insisted, though, that all such legacies carry a drive to transcendence capable of breaking through the sclerotic integument of any world order in a search to realize the universal dignity of human persons, expressed by these traditions in many different ways. But his work taken as a whole gives no formula for undertaking such breakthroughs. He

---

8. Max Weber, *The Protestant Ethic and the Spirit of Capitalism*, trans. Talcott Parsons (New York: Charles Scribner's Sons, 1958), 181; Max Weber, "Science as a Vocation," in *From Max Weber: Essays in Sociology*, trans. and ed. H. H. Gerth and C. Wright Mills (New York: Oxford University Press, 1958), 153.

offers no assurance that we will be able to surmount our current crises. What his work enables us to do is to become aware of the ways that our current challenges are inextricably connected to a deep history of cultural evolution that holds us in tension between our necessarily particularistic engagements and our hopes to live out our part of the common effort of our universal story. He inspires us to reflect on these tensions and face them realistically and responsibly. Today, as throughout history and across cultures, the transcendent Axial visions are embedded in immanent institutions, and universal moral visions are always tied to particular structures of wealth and power. Yet transcendent Axial visions always sit uneasily with immanent institutions. They always contain the possibility of criticizing embedded injustices and pushing beyond the systems of thought used to justify them.

This critical potential is enhanced by the multiplex character of the great Axial traditions. The Chinese tradition, for example, includes not only Confucianism, with its emphasis on differentiated roles and loyalties discerned through diligent study, but also Daoism, which opposes such differentiation and seeks to go beyond all conceptual knowledge, since "The Dao that is known is not the Dao."[9] Christianity includes both St. Thomas Aquinas and St. Francis—visions of an orderly world under the kingship of Christ and a universal expansion of love inspired by the Holy Spirit. Buddhism includes both the elaborate doctrine of the *tripitaka* and the vision of spontaneous enlightenment proposed by the legendary Sixth Zen Patriarch.

All the great theological and philosophical traditions emerging from the Axial Age make up multiplex dialogues that incorporate some voices more to the right and more adaptable to structures of power, and others more to the left and more critical of established power. In China, for example, the great Confucian tradition was initially persecuted by the realpolitik Legalists, but in the end, it was often coopted by emperors who ruled according to Legalist principles while relying on Confucian scholars to give their regime a veneer of morality. Meanwhile, Daoism flowed "like water" in a great subterranean stream that inspired ordinary people through the rise and fall of empires.[10] All traditions, moreover, contain dogmatic voices that draw strong boundaries between those who can and cannot be saved, while other voices push beyond such boundaries toward

---

9. Daodejing, chapter 1, verse 1, trans. Richard Madsen.
10. Daodejing, chapter 8, trans. Richard Madsen.

the universal dignity of all human beings. As Hans Joas shows in chapter 7, the medieval Catholic Church, for example, understood itself as the Mystical Body of Christ, encompassing many different kinds of people, saints and sinners, all finding a place in the One Body. But theologians also proclaimed the doctrine that "outside the Church there is no salvation," and outsiders like Jews were persecuted. On the other hand, there were those like the Jesuit Matteo Ricci, who recognized in non-Christian Chinese a rationality that comprehended universal moral principles.

Every Axial tradition adapted itself to various types of political regimes, including monarchy, aristocracy, and (often uneasily) democracy. Those inspired by each tradition strove to keep such regimes from degenerating into injustice and oppression (e.g., to keep monarchies from descending into tyrannies). But they did so with uneven success, and the same dynamics hold true in the modern world.

In the United States today, so-called Christian nationalists fight cultural and religious diversity.[11] Another theological tradition, also drawing on a permutation of Axial traditions rooted in Athens and Jerusalem, equates free market neoliberalism with God's will. Meanwhile in China, the Xi Jinping regime blesses itself with Confucian rhetoric and Marxist-Leninist theory but forbids any talk of "universal human values."[12] And in Myanmar, Buddhist monastic backers of a military dictatorship incite brutal ethnic cleansing against the Rohingya. At the same time, Christian leaders like Pope Francis call for universal brotherhood and sisterhood, while New Confucians and Engaged Buddhists across Asia inspire efforts to offer compassionate care around the globe to promote reconciliation and peace.

Beyond the boundaries of formal religious institutions, Axial ideas have penetrated and patterned the entire fabric of modernity. Western modernity, for one, is a product of Western Axial traditions. Bellah accepted the argument of Charles Taylor[13] (and, before him, Max Weber) that Western modernity was shaped not by abandoning medieval religious ideas but by reforming them. Yet the outcome of these reformations has been deeper differentiations in culture and

---

11. See Philip Gorski and Samuel Perry, *The Flag and the Cross: White Christian Nationalism and the Threat to American Democracy* (New York: Oxford University Press, 2022).

12. Chinese Communist Party Central Committee Document 9, "Communique on the Current State of the Ideological Sphere," trans. China File, November 8, 2013, www.chinafile.com.

13. Charles Taylor, *A Secular Age* (Cambridge, MA: Belknap Press of Harvard University Press, 2007).

society—differentiations, among others, between the spheres of economy, science, politics, religion, and familial life. This has made possible the efflorescence of modern science, which has enabled humans to push back against the natural constraints of famine and pestilence, described by Kyle Harper, that so limited lifespans before the Industrial Revolution. It has also underwritten the idea of universal human rights. Although there are indeed "multiple modernities,"[14] the ideas and institutions of modern science and human rights have been appropriated and adapted to Indigenous traditions around the world. We want to build on this moral dimension of modernity, not reject it.

Yet the Western Axial traditions, now in necessary dialogue with all the Axial traditions of a globalized world, give us ample reason to criticize our current incarnations of modernity. We have created an interdependent world connected through a globalized market economy, with its hegemony supported by powerfully organized states. Their citizens, especially the elites, can benefit from global commerce, but this has led to gross disparities between rich and poor. It has promoted one-dimensional aspirations to happiness based solely on materialistic consumption, all of which is generating unsustainable, "thermostatless" growth.

Modern science enables us to discern this interdependence. Modern languages and techniques of technocratic administration have enabled us to create and even bring a fragile semblance of order to our interdependence. But these by themselves cannot solve the problems that they create. By the middle of a horrendous twentieth century of war and revolution, the two surviving candidates for establishing a world order with a semblance of justice and peace were the state socialist system of the Soviet bloc and the liberal world order, led by the United States. Both were supposedly constructed on the basis of scientific reason and governed by bureaucrats employing supposedly universal technologies for social organization. In different ways, both systems engendered privileged social classes that lorded over others, and both bred alienation among people who found little meaning or purpose in their systems of domination. Both justified themselves primarily by promising to deliver the goods of material production in the name of perpetual progress, which led to despoiling the global environment.

The state socialist system lost the capacity to be sufficiently productive and collapsed. But perceptive statesmen like Vaclav Havel weighed with care the

---

14. S. N. Eisenstadt, "Multiple Modernities," *Daedalus* 129, no. 1 (Winter 2000): 1–29.
15. See Vaclav Havel, "The End of the Modern Era," *New York Times*, March 1, 1992.

victory of the liberal world order, with its mixture of market economy, democratic governance, individualistic society, and technocratic administration.[15] The neoliberal economy of the West has generated enormous inequalities, which have turned democracies into near-oligarchies. Its technocratic systems of governance have alienated many citizens who were already bereft of meaningful community and adrift in a cultural sea of individualism. The current pandemic has laid these problems bare and exacerbated them. The main candidates promising to build large-scale moral communities based on a common purpose seem to be champions of the authoritarian nationalism expressed in China by Xi Jinping's project for a "great revival of the Chinese nation" and in the United States by Donald Trump's vow to "make America great again." These have become models for projects throughout Europe and Asia.

In the twentieth century, fascist efforts to remedy the problems of modernity led to unspeakable tragedy. We need better alternatives. These lie in what Bellah termed a "double vision" that complements the world revealed by a "single vision" of scientific rationality. Thus Bellah quoted Blake: "Twofold always. May God us keep / From single vision and Newton's sleep."[16] In this binocular vision, the language of rationally articulated theory is coupled with the kinds of rich, emotionally resonant, symbolic representation and action developed over the course of cultural evolution, not just in words but in embodied movement and gesture, in myth and ritual. Such symbols express and bring into being the sacred realities that incarnate common meaning and purpose in moral communities.

These are the kinds of symbols that we call "religious," but they are by no means confined to the formal denominations and congregations of organized religion. Indeed, as Bellah characterized modern religion in 1964 and Philip Gorski writes now, such symbolic representation and action are now spread across the cultural landscape, offering no lack of meaning but indeed a surfeit of meanings. Does the multiplication and division of moral meaning necessarily lead to a culture war of all against all? Or is it possible to arrive at some multivalent religious consciousness that can sustain shared responsibility to come together to meet the common threats facing humanity?

Mobilization of religious symbols has indeed brought about some of the worst atrocities in human history, and those manipulating these symbols today are

---

16. Quoted by Robert Bellah in his review of *Love's Body* by Norman O. Brown, which appears in Robert N. Bellah, *Beyond Belief* (Berkeley: University of California Press, 1970), 230–236.

capable of terrible deeds. But those who tried to eliminate such symbols also created some of the worst disasters of the twentieth century. The only remedy for bad religion is good religion. It can enable a diverse, broken humanity to seek a larger purpose in a meaningful cosmos through the work of a multicultural conversation among poets, prophets, and citizens, enacted in practices of mutual care and responsibility. Neither Bellah's work nor the chapters in this volume tell us precisely how to do this. But the capacity for transcendence that is a living legacy of the Axial Age, never completely lost or suppressed, can still lead us forward to pursue diverse goods in common, along uncharted paths.

SUMMING UP AND MOVING FORWARD

The present moment confronts us with challenges that require our sustained resilience. Yet economic and social stress narrows perspective and pinches empathy when we most need to expand our horizon. Here, Robert Bellah's perspective encourages the countervailing impulse to find sources of resilience not by narrowing but by extending our moral sympathy into wider circles of concern. It stresses our common roots in the human and natural past by placing the human story within a narrative of deep evolutionary time to confront the problematic present. This requires building upon that past, now seen in all its contingency, while searching for the practical wisdom to open up our horizon here and now.

This evolutionary vision focuses less on the biophysical and technological aspects of modernity that have powered our material progress than on the social and cultural capacities of humanity that can guide us toward a livable future. This vision strengthens the promise of large-scale cooperation by revealing both cooperation and competition as interlinked social processes actualized within an encompassing cultural web of symbolic meaning. At the micro level of interpersonal intimacy, as well as the macro level of large-scale groups and whole societies, these symbolic meanings deeply shape and closely connect human bodies and psyches through social interaction. These tissues of meaning take their form from the sacred or religious realm, Bellah argues. They inspire humanity's most basic sense of the world while animating the symbols and moral bonds that enable the growth of human solidarity throughout the evolution of the species. Above all, Bellah judges, it is through the experience of ritual—those heightened practices in which social identity is enacted and confirmed—that human social bonds expand and meaning evolves. In the new experiments and breakthroughs of our era, for all its contradictions and breakdowns, this moral drama continues to unfold.

This perspective centers on an expansive understanding of the religious dimension of human evolution at the heart of our historical moment. Religion, by this account, has given humanity its most important resource for facing our ecological crisis: the inchoate awareness of participating within a larger reality on which we ultimately depend. With awareness of this mutual dependence comes the realization of our inescapable interconnection and the ethical imperative of our shared responsibility. Religious symbols continue to articulate this fundamental situation, even as some human societies have grown more internally complex and their global interconnections have grown wider and denser. These developments made possible the breakthroughs of Axial Age cultures, Bellah concludes, to crystallize universal ideals of individual human dignity and interdependent human flourishing.

This reciprocal sense of mutual dependence and responsibility within a larger reality also provides a key to a more mature awareness of modern possibilities. We aspire to universal moral equality. Modernity has spread this ideal worldwide and, for the first time in history, institutionalized it in democratic society. But it remains precarious. Like awareness of ecological interdependence, the aspiration for universal human rights and hopes for an equitable economy face serious, even violent threats from within global society itself. The great successes of modernity in enhancing human powers and well-being may turn out to be fleeting, even self-undermining, unless they can be integrated and sustained within larger-scale, longer-term natural processes. Similarly, the achievements that undergird individual freedom and social cohesion depend upon securing norms and institutions that can be woven together to stabilize the conflicting forces analyzed by the chapters in this volume. In fact, achieving stable forms of interdependence within our species and with our natural environment poses the great challenge of modernity.

Conversation among the authors of this volume has centered on the difficult question of what basis, and how much of a basis, humanity's inherited cultural resources can provide in our quest for a resilient modernity. Can we reimagine the insights embedded in the world religions of the Axial Age to further the modern project? Can we find signs of new, imaginative possibilities for living within a fragile, interconnected world, and can we then foster their growth? Or has modernity so undermined the actual conditions for fulfilling its ideals that a "hard ceiling" is inevitable?

This conversation has opened up divergent answers to such questions. Tensions among these answers, we believe, will provoke new investigation, contemporary and historical, to better understand the problems and possibilities that we face, not only to incite further conversation but also to inspire the confidence that we need to confront the challenge before us. Let us embrace a critical reverence for the deep past and press on with a radical openness to the contingency of a future that transcends our present peril.

CONTRIBUTORS

Ana Marta González is a professor of philosophy at the University of Navarra (Spain), where she teaches moral theory and social theory. Her research is focused on fundamental ethics and the relationship between moral philosophy and social sciences. She has published extensively on Aquinas's natural law and Kant's moral and social philosophy. In 2016, she was appointed as an ordinary member of the Pontifical Academy of Social Sciences.

Philip Gorski is the Frederick and Laura Goff Professor of Sociology and Religious Studies at Yale University. He writes on religion and politics in early modern and modern Europe and North America. His most recent book, with Samuel L. Perry, is *The Flag and the Cross: White Christian Nationalism and the Threat to American Democracy* (2022).

Kyle Harper is the G. T. and Libby Blankenship Chair in the History of Liberty at the University of Oklahoma. He is also a Fractal Faculty member at the Santa Fe Institute. He writes on the history of humans as agents of ecological change and asks how we can approach questions such as biodiversity, health, and environmental sustainability from a historical perspective. He is the author of *Slavery in the Late Roman World* (2011), *From Shame to Sin: The Christian Transformation of Sexual Morality* (2013), *The Fate of Rome: Climate, Disease, and the End of an Empire* (2017), and *Plagues upon the Earth: Disease and the Course of Human History* (2021), a global history of infectious disease spanning from human origins to COVID-19.

Hans Joas is the Ernst Troeltsch Professor for the Sociology of Religion at the Humboldt University of Berlin. For more than twenty years he was

Visiting Professor of Sociology and in the Committee on Social Thought at the University of Chicago. Among his numerous books in English are *The Power of the Sacred: An Alternative to the Narrative of Disenchantment* (2020) and *The Axial Age and Its Conseq*uences, coedited with Robert N. Bellah (2012).

Richard Madsen is a distinguished research professor and director of the Fudan-UC Center on Contemporary China at the University of California, San Diego. He is a coauthor of *Habits of the Heart: Individualism and Commitment in American Life* (1985) and *The Good Society* (1991), as well as other books on moral order and religion in the United States and China. They include *Democracy's Dharma: Religious Renaissance and Political Development in Taiwan* (2007) and, most recently, *The Chinese Pursuit of Happiness: Anxieties, Hopes, and Moral Tensions in Everyday Life* (2019), coedited with Becky Yang Hsu.

Joel Robbins is the Sigrid Rausing Professor of Social Anthropology at the University of Cambridge. His work focuses on religion, values, ethics, and anthropological theory. He is the author of the books *Becoming Sinners: Christianity and Moral Torment in a Papua New Guinea Society* (2004) and *Theology and the Anthropology of Christian Life* (2020).

Hartmut Rosa is the director of the Max Weber Center at Erfurt University and the chair of sociology and social theory at Friedrich Schiller University in Jena, Germany. He has been a visiting professor at the New School for Social Research in New York from 2001–2006 and at the FMSH/EHESS in Paris. His publications include *Alienation and Acceleration* (2007), *Social Acceleration: A New Theory of Modernity* (2013), *Resonance: A Sociology of Our Relationship to the World* (2019), and *The Uncontrollability of the World* (2020).

Alan Strathern is an associate professor of history at the University of Oxford and a fellow and tutor of history at Brasenose College. Much of his earlier work has concerned Sri Lankan history, but he now works on the global comparative history of religion. His recent publications include *Unearthly Powers: Religious and Political Change in World History* (2019) and *Sacred Kingship in World History: Between Immanence and Transcendence*, coedited with Azfar Moin (2022).

William M. Sullivan was formerly a senior scholar at the Carnegie Foundation for the Advancement of Teaching. A coauthor of *Habits of* the Heart: Individualism and Commitment in American Life (1985) and The Good Society (1991), he writes about civic democracy, philosophy of the social sciences, the professions, and higher education. He is the author of Reconstructing Public Philosophy, Work and Integrity, and Liberal Learning as a Quest for Purpose (2022).

Ann Swidler is a professor of the Graduate School in the Department of Sociology at the University of California, Berkeley. A coauthor of Habits of the Heart: Individualism and Commitment in American Life (1985) and The Good Society (1991), she currently writes about religious congregations, chiefs, and collective goods in sub-Saharan Africa. Her most recent book, with Susan Cotts Watkins, is A Fraught Embrace: The Romance and Reality of AIDS Altruism in Africa (2017).

Steven M. Tipton is the Charles Howard Candler Professor Emeritus of Sociology of Religion at Emory University and its Candler School of Theology. He is the author of Public Pulpits and Getting Saved from the Sixties (2008), and a coauthor of Habits of the Heart: Individualism and Commitment in American Life (1985) and The Good Society (1991).

INDEX

Abduh, Muhammad, 211
acceleration: global warming from socioeconomic, 72–73; innovations and, 68–69; social development, 67; of societies, 86–87; of technology, 71
achsenzeit (radical cultural transformations), 166n22
acquisition, 180n60
Acts 17:34, 97n7
Adam and Eve, 113, 116–19, 117n28, 124
Adorno, Theodor W., 79
adverse sacralization, 197
Af←fection, 80, 80n51
Age of Revolutions in Global Context, The (Armitage and Subrahmanyam), 210
agriculture, 29–30
Akbar (king, 1556–1605), 195
alienation, 73
Allegory of the Cave, 97–98
Amstutz, Galen, 208n91
ancient state, 238n39
Anna Karenina (Tolstoy, L.), 135, 137
antagonistic symbiosis, 197–98
antanairetiké (logos as), 160n3
Anthropocene period, 4, 72
antisyncretic, 289
Antonine Plague, 48
Arab tribal warriors, 253
arche (beginning), 96
Arendt, Hannah, 83
Areopagitica (Milton), 114

Aristotle, 101–3; natural art of acquisition from, 180n60; non-natural chrematistics and, 180; texts on logic by, 163; virtue and justice approach of, 161
Armitage, David, 210–11
artwork: beauty expressed through, 148; feelings conveyed through, 149; hedonism in, 148–49; science distinguished from, 146–47; Tolstoy attacking, 149–50
ascetic vocational ethic, 248–55
Asia, 211–12
Asian transcendentalism, 206–12
Assmann, Jan, 188, 190
astronomy, 100–101
Augustine, Saint (354–430 CE), 102, 112n20, 161, 174
Aurangzeb (1658–1707), 195
Australian Baptist missionaries, 288–89
authoritarianism, 3, 215
authoritarian nationalism, 331–32, 336
autocratic monarchism, 203n69
autonomy: Bellah on attainment of, 10; in cultures, 64; for humanity, 168–69; independence decisions and, 60–61; individual, 7, 62, 329; Kant and, 272, 274–75; principles of, 61; of selfhood, 192
Axial Age, 220; Bellah discussing breakthroughs of, 6; Bellah tracing legacies of, 332–37; global consciousness from, 166n23; India after, 256; Jasper's idea of, 326; legacy of, 18; *logos* in, 171;

Axial Age (*continued*)
    religious symbolism from, 11; sacralization
    in, 321–22; transcendentalist religion
    after, 185; universal moral visions of, 16;
    values from, 166
Axiality, 183; Asian, 212–13; non-Western,
    206–7; theory of, 206–7

Banerjee, Milinda, 211
Barrow, Samuel, 112
Bateson, Gregory, 28
Baucis, in *Faust*, 128
Bayly, Chris, 211–12
Beatrice, 105n15
Beck, Ulrich, 283
Beck-Gernshiem, Elisabeth, 283
beginning (*arche*), 96
Being (*On*), 101
being-in-and-to-the-world, 61
Bellah, Robert, 55; Axial Age legacies from,
    332–37; axial breakthroughs from, 6; on
    Christianity, 182–83; differentiation
    in evolutionary processes from,
    9–11; on Enlightenment, 187; ethical
    challenges concern of, 173; evolution as
    metanarrative from, 4–8; "Flaws in the
    Protestant Code" by, 285, 293; human
    project of, 1–3; human rights idea of,
    168; on India after Axial Age, 256; India
    portrayal by, 258; intellectual ambitions
    of, 166–67; on Joas's work, 192n34;
    metanarrative interest of, 166, 173–74,
    219n136, 222; modernity and, 167; "The
    Modern Project in the Light of Human
    Evolution" by, 15, 37, 57–58; *The Modern
    Project in the Light of Human Evolution*
    by, 6, 36; Notre Dame lecture by, 57–59;
    organic social ethic references of, 255–56,
    258–59; "Paul Tillich and the Challenge of
    Modernity" by, 7, 16–17; religion defined
    by, 9; *Religion in Human Evolution* by, 2, 5,
    12, 159, 167, 216n125, 225–26, 325, 328–29;
    on religious evolution, 10–11; "Religious
    Evolution" by, 9–12, 17, 186n12, 225n1,2,

321n27; religious evolution stages from,
    13–14; social development acceleration
    from, 67; thermostat interest of, 49, 326;
    thermostatlessness of modern society
    from, 71; Weber terms used by, 226–34
Bentham, Jeremy (1748–1832), 275
Bible, 96, 105, 139–40, 288. *See also* Old
    Testament; *specific verses*
birth rate (fertility), 39–41
Black Death, 47
bleeding heart (Christian symbol), 308–9
Boethius, 163n13
Bohemian Hussites, 189
Book of Memories, 94
Bortolini, Matteo, 282
Boulton, Matthew, 30
boundary problems, 23–24
Bourdieu, Pierre, 314–15
Bourgeois Principle, 269, 272
Bourgeois Spirit, 274–75
Bouwsma, William, 106–8, 108n18
Boyarin, Daniel, 93, 95–96, 95n4
Boyhood (Tolstoy, L.), 133–34
Boyle, Nicholas, 123n40
Brecht, Bertolt, 230
Breuer, Stefan, 252n94
Brexit, in United Kingdom, 220n137
British Civil War, 190, 205
brotherly love, 148, 151, 260
Buddhism, 212, 214–15, 254, 333–34
Burke, Kenneth, 115

Caesar, Julius, 103
Caliban model, 210n101
Callicles, 99
Calvin, John (1509–1564), 105–6, 187;
    depravity in, 108n18; *Institutes of the
    Christian Religion* by, 108; Pascal and, 111;
    Protestant Reformation joined by, 11, 107,
    110; superiors respected by, 109; teachings
    of, 110; weekly communion by, 110–11
capitalism: industrial, 273, 276; innovations
    and acceleration in, 68–69; Marx on, 68;
    modern, 29; science making breakthrough

for, 31; thermostatlessness created by, 28, 37–38; Weber on, 28–29, 68

caste system, 258, 258n111

catastrophic end (in Kant), 176

Catholicism, 199, 227, 278; Catholic substance, 283, 300; Church as hierarchic spiritual state, 238; medieval, 192n33; Protestantism corrective of, 279; Protestant Principle and, 280, 285; reconciliation in, 246–47; sacramental religion in, 169; Troeltsch on medieval, 242–48

Cawelti, John G., 299

CCP. See Chinese Communist Party

Chardin, Teilhard de, 93

charismatic faith, 289

Charles I (king), 112, 187

Charles II (king), 112

Childhood (Tolstoy, L.), 133–34

chimpanzees, 38–39

China, 213; boundary problems of, 23–24; Confucianism in, 333; cultural essentialism in, 214n118; hard ceiling facing, 24–25; supernatural utopianism of, 215–16; transcendentalist paradigm of, 215–16; Weber on, 259n114

Chinese Communist Party (CCP), 215, 216n124

Chorus Mysticus, 131–32

Christianity, 32, 139; Axial theory in, 206–7; Bellah on, 182–83; body of Christ in, 230–31, 231n19; catastrophic end from, 176; ethos of love in, 232; evangelical, 278; God's human intervention in, 170–71; historical approach of, 173–75; human agency in, 177–78; Jesus attention in, 184n4; Jewish prophetism in, 191–92, 270–71; Kant on decisive role of, 176n51; logos and, 171–73; model of humanity in, 294; monarchism and, 186–92, 201; moral universalism of, 243–44; Moses and, 98–99; Old Testament in, 271; orderly world from, 333; organic metaphor in, 230; patriarchalism in, 244–45; reform

movements within, 188–90; rules divinized in, 194–95, 211n104; salvation in, 231–32; scriptures of, 102; social teachings of, 242; Ten Commandments in, 97–98; Tillich on, 169; transcendental purpose in, 235; as true philosophy, 174–75; universalism in, 250–51; universalism of medieval, 242–48; Urapmin people's life of, 287–92, 300–301, 330; Western, 313; Yahweh in, 100

Christian nationalism, 302, 334

churches, 284; ancient state differences with, 238n39; body of Christ in, 240; Durkheim on formation of, 310–11; during Enlightenment, 312; growth specialists hired by, 318–19; humanity's tensions with, 237; as institution of salvation, 248; kingdom of God in, 236; right to revolution of, 246; sect distinction from, 251; secularization of, 317; Troeltsch's understanding of, 248

Church of the Sacred Heart, 309

Citio, Zeno de, 160

City of God (Augustine), 102, 174

civilizing mission, 200

Clark, Gregory, 42

Clastres, Pierre, 202

clerisy dialogue, 197–99

climate change, 48, 324

climate crisis, 3–4, 66, 216–21

Collected Essays on the Sociology of Religion (Weber), 152n74

colonialism, 308

Commentary on St. John's Gospel, 161

common good, 82–85, 204n74

Commonwealth of England (1649–53), 111

communal economy, 259–60

communion, in Calvin's thought, 110–11

communism, 189n20, 266

communities, 218, 248

Confession, A (Tolstoy, L.), 135–37

Confessions (Augustine), 102

Confessions (Rousseau), 135–36

Confucianism, 11, 31, 157, 213–15, 333

Confucian-Legalist authority, 216n124

consciousness, relational, 220n139

Constantine (emperor), 236

Converting Kings (Strathern), 213n112

Copernicus (1473–1543), 111

Corinthians I, book of, 230

Coriolanus (Shakespeare), 229

Coronavirus Pandemic. *See* COVID-19 pandemic

Corrosion of Character, The (Sennett), 66

cosmic evolution, 13

cosmology, 94, 99, 185

Courage to Be, The (Tillich), 268–69, 282

COVID-19 pandemic, 3, 219–20, 324, 331

creation stories, 93–95, 99–102, 113, 118, 175, 238

Critique of Pure Reason (Kant), 120

Cromwell, Oliver, 111–12

Cultural Revolution, 216

culture: autonomy in, 64; essentialism, 214n118; evolution of, 12; individualism in, 324; modernization of, 61; moral, 175–76; religion and, 168–71; resources of, 167, 338–39; role models of, 26

Danowski, Déborah, 218

Dante (1265–1321), 103–4, 105n15, 113–15

Daoism, 333

Darkness of God, The (Turner), 97n7

Darwin, Charles, 40, 40n10, 157

Dawn of Everything (Graeber and Wengrow), 205n78

Deacon, Terrence, 9

death rate (mortality), 39–41

Deaton, Angus, 50

deBary, Wm Theodore, 214n117

Declaration of Independence, 32–34, 60–67, 78

Declaration of the Rights of Man, 32–34

Demiurge, 100–101

democracy, 33, 72–73, 82–85, 191, 202–3

Democracy in America (Tocqueville), 31

demographic transition, 50

density-dependent mechanism, 39

Denys the Areopagite, 97, 103

desacralization, of divine kingship, 194n40

desynchronization, 72–73

devil symbolism, 153n76

diairetic technique, 162n11

Difference Principle, 260

differentiation theory, 304–8, 323–24

Dillenberger, John, 107

Dilthey, Wilhelm, 233, 235, 239–41

disenchantment, 304–6, 321–23

disestablishment, 323–24

Divina Commedia (Dante), 112, 124

divine kingship, 188, 193–95, 194n40

division of labor, 165, 175, 178–80, 228–30

Donald, Merlin, 12, 92, 159

dreaming innocence, 277–78

Duara, Prasenjit, 221

Dumont, Louis, 256–58, 286; *Essays on Individualism* by, 295; hierarchy in, 257; hierarchy of values in, 193, 301; hierarchical opposition of values in, 297; on individualism, 296–97, 302; on social formations, 297n23; values approach of, 295–300

Durkheim, Émile, 3, 59, 179, 277, 284; on church formation, 310–11; *Elementary Forms* by, 310; sacred experiences of, 309–10

dynamic stabilization, 67–72, 75–79, 81

Eagleton, Terry, 280

Earth Spirit, 125

East Asia, manufacturing by, 29

ecological critique, 219

economics: growth in, 50, 69; industrial revolution's growth in, 42–43; inequality in, 2; market, 335; non-natural chrematistics in, 180; productivity from technology in, 74; socioeconomics in, 72–73

Economy and Society (Weber), 143, 249–50

efflorescence periods, 44, 48–49

egalitarianism, 202n68; monarchy not needed in, 201–2; moral universalism's tensions with, 260; transcendentalist traditions in, 221–22; unqualified, 122

Ehrenberg, Alain, 65, 73

Einstein, Albert, 91

Eisenstadt, S. N., 166n22, 194, 200n56, 205n80, 210n99, 214, 215n119, 321n29, 335n14

Elementary Forms (Durkheim), 310

Eliot, T. S., 157

Emancipation Proclamation (of 1863), 33

emic vs. etic concepts, 184–85, 195

E→motion, 80, 80n52

encompassment (Dumont), 297

energy, 25, 27, 40–41

England, 30, 191

English Civil War (1642–51), 111

Enlightenment, 32, 40, 54, 66, 192n34; Bellah on, 187; churches during, 312; Declaration of Independence and, 62–63; humanities principles of, 59–60; Kant as central figure in, 119–20, 274; Protestantism leading to, 272

enunciations, 163, 163n13

environment, exploitation of, 84

environmental awareness, 79

epidemics, 47

equality, 33, 122, 201–2, 211, 260, 298–99, 330–31

Erasmus (1466–1536), 107

Essarhaddon (king), 188

Essay on the Principle of Population (Malthus), 30

Essay on the Principle of Population, An (Franklin), 40, 40n10

Essays on Individualism (Dumont), 295

eternalization, 247

ethic of conviction (*Gesinnungsethik*), 145, 153, 154n79

ethic of responsibility (*Verantwortungsethik*), 153, 155

ethics: of brotherliness, 144; of care, 85; challenges of, 173; conscience with, 180; preoccupations with, 185

Eurasia, 203

Eurocentrism, 206n83

Europe, 105–6, 210n101

evangelical Christianity, 278

Evans-Pritchard, E. E., 297

evolution, Bellah's theme of, 4–8

evolutionary optimists vs. pessimists, 13

Exodus 19–20, 97

exposed zone, 203–4

extensive vs. intensive growth, 43

fascism, 279, 336

Faust (Goethe), 123–24, 185–86; Baucis and Philemon in, 128; Chorus Mysticus in, 131–32; Faust falls down dead, 129; Faust's spirit in heaven in, 130; Gretchen in, 127, 130–31; knowledge is meaningless in, 125; land reclamation project in, 128; Mephistopheles in, 126–29, 131; sins committed in, 130; spirit leaves body in, 129–30; Spirit of Care in, 129; supernatural revelations in, 125–26

felix culpa (happy fall), 117, 117nn28–29

fertility, 39–41, 45, 52

"Flaws in the Protestant Code" (Bellah), 285, 293

forbidden fruit (Milton), 118–19

fossil fuels, 52–53

Fox, Everett, 93

fragmentation theory, 304, 321–23

Francis (pope), 334

Francis (Saint), 333

Frankish Empire, 238

Franklin, Benjamin, 40

freedom, for humanity, 168–69

French Revolution, 32–34, 274, 277

frenetic standstill, 77

Gaia hypothesis, 100

Galileo (1564–1642), 111

Gandhi, Mahatma, 211n105, 254

Garden of Eden, 119

Gaudium et Spes (Vatican II Pastoral Constitution), 35–36

Genesis 1, 94–96, 99, 101

Genesis 3, 116, 118

German Law of Associations, The (Gierke), 234

Germany, 189, 189n20, 266–68

Gesinnungsethik (ethic of conviction), 145, 153, 154n79

Gierke, Otto von, 238n39, 252n94; organism metaphor and, 239n42; organological societal conceptions from, 234–35; profound Pauline allegory from, 237

global consciousness, 166n23, 180

global social processes, 3, 4, 7, 15, 60, 68, 94, 167, 179, 198, 331, 335, 338

global warming, 3–4, 27, 37, 56, 72–73, 332

God, 93–108, 122–23, 125–30; Adam and Eve created by, 116–17, 117n28; Christianity with human intervention by, 170–71; church with kingdom of, 236; everything created through word of, 171; final intervention by, 177, 177n56; human dealt with personally by, 290; image of, 108n18; Kant on existence of, 120–21; Kant with intervention from, 176–77; King-God, 194–95, 194n39; obedience to, 238; reason based on, 120–21; Satan's battle with, 114–16, 124; Son begotten by, 115n26; sovereignty of, 109, 186–87, 190n27; Tillich's conception of, 275–76; L. Tolstoy beliefs in, 139

Goethe, Johann Wolfgang von (1749–1832), 132; *Faust* by, 123–31, 185–86; *The Sorrows of Young Werther* by, 125

Goldmann, Lucien, 283–84

Goldstone, Jack, 44

González, Ana Marta, 16, 330–31

good and evil, struggle between, 117–18

good life, 75–76, 82

Good Society, 79n50, 81n53, 87

good thinking, in Urapmin moral psychology, 292

Gopal, Priyamvada, 210n101

Gorgias (469b-c), 99

Gorski, Philip, 17–18, 218, 336

Gospels, 139–40

Graeber, David, 197, 205n78

grand theory, 92

gravitational field, 313–14

great escape (Deaton), 50, 56

Greek cosmogony, 94

Green New Deal, 4

Gretchen, in *Faust*, 127, 130–31

Guhin, Jeffrey, 285

Gunawardena, R. A. L. H., 197

Habermas, Jürgen, 60, 165, 169–70, 178, 295–96

Habits of the Heart, 283–84, 298–301

Halton, Eugene, 220, 220n139

Han Dynasty, 24

happy fall (*felix culpa*), 117, 117nn28–29

hard ceiling, 7, 23–25, 30, 67, 77, 339

Harper, Kyle, 15, 329, 335

Havel, Vaclav, 335

heart, in Urapmin moral psychology, 292

heart icon, 308–9

Heaven and Hell, in Dante, 104; in Goethe, 124–26, 130–32; in Milton, 113–14

Heavenly Paradise, 104, 105n15

hedonism, 148–49

Hegel, Georg Wilhelm Friedrich, 170n36, 178n57

Heidegger, Martin, 181

hen (One), 101

Henry III (king), 189

Henry IV (king), 189

Hesiod, 94

heteronomous fields, 315–16

hierarchy and universalism. *See* universalism

Hinduism, 11, 253–54, 257

Hintze, Otto, 234n25, 252n94

Historical School of Jurisprudence, 234

History Begins at Sumer (Kramer), 23

Hitler, Adolf, 267, 278

Hobbs, Thomas, 190, 190n28

Hölderlin, Friedrich, 181

holism, 257, 301–2

Holmes, Stephen, 290

homo hierarchicus, 257

Hong Xiuquan, 208

Honneth, Axel, 65
horizon of accessibility, 75–76
Horkheimer, Max, 79
Hübinger, Gangolf, 252n94
human beings: adaptation by, 325–26; God
    directly dealing with, 290; individualism
    with sacredness of, 279; inequality
    among, 227; metanarratives needed by,
    92; metapersons difference with, 196;
    psychology of, 220; resonance with
    commonality of, 331
humanity: awareness of, 2; Bellah's project on,
    1–3; Christianity and agency of, 177–78;
    Christianity's model of, 294; churches
    tensions with, 237; cultural resources
    of, 338–39; energy use of, 40–41, 52–53;
    Enlightenment principles of, 59–60;
    evolution of, 8–14, 46, 54–55; freedom
    and autonomy for, 168–69; fundamental
    unity of, 328; God's intervention of,
    170–71; as infinite-possibility thing,
    17–18; interpersonal intimacy in, 337–38;
    as living participants, 5–6; metanarratives
    needed by, 92; monarchism and social
    life of, 201; moral laws of, 121; person's
    sacredness and, 36; religion as resource
    for, 338; religion of, 5–6; religious
    meaning systems of, 323; resonance
    longing of, 81n54; in social development
    index, 22; societies and dignity of, 36;
    society with connections of, 9; unity of,
    237, 328; worldly polity and, 234–39
human rights, 58, 211, 277; Bellah's ideas on,
    168; for equality, 330–31; ideological roots
    of, 209n96; individual autonomy in, 7;
    Joas seeking roots of, 31–32; language of,
    123; as social movement, 33; universal, 32
Hus, Jan (1369–1415), 105
Husserl, Edmund, 165

Ibn Taymīya (1263–1328), 193
Ikko ikki, 207–9, 212
immanentism, 214n114; characteristics
    of, 223; divine kingship and, 193–95;

Protestantism assault on, 208n91;
    religiosity in, 184–87; royal agency
    constricted in, 195–97; Tolstoy appalled
    by elements of, 187; vanishing of, 217–18
imperialism: authority in, 199–201; of Europe,
    210n101; of Western countries, 206–7,
    206n83
Incarnation of the Word, 172
incomes, per capita, 42, 53
independence, 60–61
India, 211n104, 256–58, 301
Indic transcendentalisms, 211
Indigenous critique, 205n78
individualism, 31, 274; caste system and, 258;
    cultural, 324; Dumont on, 296–97, 302;
    emergence of, 256–57; holism distinction
    with, 257; human beings sacred in, 279;
    instrumental, 217; morality of, 283,
    300; Protestantism leading to, 286–95;
    Protestant Principle with, 283–85;
    sociology as rejection of, 283; United
    States valuing, 298; of Urapmin people,
    291–94; utilitarian, 277
individuals: autonomy of, 7, 62, 329; leading a
    life by, 65; resonance between, 82–84; in
    sacrality, 319–20; sacredness of, 277
industrial capitalism, 273, 276
industrial revolution, 25, 30–31, 42–43, 52–53,
    285
inequality, 122, 199n54, 219, 227
infant mortality, 47
infectious diseases, 47, 51–52
Inferno (Dante), 103
injustice, 2, 148; Axial critique of, 99, 122,
    333–34
Innocent III (pope), 303
innovations: acceleration and, 68–69; in
    industrial revolution, 53; social change
    and, 64; in technology, 54–55
Institutes of the Christian Religion (Calvin), 108
institutionalization, 33, 199n54
instrumental individualism, 217
Insurgent Empire: Anticolonialism and the
    Making of British (Gopal), 210n101

Intellectual ambitions, 166–67

intellectual traditions, 210

interdependence, 2, 17, 129, 179, 326, 330, 331, 335, 338

"Intermediate Reflections" (Weber), 143–44, 152, 226–27, 249; moral universalism in, 260; universal accessibility of salvation from, 253–54

interpersonal intimacy, 337–38

interpretations (Aquinas), 163, 163n13

Islam: modernization and traditional, 255–56; monarchism in, 193; organic social ethic lacking in, 252; rules divinized in, 194–95, 211n104; universalism in, 250–51

James, Henry, 112n20

Japan, work ethic in, 29

Jaspers, Karl, 9, 156, 215, 326–28

Jefferson, Thomas, 140

Jehovah's Witnesses, 221n140

Jellinek, Georg, 142

Jerusalem, 322

Jesus Christ, 115–16, 119, 171n40; Christianity as body of, 230–31, 231n119; historical perspective on, 184n4; mystical body of, 334; state and humanity as body of, 240; as true king, 231; and Weberian value spheres, 305

Jewish prophetism, 191–92, 270–71

Jews, persecution of, 190n28

Joas, Hans, 16; Bellah on work of, 192n34; Declaration of Independence and, 34; human rights sought by, 31–32; institutionalization from, 33; organic social ethics and, 199; Power of the Sacred by, 194n40; The Sacredness of the Person by, 31, 167, 276

Jōdo Shinshū, 207–8, 208n91

John 1:1, 95–96, 95n4

Joyce, James, 311

Judaism, 11, 170

Judas Iscariot, 103

Judeo-Christian prophetism, 205–6

kairos, 266, 280–81, 326

Kant, Immanuel (1724–1804): autonomy and, 272, 274–75; Christianity's decisive role in commitment to virtue, 176n51; Critique of Pure Reason by, 120; in Enlightenment, 119–20, 274; on equal rights of humanity, 122; on God's existence, 120–21; God's intervention in history, 176–77; and Habermas on practical reason, 169; moral culture and material progress, 175–76; quiet sociable life of, 274; republican justice, 121–22; secular hermeneutics of, 174

Kaufmann, Walter, 132n41

Khan, Syed Ahmad, 211

Kierkegaard, Søren, 327

"Kingdom of God is within You, The" (art), 149

King-God, 194–95, 194n39

kingship, 197n50, 201n64, 205, 231

Kirill, Patriarch, 217n131

knowledge: fields of, 124–25; inequality maintained by, 219; as machine of modern empiricist science, 55; as meaningless, 125; L. Tolstoy search for, 137–38; to treasure or expand, 69–70

knowledge-research-increased knowledge (kn-r-kn'), 70

Kramer, Samuel Noah, 23

Kreutzer Sonata, The (Tolstoy, L.), 140

Ladwig, Patrice, 212

Lanatus, Agrippa Menenius, 229

language, 26, 123

leading a life, 65

League of Nations, 247

Leo XIII, 36

"Let there be light," 99

Levi-Strauss, Claude, 301

liberty, 298

Lieberman, Victor, 203, 204n74

life expectancy, 42, 51

linear thinking, 28

listening society, 82

Literal Commentary to Genesis, 161

logic, 162–63

logismós (science), 160n3

logos (word), 96–97, 160–62, 160n3; Christianity and, 171–73; nature of being in, 161n9; Tillich on sacramental dimensions of, 172

logos-nomos paired as model of reasoning, 160

love, ethos of, 232

Lowe, Alfred, 268

Lucifer, 115

Luckert, Karl W., 94

Luhmann, Niklas, 59, 69

Luke 10:18, 104

Lutheranism, 272

2 Maccabees, 93

Machiavelli, Niccolò, 108

MacIntyre, Alasdair, 74, 295–96

Magic Mountain (Mann), 187

Malik, Charles, 35

Malthus, Thomas, 30, 40–49

Malthusian model, 42; intensive growth phases and, 44; population movements and, 44–46; thermostatlessness and, 47; wages and fertility linked in, 45; zero growth prediction from, 43–44

Mandate of Heaven, 213

Mann, Thomas, 182, 187

Margaret Mary (saint), 309

Maritain, Jacques, 34

market economies, 335

marriage, 152

Marsilius of Padua, 240

Martin Luther (1483–1546), 105, 155

Marx, Karl, 28, 68, 272–73

Marxism, 276

masculinity, 200, 299

mathematics, 160–62

Matthew: 25, 290

Matuštík, Martin Beck, 166n23

m-c-m'. See Money–Commodity–Money'

McNeill, John, 52

meaninglessness, 323

Measure of Civilization, The (Morris), 21, 24

medieval Catholicism, 192n33

medieval Christianity, 242–48

medieval metaphysics, 239–41

medieval religions, 334–35

Melancholia (film), 15, 158, 175

Mephistopheles, 124, 126–29, 131

Mesopotamia, 23

metanarratives: Bellah's interest in, 166, 173–74, 219n136, 222; of cosmic and biological evolution, 325; as human necessity, 92

metapersons, 184, 196

metaphysics, 100

Michael (angel), 119

microbial infection, 329

Middle Ages, 105, 107, 234, 238, 241

Midgley, Mary, 14

millenarianism, 207, 212

Mills, C. Wright, 268

Milton, John (1608–1674), 111–13, 115n26, 187; *Areopagitica* by, 114; *Paradise Lost* by, 124

Mind (*Nous*), 101

modern capitalism, 29

modern democracy, 203

modernity: Bellah and, 167; challenges to, 3–4; climate crisis in, 216–21; mastery of nature in, 3–4; organized, 63; project of, 65–66, 76, 80; Tillich challenged by, 268; Weber's diagnosis of, 324; of Western countries, 73–74, 334–35

modernization, 59, 61, 67–71, 255–56

Modern Project in the Light of Human Evolution, The (Bellah), 6, 36

"Modern Project in the Light of Human Evolution, The" (Bellah), 6, 15, 37, 57–58

modern religion, 11–12, 314–21

modern societies: dynamic stabilization of, 71, 75–77; empirical science and, 165; global economy and, 4; scientific knowledge in, 69–70; thermostatlessness of, 71

modern sociology, 141

Mokyr, Joel, 55

monarchism, 201n62; autocratic, 203n69; Christianity and, 186–92, 201; clerisy dialogue and, 197–99; disenchantment of, 193–95; human social life in, 201; immanentism in constriction of, 195–97; in Islamic history, 193; moral arbitration in, 198–99; republicanism and, 191n30; Tlaxcalans resisting, 202n67; transcendentalism and subordination of, 192–205; unneeded in small-scale societies, 201–2

Money–Commodity–Money' (m-c-m'), 68, 70

Mongol hegemony, 212n108

morality, 336; in communities, 218; of humanity, 121; of individualism, 283, 300; psychology and, 292–93; in transcendentalism, 187

moral universalism, 5, 247–48, 254, 324; of Christianity, 243–44; egalitarianism's tensions with, 260; in "Intermediate Reflections," 260

Morris, Ian, 6, 57; hard ceiling from, 23; *The Measure of Civilization* by, 21, 24; social development index from, 22, 49, 67, 77, 167; *Why the West Rules—for Now* by, 21, 49, 203n70

mortality, 39–41, 45, 47, 51

Mortimer, Sarah, 204n74, 205n79

Moses, 97–99, 119, 171n40

Mount Sinai, 97

Mount Zion, 97–98

Mughal emperors, 195

Mumford, Lewis, 220n139

Müntzer, Thomas, 189n20

Muslims, religious war for, 253

mystical body, 231n19, 233, 334

mythical powers of origin, 269, 271–72

myth of origin, 16–17

"Myths of Violence in American Popular Culture" (Cawelti), 299

Narai of Ayutthaya (king, 1656–1688), 196–98

narrative, 5–6, 13–14, 91–92, 95–97, 159–66

National Socialist German Workers Party (the Nazis), 267

nation-state, 308, 314–17, 320

natural law, 169n32, 205, 232, 234, 240, 256–57

nature: modernity's mastery of, 3–4; regulatory mechanisms in, 38–39, 56; thermostats of, 38–39, 53–54

negative theology, 103

Nelson, Eric, 190

neoliberalism, 301, 334

Neo-Platonism, 101–2

New Revised Standard Version (NRSV), 95n4

New Testament, 96

New World, 106

Niebuhr, H. Richard, 231, 268

Nikolajeva, Maria, 172

nominalists, 105

non-natural chrematistics, 180

normative consciousness, 178

"nothing is ever lost," Bellah's maxim that, 110, 121, 186

Notre Dame lecture (Bellah, chapter 1 of this volume), 6–7, 15, 53, 57–59, 167, 192n34, 199n54, 326

Nous (Mind), 101

NRSV. *See* New Revised Standard Version

Número y logos (Zellini), 159

objectivism, 276

occidental rationalism, 260

Odyssey (Zellini), 159

OECD. *See* Organisation of Economic Co-operation and Development

Old Testament, 254, 271

On (Being), 101

One (*hen*), 101

orderly world, 333

organic life process, 152

organic metaphor, 230

organic religion, 145

organic social ethics: ascetic vocational ethic compared to, 248–55; Bellah's references to, 255–56, 258–59; Islam lacking, 252; Joas

and, 199; reactive organicism as distinct
from, 247; from Thomas Aquinas, 231–32;
Weber on, 16; Weber's understanding of,
249–50; Weber usage relativized, 233
organic theory of state, 235n27
organic vocational ethic, 227, 250
Organisation of Economic Co-operation and
Development (OECD), 85
organism, creation as one, 238
organism metaphor, 239n42
organized modernity, 63
original sin, 116–17
origin myth, 168
Ottoman Empire, 210

pandemic, reaching Roman Empire, 48–49
Papua New Guinea, 286–95
Paradise Lost (Milton), 111–13, 115–16, 124
paradox of development, 23
parasites, 39, 46–47
Parsons, Talcott, 59, 269
Pascal, Blaise (1623–1662), 111
patriarchalism, in Christianity, 244–45
Paul (Saint), 176, 179
Pauline allegory, 237, 239
"Paul Tillich and the Challenge of
Modernity" (Bellah), 7, 16–17
Peasants' War (1524–1526), 189, 189n20
Penitent Women, 130
"Permanent Significance of the Catholic
Church for Protestantism, The" (Tillich),
279
personal appropriation, 170
pestilence, 45
pets, resonance from, 86
Philemon, in *Faust*, 128
Philo of Alexandria (20 BCE- 50 CE), 96,
98, 171
philosophical theology, 121
philosophy, 120, 163n13, 327; division from
science, 165–66; relation to religion,
170n36, 175; and truth of Christianity,
174–75; Weber and, 147
Pines, Yuri, 214

PISA. *See* Programme for International
Student Assessment
Plato (427 BCE-347 BCE), 97–102, 119,
162n11
poetry, 103, 112, 115
Polanyi, Karl, 294
politics: Kant's interest in, 121–22; and moral
universalism, 244; oppositions in, 78;
political liberty, 205n78; religion in, 319;
sociopolitical system in, 83–84
"Politics as a Vocation" (Weber), 153–54
populations, 27, 44–46
populist movements, 3
poverty, 40–42, 50, 74, 335
power, distribution of, 229–30
Power of the Sacred (Joas), 194n40
predators, 39, 46–47
predestination, doctrine of, 108–9, 145
pre-human flux (Lukert), 94
preventative check, 41
primary goods, 74
primordial human situation, 270
"Prisoner of the Caucasus, The" (art), 149
prisoners, 140
"Profession of Faith of a Savoyard Vicar"
(Rousseau), 123
Programme for International Student
Assessment (PISA), 85
prophecy, rejection of, 151
prophetic word, 168
prophetism, 168–69, 191–92, 205–6, 270–71
Protestant Era, The (Tillich), 281
Protestant Ethic and the Spirit of Capitalism, The
(Weber), 143, 147
Protestantism, 187; assault on immanentism,
208n91; and emergence of Enlightenment,
272; indifference to sacramental
thinking, 278; and individualism,
286–95; Lutheranism and, 272; need of
Catholicism corrective, 279; theologians
of, 244n61
Protestant Principle, 193n36, 272, 277–80,
283–85
Protestant prophetism, 168–69

Protestant Reformation: Bible as source for, 105; Calvin joining, 11, 107, 110; European society transformed by, 105–6; preceding modern religion, 11

Proverbs 8:22–31, 95

Pseudo-Dionysius the Areopagite, 97n7

psychology, 220, 292–93

Puett, Michael, 213n112

punishment, 117n28

pure reason, 102

purgatory, 103, 104

Puritanism, 190

quasi-democratic systems, 202–3

racism, 33

radical cultural transformations (achsenzeit), 166n22

radicalism, 212

Radical Reformation, 109

railway, 73

Rand, Ayn, 276

Raphael, conversations with, 113–14

rationalization, 306

Rawls, John, 74, 260

reactive organicism, 247

reality, 12–13

reason: God as basis of, 120–21; inspired by religion, 170; Kant on practical, 169; mathematics as model of, 160–61; pure, 102; truth in, 164n17

Reform, Resistance, and Reason of State (Mortimer), 204n74, 205n79

reformists, 186

reform movements, 188–90

regulatory mechanisms: in nature, 38–39, 56; preventative check in, 41; thermostats and, 47

relational consciousness, 220n139

relationalism, 17, 291–93

relations, hierarchical, 330

relations between relations, 297

religion: of Axial Age world-rejection, 11; Axial legacies of, 16–17; Bellah on evolution of, 10–11, 13–14; Bellah on meaning of, 9; Catholic sacramental, 169; culture and, 168–71; defined by Durkheim and Weber, 310; in ecological awareness, 338; everyday reality and, 12–13; forms of, 184–85; genuine brotherliness in, 151; gravitational field of, 313–14; in human evolution, 8–14; of humanity, 5–6; in immanentism, 184–87; inspiring commitment to reason, 170; meaning systems in, 323; medieval, 334–35; modern, 11; modern fragmenting and weakening of, 318–19, 324; Muslim wars for, 253; mythical origins of, 269; organic, 145; philosophy's relation to, 170n36, 175; politicization of, 319; Rousseau's view on, 123n39; secularization and decline in, 306–7; socialism in, 266; sociology of, 145–46, 315; spirituality and, 320; symbols of, 336–38; tolerance in, 211–12; and transcendence, 336–37; transcendentalist, 185–86; universalism in, 250–51; wars of, 186–87; Weber on intellect and, 150–51

Religion in Human Evolution (Bellah): human evolution in, 2, 5, 12, 159, 167, 216n125, 225–26, 325, 328–29; universal criticism in, 14

"Religious Evolution" (Bellah), 9, 17

Religious Situation, The (Tillich), 268

Remonstrance of a Thousand Citizens, A, 190

Republic 7, 97–99

republicanism, 191n30, 201

republics, reform of, 121–22

Rerum Novarum (Leo XIII), 36

resistance, right of, 246

resonance, 329; dynamic stabilization contrary to, 81; elements of, 80–81; ethics of care and, 85; human commonality in, 331; humanity longing for, 81n54; between individuals, 82–84; pets providing, 86; Rosa's theory of, 311; in societies, 84–85; visions of harmony in, 87

responsibility, Bellah's theme of, 4–8

"Restoration of Hell, The" (Tolstoy, L.), 138n53

Resurrection (Tolstoy, L.), 140

Revelation, book of, 174

Revised Standard Version (RSV), 95n4

Ricci, Matteo, 334

righteous kingship, 194

ritual, 7–8, 12, 69, 185, 331, 336–38

ritual enactment, 7

ritual initiation, 288

ritualization trap, 195–97

Robbins, Joel, 17, 187, 193, 193n36, 204, 330

role models, 26

Roman Empire, 22; boundary problems of, 23–24; fall of, 48–49; pandemic reaching, 48–49; Roman Climate Optimum, 48; technology of, 54

Roosevelt, Eleanor, 35

Rosa, Hartmut, 15, 311, 329, 331

Rousseau, Jean-Jacques, 123, 123n39, 135–36, 205n78, 273

Roy, Rammohan (1772-1833), 204, 211

RSV. *See* Revised Standard Version

ruling elites, 194, 202–3

Russell, Bertrand, 162n10

Russia, at war, 139

Russian Orthodox Church, 139

sacerdotium, 240

sacrality, of the individual, 319–20

sacralization, 314; adverse, 197; in Axial Age, 321–22; desacralization and, 194n40; fragmentation of, 218n133; process of, 308–11; supernatural blessings in, 196–97

sacred canopy, 15

sacred hearts, 309

sacredness, of individuals, 277

Sacredness of the Person, The (Joas), 31, 167, 276

Sahlins, Marshall, 184, 195, 298

salvation, 185; in Christianity, 231–32; church as institution of, 248; in transcendentalism, 200, 220–21; universal accessibility of, 253–54

Samaritan woman, 130

Satan, 113–16, 124

Satnamis revolt, 208n92

Schluchter, Wolfgang, 154–56

Schnitger, Marianne, 142

science: critical to rise of industrial society, 31; distinguished from art, 146–47; divided from philosophy, 165–66; ecological critique of, 219; empirical, 165; *logismós* as, 160n3; revolution in, 106; role in thermostatless economic growth and climate crisis, 28, 37–38; Sermon on the Mount and, 154; truth and good of, 150; as vocation, 70; Weber on progress of, 146; Weber on works in, 70

"Science as a Vocation" (Weber), 8, 151, 153, 156

scientific knowledge, 69–70

sect, 251

Secular Age, A (Taylor), 312

secularization, 217, 217n127; of churches, 317; components of, 312; religion's decline and, 306–7

secular rulers, 222

self-consciousness, 178n57, 185

self-destruction, 28, 81–82

self-determination, 61, 65, 178n57

self-governance (*swaraj*), 211n105

self-realization, 178n57

Sennett, Richard, 66

Sermon on the Mount, 154

sex, hatred of by L. Tolstoy, 140

Shakespeare, William, 149, 229

Shields, James Mark, 212

Sikhs, 208, 209, 211

Simmel, Georg, 73, 166

sin: Faust saved without repenting, 130; original, 116–17; practices of, 293

skepticism, 134

slavery, 29, 33

Sloterdijk, Peter, 1

Smith, Adam, 29, 273

Smith, James K. A., 309

Smith, Wilfred Cantwell, 9

social change, 64, 71

Social Darwinism, 275

Social Democratic Party (SPD), 266–67

social development index, 6–7; Bellah on acceleration of, 67; of energy capture per capita, 22; exponential growth in, 25–26; from Morris, 22, 49, 67, 77, 167

social dynamics, 41, 43

social evolution, 5–6, 9, 27, 143n57. *See also* "Religious Evolution"

social fields, 314, 316–17

social formations, 297n23

socialism, 150, 212, 266, 269

Socialist Decision, The (Tillich), 267–69

social movement, 33

social organization, 57, 292; differentiation from symbols, 9

social power, 200–201

social radicalism, 140

social structures, 9, 60, 73, 292

Social Teaching of the Christian Churches, The (Troeltsch), 233, 249, 256

societies: ecological disaster as hammer of doom to, 66–67; good of resonance in, 84–87; human connections in, 9; human members dignity in, 36; imperatives of acceleration in, 86–87; language in, 26; listening, 82; medieval metaphysics and, 239–41; modern, 4, 69–71, 75–77, 165; organological conceptions of, 234–35; stateless, 201n64; L. Tolstoy time outside, 134

Society against the State (Clastres), 202

socioeconomics, 72–73

sociology: of domination, 252, 311; ecological models in, 47–48; individualism rejected by, 283; modern, 141; of religion, 145–46, 315

"Sociology of Domination" (Weber), 251

"Sociology of Law" (Weber), 235

"Sociology of Religion" (Weber), 233n23, 251

sociopolitical system, 83–84

Socrates, 99, 162n11

Song Dynasty, 23, 26, 273

Sophia (Wisdom), 96

Sophist, 162n11

Sorrows of Young Werther, The (Goethe), 125

sovereignty, 61, 109, 186–87, 190n27

Soviet Union, 34

SPD. *See* Social Democratic Party

spheres of life, 148–49

spirit, taken to heaven in *Faust*, 129–30

Spirit of Care, 129

spiritual Declaration of Independence central to modern project, 60–67, 78

spiritual independence, 74

spirituality, 228, 320, 323

stabilization, dynamic, 67–81

Stasavage, David, 202–4

stateless societies, 201n64

state socialist system, 335–36

steam engines, 25, 30, 36, 73

Stevens, Wallace, 157

storytelling. *See* narrative

Strathern, Alan, 16, 213n112, 329

Strevens, Michael, 55

Stuart-Glennie, John, 220n139

Stumme, John R., 268

Subrahmanyam, Sanjay, 210–11

subsistence-level existence, 51

Sulh-i Kull (total peace), 212, 212n108

superiority, opposed to social justice in Kant, 122

supernatural blessings, 196–97

supernatural revelations, 125–26, 185

supernatural utopianism, 207, 207n88, 209, 215–16

supernovas, 313–14

supramundane order, 305

sustainability, 27, 79, 180, 221

swaraj (self-governance), 211n105

symbolic forms, 9

Systematic Theology (Tillich), 270

Taiping Rebellion, 208–9, 209n94

Taylor, Charles, 60, 217–18, 312–14, 319

teachings, of Calvin as the spirit of the Protestant Reformation, 110

technology: acceleration of, 71; accessibility from, 75–76; climate change and,

324; economic productivity from, 74; innovations in, 54–55; of Roman Empire, 54

teleological, 183–84

Ten Commandments, 97–98

Tezcan, Baki, 209

Thales (Greek philosopher), 94

Theaetetus (Plato), 162n11

theology, 103, 121, 170n36, 208

theonomy, 275, 277, 300

Theory of Justice, A (Rawls), 260

theory of values, 296–98

Theravada Buddhist, 197–98

thermodynamic equilibrium, 54

thermostat, 24; Bellah's interest in, 49, 326; density-dependent mechanism as, 39; global warming and, 37; humanity turning off, 56; Malthus and, 40–49; of nature, 38–39, 53–54; regulatory mechanisms and, 47

thermostatlessness, 15, 331; Malthusian model and, 47; of modern society, 71; science and capitalism causing, 28, 37–38; self-destruction and, 81–82; and unsustainable growth, 335

thinking about thinking, 12

this-worldly transcendence, 214–15

Thomas Aquinas (1225–1274), 102–3, 124, 163, 227, 333; authority of, 105; organic social ethics exemplified by, 231–32

Thrasymachus, 99

Tillich, Paul, 168; at Battle of Verdun, 266; Catholic substance from, 283, 300; on Christianity, 169; correlation theology from, 265; *The Courage to Be* by, 268–69, 282; dreaming innocence from, 277–78; early life of, 265–66; Jewish prophetism from, 191–92, 270–71; mythical powers of origin of religion from, 271–72; Nazi Germany banning book of, 267–68; "The Permanent Significance of the Catholic Church for Protestantism" by, 279; primordial human situation from, 270; *The Protestant Era* by, 281; on Protestant Principle, 277–78; *The Religious Situation* by, 268; religious socialism to renew modernity, 268; sacramental dimensions of logos from, 172; socialism advocated by, 269; *The Socialist Decision* by, 267–69; *Systematic Theology* by, 270; theonomy as conception of God in, 275–76

Timeaus (Platonic dialogue), 99–100, 103–4

Tlaxcalans, 202, 202n67

Tocqueville, Alexis de, 31

Tolstoy, Leo (1828–1910), 123; *Anna Karenina* by, 135, 137; appalled by immanentism, 187; art attacked by, 149–50; *Boyhood* by, 133–34; captivated by adolescent skepticism, 134; *Childhood* by, 133–34; *A Confession* by, 135–37; as diarist, 133–34; existential anxieties of, 138; God beliefs of, 139; Goethe not appreciated by, 132; Gospels rewritten by, 139–40; image created for self by, 133; *The Kreutzer Sonata* by, 140; "The Restoration of Hell" by, 138n53; *Resurrection* by, 140; search for knowledge of, 137–38; sex hated by, 140; social radicalism of, 140; time outside society to think, 134; trilogy by, 133–35; true science and, 150; *War and Peace* by, 135, 141; Weber opposed to yet affinity with and respect for, 148, 150; *What I Believe* by, 132; *Youth* by, 133, 135

Tolstoy, Sophia, 141

total peace (*Sulh-i Kull*), 212, 212n108

transcendentalism, 311; Asian, 206–12; after Axial Age, 185; axiality and, 183; in Buddhism, 214; central authority threatened by, 190; characteristics of, 223–24; China's paradigm of, 215–16; Christian purpose in, 235; in egalitarianism, 221–22; imperial authority in, 199–201; Indic, 211; monarchy subordination and, 192–205; morality in, 187; of religions, 185–86; ruling elites in, 194; salvation in, 200, 220–21; secular rulers and, 222; social power of, 200–201; supernatural utopianism of, 209

Transformation, 80

Trier, Lars von, 15, 158, 175

Triple A Approach, to good life, 75–76

Troeltsch, Ernst, 142, 233, 235; on medieval
Catholicism, 242–48; on moral
universalism, 247–48; Protestant
theologians and, 244n61; *The Social Teaching
of the Christian Churches* by, 233, 249, 256;
understanding of the church by, 248

True Pure Land Buddhism, 207

Turner, Denys, 97n7, 98, 102–3

unconditional basic income, 86–87

United Kingdom, 34, 220n137. *See also*
England

United States, 34; Christian nationalism
in, 302, 334; faith-based community
organizations in, 317; individualism's
value in, 298; religious field in, 318, 324

universal accessibility of salvation, 253–54

Universal Declaration of Independence, 34

universal human rights, 8, 32, 34, 330–31, 335, 338

universalism, 231–32; in Christianity, 250–51;
and hierarchy, 257, 330; in Islam, 250–51;
issue of, 240; of medieval Christianity,
242–48; moral, 5, 243–44, 247–48, 254,
260, 324; Old Testament, 254; and
particularism, 333; political, 244; in
religion, 250–51

universal moral visions, 16, 333

unqualified egalitarianism, 122

Urapmin people, 295; Australian Baptist
missionaries with, 288–89; Bible study
of, 288; charismatic faith of, 289;
Christian life of, 287–92, 300–301, 330;
moral psychology of, 292; Protestant
individualism of, 291–94; ritual initiation
of, 288; social organization of, 292

utilitarian individualism, 277

Valignano, Alessandro (1539–1606), 208

values: from Axial Age, 166; Dumont's
approach to, 295–300; of holism, 301–2;
theory of, 296–98

value spheres, 74; components of, 307–8;
differentiation of, 145, 306; social
fields compared to, 314; warring gods
differentiated from, 332; Weber on,
143–44, 297n23, 308

Vatican II Pastoral Constitution on the
Modern World (*Gaudium et Spes*),
35–36, 279

Verantwortungsethik (ethic of responsibility),
153, 155

Verdun, Battle of, 266

Virgin Mary, 109, 119

virtue, 135, 161

Viveiros de Castro, Eduardo, 218, 221

Vlastos, Gregory, 100

Vries, Jan de, 45

wages, 44–45

Wagner, Peter, 63

Walzer, Michael, 190

War and Peace (Tolstoy, L.), 135, 141

warring gods, 17, 322, 332

Watt, James, 30

weak fields, theory of, 316

weapons, 22, 24, 46

Weariness of Self, 73

Weber, Max, 3; on Arab tribal warriors,
253; Bellah using terms from, 226–34;
capitalism comments by, 28–29; on
capitalist economy, 68; caste system
understanding of, 258n111; on China,
259n114; *Collected Essays on the Sociology of
Religion* by, 152n74; communal economy
from, 259–60; on desacralization of divine
kingship, 194n40; devil symbolism and,
153n76; dynamic stabilization and, 71; early
childhood of, 141–42; *Economy and Society*
by, 143, 249–50; ethic of brotherliness
from, 144; failing health of, 142–43; flood
of ideas from, 157; on inherently outdated
works in science, 70; "Intermediate
Reflections" by, 143–44, 152, 226–27, 249,
253–54, 260; modern condition diagnosed
by, 324; modern man embodiment by,

156–57; modern sociology from, 141; Old Testament universalism interest of, 254; as opposite of Tolstoy, 148; on organic social ethics, 16; organic social ethics understanding of, 249–50; organic social ethics used by, 233; organic theory of state by, 235n27; on organic vocational ethics, 250; philosophy and, 147; "Politics as a Vocation" by, 153–54; prisoner treatment from, 140; professorship of, 142; *The Protestant Ethic and the Spirit of Capitalism* by, 143, 147; religion and intellect from, 150–51; "Science as a Vocation" by, 8, 151, 153, 156; science distinguished from art by, 146–47; on scientific progress, 146; on scientific works, 70; social differentiation theory of, 304–8; social evolution rejected by, 143n57; on social spheres of life, 148–49; "Sociology of Domination" by, 251; sociology of domination from, 252, 311; "Sociology of Law" by, 235; on sociology of religion, 145–46, 315; "Sociology of Religion" by, 233n23, 251; Tolstoy respected by, 150; on value spheres, 143–44, 297n23, 308; *Wissenschaft als Beruf* by, 165; on world-denying love as compromise formation, 227n4

Weil, David, 54

Weimar Republic, 266

Weinberg, Steven, 91

welfare state, 63, 69, 71, 259n114, 260

Wengrow, David, 203n69, 205n78

Western Christianity, 313

Western countries: hard ceiling facing, 24–25; imperialism of, 206–7, 206n83; modernity of, 73–74, 334–35; organized modernity of, 63; religious field weakening in, 318–19, 324

What I Believe (Tolstoy, L.), 132

Whitehead, Alfred North, 162n10

Why the West Rules—for Now (Morris), 21, 49, 203n70

Wilson, E. O., 39

Winstanley, Gerrard, 190

Wisdom, 95–96

Wissenschaft als Beruf (Weber), 165

Women's Suffrage movement, 33

Wood, Allen, 122

word (*logos*), 96–97, 160–62, 160n3, 161n9, 171–73

work, 179–80

work ethic, of Japan, 29

worldly polity, 234–39

Wycliffe, John (1320-1384), 105

Xi Jinping, 334, 336

Yahweh, in Christianity, 100

Yelle, Robert, 190, 190n28

Yellow Turban revolt (184 CE), 216

You Must Change Your Life (Sloterdijk), 1

Youth (Tolstoy, L.), 133, 135

Zellini, Paolo, 159–62

zero growth prediction, 43–44

Zeus, 99, 128

Zhang Zai, 328

Zhou empire, 213

Zhu Yuanzhang, 216n124

Zolotov, Viktor, 217n131